Breaking Through

ANNOTATED INSTRUCTOR'S EDITION

D1313933

Breaking Through

College Reading

FIFTH EDITION

ANNOTATED INSTRUCTOR'S EDITION

Brenda D. Smith

Georgia State University

An imprint of Addison Wesley Longman, Inc.

New York • Reading, Massachusetts • Menlo Park, California • Harlow, England
Don Mills, Ontario • Sydney • Mexico City • Madrid • Amsterdam

To my mother and father.

Editor-in-Chief: Patricia Rossi
Acquisitions Editor: Steven A. Rigolosi
Developmental Editor: Susan Moss
Marketing Manager: Ann Stypuloski
Supplements Editor: Donna Campion
Technical Reviewer: Jacqueline Stahlecker
Project Coordination and Text Design: Ruttle, Shaw & Wetherill, Inc.
Cover Design/Manager: Nancy Danahy
Cover Illustration: © James Kaczman/Laughing Stock
Full Service Production Manager: Joseph Vella
Photo Researcher: Photosearch, Inc.
Electronic Page Makeup: Ruttle, Shaw & Wetherill, Inc.
Senior Print Buyer: Hugh Crawford
Printer and Binder: Courier/Westford, Inc.
Cover Printer: Phoenix Color Corp.

For permission to use copyrighted material, grateful acknowledgment is made to the copyright holders on pp. 413–416, which are hereby made part of this copyright page.

Copyright © 1999 by Addison-Wesley Educational Publishers Inc.

All rights reserved. No part of this publication may be reproduced, stored in a retrieval system, or transmitted, in any form or by any means, electronic, mechanical, photocopying, recording, or otherwise, without the prior written permission of the publisher. Printed in the United States.

Please visit our Website at http://longman.awl.com

ISBN 0-321-01655-6 (Student's Edition)
ISBN 0-321-40874-8 (Instructor's Edition)

2345678910—CRW—010099

Brief Contents

Detailed Contents   vii

Reading, Vocabulary, Critical Thinking Skills,
   and Internet Exploration   xvii

Preface   xxi

CHAPTER 1 Student Success   1

CHAPTER 2 Stages of Reading   23

CHAPTER 3 Vocabulary   55

CHAPTER 4 Main Idea   83

CHAPTER 5 Supporting Details and
            Organizational Patterns   129

CHAPTER 6 Textbook Learning   177

CHAPTER 7 Test-Taking Strategies   223

CHAPTER 8 Efficient Reading   249

CHAPTER 9 Analytical Reading   271

CHAPTER 10 Inference   309

CHAPTER 11 Critical Reading   339

CHAPTER 12 Independent Textbook Assignments   385

APPENDIX 1 Pronunciation Review   399

APPENDIX 2 Spelling Confusing Words   407

APPENDIX 3 Word Parts: Prefixes, Roots, and Suffixes   409

Acknowledgments 413

Index 417

Copyright ©1999 by Addison-Wesley Educational Publishers Inc.

Detailed Contents

Reading, Vocabulary, Critical Thinking Skills, and Internet Exploration   xvii
Preface   xxi

CHAPTER 1   *Student Success*   *1*

Think Success   2

Set Goals   2

Create a Positive Attitude   3

Seek Excellence   3

> "MAKING CHOICES FOR SUCCESS"
> from *Live Your Dream* by Les Brown   4
> *"Ask yourself if you are leaving a trail that others may want to follow."*

Plan for Success   6

Manage Your Time   6

> "MAKING THE MOST OF PRIORITIES"
> from *How to Get Control of Your Time and Your Life* by Alan Lakein   6
> *"People at the top and people at the bottom both know about To Do Lists, but one difference between them is that the people at the top use a To Do List every single day. . . ."*

Plan Your Week   8

Study the Syllabus   9

Use a Calendar to Decode a Syllabus   12

Act Successful   12

Attend Class   13

Be on Time for Class   13

Be Aware of Essential Class Sessions   13

Be Equipped for Success   14

Mark Your Text   14

Communicate with Your Instructor   15

Review Your Lecture Notes   15

Network with Other Students   15

Collaborate to Divide Work   16

Look at an A Paper   16

Use Technology to Communicate   16

Consider a Tape Recorder   17

Pass the First Test   17

Copyright © 1999 by Addison-Wesley Educational Publishers Inc.

Watch Videos   17

Predict Exam Questions   17

Change Your Behavior   17

"ACTIONS FOR SUCCESS"
from *The Magic of Thinking Big* by David Schwartz   17
"Act the way you want to feel."

◆ **Points to Ponder   20**

◆ **Explore the Net   21**

CHAPTER 2   *Stages of Reading*   **23**

Grow as a Learner   24
What Is the Reading Process?   24
Stages of Reading   24

Stage One: Previewing   24

Stage Two: Integrating Knowledge   28

Stage Three: Recalling   32

Assess Your Progress as a Learner   35

Levels of Reading Comprehension   35

◆ **Points to Ponder   36**

SELECTION 1 ◆ PSYCHOLOGY   37

"HYPNOSIS"
from *Psychology: What It Is/How to Use It* by David Watson   37
"Hypnotized people can be programmed by a suggestion of the hypnotist to forget all they have seen or heard while hypnotized."

◆ **Explore the Net   43**

SELECTION 2 ◆ HISTORY   43

"SQUANTO"
from *America and Its People* by James Martin et al.   44
"When he returned the next spring, his Patuxet fathers fed him poisonous herbs for days on end. . . ."

◆ **Explore the Net   48**

SELECTION 3 ◆ ANTHROPOLOGY   48

"DRESS CODES AND SYMBOLISM"
from *Cultural Anthropology: A Global Perspective* by Raymond Scupin   49
"In the 1950s, during the early phase of the Rastafarian movement, some male members began to grow their hair in 'locks' or 'dreadlocks' to symbolize their religious and political commitments."

◆ **Explore the Net   54**

CHAPTER 3   *Vocabulary*   **55**

Learning New Words   56
Remembering New Words   57

Use Association   57

Copyright © 1999 by Addison-Wesley Educational Publishers Inc.

Use Concept Cards   57
Practice Your New Words   58
Unlocking the Meaning of New Words   58
Use Context Clues   58
Use Knowledge of Word Parts   58
Use the Glossary and the Dictionary   58
Types of Context Clues   59
Multiple Meanings of a Word   64
Words Parts   65
Roots   66
Prefixes   67
Suffixes   68
The Dictionary   69
Guide Words   70
Pronunciation   70
Spelling   70
Word Meaning   70
Parts of Speech   70
Word History   70
Word Origins   72
Etymology   72
Textbook Glossary   74
Thesaurus   74
Analogies   77
Easily Confused Words   79
Vocabulary Enrichment   81
◆ **Points to Ponder   81**
◆ **Explore the Net   81**

CHAPTER 4   *Main Idea*   *83*

What Is a Main Idea?   84
Recognize General and Specific Words   84
Recognize General and Specific Phrases   85
Recognize the General Topic for Sentences   86
Recognize General and Supporting Sentences   88
Differentiate Topic, Main Idea, and Supporting Details   91
Questioning for the Main Idea   93
Stated Main Ideas   94
Unstated Main Ideas   97
Differentiating Distractors   100
Getting the Main Idea of Longer Selections   102
◆ **Points to Ponder   103**

SELECTION 1 ◆ PSYCHOLOGY   104

"SLEEPING AND DREAMING"
from *Psychology: What It Is/How to Use It* by David Watson   104
"Everyone dreams about 20 percent of the time they are sleeping—that is, they show REM sleep about that much."

◆ **Explore the Net   110**

SELECTION 2 ◆ ESSAY   111

"THE SCHOLARSHIP JACKET"
from *Growing Up Chicana/o: An Anthology* by Marta Salinas   111
"This one, the scholarship jacket, was our only chance."

◆ **Explore the Net   119**

SELECTION 3 ◆ HISTORY   119

"BLACKS IN BLUE: THE BUFFALO SOLDIERS IN THE WEST"
from *America: Past and Present* by Robert Divine et al.   120
". . . more than 2000 black cavalrymen served on the western frontier between 1867 and 1890."

◆ **Connect: "Jones Morgan, 110, Thought to Be Last of Buffalo Soldiers"**
from *The Atlanta Journal/The Atlanta Constitution*   127

◆ **Explore the Net   128**

CHAPTER 5   *Supporting Details and Organizational Patterns*   **129**

What Is a Detail?   *130*
Recognize Levels of Importance   130
Distinguish Major and Minor Details   133
Patterns of Organization   *138*
Listing   139
Definitions with Examples   141
Time Order and Sequence   144
Comparison and Contrast   146
Cause and Effect   149

◆ **Points to Ponder   152**

SELECTION 1 ◆ PSYCHOLOGY   153

"BECOMING HEALTHY"
from *Psychology: Introduction to Human Behavior* by Morris Holland   154
"To learn about yourself and others, to love and to be loved, and to live actively and productively—all are growth-producing."

◆ **Explore the Net   160**

SELECTION 2 ◆ HISTORY   160

"AMERICA'S FIRST AGE OF REFORM"
from *America and Its People* by James Martin et al.   161
"As Sojourner Truth, she became a legend in the struggle to abolish slavery and extend equal rights to women."

◆ **Explore the Net   168**

SELECTION 3 ◆ PSYCHOLOGY   168

"OBEDIENCE"
from *Psychology* by John Dworetzky   169
"Every time he made an error, the teacher was to administer a shock, starting with the lowest level and gradually increasing."

◆ **Explore the Net** 175

◆ **Connect: "Criticisms of the Milgram Experiment" from** *Essentials of Psychology* **by Josh Gerow** 176

| CHAPTER 6 | *Textbook Learning* | *177* |

Expect Knowledge to Exist 178

Annotating 178

When to Annotate 178

How to Annotate 178

Notetaking 181

When to Take Notes 181

How to Take Notes 181

Summarizing 184

When to Summarize 184

How to Summarize 184

Outlining 187

When to Outline 187

How to Outline 187

Mapping 191

When to Map 191

How to Map 191

Take Organized Lecture Notes 193

◆ **Points to Ponder** 194

SELECTION 1 ◆ HISTORY 195

"TIMBUKTU"
from *Before the Mayflower* **by Lerone Bennett, Jr.** 196
"Youths from all over the Moslem world came to Timbuktu to study law and surgery at the University of Sankore; scholars came from North Africa and Europe to confer with the learned historians and writers of the black empire."

◆ **Explore the Net** 203

SELECTION 2 ◆ BIOLOGY 203

"ECHOLOCATION: SEEING IN THE DARK"
from *Biology: Exploring Life* **by Gil Brum, Larry McKane, and Gerry Karp** 204
"How could an animal's ears and mouth be of more importance than its eyes in guiding flight?"

◆ **Explore the Net** 210

SELECTION 3 ◆ COMMUNICATION 210

"EFFECTIVENESS IN INTERPERSONAL CONFLICT"
from *Essentials of Human Communication* **by Joseph DeVito** 211
"It is not so much the conflict that creates the problem as the way in which the individuals approach and deal with it."

◆ **Explore the Net** 219

◆ **Connect: "How Do You Fight?" from** *Essentials of Human Communication* **by Joseph DeVito** 219

Copyright © 1999 by Addison-Wesley Educational Publishers Inc.

CHAPTER 7   *Test-Taking Strategies*   **223**

Achieve Your Highest Potential   **224**
Be Prepared   **224**
Stay Alert   **225**
Seek Feedback   **226**
Standardized Reading Tests   **227**
   Read to Comprehend   228
   Interact   228
   Anticipate   228
   Relax   228
   Read to Learn   228
   Recall   228
Understand Major Question Types   **229**
   Main Idea Questions   230
   Detail Questions   232
   Implied Meaning Questions   233
   Purpose Questions   234
   Vocabulary Questions   236
Hints for Taking Multiple-Choice and True-False Tests   **237**
Hints for Taking Essay Exams   **241**
   Reword the Statement of Question   242
   Answer the Question   242
   Organize Your Answer   242
   Use a Formal Writing Style   243
   Be Aware of Appearance   243
   Predict and Practice   243
   Notice Key Words   244
   Write to Earn Points   244
   Read an "A" Paper for Feedback   245
      ◆ **Points to Ponder**   **246**
      ◆ **Explore the Net**   **247**

CHAPTER 8   *Efficient Reading*   **249**

What Is Your Reading Rate?   **250**
   What Is an Average Reading Rate?   251
How Can You Increase Your Reading Speed?   **252**
   Be Aggressive—Attack!   252
   Concentrate   253
   Stop Regressions   255
   Avoid Vocalization   255
   Expand Fixations   256
   Use a Pen as a Pacer   258
   Preview Before Reading   262
   Set a Time Goal for an Assignment   262

Be Flexible   262

Practice   263

◆ **Points to Ponder**   263

TIMED READING 1   263

"DARKNESS AT NOON"
by Harold Krents, *The New York Times*   263
"There are those who assume that since I can't see, I obviously also cannot hear."

TIMED READING 2   266

"REMEMBERING LOBO"
from *Nepantla: Essays from the Land in the Middle* by Pat Mora   266
"Lobo saved her money to take us out to dinner and a movie, to take us to Los Angeles in the summer, to buy us shiny black shoes for Christmas."

TIMED READING 3   268

"CHILDBIRTH IN EARLY AMERICA"
from *America and Its People* by James Martin et al.   268
"In their letters, women often referred to childbirth as 'the Dreaded apparition.'"

◆ **Explore the Net**   270

CHAPTER 9   *Analytical Reasoning*   *271*

Identify Analytical Thinking   272

An Unsuccessful Student   272

A Successful Student   272

Engage in Problem Solving   274

Analytical Reasoning in Textbooks   276

◆ **Points to Ponder**   285

SELECTION 1 ◆ PSYCHOLOGY   285

"COPING WITH SHYNESS"
from *Using Psychology* by Morris Holland   285
"In college I spent many nights alone in my dorm room. It was depressing, but it was easier than going out and facing the world."

◆ **Connect:** *"Attraction and Personal Relationships"* from *Psychology* by Henry Roediger et al.   292

◆ **Explore the Net**   293

SELECTION 2 ◆ BIOLOGY   293

"SCIENTIFIC LOGIC"
from *Focus on Human Biology* by Carl Rischer and Thomas Easton   293
"The researchers' hypothesis . . . was that prolonged contact between the zinc compound and the tissues lining the throat and mouth may somehow shorten the duration of the cold."

◆ **Explore the Net**   298

SELECTION 3 ◆ BUSINESS   298

"MOTIVATING YOURSELF"
from *Your Attitude Is Showing* by Elwood Chapman   299
"How can you motivate yourself to live close to your potential despite a negative environment?"

◆ **Explore the Net**   307

Copyright ©1999 by Addison-Wesley Educational Publishers Inc.

CHAPTER 10 *Inference*   *309*

What Is an Inference?   *310*

Inference from Cartoons   310

Recognizing Suggested Meaning   312

Connecting with Prior Knowledge   313

Recognizing Slanted Language   314

Drawing Conclusions   316

     ◆ **Points to Ponder**   **322**

SELECTION 1 ◆ NARRATIVE ESSAY   322

"MY BROTHER"
by Rick Theis   **322**
    "Now he'd be arriving the very next morning; back after three long years at war."

SELECTION 2 ◆ LITERATURE   328

"THE ALCHEMIST'S SECRET"
by Arthur Gordon   **329**
    "She died, I believe, poor woman. Quite suddenly."

SELECTION 3 ◆ ESSAY   332

"AMERICANIZATION IS TOUGH ON 'MACHO'"
by Rose Del Castillo Guilbault from Henderson et al.   **332**
    "What is macho*? That depends which side of the border you come from."*

CHAPTER 11 *Critical Reading*   *339*

What Do Critical Readers Do?   *340*

Recognize the Author's Purpose or Intent   340

Recognize the Author's Point of View or Bias   343

Recognize the Author's Tone   346

Distinguish Fact from Opinion   350

Recognize Valid and Invalid Support for Arguments   352

     ◆ **Points to Ponder**   **359**

SELECTION 1 ◆ NARRATIVE ESSAY   359

"AS THEY SAY, DRUGS KILL"
by Laura Rowley from *Models for Writers* edited by Alfred Rosa and Paul Eschholz   **360**
    "My hands began to shake and my eyes filled with tears for someone I didn't know."

     ◆ **Connect: "Conformity" from *Psychology* by Henry Roediger et al.**   **366**

     ◆ **Explore the Net**   **366**

SELECTION 2 ◆ PSYCHOLOGY   366

"ASTROLOGY—THE EARLIEST THEORY OF PERSONALITY"
from *Psychology: What It Is/How to Use It* by David Watson   **367**
    "The fate and acts of each human being are controlled by how the stars were arranged at the moment of that person's birth."

     ◆ **Connect: *"Angels All Around Us"* by Joan Webster Anderson**   **374**

     ◆ **Explore the Net**   **374**

SELECTION 3 ◆ BUSINESS   375

"THE JOB MAKES THE PERSON"
by Rosabeth Moss Kanter from *Understanding Diversity by Carol Harvey and*
M. June Allard   375

> *"I'd never work for a woman, a woman draftsman told me. 'They are too*
> *mean and petty.'"*

◆ **Explore the Net**   383

CHAPTER 12 *Independent Textbook Assignments*   *385*

Apply What You Have Learned   386

INDEPENDENT ASSIGNMENT 1 ◆ PSYCHOLOGY   386

"THE JOY OF SMOKING"
from *Biology: The World of Life* **by Robert Wallace**   386
"SMOKING: HAZARDOUS TO YOUR HEALTH"
from *Psychology in Action* **by Karen Huffman et al.**   397

> *". . . cigarette smoking is the single most preventable cause of death and*
> *disease in the United States."*

INDEPENDENT ASSIGNMENT 2 ◆ HISTORY   392

"THE SURGE WESTWARD"
from *America and Its People* **by James Martin et al.**   396

> *"Still, despite the hardships of the experience, few emigrants ever*
> *regretted their decision to move west."*

APPENDIX 1 *Pronunciation Review*   399

APPENDIX 2 *Spelling Confusing Words*   407

APPENDIX 3 *Word Parts: Prefixes, Roots, and Suffixes*   409

Acknowledgments 413

Index 417

Copyright ©1999 by Addison-Wesley Educational Publishers Inc.

Reading, Vocabulary, Critical Thinking Skills, and Internet Exploration

This new edition of *Breaking Through* contains a wealth of material designed to help students become more effective readers and learners.

- ◆ **Reading and study skills** are introduced and explained in each chapter.
- ◆ **Vocabulary enrichment** sections in each chapter help students increase their word power in the context of academic reading selections.
- ◆ Exercises throughout the text emphasize **critical thinking** as an important aspect of the college experience.
- ◆ For students and professors with access to the World Wide Web, opportunities for **Internet exploration** are presented throughout.

The following chart presents just a sampling of these features, which are found throughout the text.

	Reading or Study Skills	Vocabulary Enrichment	Critical Thinking Topics	Ideas for Internet Exploration

Chapter 1 **Student Success**	Setting Goals 2
	Managing Time 6
	Interpreting a
	   Syllabus 9
	Networking 15
	Motivating
	   Yourself 17
				Locating Relevant
				Web Pages 21

Chapter 2 **Stages of Reading**	Previewing 24
	Integrating
	   Knowledge 28
	Recalling 32
	Assessing
	   Progress 35
			Terrorists and
			   Hypnotism 40
			Cultural
			   Values/Goals:
			   Native
			   Americans vs.
			   Europeans 45
			Symbols of
			   Defiance in Your
			   Community 51
				Other Uses of
				   Hypnotism 43
				Historic Attractions
				   in Plymouth
				   Bay 48
				Connection
				   Between
				   Rastafarians and
				   Ethiopia 54

Chapter 3 **Vocabulary**	Using Context Clues 58–64
	Understanding Multiple Meanings 64
	Knowing Word Parts 65–69
	Using a Dictionary 69–71
	Knowing Word Origins 72–74
	Using a Glossary 74
	Using a Thesaurus 74
	Understanding Analogies 77–78
	Differentiating Easily Confused
	   Words 79–80
				Vocabulary-
				   building Tips or
				   Programs 81

Copyright ©1999 by Addison-Wesley Educational Publishers Inc.

	Reading or Study Skills	Vocabulary Enrichment	Critical Thinking Topics	Ideas for Internet Exploration
Chapter 4 **Main Idea**	Finding Main Idea 84 Differentiating Topic, Main Idea, and Supporting Details 91–93 Recognizing Stated Main Idea 94–96 Recognizing Unstated Main Idea 97 Differentiating Distractors 100 Getting the Main Idea—Longer Selections 102	Acronyms 109 Context Clues 110 Prefixes 117 Word Roots 125	Correlation Between Quality of Life and Good Sleep 107 Rich vs. Poor: Treatment in Education, Business, Medicine, and Law 115 Defense of Native American Raids in 1880s 123	Techniques for Overcoming Insomnia 110 Scholarship Services 119 Buffalo Soldiers and Congressional Medal of Honor 128
Chapter 5 **Supporting Details and Organizational Patterns**	Recognizing Levels of Importance 130 Distinguishing Major and Minor Details 133 Identifying Organizational Patterns 138 Identifying Transitional Words That Signal Patterns 139–152	Invented Words 158 Transitional Words 166 Context Clues 174 Thesaurus Use 175	Ways That Learning Can Foster Good Health 156 Evaluating Character and Beliefs Through Behavior 163 Accounting for Nazi War Crimes Through Research 172	Frequently Asked Medical Questions 160 Writings of Frederick Douglass 168 Ethics in Human Research 175
Chapter 6 **Textbook Learning**	Understanding and Using Annotation 178 Taking Notes 181 Summarizing 184 Outlining 187 Mapping 191	Words from Literature 201 Analogies 202 Words from Science 208 Similar-Sounding Words 217	Greatness of Askia Mohammed 199 Comparing Scientific Research Techniques: Humans vs. Bats 206 Evaluating Productive and Nonproductive Behaviors During Conflict 215	Timbuktu—Current Boundaries and Economics 203 Types of Bats and Myths About Them 210 Help Lines and Abuse Prevention Programs 219
Chapter 7 **Test-Taking Strategies**	Preparing 224 Predicting 237 Recognizing Tricks and Flaws 240 Organizing an Essay Response 242			Availability of Sample Standardized Tests 247 Graduate School Admissions Tests 247

	Reading or Study Skills	Vocabulary Enrichment	Critical Thinking Topics	Ideas for Internet Exploration
Chapter 8 **Efficient Reading**	Assessing Reading Rate 251 Using Strategies for Increasing Reading Speed 252–263			Reading Rate Improvement Programs 270
Chapter 9 **Analytical Reasoning**	Identifying Analytical Thinking 272 Differentiating Successful vs. Unsuccessful Student Characteristics 272 Engaging in Problem Solving 274 Visualizing Complex Information Through Graphic Illustrations 276–277	Context Clues 297 Easily Confused Words 305 Suffixes 306	Plastic Surgery and Self-Image 302	Overcoming Shyness 293 Traditional Uses of Zinc Gluconate 298 Psychocybernetics 307 Application of Maslow's Hierarchy of Needs to Business Management 307
Chapter 10 **Inference**	Understanding Implied Meaning 312 Recognizing Slanted Language 314 Drawing Conclusions 316	Idioms 327 Figurative Language 331 Similes 331 Personification 337 Irony 337	Application of Author's Message to War 325	
Chapter 11 **Critical Reading**	Recognizing Author's Purpose or Intent 340 Recognizing Point of View or Bias 343 Recognizing Tone 346 Distinguishing Fact from Opinion 350 Recognizing Fallacies 352	Similar-Sounding Words 364 Context Clues 365 Analogies 373 Transitional Words 373	Drugs and Fatality 362 Relevance of Horoscopes 369 Strategies for Motivating Employees 379	Drug Abuse Hotlines 366 Instructional Sources for Astrology 374 Organizational Change 383
Chapter 12 **Independent Textbook Assignments**	Applying Your Learning 386 Preparing for Exams 396			

Copyright ©1999 by Addison-Wesley Educational Publishers Inc.

Preface

The Goals of the Fifth Edition ◆◆◆◆◆◆◆◆◆◆◆◆

In reading the reviews for this fifth edition, I was struck by the logic and simplicity of the following description, written by Professor Dorothy Traughber at Murray State College, a reviewer who has used *Breaking Through* for many years. Her description summarizes what I want my book to do, and what I teach my own students.

> . . . In previewing *Breaking Through* with students at the beginning of the semester, I point out that reading is "thinking" and they can monitor their comprehension with questions which follow the chapter sequence in the book. For example, after they learn to apply the reading-study strategy, they ask the following questions while reading: Who or what is the passage about? What is it the author wants me to understand about the subject matter? What is it the author wants me to infer and understand about the subject matter? What does the author want me to know in order to understand more about the main idea (the supporting details)? How does the author organize the material he or she is presenting (the five most commonly used patterns)? What techniques (annotating, outlining summaries, etc.) can be used in order to help me remember what I read? Finally, based on the information in the passage, what inferences does the author want me to make (opinion vs. fact, implied meaning, etc.)? I give the class a handout that shows this as a hierarchy.

The ultimate goal of *Breaking Through*, of course, is to develop successful independent learners. The techniques are to teach, to model, and to offer practice in the reading and study skills most essential for understanding and retaining the material in freshman college texts. Further goals are to motivate students to achieve success and to help students draw on previous knowledge in order to integrate new and old ideas.

This fifth edition includes two chapters of expanded instruction on main idea and supporting details skills, a separate chapter on vocabulary building, a combined chapter on motivation and activities for college success, new practice exercises, and eleven new longer textbook selections. *Personal Feedback* questions have been inserted in the chapters to encourage students to communicate academic and personal concerns to the instructor. Comprehension questions have been labeled as *main idea, detail,* or *inference* to help students evaluate strengths and weaknesses, and *Vocabulary Preview* and *Vocabulary Enrichment* sections have been added to the longer reading selections to reinforce vocabulary-building skills. Longer selections are also followed by *React, Reflect,* and *Think Critically* questions to stimulate thought and encourage thoughtful written responses. A new feature, *Explore the Net,* at the end of each longer selection offers students an opportunity to seek additional information on a related subject by searching the Internet.

Copyright ©1999 by Addison-Wesley Educational Publishers Inc.

Organization ◆◆◆◆◆◆◆◆◆◆

Breaking Through opens with a chapter on motivation, attitude, and action. Success starts with a vision and is built on determination, perseverance, and activity. Chapter 2 moves to theories of reading and the strategies used by good readers. To control the process, readers must understand it. Reading is thinking and interacting with the printed page in three stages: before, during, and after the process. Chapter 3, a new separate chapter on vocabulary, includes explanations and exercises on context clues and word parts; using the dictionary, glossary, and thesaurus; and analogies.

Understanding the main idea, the most important reading comprehension skill, begins with models and practice exercises in Chapter 4 and extends into Chapter 5 with attention to supporting details, organizational patterns, and the beginning stages of notetaking. Chapter 6 explains annotating, notetaking, outlining, and mapping.

Chapter 7 offers advice on test-taking on multiple-choice and true-false tests, as well as essay responses. Heightened awareness and insight into expectations can give students a winning edge and help improve test scores. The efficient reading discussion in Chapter 8 presents techniques for rate improvement and provides exercises to assess student reading rates.

Chapter 9 recognizes college students as analytical reasoners and problem solvers, with exercises provided to help students develop and refine analytical reasoning skills. Chapter 10, on implied meaning, and Chapter 11, on critical reading, focus on unstated attitudes and assumptions. These chapters are designed to help students become more aware of suggested meaning and to be more critical of what they read. Success in college depends on being able to transfer reading skills to daily textbook assignments. Chapter 12 includes models of outlining and notetaking activities and contains three longer textbook selections for transferring skills, studying content, and demonstrating learning.

Special Features of the Fifth Edition ◆◆◆◆◆◆◆◆◆◆◆

- ◆ Instruction on **main idea** and **supporting details** is expanded into two Chapters (4 and 5).
- ◆ **Vocabulary-building** instructions and exercises are presented in a separate early chapter, followed by reinforcing vocabulary enrichment activities for the longer reading selections.
- ◆ Responsibilities, resources, and actions for **college success** have been blended with motivation in Chapter 1.
- ◆ Eleven **new high-interest textbook selections** reflect the cultural diversity and evolving interests of student readers. For a complete list of textbook selections, please see the inside front cover.
- ◆ **New practice exercises** are interspersed throughout the text.

- ◆ *React, Reflect,* and *Think Critically* questions prompt personal interaction with the material.
- ◆ *Personal Feedback* questions offer opportunities for self-assessment and communication of academic and personal concerns.
- ◆ **Reader's Tips** present concise, practical tips and suggestions to help students make the most of their reading.
- ◆ **Points to Ponder** summarize the key concepts of each chapter in a concise, easy-to-read format.
- ◆ **Comprehension questions** are labeled as *main ideas, detail,* or *inference* to help students evaluate their own strengths and weaknesses.
- ◆ *Explore the Net* activities suggest subjects related to the longer readings as topics for research on the Internet.

Continuing Features ◆◆◆◆◆◆◆◆◆◆

- ◆ Reading selections and practice exercises are taken from actual freshman-level college textbooks.
- ◆ Three reading levels in each chapter permit individualization of assignments to meet student needs.
- ◆ Textbook reading selections cover a variety of college courses, including history, communication, psychology, sociology, literature, biology, anthropology, and management.
- ◆ "Connect" articles help students relate old knowledge to new ideas.
- ◆ Skills are presented in the recommended teaching order, but each chapter is self-contained to provide flexibility in teaching.
- ◆ An explanation of the thinking strategies involved in reading includes a discussion of the stages of reading, schema theory, and metacognition.
- ◆ Five strategies are presented for organizing material for later study. (Separate lecture material for notetaking practice is provided in the Instructor's Manual.)
- ◆ Test-taking strategies include advice on multiple-choice, true-false, and essay exams.
- ◆ Selections are followed by multiple-choice, true-false, and sentence completion questions on both the literal and the interpretive levels of comprehension.
- ◆ Selections are followed by ten vocabulary words that are presented with contextual clues and line references to their location in the passage. (Vocabulary quizzes are provided in the Instructor's Manual for further practice.)
- ◆ Pages are perforated so that students can submit their assignments.

Teaching and Learning Package ◆◆◆◆◆◆◆◆◆◆

Each component of the teaching and learning package has been crafted to ensure that the course is a rewarding experience for both instructors and students.

- ◆ The **Annotated Instructor's Edition** is an exact replica of the student edition, but includes all answers printed directly on the fill-in lines provided in the text. (0-321-40874-8)
- ◆ The **Instructor's Manual** contains additional vocabulary and comprehension questions for each selection, which can be used as prereading quizzes to stimulate interest or as evaluation quizzes after reading. (0-321-02670-5)
- ◆ A **test bank,** prepared by Bob Brannan of Johnson County Community College, includes additional reading selections, chapter tests, vocabulary tests, and midterm final exams. It is available upon request. (0-321-02762-0)

Electronic and Online Offerings

- ◆ **Longman Reading Journeys Multimedia Software.** This innovative and exciting multimedia reading software is available either in CD-ROM format (0-321-04432-0) or as a site license. The package takes students on a tour of 15 cities and landmarks throughout the United States. Each of the 15 modules corresponds to a reading or study skills (for example, finding the main idea, understanding patterns of organization, and thinking critically). All modules contain a tour of the location, instruction and tutorial, exercises, interactive feedback, and mastery tests. Please contact your Addison Wesley Longman sales consultant for a demonstration disk. (0-321-04619-6)
- ◆ **The Longman English Pages Web Site.** Both students and instructors can visit our free content-rich Web site for additional reading selections and writing

Copyright ©1999 by Addison-Wesley Educational Publishers Inc.

exercises. From the Longman English pages, visitors can conduct a simulated Web search, learn how to write a résumé and cover letter, or try their hand at writing poetry. Stop by and visit us at **http://longman.awl.com/englishpages.**

◆ **The Basic Skills Electronic Newsletter.** Twice a month during the spring and fall, instructors who have subscribed receive a free copy of the Longman Basic Skills Newsletter in their e-mailbox. Written by experienced classroom instructors, the newsletter offers teaching tips, classroom activities, book reviews, and more. To subscribe, visit the Longman Basic Skills Web site at **http://longman.awl.com/basicskills,** or send an e-mail to **BasicSkills@awl.com.**

The Longman Basic Skills Package ◆◆◆◆◆◆◆◆◆◆

In addition to the book-specific supplements discussed above, a series of other skills-based supplements are available for both instructors and students. All of these supplements are available either free or at greatly reduced prices.

For Additional Reading and Reference

◆ **The Dictionary Deal.** Two dictionaries can be shrinkwrapped with any Longman Basic Skills title at a nominal fee. *The New American Webster Handy College Dictionary* (0-451-18166-2) is a paperback reference text with more than 100,000 entries. *Merriam Webster's Collegiate Dictionary,* tenth edition (0-87779-709-9), is a hardback reference with a citation file of more than 14.5 million examples of English words drawn from actual use.

◆ **Penguin Quality Paperback Titles.** A series of Penguin paperbacks is available at a significant discount when shrinkwrapped with any Longman Basic Skills title. Some titles available are: Toni Morrison's *Beloved* (0-452-26446-4), Julia Alvarez's *How the Garcia Girls Lost Their Accents* (0-452-26806-0), Mark Twain's *Huckleberry Finn* (0-451-52650-3), *Narrative of the Life of Frederick Douglass* (0-451-52673-2), Harriet Beecher Stowe's *Uncle Tom's Cabin* (0-451-52302-4), Dr. Martin Luther King, Jr.'s *Why We Can't Wait* (0-451-62754-7), and plays by Shakespeare, Miller, and Albee. For a complete list of titles or more information, please contact your Addison Wesley Longman sales consultants.

◆ **80 Readings.** This inexpensive volume contains 80 brief readings (1 to 3 pages each) on a variety of themes: writers on writing, nature, women and men, customs, and habits, politics, rights and obligations, and coming of age. Also included is an alternate rhetorical table of contents. (0-321-01648-3)

◆ **100 Things to Write About.** This 100-page book contains 100 individual assignments for writing on a variety of topics and in a wide range of formats, from expressive to analytical. Ask your Addison Wesley Longman sales representative for a sample copy. (0-673-98239-4)

For Instructors

◆ **CLAST Test Package.** These two 40-item objective tests evaluate students' readiness for the CLAST exams. Strategies for teaching CLAST preparedness are included. Free with any Longman English title. (Reproducible sheets: 0-321-01950-4 Computerized IBM version: 0-321-01982-2, Computerized Mac version: 0-321-01983-0)

◆ **TASP Test Package.** These 12 practice pre-tests and post-tests assess the same reading and writing skills covered in the TASP examination. Free with any Longman English title. (Reproducible sheets: 0-321-01959-8, Computerized IBM version: 0-321-01985-7, Computerized Mac version: 0-321-02984-9)

◆ *Teaching Online.* Ideal for instructors who have never surfed the Net, this easy-to-follow guide offers basic definitions, numerous examples, and step-by-step information about finding and using Internet sources. Free to adopters. (0-321-01957-1)

◆ *Reading Critically:* **Texts, Charts, and Graphs.** For instructors who would like to emphasize critical thinking in their courses, this brief book (65 pages) provides additional critical thinking material to supplement coverage in the text. Free to instructors. (0-673-97365-4)

For Students

◆ *Researching Online.* A perfect companion for a new age, this indispensable new supplement helps students navigate the Internet. Adapted from *Teaching Online,* the instructor's Internet guide, *Researching Online* speaks directly to students, giving them detailed, step-by-step instructions for performing electronic searches. Available at a nominal charge when shrinkwrapped with any Longman Basic Skills text. (0-321-02714-0)

Acknowledgments ◆◆◆◆◆◆◆◆◆◆

I would like to thank several people for their contributions to this book. First, Susan Moss, my Developmental Editor, has been both a partner and an inspiration in seeking to meet the needs of the teachers and students who use my books. I appreciate the support of my acquisitions editor, Steven Rigolosi. I would also like to acknowledge the help and suggestions that I received from the following people who reviewed the text:

Cheryl Altman, Saddleback College

Acquanetta L. Bracey, Alabama State University

Marlene King Bush, South Georgia College

Elaine Caplan, Broward Community College

Dianne Cates, Central Piedmont Community College

Gertrude Coleman, Middlesex County College

Kathy R. Griffin, Community College of Allegheny County

Judy Hayman, Houston Community College Southwest

Gary Kay, Broward Community College

Wei Li, North Harris College

Rick Richards, St. Petersburg Junior College

Judith Riordan, Rio Hondo College

Sandy Sampson, Tallahassee Community College

Jacqueline Stahlecker, St. Philip's College

Sheila R. Swanson, Wright State University

Martha M. Stearns, Central Piedmont Community College

Donald G. Taylor, University of Akron

Dorothy Traughber, Murray State College

Jacqueline S. Tyler, Anne Arundel Community College

Brenda D. Smith

Copyright © 1999 by Addison-Wesley Educational Publishers Inc.

Student Success

- ◆ *Are you a winner?*
- ◆ *What is the "can do" spirit?*
- ◆ *Do you set high standards?*
- ◆ *Do you plan for success?*
- ◆ *How can you efficiently manage time?*
- ◆ *What are the behaviors of success?*
- ◆ *How can fellow students be learning resources?*
- ◆ *What student responsibilities determine success in college?*

Copyright ©1999 by Addison-Wesley Educational Publishers Inc.

Think Success ◆◆◆◆◆◆◆◆◆◆

Are you mentally ready to go to college? Do you have a desire to achieve? Have you set goals for yourself, and are you ready to plan, labor, and sacrifice to achieve those goals? College and college work are fun, but they require extra effort. Students need to cultivate an attitude for success.

Most of this book focuses on strategies for reading college texts. Before you concentrate on the books, however, take a look at yourself and your dreams. You are now shaping your future. To become a winner, you must first think like a winner. Studies show that not only do college graduates enjoy more social and self-esteem benefits, but they also earn 18.3% to 46.5% more than those with only high school diplomas.[1]

This chapter will help you shape your thinking and behaviors by presenting the thoughts and describing the actions of successful people. Working on yourself can be as important as working on the books.

Set Goals

Entering college is a major turning point in life. College offers freedom, variety, and increased responsibility. Success in college requires a commitment of time, money, and energy. College is an investment in the future that requires a sacrifice in the present.

Students enter college with dreams, enthusiasm, and anxieties. Put your thoughts into words and strengthen your determination by communicating with your instructor. Share information about yourself in order to build a learning partnership with him or her. This partnership will be only as strong as each of you allow it to be. Your instructor is not a mind reader, so reveal who you really are. Respond thoughtfully to the **Personal Feedback** sections that appear throughout this text and pass them in to your instructor. Move beyond the

[1]E. T. Pascarella and P. T. Terenzini, *How College Affects Students: Findings and Insights from Twenty Years of Research* (San Francisco: Jossey-Bass Publishers, 1991).

academic and respond to questions regarding your habits, responsibilities, joys, and stresses. Your instructor wants to know you as a person and wants to help you be successful.

For the first one, think about your feelings as you begin your college career, and then respond to the following questions:

PERSONAL FEEDBACK 1

Name_____

1. What three dreams and/or influences motivated you to come to college?

   (a) _____

   (b) _____

   (c) _____

2. In five years what do you hope to be doing both professionally and personally?

   (a) Professionally: _____

   _____

   (b) Personally: _____

   _____

3. Explain three anxieties that you have as you begin college.

   (a) _____

   (b) _____

   (c) _____

4. What will you do to celebrate on the day you receive your college degree or certificate? _____

   _____

Create a Positive Attitude

Your dreams are your goals. Hold them in a corner of your mind as you go through college. On rough days, think of the dreams and picture the excitement of achieving your goals. Imagine your graduation celebration and think about those who will join in the fun. Allow your dreams to renew your enthusiasm and keep you focused on your goals. Let motivation overshadow your anxieties. Program your mind to think of success rather than failure. Don't worry about why something *cannot* be done. Instead, think about how it *can* be accomplished. What you think of yourself determines what you will become.

Seek Excellence

All of us would like to do well. Some people, however, set higher goals and eventually achieve more than others. What explains the difference? In his book, *Live Your Dreams*, Les Brown offers a blueprint for success that starts with high

Copyright ©1999 by Addison-Wesley Educational Publishers Inc.

expectations. Although he was born into poverty, adopted and raised by a single mother, and at one time was labeled "educable mentally retarded," Les Brown became a disc jockey, a three-term Ohio legislator, and an acclaimed public speaker. He energizes audiences around the country in professional seminars and on television, sharing his dreams and summarizing his strategies for success. He recognizes the difficulties faced by many, but passes along George Washington Carver's advice that we should judge people not by what they have, but by what they have had to overcome to succeed. The following is an excerpt from Brown's book.

MAKING CHOICES FOR SUCCESS

FIX YOUR FOCUS

Whatever dream you decide to go after, whether it is a family, or a career goal, you must consciously decide that it is your *life's mission.* Benjamin Disraeli said, "The secret of success is constancy to purpose." You must go at it obsessively and set high standards for yourself along the way. There is no room for compromise when you are charting a course for your life or your career.

I spoke to a group of sharp young people not long ago, and when I finished, some of the fellows came up and said they were interested in becoming professional speakers. They invited me to go out with them that evening to have a good time. These fellows looked as though they knew how to have a *serious* good time. I had planned to work on my delivery that night by listening to my tape of my speech. I tape my speeches and listen to them later so I can study what works and what does not work with a particular audience. In effect, I listen to the audience listening to me.

I was tempted to go with these fellows, and back when I was their age I probably would have given in to that temptation and gone. But I have become more disciplined and more committed to my craft.

A friend of mine, Wes Smith, wrote a humor book called *Welcome to the Real World,* and in it he offered advice to fresh high school and college graduates. He had a line in the book that pertains to the situation I faced that night. It said, "Having a drink with the boys after work every night is a bad idea. Notice that the boss doesn't do it. That is why *he* is the boss and *they* are still the boys."

Wes told me that he wrote that line with one particular group of hard-partying young businessmen in mind, and five years after the book came out, he ran into one of them. The guy volunteered that he'd read that line in Wes's book and decided never to go drinking after work again. It paid off, he said. He had risen to a vice-presidency at a savings and loan.

In my drive to become a public speaker, I developed that kind of *focus,* too. There is not a lot of time for hard partying if you are pursuing greatness. It was not that these young fellows were not serious about their interest in professional speaking, but they were just as serious about having a good time. I don't believe they were focused on their goals. They were seeking a profession but they were not on a mission to make a dramatic difference in the world. I am. You should be too.

Rather than the party crowd, I prefer to seek out people with knowledge that might be useful. I like to find out what books successful and intelligent people are reading. I want access to the information that contributes to their success and intelligence.

SEEK SUPPORT

I have come to believe that, to a certain degree, when the student is ready, the teacher appears. I first met Mike when I attended a meeting at which he spoke. I was impressed with his intelligence and articulate presentation. We became friends and Mike came to see things in me that I did not see in myself. Through his patience and example, he helped me reach a higher level. It has not always been easy for either of us. Mike is hard on me sometimes, and I have been known to be a somewhat inattentive pupil.

When I became a program director at the radio station, I hired Mike to work as my news director. I was still undisciplined at that time in my life, and I liked to sneak out of the office to shoot pool now and then. Mike made me feel guilty about it, so I would duck down and duck-walk past his office window. Sometimes he'd catch me in the parking lot and say, "Brown! Where are you going?" I wanted to be broadcasting at that point, but I wasn't committed enough to be in the building all day long being focused on my goal. I was creative, but I didn't like to keep my nose to that grindstone.

Mike convinced me that there were greater possibilities for my humble gifts than being a radio entertainer. He had a greater vision of what I could do to help others, and he has stayed with me to keep me on the path that he first envisioned. He developed the nine principles for life enrichment. He is a beacon that lights my way.

I believe that as you grow in consciousness you begin to attract people who facilitate your growth. Be on the lookout for these sorts of people, the masters, the mentors and the people who see things for you that you do not see for yourself. Find those who can look at your performance objectively and critically but positively.

We all need to have friends who hold our feet to the fire and challenge us. You need mutually enhancing relationships. As my relationship with Mike developed, he imparted some of his work habits to me. Look for the sort of friends who help you work on your weaknesses, not just those who feed your habits and congratulate you on your strong points.

—*Live Your Dream* by Les Brown

No one says that achievement is easy. Set your goals high and pull out of your comfort zone to seek your dreams. Persistence and a willingness to do the work that others are reluctant to do will make the difference.

PERSONAL FEEDBACK 2

Name_____

1. Identify three people on your personal support team.

   (a) _____

   (b) _____

   (c) _____

2. Define the word *mentor*. Describe one of your mentors.

   Mentor: _____

   Who? _____

3. What are three things you want to learn from this reading course?

   (a) _____

   (b) _____

   (c) _____

4. What grade will you realistically seek to make in this course?

   Grade: _____

   Explain: _____

Copyright ©1999 by Addison-Wesley Educational Publishers Inc.

5. List four responsibilities you have as a college student who wants to be a high achiever with excellent grades.

   (a) _____

   (b) _____

   (c) _____

   (d) _____

6. Describe one of your high school teachers who you thought was an excellent instructor. _____

   _____

7. What do you expect from a college instructor? List four responsibilities of a good instructor.

   (a) _____

   (b) _____

   (c) _____

   (d) _____

Plan for Success ◆◆◆◆◆◆◆◆◆◆◆

A business maxim known as Parkinson's Law states that work expands to fill the time available for its completion. Have you ever had all Saturday to finish an assignment and found that it did in fact take all day, whereas if you had planned to finish it in four hours, you probably could have done so?

Time is limited, and everyone has only twenty-four hours in a day, even the President of the United States. Does the President get more done than you do? The key to success is to plan and use the minutes and hours wisely. Establish a routine and stick to it. Plan for both work and play.

Manage Your Time

Alan Lakein, a time management consultant, works with business people all over the country. In his book *How to Get Control of Your Time and Your Life,* he offers the following daily method of planning for achievement.

MAKING THE MOST OF PRIORITIES

The main secret of getting more done every day took me several months of research to discover. When I first started delving into better time use, I asked successful people what the secret of their success was. I recall an early discussion with a vice-president of Standard Oil Company of California who said, "Oh, I just keep a 'To Do' list." I passed over that quickly, little suspecting at the time the importance of what he said. I happened to travel the next day to a large city to give a time management seminar. While I was there I had lunch with a businessman who practically owned the town. He was chairman of the gas and light company, president of five manufacturing companies, and had his hand in a dozen other enterprises. By all standards he was a business success. I asked him the same question of how he managed to get more done and he said, "Oh, that's easy—I keep a To Do List."

ONLY A DAILY LIST WILL DO

People at the top and people at the bottom both know about To Do Lists, but one difference between them is that the people at the top use a To Do List every single day to make better use of their time; people at the bottom know about this tool but don't use it effectively. One of the real secrets of getting more done is to make a To Do List every day, keep it visible, and use it as a guide to action as you go through the day.

Because the To Do List is such a fundamental time planning tool, let's take a closer look at it. The basics of the list itself are simple: head a piece of paper "To Do," then list those items on which you want to work; cross off items as they are completed and add others as they occur to you; rewrite the list at the end of the day or when it becomes hard to read.

Some people try to keep To Do Lists in their heads but in my experience this is rarely as effective. Why clutter your mind with things that can be written down? It's much better to leave your mind free for creative pursuits.

WHAT BELONGS ON THE LIST

Are you going to write down everything you have to do, including routine activities? Are you only going to write down exceptional events? Are you going to put down everything you *might* do today or only whatever you decided you *will* do today? There are many alternatives, and different people have different solutions. I recommend that you not list routine items but do list everything that has high priority today and might not get done without special attention.

Don't forget to put the A-activities for your long-term goals on your To Do List. Although it may appear strange to see "begin learning French" or "find new friends" in the same list with "bring home a quart of milk" or "buy birthday card," you want to do them in the same day. If you use your To Do List as a guide when deciding what to work on next, then you need the long-term projects represented, too, so you won't forget them at decision time and consequently not do them.

Depending on your responsibilities, you might, if you try hard enough, get all the items on your To Do List completed by the end of each day. If so, by all means try. But probably you can predict in advance that there is no way to do them all. When there are too many things to do, conscious choice as to what (and what not) to do is better than letting the decision be determined by chance.

I cannot emphasize strongly enough: You must *set priorities*. Some people do as many items as possible on their lists. They get a very high percentage of tasks done, but their effectiveness is low because the tasks they've done are mostly of C-priority. Others like to start at the top of the list and go right down it, again with little regard to what's important. The best way is to take your list and label each item according to ABC priority, delegate as much as you can, and then polish off the list accordingly.

—*How to Get Control of Your Time and Your Life* by Alan Lakein

EXERCISE 1　Answer the following questions and make a To Do List.

1. What does the author believe is the difference between the To Do List of people at the top and those of people at the bottom? <u>People at the top use them consistently and effectively; people at the bottom know about them but do not use them, or use them ineffectively.</u>

Copyright ©1999 by Addison-Wesley Educational Publishers Inc.

2. Prior to reading this passage, what method have you used to keep up with things you need to remember to do? _____

_____

3. What kinds of things does the author say belong on a To Do List?
   <u>High-priority items needing special attention, not routine items.</u>

4. How can you indicate levels of priority on your To Do List? <u>Mark items with</u>
   <u>A, B, or C.</u>

5. Why do you think a student would feel that it is not necessary to keep a daily To Do List? _____

_____

6. Make out your own To Do List today. In the left margin, indicate priorities. Keep your list in a notepad or in your assignment book so that it is always handy.

> *Example*
> A (1) Pay rent
> B (2) Change oil in car
> A (3) Call Maria
> C (4) Buy dictionary
> B (5) Get breakfast foods

To Do List

_____ (1) _____

_____ (2) _____

_____ (3) _____

_____ (4) _____

_____ (5) _____

_____ (6) _____

_____ (7) _____

Plan Your Week

Organize yourself on a weekly basis. Project your schedule for next week and put it on the time chart on page 22. Be specific about each item and note what you anticipate studying when listing a study time. Be realistic about your activities and plan recreation as well as work time.

The majority of your activities will remain routine. For example, your class hours are probably the same each week. Put them on the chart first. If you have a job, plug in your work hours. If you work while attending college, you will have even fewer minutes to waste and thus you must become a super-efficient time manager. Put in your meal times and your bedtime. If you can't live without a favorite television show, plug that in as well. It's better to plan for your weaknesses than to pretend that you are going to be studying and then not live up to your expectations.

Lay out your life the way you would like to live it for the week, and then try to stick to the plan. At the beginning of each week, adjust your plan for any changes that you foresee. Use your weekly schedule as a goal.

READER'S TIP

TIME SAVERS

Using time wisely becomes a habit. Analyze your current problems according to the following principles of time management to gain greater control of yourself and your environment.

1. Plan. Keep an appointment book by the day and hour. Write a daily To Do List.
2. Start with the most critical activity of the day and work your way down to the least important one.
3. Ask yourself, "What is the best use of my time right now?"
4. Don't do what doesn't need doing.
5. Concentrate completely on one thing at a time.
6. Block out big chunks of time for large projects.
7. Make use of five-, ten-, and fifteen-minute segments of time.
8. Keep phone calls short or avoid them.
9. Listen well for clear instructions.
10. Learn to say "No!" to yourself and others.
11. Wean yourself from TV. Business executives do not watch soap operas.
12. Strive for excellence, but realize that perfection may not be worth the cost.

Study the Syllabus

On the first day of class almost every professor distributes a syllabus. This is an outline of the goals, objectives, and assignments for the entire course. The syllabus includes examination dates and an explanation of the grading system. Depending on the professor, the syllabus may be a general overview or a more detailed outline of each class session. Keep your syllabus for ready reference; it is an invaluable tool. It is your guide to the professor's plan for your learning. Passive learners show their lack of sophistication by using class time to ask questions about test dates or details that could be found by looking at the syllabus.

EXERCISE 2   Review the following history syllabus and answer the questions.

Copyright ©1999 by Addison-Wesley Educational Publishers Inc.

United States History Syllabus

Class: 9–10 daily   10-Week Quarter: 1/4–3/12
Dr. J. A. Johnson   Office Hrs.: 10–12 daily
Office: 422G   Phone: 562-3367
     E-mail: jajlsp.edu

Required Texts
(1) *A People and a Nation* by Norton et al.
(2) One paperback book on immigration selected from the list for a report.

Course Content

This course is a survey of United States history from the early explorations to the present. The purpose is to give you an understanding of the major forces and events that have interacted to make modern America.

Method of Training

Thematic lectures will be presented in class. You are expected to read and master the factual material in the text as well as take careful notes in class. Tests will cover both class lectures and textbook readings.

Grading

Grades will be determined in the following manner:

> Tests (3 tests at 20% each)
> Final Exam
> Written Report

Tests will include both multiple-choice or identification items and two essay questions.

Important Dates

Test 1: 1/22	Final Exam: 3/18
Test 2: 2/11	Written Report: 3/10
Test 3: 3/3	Makeup Test (with permission): 3/16

Written Report

Your written report on immigration should answer one of the three designated questions and reflect your reading of a book from the list. Each book is approximately 200 pages long. Your report should be at least six typed pages. More information to follow.

Assignments

Week 1: Ch. 1 (pp. 1–27), Ch. 2 (pp. 28–49), Ch. 3 (pp. 50–68)
Week 2: Ch. 4 (pp. 69–86), Ch. 5 (pp. 87–103), Ch. 6 (pp. 104–122)
Week 3: Ch. 7 (pp. 123–139), Ch. 8 (pp. 140–159), Ch. 9 (pp. 160–176),
  Ch. 10 (pp. 177–194)

Test 1: Chaps. 1–10

Week 4: Ch. 11 (pp. 195–216), Ch. 12 (pp. 217–236), Ch. 13 (pp. 237–253)

Week 5: Ch. 14 (pp. 254–272), Ch. 15 (pp. 273–288), Ch. 16 (pp. 289–304),
  Ch. 17 (pp. 305–320)

Week 6: Ch. 18 (pp. 321–344), Ch. 19 (pp. 345–358), Ch. 20 (pp. 359–375)

Test 2: Chaps. 11–20

Week 7: Ch. 21 (pp. 376–391), Ch. 22 (pp. 392–410), Ch. 23 (pp. 411–428)

Week 8: Ch. 24 (pp. 429–450), Ch. 25 (pp. 451–466), Ch. 26 (pp. 467–484),
  Ch. 27 (pp. 486–504)

Week 9: Ch. 28 (pp. 505–520), Ch. 29 (pp. 521–533), Ch. 30 (pp. 534–553)

Week 10: Ch. 31 (pp. 554–569), Ch. 32 (pp. 570–586), Ch. 33 (pp. 587–599)

Test 3: Chaps. 21–28

Final Exam: Chaps. 1–33

1. What is the stated purpose of this history course? <u>To give students an</u> <u>understanding of the major forces and events interacting to make modern</u> <u>America.</u>

2. How will your grade be determined? <u>three tests, a final exam, and a written</u> <u>report</u>

3. How many pages do you have to read the first week? <u>68</u>
   Second week? <u>54</u> Third week? <u>72</u>

4. On the average, how many pages should you read each day for the first week? <u>approximately 10</u>

5. Will you have any pop quizzes? <u>No; they are not listed as part of the grade.</u>

6. Does the final exam count more than the individual tests? <u>% unclear</u>

7. What questions might you ask about the tests? <u>Ex: How much do final exam</u> <u>and written report count?</u>

8. Do you have questions that are not answered by this syllabus?
   _____

PERSONAL FEEDBACK 3

Name_____

1. When did you receive the syllabus for this reading course? Where is it now?

   _____

2. When is your next test and how much does it count toward your final grade?

   _____

3. What material does your next major exam cover? Will the questions be multiple-choice or essay?

   _____

4. Is there a penalty for turning work in late?

   _____

5. What is the purpose of this course?

   _____

6. What questions do you have about how your final grade will be determined?

   _____

7. What questions do you have about the syllabus or the course?

   _____

Copyright ©1999 by Addison-Wesley Educational Publishers Inc.

Use a Calendar to Decode a Syllabus

Students who just glance at the course syllabus might think there is no immediate assignment because the first test is four weeks away. Wrong! These students will find themselves falling behind by the second class session because of their "slow start" or "no start" strategy. Avoid this pitfall. As soon as the course begins, use your calendar along with the syllabus and divide your work according to the days and weeks of the course.

Be cautious of unlimited freedom. It could become the freedom to fail. Some professors make short-term goal setting entirely the student's responsibility. For example, such a professor would say that the syllabus clearly states that the exam will cover the first twelve text chapters. Period. No interim goals are provided. Thus, it is up to the student to take control and design his or her own detailed learning plan.

To make a learning plan, use a calendar with your syllabus, and break up all your reading assignments according to the number of days and weeks available. Mark exam dates and assignment deadlines. Plan to finish textbook and supplemental reading several days before test dates so that the last few days can be used for study only. Total the pages assigned and divide to determine how many pages you should read each day. Write these on your calendar and give yourself a projected weekly page average. Do the same scheduling for term papers, critiques, or special projects. Mark the date you need to start special assignments, divide the work into small steps, and indicate your projected goals for each day. Use your calendar of expected achievements to stay on schedule in each of your classes.

◆◆◆ READER'S TIP

MAKING A LEARNING SCHEDULE

Use your assignment calendar to devise a learning schedule. Mark important dates for this class.

- ❖ Enter all test dates and due dates for papers.
- ❖ Divide reading assignments in text according to daily and weekly goals. Leave several days for study and review before tests.
- ❖ Divide extra reading and project goals.
- ❖ Designate date for first draft of written report.

Act Successful ◆◆◆◆◆◆◆◆◆◆◆◆

Successful people share certain observable characteristics. Study those characteristics and discover the accompanying behaviors. Then imitate the behaviors of successful people. The following example demonstrates students behaving in the opposite manner.

COLLEGE PROFESSOR "TAKES" AMERICAN HISTORY

In order to prepare for a course to assist students in learning history, I recently "took" American History 113. I put the word *took* in quotation marks because I skipped the hard part; I did not take the exams. I did, however, attend class, take notes, observe, and learn.

Since the university operates on the quarter system, classes meet for ten weeks with an extra week for exams. My particular class met on Tuesdays and Thursdays from 10:50 to 1:05, which means the class lasted for two hours and fifteen minutes. I attended all but one class.

I had an excellent professor who seemed concerned that students learn and make good grades. In fact, after the first class, I would have been astonished if any student could fail. To my amazement, the professor actually distributed a list of ten questions from which he would choose the two essay questions on the first exam. After talking with students in other classes, I learned that this was not unusual; many professors distributed lists of possible exam questions.

As the course progressed, I noticed that some students were their own worst enemies. I could see opportunities for learning that students were ignoring. I began taking notes on student behaviors, as well as my regular notes on the history lectures. From my observations, not just of a few class sessions, but of the entire duration of the course, I formed some opinions about why some students make A's and others barely pass or even fail. For example, I observed that many students skipped class or came late; some took very sketchy lecture notes; students rarely talked to each other; and many students did not seem to have the master plan of the sequence of events that is so necessary for being successful. Although my observations were made only in a history course, after talking to other students and professors, I believe that the behaviors necessary for success apply to most college courses. I wanted to say to some individuals, ''You are shooting yourself in the foot.'' Some of the suggestions outlined below are simple and obvious, yet many students ignored them.

Attend Class

"I missed the last class. Did we do anything?" Does this sound familiar? Never mind that the class lasted almost two and a half hours and covered too much to repeat, some students seem unconvinced that an absence puts them at a disadvantage. In my history class, the professor used the exam questions as a guide to the lectures. I was astounded at how many students skipped classes. While 40 students were registered for the course, no more than 33 ever showed up at any one session. At the session after the midterm, only 17 students were present. I asked myself, "Why would a student pay for a course, yet not take advantage of the instruction?" Professors cannot teach students who are not there.

Assume some of the responsibility for your class sessions. If your interest is not sufficiently stimulated, move beyond blaming it all on the professor. Ask questions and participate in class discussions. Arrive prepared so class sessions will be more meaningful. Talk with other students. Suggest ideas to the professor. Every class period can be significant if you, the professor, and other class members make it important.

Be on Time for Class

Professors usually begin with important reminders about test questions, assignments, or papers, and then give an overview of what will be discussed in class that day. If you come late, you arrive for the details and miss the "big picture." You put yourself at a disadvantage and must scramble to catch up. In my history class, sometimes as many as seven students arrived late, strolling into class with sodas and snacks, suggesting they did not make class their first priority.

Be Aware of Essential Class Sessions

Every class session should be important, but have you ever heard a student ask, "Why attend on the first day if the professor only explains the syllabus and overviews the course?" This student doesn't know you can get a "fast start."

Copyright ©1999 by Addison-Wesley Educational Publishers Inc.

Always strive for a solid beginning rather than a shaky one. At the first class meeting students usually ask questions to clarify the syllabus, and the professor responds with important, unwritten details that can help you improve your grades. For example, does your history professor expect you to memorize dates, to understand the causes and effects of social change, or to critique historical interpretations? Goals such as these will be explained on the first day.

Students who do not attend the last class before an exam put themselves at an extreme disadvantage. By this time, the professor has usually written the exam and feels pressured to cover anything that he or she will ask on the test that has not been discussed previously in class. Student questions usually prompt a brief but extremely helpful review that pinpoints essential areas of study. Hearing the professor comment, "That's not really important," helps you eliminate study areas and save time. In addition, be sure you have studied enough before this session so that you know which things you need to clarify.

Never miss an exam unless you are on your death bed! The exam "make up" may be in a noisy study area or scheduled two weeks later. This could mean you receive feedback on your work too late to use it to improve. "Make up" is just what the phrase implies, trying to move from behind to regain a position. Unfortunately, I observed that some students did not start studying or take the course seriously until after the first exam. Be sure to be in class when exams are returned. Listen to the professor's description of a good answer. Learn from the professor's responses to other students. Find out what you did right, what you did wrong, and exactly what is expected. Also, find out who made the best grades and ask those students how they studied. The exam and subsequent discussions help you understand expectations and set your future learning goals.

Be Equipped for Success

Some students arrive on the first day of class without paper and end up writing lecture notes on the back of the syllabus. Others arrive prepared to get organized and learn. Every college student should have the equipment listed below.

EXERCISE 3

Put a check mark next to each item of equipment that you have with you. Your instructor may want you to do this during the second week of class to give you time to purchase all the items.

_____ Assignment calendar with large daily spaces

_____ Three-ring notebook for organizing papers

_____ Spiral notebook for lecture notes

_____ Three-ring plastic hole puncher for putting handouts in notebook

_____ Notebook paper

_____ Notebook dividers (at least five) for organizing by topic

_____ Some sort of container in which to keep the following:

_____pencil _____regular pen _____erasable pen _____highlighter

_____white out _____small pencil sharpener _____small stapler

_____small "Post-it" notes _____small binder clips

Mark Your Text

Get the most from your books and use them as learning tools. Read your textbooks with a pen or highlighter in hand and mark information that you will most likely need to know later. A well-marked textbook is much more of a treasure than an unmarked one, a treasure that you may want to keep as a reference for later courses.

Don't miss an opportunity to learn by being reluctant to mark in your text. Marking your text actively involves you in reading and studying. Some books, such as this one, are workbooks. The small amount of money that you receive in a textbook resale may not be worth what you have lost in active involvement. Use this book to practice, to give and get feedback, and to keep a record of your progress.

Communicate with Your Instructor

Don't be an anonymous student. Let your professor know who you are. Get your money's worth and more. Make a special effort to speak to your professor about something you found interesting or something you did not understand. Overcome your fear and seek help when you need it. Contrary to popular opinion, good students are more likely to seek help than weak ones. Visit during office hours. Professors want their students to be successful.

Review Your Lecture Notes

Review your lecture notes after each class session. Recite to yourself what the professor said. Identify gaps of knowledge and seek clarification. This kind of review reinforces your learning and reminds you of what the professor thinks is important. Unfortunately, most students wait until test time to review notes, thus missing these easy opportunities to solidify learning. Your own notebook is a valuable resource; use it.

Network with Other Students

Use the other students in the classroom as learning resources. For the first four weeks of my history class, almost none of the students spoke to each other. I was amazed. Even when I arrived five or ten minutes early to observe behavior, no one spoke. Most stared straight ahead, some read the history text, and some read the newspaper. After the first exam, however, students started to compare scores and to talk about correct answers.

Research with college students all over the country has shown that students who are part of a study group are less likely to drop out of school. However, many bright college students are loners. They do not know how to network and think that studying in groups is cheating. In fact, study groups teach students to collaborate and to form academic bonds. Networking is important for all students, including older, returning students who may initially feel out of the mainstream.

Start your network on the first day of class. In each course, ask for the name, telephone number, and e-mail address of at least two other students. Write this information in your text or lecture notebook so you won't lose it. These names and numbers are insurance policies. If you are absent or are unclear on an assignment, call a classmate for clarification, homework, and lecture notes. Students *can* help other students. Begin your network right now with two people. Don't be bashful.

Classmate _____   Phone _____   E-mail _____

Classmate _____   Phone _____   E-mail _____

Copyright ©1999 by Addison-Wesley Educational Publishers Inc.

Collaborate to Divide Work

Find a "study buddy" to share the work. In my history class, only two essay questions would be chosen for the exam from the list of ten distributed on the first day. The professor expected answers to include information from the lectures, as well as details from the history text. To be thoroughly prepared for the exam, each student should have a study outline to answer each of the ten questions. Such an assignment presents an obvious opportunity to cut work in half. Why not get a "study buddy" and each prepare five possible essay answers and share? Seize every opportunity to collaborate and efficiently divide work.

Look at an A Paper

When exams are returned, always find out the correct answers. For essay responses, always ask to see an A paper. Ask the professor or a top-scoring student to allow you "an opportunity to read an excellent paper." Who would deny such a request? Analyze the A paper to determine how you can improve. Ask yourself, "What is this student doing that I'm missing?" Even if you made an A yourself, read another paper. Maybe your next exam will earn an A+. In my history class, I noticed that the good students sought examples, but the weak students slipped out of the room without seeking any help or insight from others.

Use Technology to Communicate

Do you need to meet face to face to study together? Conflicting class and work schedules make getting study groups together difficult. The telephone, the fax machine, and e-mail can eliminate some of those barriers. Outlines, lecture notes, and mathematics problems can be discussed and sent back and forth rapidly. You and your "study buddy" can communicate without wasting time commuting.

Consider a Tape Recorder

If your professor talks fast and you have trouble taking notes, try using a tape recorder. Do not use the recorder as an excuse to postpone the organizing and priority-setting involved in notetaking. Instead, use the audio replay as another sensory tool for learning. The tiny tape recorders now available make this option fairly convenient. One history student said she listened to the replays while driving her car or fixing dinner.

Pass the First Test

Always overprepare for the first exam. Success on the first exam builds confidence, allays fears, and saves you from trying desperately to come from behind.

Watch Videos

Visual learning is powerful. Find videos on subjects covered in your text. Use the college library, the public library, and well-stocked video stores. If you are studying the Great Depression, check out a video of newsreel clips or watch *The Grapes of Wrath*, a drama set in that period. For an introductory psychology course, check the college for a movie on Sigmund Freud or theories of personality.

Predict Exam Questions

Predict both essay questions and multiple-choice items for exams. Not all professors provide possible essay questions and study guides. On your own you can review your textbook's table of contents and turn major headings into possible essay questions. Turn chapter titles into essay questions. Consider subheadings and boldface print a ripe source of multiple-choice items. Review lecture notes for any indication the professor gave about areas of special importance. Ask previous students about the professor's exams. The format and questions on a major exam should not come as a total shock to you. Predict and be prepared. The way we act not only mirrors our feelings, but can also initiate a change in our attitude. When you feel defeated, stand up straight. When you feel sad, put a smile on your face.

Change Your Behavior

David Schwartz was a marketing professor at Georgia State University for many years. Among the many academic and popular books he authored, his favorite was *The Magic of Thinking Big*, in which he suggests that our behaviors can lead to success.

ACTIONS FOR SUCCESS

Act the way you want to feel. Below are five confidence-building exercises. Read these guides carefully. Then make a conscious effort to practice them and build your confidence.

1. Be a Front Seater. Ever notice in meetings—in church, classrooms, and other kinds of assemblies—how the back seats fill up first? Most folks scramble to sit in the back rows so they won't be "too conspicuous." And the reason they are afraid to be conspicuous is that they lack confidence.

Sitting up front builds confidence. Practice it. From now on make it a rule to sit as close to the front as you can. Sure, you may be a little more conspicuous in the front, but remember there is nothing inconspicuous about success.

Copyright ©1999 by Addison-Wesley Educational Publishers Inc.

2. Practice Making Eye Contact. Usually, failure to make eye contact says one of two things. It may say, "I feel weak beside you. I feel inferior to you. I'm afraid of you." Or avoiding another person's eyes may say, "I feel guilty. I've done something or I've thought something that I don't want you to know. I'm afraid if I let my eyes connect with yours, you'll see through me."

You say nothing good about yourself when you avoid making eye contact. You say, "I'm afraid. I lack confidence." Conquer this fear by *making* yourself look the other person in the eye. Looking the other person in the eye tells him, "I'm honest and above board. I believe in what I'm telling you. I'm not afraid. I'm confident."

Make your eyes work for you. Aim them right at the other person's eyes. It not only *gives* you confidence. It *wins* you confidence, too.

3. Walk 25 Percent Faster. Psychologists link slovenly postures and sluggish walking to unpleasant attitudes towards oneself, work, and the people around us. But psychologists also tell us you can actually change your attitudes by changing your posture and speed of movement. Watch, and you discover that body action is the result of mind action. The extremely beaten person, the real down-and-outers, just shuffle and stumble along. They have zero self-confidence. Average people have the "average" walk. Their pace is "average." They have the look of "I really don't have very much pride in myself."

Then there's a third group. Persons in this group show super-confidence. They walk faster than the average. There seems to be a slight sprint in the way they walk. Their walk tells the world, "I've got someplace important to go, something important to do. What's more, I will succeed at what I will do fifteen minutes from now."

Use the walk-25-percent-faster technique to help build self-confidence. Throw your shoulders back, lift up your head, move ahead just a little faster, and feel self-confidence grow. Just try and see.

4. Practice Speaking Up. In working with many kinds of groups of all sizes, I've watched many persons with keen perception and much native ability freeze and fail to participate in discussions. It isn't that these folks don't want to get in and wade with the rest. Rather, it's a simple lack of confidence. The conference clam thinks to himself, "My opinion is probably worthless. If I say something I'll probably look foolish. I'll just say nothing. Besides, the others in the group probably know more than I. I don't want the

others to know how ignorant I am." Each time our clam fails to speak, he takes one more dose of confidence poison. He becomes less and less confident of himself. But on the positive side, the more you speak up, the more you add to your confidence, and the easier it is to speak up the next time. Speak up. It's a confidence-building vitamin.

And never worry about looking foolish. You won't. For each person who doesn't agree with you, odds are another person will. Quit asking yourself, "I wonder if I dare speak?"

5. Smile Big. Make this little test. Try to feel defeated and smile big at the same time. You can't. A big smile gives you confidence. A big smile beats fear, rolls away worry, defeats despondency.

And a real smile does more than cure just your ill feeling. A real smile melts away opposition of others—and instantly, too. Another person simply can't be angry with you if you give him a big sincere smile. Just the other day, a little incident happened to me that illustrates this. I was parked at an intersection waiting for the light to change when BAM! The driver behind me let his foot slip off the brake and had put my rear bumper to a test. I looked back through my mirror and saw him getting out. I got out, too, and forgetting the rule book, started preparing myself for verbal combat. I confess I was ready verbally to bite him to pieces.

But, fortunately, before I got this chance, he walked up to me, smiled, and said in the most earnest voice, "Friend, I really didn't mean to do that." That smile matched with his sincere comment, melted me. I mumbled something about "That's O.K. Happens all the time." Almost in less time than it takes to wink an eye, my opposition turned into friendship.

Smile big and you feel like "happy days are here again." But smile *big*. A half-developed smile is not fully guaranteed. Smile until your teeth show. That large-size smile is fully guaranteed. I've heard many times, "Yes, but when I fear something, or when I'm angry, I don't feel like smiling."

Of course you don't. No one does. The trick is to tell yourself forcefully, "I'm going to smile."

Then smile.

Harness the power of smiling.

—*The Magic of Thinking Big* by David Schwartz

Adopt the behaviors of successful people. *Act successful as you become successful.*

Copyright ©1999 by Addison-Wesley Educational Publishers Inc.

PERSONAL FEEDBACK 4

Name_____

1. You have already chosen your seat for this course.

   Where is it? _____

   Why did you choose it? _____

2. Observe the physical behaviors of your fellow classmates. Name or describe several students who seem to be self-confident.

   _____

   Why do you feel they are self-confident?

   _____

   Identify a student who walks fast and explain what makes you notice.

   _____

Identify the students who participate the most in class discussions.

_____

Why might speaking up in class be considered risk taking? _____

_____

What are the rewards for speaking up in class? _____

_____

Identify several students who have big smiles and friendly greetings.

_____

3. Describe a student in one of your classes who arrives late. _____

_____

From the actions, what does the student's attitude seem to be? _____

_____

What are the consequences? _____

_____

4. Describe a situation in which you have individually talked with a college instructor. _____

_____

POINTS TO PONDER

▲ To become a winner, think like a winner.
▲ Formulate a dream that you turn into reality.
▲ Create the self-image of a star. Believe in your possibilities, and feel "born to win."
▲ Imitate the characteristics and behaviors of successful people.
▲ Decode your syllabus on the first day and keep it for ready reference.
▲ Use a calendar to list your test dates, as well as daily and weekly learning goals.
▲ Beware of unlimited freedom.
▲ Attend class on time and participate in making it successful.
▲ Ask to read the papers of top-scoring students.
▲ Talk to fellow students about class assignments.
▲ Review lecture notes after each class and seek clarification from fellow students.
▲ Ask someone to be your "study buddy."
▲ Use technology to help you learn.
▲ Predict exam questions.

PERSONAL FEEDBACK 5

Name_____

Name_____

Address_____

_____

Home Phone _____

E-mail address _____

Other classes this term with class hours:

_____

_____

_____

Place of work _____

Work schedule _____

Work phone _____

Explain any special concerns about this course or your learning that might be helpful to your instructor.

_____

_____

_____

List any questions that you would like to ask your instructor.

_____

_____

_____

EXPLORE THE NET

- Send an e-mail message to your instructor, just to say, "Hi! I exist, and I want to do well."
- Locate the Web page for your college or another college in the state. Describe the type of information that is included and comment on its usefulness to you.
- Do any of your professors have Web pages? If so, what do you like about them?

For additional readings and exercises, visit the Longman English Skills Web page at:

http://longman.awl.com/englishpages

For a user name and password, please see your instructor.

Copyright ©1999 by Addison-Wesley Educational Publishers Inc.

CHAPTER APPENDIX Weekly Time Chart

TIME	SUNDAY	MONDAY	TUESDAY	WEDNESDAY	THURSDAY	FRIDAY	SATURDAY
8–9							
9–10							
10–11							
11–12							
12–1							
1–2							
2–3							
3–4							
4–5							
5–6							
6–7							
7–8							
8–9							
9–10							
10–11							
11–12							

2 *Stages of Reading*

◆ *What is reading?*
◆ *Do you know when you don't know?*
◆ *What is schema?*
◆ *What do good readers think about as they read?*
◆ *How can you remember what you read?*

Copyright ©1999 by Addison-Wesley Educational Publishers Inc.

Grow as a Learner ◆◆◆◆◆◆◆◆◆◆

In most college courses you will be taught a procedure or process for learning and performing. Seek to understand the process and consciously try to follow it.

Learn from, rather than arguing against, new information. For example, in English classes students are taught the importance of brainstorming and then outlining before writing a paper. All students are taught, yet some follow the procedures while others refuse. Despite years of research by writing professionals, some students continue to start writing without a plan, saying, "I don't need an outline." Be open to trying new methods and changing old habits.

What Is the Reading Process? ◆◆◆◆◆◆◆◆◆◆

In the past, experts thought of reading comprehension as a *product*. They assumed that if the reader could pronounce the words fluently, he or she would automatically be able to comprehend. Instruction focused on practicing and checking for the correct answers rather than on explaining comprehension skills. Newer approaches, by contrast, teach reading comprehension as a *process* in which the reader needs to understand the parts to achieve understanding of the whole. Students are taught how to predict upcoming ideas, activate existing knowledge, relate old information with new, form a main idea, and make inferences.

Stages of Reading ◆◆◆◆◆◆◆◆◆◆

To understand and improve your own reading, visualize the process. Good reading is divided into the following three thinking stages:

1. Before reading, readers *preview* to find out what the material is about, what they already know about the topic, and what they need to find out while reading.
2. During reading, readers *anticipate* upcoming information, visualize and integrate old and new knowledge, and assess their own understanding in order to make adjustments.
3. After reading, readers *recall and react* to what they have learned.

During the past fifty years, many experts have devised study skills strategies that break these thinking stages into small steps. A historical example is SQ3R, which was devised by Francis P. Robinson at Ohio State University. The letters stand for Survey, Question, Read, Recite, and Review. Any of the systems can be successful, but all are systematically designed to engage the reader in thought *before, during,* and *after* reading.

Stage One: Previewing

Previewing is a method of assessing the material, your knowledge of the subject, and your goals for reading. You try to connect with the topic and get an overview of the assignment before starting on the first paragraph. At the beginning of each new course, you should preview your new text to get an overview of the scope of the material. Then, before reading each chapter, preview in greater detail so that you can anticipate what you will be learning. Textbooks proceed by offering signposts such as subheadings, boldface or italic type, and summaries.

Copyright ©1999 by Addison-Wesley Educational Publishers Inc.

Before → **Preview**
Set goals
Activate Schema

After ← **Recall**
React

During
Predict
Picture
Relate
Monitor
Correct

To preview before reading, use these and other signposts to answer the following questions:

1. What is the topic of the material?
2. What do I already know about the subject?
3. What is my purpose for reading?
4. How is the material organized?
5. What will be my plan of attack?

Previewing can energize your reading and help you become an active learner. Clayton Pinette, a professor at the University of Maine, says, "Passiveness in reading at any stage is a form of academic rigor mortis. Without a true inquisitive, active mind, alert and perceptive, the process of reading can be deadly, boring, and often meaningless. Students must be convinced beyond any doubt of the value of energizing."

Signposts for Previewing. The following are typical features of college textbooks that you should consider when you preview.

Learning Questions. Many textbook chapters start with questions designed to heighten your interest and stimulate your thinking. Such questions directly relate to what the material will cover and thus help set goals for the reader.

Title. The title of a book, chapter, or article is the first clue to its meaning. Some titles are designed to be clever to attract attention, but most try to communicate the important thought in the text. Identify the *who, what,* or *why* of the title to anticipate the content of the material and its importance to you.

Introductory Material. For an overview of a textbook, read the table of contents and the preface. The first highlights the book's contents, and the second gives the author's perspective on the subject. Many texts have a detailed outline that serves as a table of contents for each chapter. Others list probing questions that will be answered in each chapter, or begin with a summary of the chapter. Regardless of the specific feature provided, be sure to read the material to anticipate the content.

Subheadings. Subheadings are the titles of the sections within chapters which, like the major titles, describe the content. Usually subheadings appear in bold or italic type and outline the author's message. Turn the subheadings into questions to anticipate what you will need to know from the reading. For example, the subheadings in a marketing text, "Estimating Revenue Potential" and "Simulated Market Test," could be changed to "How Do You Estimate Revenue Potential?" and "What Is a Simulated Market Test?"

Italics, Boldface, and Numbers. Italic and bold type highlight words that merit special emphasis. These are usually terms that you will need to define and remember. Numbers are also used to list important details that you may need to learn.

Visual Aids or Marginal Notations. A biology professor at a major university tells his students to at least look at the illustrations and read the captions in the assigned material before coming to class, even if they don't read the assignment. He wants his students to have a visual overview. Authors use pictures, charts, and graphs to enhance meaning, heighten interest, and help readers visualize information. Additional notations and definitions may be added in the page margins to further simplify the material for the reader.

Concluding Summary or Review. Most textbook chapters end with a summary of the most important points. This may be several paragraphs or a list of the important ideas. Regardless of its form, the summary helps you to recall the material and reflect on its importance.

Read the table of contents of this text and glance through the chapters. Notice the format of the chapters and selectively scan the subheadings. Preview the text to answer the following questions:

1. How many major sections are in this book? 12

2. Many chapters follow a similar format or organization. Which chapters differ? 1, 3, 7, 8, and 12

3. Describe the format of a typical chapter. Introduce a new skill, short practice exercises, and then three longer text selections.

4. What is the purpose of "Points to Ponder"? Review important points in the chapter; a type of summary.

5. In which chapter would you find information on drawing conclusions? 10

6. In the chapter on the main idea, what is the progression of ideas presented for developing the skill? Find topic, then stated main idea, then unstated main idea, and distinguish between distractors.

7. Name five college subjects represented in the longer selections at the end of the chapters. Psychology, Business, Biology, History, Communication

8. In which chapter would you learn more about patterns of organization? 5

9. How does the final chapter differ from the previous chapters? Teaches no new skill and does not include questions for text.

10. In which chapter would you find hints on time management? 1

EXERCISE 2

To get an overview of this chapter, look at the questions on the first page. Read the "Points to Ponder" on page 36 and scan to understand the subheadings and the bold-faced and italicized words. Preview the chapter to answer the following questions:

1. What is metacognition? Knowing about knowing.

2. What is a schema? The "computer chip" in the brain that stores information on the topic. *or* The skeleton of knowledge in your mind on a particular subject.

3. What five thinking strategies do good readers use? Predict, picture, relate, monitor, and correct.

4. What college subjects are represented by the longer reading selections at the end of this chapter? Psychology, Anthropology, and History.

The Power of Prior Knowledge. Experts say that prior knowledge is the most important factor in reading comprehension. The good news is that the more you know, the easier it is for you to read and learn. Every new idea added to your framework of knowledge about a subject makes the next reading assignment on the topic a little bit easier. On the other hand, the bad news is that if you know very little about a subject, the initial reading in that area will be difficult.

Students who already know a lot about history may think that American History assignments are easy. On the other hand, students who perhaps excel in science and know little history might disagree. Most students would probably agree that senior-level college courses are much easier than freshman survey courses.

PERSONAL FEEDBACK 1

Name_____

1. What was your favorite subject in high school and why? _____
_____
_____

2. What magazines do you like to read? _____
_____

3. What sections do you like to read in the newspaper? _____
_____

4. What magazines did your family subscribe to during your high school years? _____
_____

5. What is the best book you have read? _____
_____

6. What television programs do you watch regularly? _____
_____

7. How does prior knowledge seem to relate to your areas of greatest interest? _____
_____

Previewing to Activate Schemata. Prior knowledge on a subject is a schema. According to theory, a **schema** (plural *schemata*) is the skeleton of knowledge in your mind on a particular subject. As you expand your knowledge, the skeleton grows. Here's another way to think about a schema: a schema is like a computer chip in your brain that holds everything you know on a particular

Copyright ©1999 by Addison-Wesley Educational Publishers Inc.

subject. You pull it out when the need arises, add to it, and then return it to storage.

Your preview of the material will help you know which "computer chips" to activate. It is your responsibility to call on what you already know and blend it with the new ideas. If you embellish the new thoughts with your past experience, your reading will become more meaningful.

Students tend to know more than they think they know. No matter how unfamiliar the topic may seem, you can probably provide some small link from your own experience. The written material provides the signals. It becomes *your* task to pick up those signals, and use them to retrieve prior knowledge and form a link of understanding with the next text.

EXAMPLE   Read the following sentence and activate your schema. Identify a knowledge link. Briefly describe an idea or image that comes to mind.

> Cuba became an obsession of American policy makers in 1959, when Fidel Castro and rebels of his 26th of July Movement ousted America's longtime ally Fulgencio Batista.
>
> —*A People and a Nation* by Mary Beth Norton et al.

EXPLANATION   You may know little Cuban history, but you probably know that Miami, Florida has a large and flourishing Hispanic population, begun by people who left Cuba. Do you know why they left Cuba? Link this knowledge of Cubans in Florida to the new information.

Stage Two: Integrating Knowledge

If you watch two students reading silently, can you tell which student comprehends better? Probably not. The behaviors of good silent readers are thinking behaviors that cannot be observed or learned by watching others. These behaviors, however, need not be mysterious to college students.

Knowing About Knowing. A myth in readings, probably inspired by the "speed reading" craze, is that good readers begin an assignment, race through it, and never stop until the last period. In fact, however, *good readers work hard* to assimilate the information they read. If they do not understand or if they get confused, they go back and reread to resolve the confusion. Good readers also understand the processes involved in reading and consciously control them. This awareness and control of the reading processes is called **metacognition,** which one expert defines as "knowing about knowing."[1]

Some students don't know when they don't know. They continue to read even though they are not comprehending. Poor readers tolerate such confusion because they either don't realize that it exists or don't know what to do about it. Poor readers focus on facts, whereas good readers try to assimilate details into a larger cognitive pattern. Good readers monitor their own comprehension. In other words, they supervise their own understanding of the material. They recognize inadequate comprehension and interrupt their reading to seek solutions.

Five Thinking Strategies of Good Readers. In order to find out what good readers do, Beth Davey studied the research on good and poor readers. She discovered that, both consciously and subconsciously, good readers use the following five thinking strategies.[2]

---

[1]Ann L. Brown, "The Development of Memory: Knowing, Knowing About Knowing, and Knowing How to Know," Vol. 2 of *Advances in Child Development and Behavior*, ed. H. W. Reese (New York: Academic Press, 1975).

[2]Adapted from Beth Davey, "Think Aloud—Modeling the Cognitive Processes of Reading Comprehension," *Journal of Reading*, 27 (Oct. 1983): 44–47.

1. Predict: Make Educated Guesses. Good readers make predictions about thoughts, events, outcomes, and conclusions. With the arrival of each new character in an Agatha Christie murder mystery, the reader will make a guess about who the culprit might be. Textbook predictions, while a little less dramatic, are equally important. While reading the facts in a science text, for example, you may be thinking about the concluding theory.

As you read, your predictions are confirmed or denied. If they prove invalid, you make new predictions. For example, in reading an economics text, you might predict that inflation hurts everyone. But after further reading, you discover that real estate investors make money be selling at the inflated prices. Thus, your prediction has proved invalid, and you must readjust your thinking on inflation. Your prediction, although erroneous, has made you more involved with the author's thinking and has helped you to learn.

EXAMPLE What are your predictions for the rest of the section based on these beginning sentences of a textbook paragraph?

> In the history of religion, few stories are more dramatic than that of the Mormons. It is a story with the haunting Biblical overtones of divine revelations and visitations, of persecution and martyrdom, of an exodus two-thirds of the way across a continent, and of ultimate success in establishing a religious society in an uninhabited desert.
>
> —*America and Its People* by James Martin et al.

EXPLANATION The rest of this section will probably be about what prompted the Mormons to move, their hardships, and their successes in a new location. From prior knowledge, some readers already know that the Mormons settled in Utah.

2. Picture: Form Images. For good readers, the words and the ideas on the page trigger mental images that relate directly or indirectly to the material. Since these mental images depend on the reader's experience, visualization is a highly individualistic process. One learner might read about Maine and picture the countryside and the rockbound coast, whereas another, with no experience in the area, might visualize the shape and location of the state on a map. Images are like movies in your head. The reader forms a visualization to enhance the message in the text. Fiction quickly moves the reader into a new world of enjoyment or terror through visualization. Expository or textbook writing may require more imagination than fiction, but the images created also strengthen the message.

EXAMPLE Describe your visualizations for the following sentence.

> A public debate over the proper role of women in the antislavery movement, especially their right to lecture to audiences composed of both sexes, led to the first organized movement of women's rights.
>
> —*America and Its People* by James Martin et al.

EXPLANATION Imagine crowds of angry women eager to speak, but told not to lecture to men. Depending on prior knowledge, you may visualize Sojourner Truth or some of the women who long ago argued for the right to vote.

3. Relate: Draw Comparisons. When you relate your existing knowledge to the new information in the text, you are embellishing the material and making it part of your framework of ideas. A phrase or a situation may remind you of a personal experience that relates to the text. For example, a description of ocean currents may remind you of a strong undertow you once fought while swimming. Such related experiences help you digest the new experience as part of something you already know.

Copyright ©1999 by Addison-Wesley Educational Publishers Inc.

EXAMPLE   Describe a previous experience that the following sentence brings to mind.

> Anyone who has used a compass to find direction knows that the earth's magnetic field has a north pole and a south pole.
>
> —*The Earth* by Edward Tarbuck and Frederick Lutgens

EXPLANATION   Were you ever in a scouting program and taught to use a compass in the woods? Why does the compass work?

4. Monitor: Check Understanding. Monitor your ongoing comprehension to test your understanding of the material. Keep an internal summary or synthesis of the information as it is presented and how it relates to the overall message. Your summary will build with each new detail, and as long as the author's message is consistent, you will continue to form ideas. If, however, certain information seems confusing or erroneous, you should stop and seek a solution to the problem. You must monitor and supervise your own comprehension. Remember that poor readers keep on going in the face of confusion, but good readers seek to resolve the difficulty. Good readers demand complete understanding, and know whether it has been achieved.

EXAMPLE   What is confusing about the following sentence?

> "Another such victory like that on July 1," wrote Richard Harding Davis, "and our troops must retreat."
>
> —*America and Its People* by James Martin et al.

EXPLANATION   You may need to reread and rethink a "retreat" after a "victory." Davis must mean that the victory was too costly.

5. Correct Gaps in Understanding. Do not accept gaps in your reading comprehension. They may signal a failure to understand a word or a sentence. Stop and resolve the problem so you can continue to synthesize and build your internal summary. Seek solutions to confusion. Usually, this means rereading a sentence or looking back at a previous page for clarification. If an unknown word is causing confusion, the definition may emerge through further reading. Changing predictions is also a corrective strategy. For example, you may be predicting that heavy rains saved a country from famine, but, as the conclusion emerges, it seems that fertilizers and irrigation were the saviors. If you cannot fill the gaps yourself, seek help from the instructor or another student.

Remember, there is no shame in looking back in the text. Rereading for clarification or admitting that a prediction was incorrect is part of good reading. The only shame is in viewing a failure to understand as a lack of ability. Researchers have called this attitude "learned helplessness."[3] Such thinking is self-defeating. When good readers experience gaps in comprehension they do not perceive them as failures; instead, they reanalyze the task to achieve full understanding.

EXAMPLE   How could you seek to better understand the following sentence?

> Gibberellins also stimulate cell division at the stem apex, leaf growth, development of sexual flower parts, and (with sugars) differentiation of phloem tissue.
>
> —*A Journey into Life* by Karen Arms and Pamela Camp

---

[3]C. S. Dweck and B. G. Licht, "Learned Helplessness and Intellectual Achievement," in *Human Helplessness: Theory and Applications*, ed. J. Garber and M. F. P. Seligman (New York: Academic Press, 1980).

EXPLANATION   To resolve this kind of confusion, which is common in science texts, you would need to look at a diagram which usually appears next to such a complex reading.

Applying All Five Thinking Strategies. The following passage illustrates the use of the five thinking strategies. Some of the reader's thoughts appear as handwritten comments in the margins. Keep in mind that each person reacts differently. This example merely represents one reader's attempt to integrate knowledge.

EXAMPLE

Do the handwritten thoughts also represent your thoughts?

FACT OR FASHION

In 1800's?
What?
How do you breathe?
Is it healthy?
Are they victims of fashion?

Nineteenth-century doctors were taught that men and women breathed differently: men used their diaphragms to expand their chests, whereas women raised the ribs near the top of the chest. Finally, a woman doctor found that women breathed in this way because their clothes were so fashionably tight that the diaphragm could not move far enough to admit air into the lungs. Some women even had their lower ribs removed surgically so that they could lace their waists more tightly.

—*A Journey into Life* by Karen Arms and Pamela Camp

EXPLANATION   The handwritten comments model the reader's conscious and subconscious thoughts. Such an analysis may seem artificial and intrusive, but be aware that you do incorporate these thinking strategies into your reading. The following exercises are designed to make you more aware of this interaction.

EXERCISE 3

For the following passages, answer the questions and make a conscious effort to use the five strategies as you read:

1. Predict (develop hypotheses).
2. Picture (develop images).
3. Relate (link prior knowledge with new ideas).
4. Monitor (clarify ongoing comprehension).
5. Use corrective strategies (solve comprehension problems).

PASSAGE 1

A SIAMESE CAT

The enzyme that makes the dark pigment melanin is unstable at body temperature, and so fur on the cat's body is light in color. The cat's ears, nose, feet, and tail are cooler. At these lower temperatures, the enzyme can work and make its product. Hence, the fur in these areas is dark.

—*A Journey into Life* by Karen Arms and Pamela Camp

1. How did you predict the chemical reaction? _____

2. Who do you know who has a Siamese cat? _____

3. Does the cat have dark feet and ears? _____

Copyright ©1999 by Addison-Wesley Educational Publishers Inc.

4. Why is a Siamese cat's tail dark? <u>Melanin affects color at tail's cooler</u> <u>temperature.</u>

5. Underline any part of the passage that you found confusing or reread.

PASSAGE 2

VESTIGIAL HAND GRASP

One of the most characteristic types of infant behavior is the grasping reflex of the hand. The response is elicited by touching the palm. Interestingly, the fingers close in a certain sequence. And what is more, the response is more strongly elicited by touching the palm with hair than with a solid object. The first thing that springs to mind, of course, is that this is a vestigial response left from the time when the mother had hair to which the infant had to cling. (Babies still hold tightly to their mother's clothing, so perhaps the pattern still has some value.) It turns out that the hand grasp is more pronounced in premature babies than in those born later, and in fact, a premature baby can be hung on a clothesline. Surprisingly, they can also grasp strongly with their feet. Much of this ability is lost later, a factor that indicates that the tendency is now only rudimentary and vestigial and is disappearing from our behavioral repertoire.

—*Animal Behavior* by Robert Wallace

1. How did you predict why the hair caused a strong response? _____

_____

2. How did you figure out the meaning of *vestigial*? _____

_____

3. Whose baby did you visualize? _____

4. Underline any part of the passage that you found confusing.

Stage Three: Recalling

Recall is your review of what you have read. Recall is self-testing and can be a silent, oral, or written recitation. When you recall, you take an additional few minutes to tell yourself what you have learned before you close the book. Poor readers tend to finish the last paragraph of an assignment, sigh with relief, and close the book without another thought. Study strategies developed by experts, however, stress the importance of a final recall or review stage. The experts emphasize that this final step improves both comprehension and memory.

As a part of monitoring their comprehension, good readers maintain a kind of running summary as they read. The end of an assignment is the time to give voice to this internal summary and review the material for gaps of knowledge. The recall step can be done in your head or on paper. To recall, talk to yourself and test your understanding. Pull the material together under one central idea or generalization, and then review the relevant details and commit them to memory.

Do not neglect this last stage. Finish the reading process with this final step to prove to yourself that you understand the material. To look at this last stage from a metacognitive point of view, you are reviewing your knowledge networks. You have created knowledge networks for new material and added related ideas to existing schemata. You are incorporating information into your own learning systems, selecting appropriate "computer chips" for storage or creating new chips. Recall makes a difference.

How to Recall. The recall stage of reading can be either an internal, organized conversation with yourself or a written reorganization. What method you choose will depend on the difficulty of the material or your purpose for learning. Keep in mind that the goal is self-testing. Rather than waiting for the professor's inquiry, answer your own question, "Do I understand this material?"

Connect and React. After recalling what an author has said, you cannot avoid evaluating its significance for you. As an active, thinking learner you will consciously or subconsciously answer the following questions: Did I enjoy the reading? Was the selection well-written? Do I agree or disagree with the author? How many of the ideas am I going to accept? Feel free to accept or reject ideas according to your prior knowledge and the logic of the presentation. Your response is subjective, but as a critical thinker, you should base it on what you already know and what you have just found out.

EXAMPLE   Read the following passage and decide what it is about and whether you agree or disagree with the author.

> Access is a very important resource for an interest group. As we have noted, a person who makes a campaign contribution will often say something like this: "I don't want any special promise from you; all I want is the right to come and talk to you when I need to." This seemingly modest request may in fact be significant. Access is power.
>
> —*American Democracy* by Fred Harris

EXPLANATION   What is your position on the issue of access and power? You may agree with the author's position. The message is that if you can manage to talk to a powerful political figure, you have an excellent chance of influencing decisions. Since face-to-face contact can be convincing, access probably does give power.

EXERCISE 4   Read the following passages and decide whether you agree or disagree with their messages. Since you are giving your *reactions* to the ideas, there are no right or wrong answers. Think and react.

Copyright ©1999 by Addison-Wesley Educational Publishers Inc.

PASSAGE 1

GENDER DIFFERENCES

Men and women differ with respect to gossip. It isn't that one group gossips and the other does not. [It is the subjects of their talks.] "When most men talk to their friends or on the phone," Tannen says, "they may discuss what's happening in business, the stock market, the soccer match, or politics." "For most women, getting together and talking about their feelings and what is happening in their lives is at the heart of friendship."

Men and women differ when it comes to lecturing and listening. Experimental studies support Tannen in finding that "men are more comfortable than women in giving information and opinions and speaking in an authoritative way to a group, whereas women are more comfortable than men in supporting others."

—*You Just Don't Understand: Women and Men in Conversation* by Deborah Tannen

1. What is the message? <u>Men and women differ in their approach to gossip,</u>
<u>lecturing, and listening.</u>

2. Why do you agree or disagree with these assertions of gender differences on gossip, lecturing, and listening?

   (a) Gossip? _____

   (b) Lecturing? _____

   (c) Listening? _____

PASSAGE 2

LOOKING FOR FRESH PERSPECTIVES

The turning point in solving a problem is typically when a useful insight is reached through an effort to see the situation from a fresh perspective.

Within the Federal Express overnight mail service company, managers were discouraged by the frequent delays in transferring mail between the airplanes that met at night at the central exchange location in Memphis, Tennessee. To keep on schedule, all packages had to be transferred within four hours. The transfer was usually completed barely in time. It was obvious that the employees were not working as fast as they could, but efforts to encourage them to work faster failed. Finally, managers learned that the employees intentionally stretched out the job to earn extra overtime pay. In other words, management had created a pay system that *rewarded slowness!* Once this perspective became clear, a solution was easy to create. The workers were guaranteed pay for a specific number of hours but could leave early if they finished early. Within a month the delays were gone.

—*The Creative Problem Solver's Toolbox* by Richard Fobes

1. What is the message? <u>Federal Express solved a delay problem by looking at</u>
<u>it from a fresh perspective.</u>

2. Describe examples of poor performance in need of a fresh perspective. What fresh perspective would you suggest?

   (a) _____

   (b) _____

Assess Your Progress as a Learner ◆◆◆◆◆◆◆◆◆◆◆

This textbook creates an artificial environment for you to learn about your own reading. Normally after reading, you do not answer ten comprehension questions and ten vocabulary questions. You read, reflect, and move on. In this book, however, the questions are provided to help you monitor your thinking. To improve your skills, you must seriously reflect on what you are getting right and what you are getting wrong. Getting a quick homework or classwork grade is part of the process, but it is not the real purpose. Understanding and improving are the goals, and they require your active participation as a learner. You must assume responsibility for your own improvement.

Levels of Reading Comprehension

In order to give you more insight into your strengths and weaknesses, the comprehension questions at the end of each long reading selection have been labeled as *main idea, detail,* and *inference.* These question types represent different levels of sophistication in reading that can be ranked and defined as follows:

1. Literal—What did the author say? These are detail questions about the facts, and the answers are clearly stated within the material. This is the beginning level of reading comprehension, and the least sophisticated level. A reader might be able to answer detail questions but not understand the overall meaning of the passage.

2. Interpretive—What did the author mean by what was said? These are main idea and inference questions. In order to answer, the reader must interpret the facts along with the author's attitude, using implied meaning to make assumptions and draw conclusions. At this level, you are considering both what is stated and what is unstated in order to figure out what the author is trying to say.

3. Applied—How does the author's message apply to other situations? These are questions that call for reaction, reflection, and critical thinking. This is the highest level of sophistication and involves analyzing, synthesizing, and evaluating. You are putting together what was said with what was meant and applying it to new situations and experiences. You are attempting to make wider use of what you have just learned.

Use the questions in this book as diagnostic information. What do your responses tell you about yourself? What kinds of questions do you always answer correctly? What do your errors tell you about your reading? Learn from your mistakes and begin to categorize your own reading strengths and weaknesses. Throughout the course, refer back to previous work as a reference for your own development. Keeping records and reflecting on your own learning are not a waste of time. They are essential parts of your improvement plan.

Copyright © 1999 by Addison-Wesley Educational Publishers Inc.

PERSONAL FEEDBACK 2

Name_____

1. When you finish a reading assignment, why would you be reluctant to recall what you have read? _____

_____

2. What have you learned in this chapter that is positive about your reading habits? _____
_____

3. What three immediate changes would you suggest for your own reading improvement? _____
   (a) _____
   (b) _____
   (c) _____

4. What did you learn in this chapter about the reading process that surprised you? _____
_____

5. What myths did you have about reading that no longer seem to be true?
_____

6. What is keeping you from becoming an excellent reader? _____
_____

7. What questions would you like to ask your instructor about the reading process? _____
_____
_____

POINTS TO PONDER

▲ Reading comprehension includes understanding the author's words as well as what they suggest, and adding appropriate details.
▲ Good readers understand the processes of reading and consciously control them.
▲ Good readers anticipate content, structure, and purpose.
▲ Good readers activate their schemata by tapping previous knowledge.
▲ Good readers predict, picture, relate, monitor, and use corrective strategies.
▲ After reading, good readers pull the material together as one central idea and review the relevant details.
▲ Good readers evaluate the significance of what they have read, and accept or reject new ideas.
▲ Good readers keep records of their own learning progress.

Copyright ©1999 by Addison-Wesley Educational Publishers Inc.

SELECTION 1	*Psychology*

THINKING BEFORE READING

Preview the selection for clues to content. What do you already know about hypnosis? Activate your prior knowledge. Anticipate the author's ideas and your purpose for reading. Think!

Is hypnosis fake?

Would you be a good candidate for hypnosis? Why or why not?

If you were hypnotized, what posthypnotic suggestion would you like to receive?

I'll read this to find out _____

VOCABULARY PREVIEW

Are you familiar with these words?

focuses	selective	distracting	suggestible	regulating
babble	speculating	anesthesia	posthypnotic	squiggly

When is a posthypnotic suggestion actually given?

Is a stock purchase considered a speculation in the market?

Your instructor may give a true-false vocabulary review before or after reading.

THINKING DURING READING

As you read, use the five thinking strategies of a good reader: predict, picture, relate, monitor, and correct. Answer the questions in the margins that reflect your active thinking.

HYPNOSIS

Hypnosis has been known and used for many hundreds of years, since ancient times. But not until the last one hundred years has scientific study begun to help us understand hypnosis.

WHAT IS HYPNOSIS?

Several different things happen when a person is hypnotized. A hypnotized person doesn't make plans or control his or her own actions or thoughts. People in deep hypnosis, for example, don't seem to think anything unless the hypnotist tells them to. People in lighter hypnosis will sit waiting for the hypnotist to tell them what to do. Also, a hyp-
5   notized person focuses attention in a very selective way. Things that would normally be distracting, such as a loud noise, aren't distracting. Attention is focused on the things the hypnotist says to focus on.

What are you visualizing?

Hypnotized people are very suggestible. If the hypnotist says, "There's a rhinoceros here, see it," they can see it. If the hypnotist points to a chair and says, "You cannot see
10   this," then they don't see it. Instead of dealing with reality themselves, they allow the hypnotist to tell them what is real and what is not. Hypnotized people will act out roles

they usually don't perform. For example, the hypnotist can suggest that the person is really only one year old. The hypnotized person then will crawl around, babble like a baby, and act the way babies are supposed to act. Hypnotized people can be pro-
15   grammed by a suggestion of the hypnotist to forget all they have seen or heard while hypnotized.

Do you know anyone who has been hypnotized? How could hypnotism be used positively?

Not all hypnotized people will show all these effects. There are different levels of hypnosis. People usually have to practice by being hypnotized several times in order to reach the deeper levels. Hypnosis is not sleep. The brain waves of hypnotized people are like
20   those of people who are awake. If you feel like speculating, consider this: The brain waves of people most easily hypnotized often show right cortex activation.

BEING HYPNOTIZED

Different techniques are used by hypnotists. Usually they ask the subject to concentrate on something. The subject has to cooperate. The hypnotist asks the subject to give up some control over the moment-to-moment events in the subject's life and turn over this
25   control to the hypnotist. The hypnotist asks the subject to imagine things under the control of the hypnotist.

Some people are more easily hypnotized than others, some are never hypnotized. Some fall into deep hypnosis readily; most can attain some degree of hypnosis with practice. No one knows clearly why there are these differences. It is possible, however, to pre-
30   dict who will or will not be hypnotized by giving a test of suggestibility. For example, the subject is asked to stand with eyes closed. After a few seconds, the experimenter says: "You're beginning to sway a little bit." Then the experimenter watches to see if the subject sways. (The experimenter must be prepared to catch the ones who really get into it.)

Would you be easy or difficult to hypnotize?

People who show some effects from the suggestions of the experimenter are more easily
35   hypnotized.

Can you hypnotize someone against the person's will? Probably not. If the person had a lot of past experience with hypnosis, and you knew what cues set off the hypnosis, you might be able to arrange for the cues to happen and the person would go under. But that would be rare.

THE EFFECTS OF HYPNOSIS

40   Hypnosis is well known for the really dramatic effects that can sometimes be achieved. Surgeons have successfully used it to suggest that the person can feel no pain. They have removed an appendix with no anesthesia. Hypnotists often suggest things such as: "Watch out for that charging rhinoceros." Then the hypnotized subject ducks and runs. The person swears he can see and hear the animal. One hypnotist held up a piece of

45   chalk and said: "This is a burning cigarette." He touched the arm of the subject with it, and a red mark appeared, just as if the subject had been burned. People can often remember things under hypnosis that they can't remember in the normal state. This may be due to their increased focus of attention.

Could hypnotism help solve crimes?

Another effect is gained by making a posthypnotic suggestion, so that the subject

50   does something after coming out of the hypnosis. The subject is hypnotized and told: "After you wake up, watch what I do. When I scratch my ear, jump up and shout: 'The building is on fire!' Then sit down. You won't remember that I told you this. Okay, now when I count to three, wake up." Then later, in the middle of a class, for example, the hypnotist casually scratches an ear. Up jumps the subject and shouts: "The building is on

55   fire!" Then the subject looks all around, sees the amused faces, gets red with embarrassment, and sits down. "Why did you do that?" asks the hypnotist. "I don't know," says the subject.

Are hypnotized subjects faking it? Not in any usual sense of the word "faking." When the subject is acting like a one-year-old, the subject really believes that he or she is

60   one year old. Of course, some people do fake it, but an experienced hypnotist can distinguish them from the truly hypnotized subjects.

Can you use hypnosis to get people to do things they wouldn't do under different conditions? For example, will people violate their own ethical principles? It has happened—not always, not predictably, but in a few cases. Under deep hypnosis a subject

65   pulled a trigger on a gun that would have killed another person if it had been loaded. People have stuck their hands into pits of snakes they thought were dangerous.

Could evil people manipulate others through hypnotism?

Is it dangerous to play around with hypnosis? Yes. It's dangerous because the subject can become emotional or very dependent on you, and you aren't trained to deal with that. Will a person go under and never come out? No.

WHAT'S GOING ON IN HYPNOSIS?

70   There are several theories. The old one was that hypnosis was a form of sleep, but research has shown this isn't true. Some researchers say: "It's a role the person plays, just like the role of mother, student, or lover. The role has certain things you're supposed to do, and other people expect you to do them. When you're hypnotized, you play the hypnotized role, doing what you think hypnotized people are supposed to do." This may be

75   part of it, but some theories go further.

Hypnosis raises important questions about the organization of the human brain. We know there are levels of organization in the brain. As you read this, for example, a lower part of your brain is regulating your body temperature without your thinking about it. Another part is organizing all these little squiggly patterns on paper into words that make

80   sense. Way up high, you are thinking. Some theorists have said that what happens in hypnosis is that levels in the brain become disconnected. The subject's conscious level is restricted to the things the hypnotist suggests; nothing else is allowed into that consciousness. If the subject's arm is hurt, and the hypnotist says, "No, it's not," the subject doesn't experience the pain at the conscious level. It might as well not exist. All we are

85   aware of is what we are conscious of. In hypnosis, goes this theory, the content of your conscious brain comes under the direction of the hypnotist. Why this happens, or how it happens, is not known.

Do you believe this?

(1,237 words)

—*Psychology: What It Is/How to Use It* by David Watson

Copyright ©1999 by Addison-Wesley Educational Publishers Inc.

THINKING AFTER READING

RECALL: Self-test your understanding. Your instructor may choose to give a true-false review.

REACT: If you were a smoker, would you try hypnosis to help you stop smoking?

REFLECT: Describe three positive uses of hypnosis.

(1) _____

(2) _____

(3) _____

 THINK CRITICALLY: How could terrorists use hypnotism to sabotage Pentagon security? Write your answer on a separate sheet of paper.

Name _____

Date_____

COMPREHENSION QUESTIONS

Answer the following with *a, b, c,* or *d,* or fill in the blank. In order to help you analyze your strengths and weaknesses, the question types are indicated.

Main Idea _____a_____ 1. The author's primary purpose in this passage is

    a. to explain hypnosis and its effects.
    b. to encourage the use of hypnosis for adjustment problems.
    c. to explain why people want to be hypnotized.
    d. to summarize the need for hypnosis in modern society.

Detail _____c_____ 2. Scientific study shows that hypnotized persons are all of the following *except*

    a. highly suggestible.
    b. concentrated in their attention.
    c. asleep.
    d. willingly controlled by the hypnotist.

Inference _____b_____ 3. The author believes that

    a. everyone can be hypnotized.
    b. most people can be hypnotized who want to be.
    c. people can be hypnotized who don't want to be.
    d. most people fall into deep hypnosis readily.

Detail _____c_____ 4. Under hypnosis people have been known to do all of the following *except*

    a. act in a manner harmful to their own bodies.
    b. violate their own ethical principles.
    c. never come out of the hypnotic state.
    d. imitate an animal behavior.

Inference 5. Some theorists believe that a person does not feel pain under hypnosis because <u>the sensation does not reach the conscious level.</u>

Inference _____b_____ 6. According to the passage, it can be concluded that

    a. hypnosis is harmful and should not be used.
    b. hypnosis can be beneficial.
    c. hypnosis has been used only during the past hundred years.
    d. hypnotists are illegitimate hucksters.

Inference _____a_____ 7. The author implies that a person who is easily hypnotized

    a. has a vivid imagination.
    b. is less intelligent than one who is difficult to hypnotize.
    c. has inadequate brain regulation.
    d. wants to maintain control.

Answer the following with *T* (true), *F* (false), or *CT* (can't tell).

Inference _____T_____ 8. Posthypnotic suggestion can make a person engage in an atypical action while not under hypnosis.

Copyright ©1999 by Addison-Wesley Educational Publishers Inc.

Inference _____CT_____ 9. Hypnosis is more popular in the United States for entertainment than for relief of pain.

Inference _____T_____ 10. Hypnosis is an example of mind over matter.

VOCABULARY

Answer the following with *a, b, c,* or *d* for the word or phrase that best defines the boldface word used in the selection. The number in parentheses indicates the line of the passage in which the word is located.

_b_ 1. "**focuses** attention" (5)

    a. applies
    b. concentrates
    c. suggests
    d. recalls

_d_ 2. "a very **selective** way" (5)

    a. general
    b. amateurish
    c. strict
    d. discriminating

_a_ 3. "would normally be **distracting**" (5–6)

    a. diverting
    b. unsafe
    c. inspiring
    d. frightening

_d_ 4. "are very **suggestible**" (8)

    a. sensible
    b. sensitive
    c. ignorant
    d. easily influenced

_c_ 5. "**babble** like a baby" (13–14)

    a. misbehave
    b. converse intelligently
    c. make meaningless sounds
    d. play

_a_ 6. "feel like **speculating**" (20)

    a. pondering
    b. talking
    c. changing
    d. remembering

_c_ 7. "with no **anesthesia**" (42)

    a. doctor
    b. mental concern
    c. painkillers
    d. antibodies

_b_ 8. "a **posthypnotic** suggestion" (49)

    a. before hypnosis
    b. after hypnosis
    c. during hypnosis
    d. nonhypnotic

_c_ 9. "is **regulating** your body temperature" (78)

    a. increasing
    b. decreasing
    c. controlling
    d. simplifying

_d_ 10. "little **squiggly** patterns" (79)

    a. straight
    b. meaningful
    c. organized
    d. twisted

ASSESS YOUR LEARNING

Review questions that you did not understand, found confusing, or answered incorrectly. Seek clarification. Indicate beside each item the source of your confusion and notice the question type. Beside confusing vocabulary items, make notes to help you remember the new word. Use your textbook as a learning tool.

EXPLORE THE NET

- Find a recent article that explores the use of hypnosis in an area that interests you.
- Is there a location near you that offers hypnosis programs for smoking, stress, or weight loss? If so, when, where, and what is the cost?

For additional readings and exercises, visit the Longman English Skills Web page at:

http://longman.awl.com/englishpages

For a user name and password, please see your instructor.

SELECTION 2   *History*

THINKING BEFORE READING

Preview the selection for clues to content. Activate your schema and anticipate what you will learn.

Why did the Pilgrims come to America?

Where did the Pilgrims land in America?

How did the Native Americans help the Pilgrims?

This selection will probably say _____

VOCABULARY PREVIEW

Are you familiar with these words?

solitude	scrawled	ecstatic	tinged	demeaned
solace	invincible	degraded	momentum	duped

What does the prefix *de* in *demeaned* and *degraded* mean?

Do you enjoy solitude?

What happens when a political campaign gains momentum?

Your instructor may give a true-false vocabulary review before or after reading.

THINKING DURING READING

As you read, predict, picture, relate, monitor, and correct. Answer the questions in the margins that reflect your active thinking.

Copyright ©1999 by Addison-Wesley Educational Publishers Inc.

SQUANTO

The Pilgrims called him Squanto, a corruption of his given name, Tisquantum. Each Thanksgiving Americans remember him as the valued native friend who saved the suffering Pilgrims from starvation. Few know the other ways in which Tisquantum's life reflected the disastrous collision of human beings that occurred in the wake of Christopher Columbus's first voyage of discovery to America in 1492. European explorers believed they had stumbled upon two empty continents, which they referred to as the "new world." In actuality, the new world was both very old and the home of millions of people. These Native Americans experienced chaos and death when they came into contact with the Europeans. A little more than 100 years after Columbus, at the time of the Pilgrims, the American Indian population had declined by as much as 90 percent. The tragic story of Tisquantum and his tribe, the Patuxets of eastern Massachusetts, vividly portrays what happened.

Born about 1590, Tisquantum acquired the values of his Algonquian-speaking elders before experiencing much contact with adventurers from overseas. Tribal fathers taught him that personal dignity came from respecting the bounties of nature and serving one's clan and village, not from acquiring material possessions. He also learned the importance of physical and mental endurance. To be accepted as an adult, he spent a harrowing winter surviving alone in the wilderness. When he returned the next spring, his Patuxet fathers fed him poisonous herbs for days on end, which he unflinchingly ate—and survived by forced vomiting. Having demonstrated his fortitude, tribal members declared him a man.

Living among 2000 souls in the Patuxet's principal village, located on the very spot where the Pilgrims settled in 1620, Tisquantum may well have foreseen trouble ahead when fair-skinned Europeans started visiting the region. First there were fishermen; then in 1605 the French explorer, Samuel de Champlain, stopped at Plymouth Bay. More fatefully, Captain John Smith, late of the Virginia colony, passed through in 1614. Smith's party treated the Patuxets with respect, but they viewed the natives as little more than wild beasts, to be exploited if necessary. Before sailing away, Smith ordered one of his lieutenants, Captain Thomas Hunt, to stay behind with a crew of mariners and gather up a rich harvest of fish. After completing his assignment, Hunt lured 20 Indians, among them Tisquantum, on board his vessel and, without warning, set his course for the slave market in Malaga, Spain.

Somehow Tisquantum avoided a lifetime of slavery. By 1617 he was in England, where he devoted himself to mastering the English tongue. One of his sponsors, Captain Thomas Dermer, who had been with Smith in 1614, asked Tisquantum to serve as an interpreter and guide for yet another New England expedition. Eager to return home, the native readily agreed and sailed back to America in 1619.

When Dermer's party put in at Plymouth Bay, a shocked Tisquantum discovered that nothing remained of his once-thriving village, except overgrown fields and rotting human bones. As if swept away by some unnamed force, the Patuxets had disappeared from the face of the earth. Trained to hide his emotions, Tisquantum grieved privately. Soon he learned about a disastrous epidemic. Thousands of natives had died in the Cape Cod vicinity. They had succumbed to diseases heretofore unknown in New England, in this case probably chicken pox carried there from Europe by fishermen and explorers. When these microparasites struck, the native populace, lacking antibodies, had no way of fending them off.

Tisquantum soon left Dermer's party and went in search of possible survivors. He was living with the Pokanoket Indians when the Pilgrims stepped ashore in December 1620 at the site of his old village. The Pilgrims endured a terrible winter in which half their numbers died. Then in the early spring of 1621 a lone Indian, Samoset, appeared in Plymouth Colony. He spoke halting English and told of another who had actually lived in England. Within a week Tisquantum arrived and agreed to stay and help the Pilgrims produce the necessities of life.

Tisquantum taught them how to grow Indian corn (maize), a crop unknown in Europe, and how to catch great quantities of fish. His efforts resulted in an abundance of

What is the author's attitude toward history?

Visualize the population difference.

This is similar to rituals in other cultures?

What kind of trouble was ahead?

How did he escape?

Why did the natives die?

SQUANTO

55   food, celebrated in the first Thanksgiving feast during the fall of 1621. To future Pilgrim Governor William Bradford, Squanto "was a special instrument sent of God for their good beyond their expectation."

What happens to him?

The story does not have a pleasant ending. Contact with the English had changed Tisquantum, and he adopted some of their practices. In violation of his childhood train-
60   ing, he started to serve himself. As Bradford recorded, Squanto told neighboring Indian tribes that the Pilgrims would make war on them unless they gave him gifts. Further, he would unleash the plague, which the English "kept . . . buried in the ground, and could

Had he changed his culture?

send it among whom they would." By the summer of 1622 Squanto had become a prob-lem for the Pilgrims, who were eager for peace. Then he fell sick, "bleeding much at the
65   nose," and died within a few days as yet another victim of some European disease.

As demonstrated by Tisquantum's life, white-Indian contacts did not point toward a fusing of Native American and European customs, values, and ideals. Rather, the west-ward movement of peoples destroyed Indian societies and replaced them with European-based communities. The history of the Americas (and of the United States) cannot be

Where else did this happen?

70   fully appreciated without considering the reasons why thousands of Europeans crossed the Atlantic Ocean and sought dominance over the American continents and their native peoples. Three groups in particular, the Spanish, French, and English, succeeded in this life-and-death struggle that changed forever the course of human history.

(943 words)

—*America and Its People* by James Martin et al.

THINKING AFTER READING

RECALL: Self-test your understanding. Your instructor may choose to give a true-false review.

REACT: Why did the Indians tolerate the European visitors and settlers?

REFLECT: What experiences might have led Squanto to "start to serve himself"?

THINK CRITICALLY: Explain how the cultural values, goals, and ethics of the Native Americans as illustrated by Squanto in his youth differed from those of Europeans, and thus caused conflict.

Copyright ©1999 by Addison-Wesley Educational Publishers Inc.

Name _____

Date _____

COMPREHENSION QUESTIONS

Answer the following with *a, b, c,* or *d,* or fill in the blank. In order to help you analyze your strengths and your weaknesses, the question types are indicated.

Main Idea ___b___ 1. The best statement of the main idea of this selection is:

    a. Squanto saved the Pilgrims from disaster by helping them produce the necessities of life.
    b. Squanto's life portrays the destructive clash between the Indian and European cultures.
    c. Each Thanksgiving, Americans remember Squanto for saving the Pilgrim colony from further suffering.
    d. Squanto learned the English language and the English ways.

Inference ___c___ 2. The author suggests that the Patuxets valued all of the following *except*

    a. bravery.
    b. endurance.
    c. wealth.
    d. strength.

Inference ___c___ 3. The history of Plymouth Bay in the 1600s suggests that it was popular because of its

    a. favorable climate.
    b. rich farm land.
    c. accessible port.
    d. friendly people.

Inference 4. The primary purpose of this selection is to explain the historical significance of Squanto.

Inference ___a___ 5. The author implies that Captain Thomas Dermer

    a. was kind to Squanto and respected his ability.
    b. brought disease to the Patuxet village.
    c. forced Squanto to stay with him in Plymouth.
    d. purchased Squanto from Captain Hunt.

Detail ___a___ 6. Squanto became a problem for the Pilgrims because

    a. he used threats to bribe the Indians.
    b. he demanded money from the Pilgrims.
    c. he sought revenge for the destruction of his village.
    d. he was inciting the Indians to revolt.

Inference ___d___ 7. The author implies that the success of Spanish, French, and English settlements in America was based on

    a. a fusing of Native American and European customs.
    b. a mutual respect and cooperation among the Spanish, French, and English.
    c. the struggle of Europeans to blend their own culture with the existing culture of the new land.
    d. destruction of the Indian culture.

Answer the following with *T* (true) or *F* (false).

Detail   _____F_____ 8. According to the passage, Samoset learned his English from Squanto.

Detail   _____F_____ 9. Captain Thomas Hunt came to Plymouth Bay to capture Indians for the slave market.

Inference   _____F_____10. Squanto was believed to have died from chicken pox.

VOCABULARY

Answer the following with *a, b, c,* or *d* for the word or phrase that best defines the boldface word used in the selection. The number in parentheses indicates the line of the passage in which the word is located.

__c__ 1. "**corruption** of his given name" (1)

    a. interpretation
    b. translation
    c. negative change
    d. misuse

__a__ 2. "disastrous **collision**" (4)

    a. clash
    b. anger
    c. momentum
    d. conclusion

__a__ 3. "in the **wake** of Christopher Columbus's" (4–5)

    a. aftermath
    b. voyage
    c. rebirth
    d. awareness

__d__ 4. "**bounties** of nature" (15)

    a. sacrifices
    b. limits
    c. refinements
    d. riches

__b__ 5. "demonstrated his **fortitude**" (20)

    a. health
    b. courage
    c. hatred
    d. loyalty

__c__ 6. "**succumbed** to diseases" (42)

    a. rejected
    b. admitted
    c. yielded
    d. encountered

__c__ 7. "**fending** them off" (45)

    a. wishing
    b. locating
    c. repelling
    d. ordering

__c__ 8. "**violation** of his childhood training" (59)

    a. contradiction
    b. anxiety
    c. breaking the rules
    d. mastery

__a__ 9. "**unleash** the plague" (62)

    a. release
    b. direct
    c. multiply
    d. create

__d__10. "**dominance** over the American continents" (71)

    a. democracy
    b. riches
    c. affection
    d. superiority

ASSESS YOUR LEARNING

Review confusing questions, seek clarification, and make notes in your text to help you remember new information and vocabulary.

Copyright ©1999 by Addison-Wesley Educational Publishers Inc.

EXPLORE THE NET

- Find out more about how Squanto helped the Pilgrims in Plymouth.
- What historic attractions are open to tourists in Plymouth Bay?

For additional readings and exercises, visit the Longman English Skills Web page at:

http://longman.awl.com/englishpages

For a user name and password, please see your instructor.

SELECTION 3 *Anthropology*

THINKING BEFORE READING

Preview the selection for clues to content. Activate your schema and anticipate what you will learn.

What is the origin of dreadlocks?

What is reggae music?

Where is Jamaica?

I'll read this to find out _____

_____

VOCABULARY PREVIEW

Are you familiar with these words?

tartan	inclination	redemption	fuses	derive
invoke	degeneration	unkempt	defiance	enhance

Do parents appreciate defiance in a child?

How do the terms *regeneration* and *degeneration* differ?

What does the prefix in *unkempt* mean?

Your instructor may give a true-false vocabulary review before or after reading.

THINKING DURING READING

As you read, use the five thinking strategies of a good reader: predict, picture, relate, monitor, and correct. Answer the questions in the margins that reflect your active thinking.

DRESS CODES AND SYMBOLISM[1]

Visualize different hairstyles.

The importance of symbols as a source of cultural diversity can be seen in the dress codes and hairstyles of different societies. In most situations, the symbolism of clothing and hairstyles communicates different messages ranging from political beliefs to identification with specific ethnic or religious groups. The tartan of a Scottish clan, the Mao jacket of a

What are the messages of each?

5 Chinese revolutionary, the black leather jacket and long hair of a motorcycle gang member in the United States, and the veil of an Islamic woman in Saudi Arabia provide a symbolic vocabulary that creates cultural diversity.

Many examples of clothing styles could be used to illustrate how symbols are used to produce cultural diversity. Consider, for instance, changing dress codes in the United

What symbolizes rebellion today?

10 States. During the 1960s, many young people wore jeans, sandals, and beads to symbolize their rebellion against what they conceived as the conformist inclinations of American society. By the 1980s, many of the same people were wearing "power suits" as they sought to advance up the corporate ladder.

An example of how hairstyles can create meaningful symbolic codes can be seen in a

15 group known as the Rastafarians (sometimes known as Rastas or Rastaman) of Jamaica. The majority of the people of Jamaica are of African descent. During the eighteenth and nineteenth centuries, they were brought to Jamaica by European slave traders to work on plantations. The Rastafarians are a specific religious group within Jamaica who believe that Haile Selassie (1892–1975), the former emperor of Ethiopia, whose original name

Who is he?

20 was Ras Tafari, was the black Messiah who appeared in the flesh for the redemption of all blacks exiled in the world of white oppression. Rastafarian religious fuses Old Testament teachings, Christian mysticism, and Afro-Jamaican religious beliefs. The Rastafarian movement originated as a consequence of harsh economic, political, and living conditions in the slums of Jamaica.

Visualize someone with dreadlocks.

25 In the 1950s, during the early phase of the Rastafarian movement, some male members began to grow their hair in "locks" or "dreadlocks" to symbolize their religious and political commitments. This hairstyle became well known in Western society through reggae music and Rasta musicians such as the late Bob Marley. Rastafarians derive the sym-

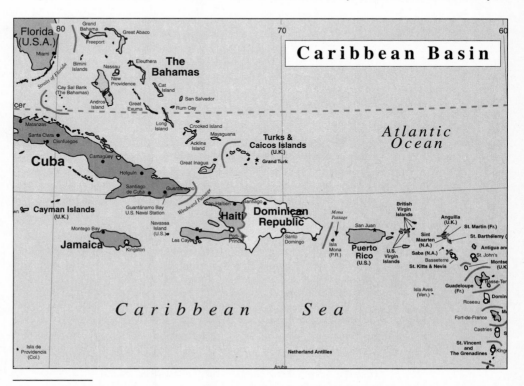

Copyright ©1999 by Addison-Wesley Educational Publishers Inc.

[1]Scupin, Raymond. From *Cultural Anthropology: A Global Perspective*, 3E by Raymond Scupin. Copyright 1998. Reprinted by permission of Prentice-Hall, Inc. Upper Saddle River, NJ.

bolism of the dreadlock hairstyle of the Rastafarians from the Bible. They view the
30   unshaven man as the natural man and invoke Samson as one of the most important figures in the Bible. Dreadlocks also reflect a dominant symbol within the Rastafarian movement, the lion, which is associated with Haile Selassie, one of whose titles was the "Conquering Lion of Judah." To simulate the spirit of the lion, some Rastas do not cut their
hair, sometimes growing their locks 20 inches or more.

35   In addition, the dreadlock hairstyle has a deeper symbolic significance in Jamaican
society, where hair was often referred to as an index of racial and social inequality. Fine,
silky hair was considered "good," whereas woolly, kinky hair was frowned on (Barrett,
1977). Thus, the Rastafarian hairstyle was a defiant symbol of resistance to the cultural
values and norms of Jamaican society.

40   The cultural symbolism of the Rastafarian dreadlocks and long beards represents sav-
agery, wildness, danger, disorder and degeneration. It sends the message that Rastafarians are outside of Jamaican society. Dreadlocks are viewed by many Jamaicans as
unkempt, dangerous, and dirty. Yet to the Rastafarians, dreadlocks symbolize power, liberation, and defiance. Through their hairstyle they announce to society that they do not
45   accept the values, beliefs, and norms of the majority of the people.

How do we each
announce that?

Thus, to a great extent, culture consists of a network of symbolic codes that enhance
values, beliefs, worldviews, and ideologies within a society. Humans go to great lengths
to create symbols that provide meaning for individuals and groups. These symbolic
meanings are a powerful source of cultural diversity.

(621 words)

—*Cultural Anthropology: A Global Perspective* by Raymond Scupin

THINKING AFTER READING

RECALL: Self-test your understanding. Your instructor may choose to give a
true-false review.

REACT: Why do some people want to look culturally different and others want to conform? _____

_____

REFLECT: What cultural symbolism is created by body piercing and tatoos?

_____

_____

THINK CRITICALLY: Describe how a cultural group in your area uses clothing and hairstyle as symbols of defiance. _____

_____

_____

Copyright ©1999 by Addison-Wesley Educational Publishers Inc.

Name _____

Date _____

COMPREHENSION QUESTIONS

Answer the following with *a, b, c,* or *d,* or fill in the blank. In order to help you analyze your strengths and weaknesses, the question types are indicated.

Main Idea   ___d___ 1. The best statement of the main idea of this selection is:

      a. Hairstyles and dress codes identify political beliefs in diverse societies.
      b. The Rastafarian movement symbolized a religious and political commitment.
      c. Symbols provide meaning and a satisfaction of biological needs in society.
      d. Hairstyles and dress codes can be important symbols of cultural diversity in different societies.

Inference   ___c___ 2. The author uses the examples of the Scottish tartan, the Mao jacket, the motorcycle jacket, and the Islamic veil to show

      a. the political power of dress codes in different societies.
      b. the diversity of clothing styles throughout the world.
      c. dress codes that symbolize different ethnic and religious groups.
      d. the resistance to change of culturally different groups.

Inference   ___c___ 3. The author suggests that the young people wearing jeans in the 1960s wore "power suits" in the 1980s because

      a. styles changed.
      b. the American government changed.
      c. their attitudes and goals changed.
      d. both outfits symbolized rebellion.

Inference   4. The author uses the term "power suits" with quotation marks to indicate _that the term has a special cultural meaning_____

Detail   ___b___ 5. All of the following are true of the Rastafarians *except*

      a. they believe that Emperor Haile Selassie was the black Messiah.
      b. they are the original natives of Jamaica.
      c. they are a religious group with political commitments.
      d. they formed as a result of harsh living conditions in Jamaica.

Detail   ___b___ 6. All of the following are true of the Rastafarians' dreadlock hairstyle *except*

      a. the hairstyle symbolizes the lion.
      b. Haile Selassie wore his hair in dreadlocks.
      c. long hair suggests the Biblical strength of Samson.
      d. dreadlocks represent liberation and defiance.

Inference   ___c___ 7. The author's primary purpose in describing the Rastafarians is to

      a. give an example of how a hairstyle creates a religion.
      b. explain cultural differences in Jamaican history.
      c. link hairstyles to religion and music.
      d. compare the cultural symbols of Jamaica with those of the world.

Answer the following with *T* (true) or *F* (false).

Detail   __F__   8. Samson was known as the "Conquering Lion of Judah."

Detail   __T__   9. The Rastafarian movement began while Haile Selassie was still alive.

Inference   __F__ 10. The author suggests that the majority of people in Jamaica are Rastafarians.

VOCABULARY

Answer the following with *a, b, c,* or *d* for the word or phrase that best defines the boldface word used in the selection. The number in parentheses indicates the line of the passage in which the word is located.

__b__ 1. "**tartan** of a Scottish clan" (4)

     a. jacket
     b. plaid cloth design
     c. hair
     d. religion

__a__ 2. "conformist **inclinations**" (11)

     a. preferences
     b. rejections
     c. emotions
     d. difficulties

__c__ 3. "**redemption** of all blacks" (20–21)

     a. nourishment
     b. leadership
     c. freedom
     d. foundation

__d__ 4. "**fuses** Old Testament teachings" (21–22)

     a. separates
     b. confuses
     c. reduces
     d. combines

__b__ 5. "**derive** the symbolism" (28–29)

     a. teach
     b. originate
     c. learn
     d. read

__a__ 6. "**invoke** Samson" (30)

     a. call upon
     b. worship
     c. nominate
     d. picture

__a__ 7. "disorder, and **degeneration**" (41)

     a. deterioration
     b. disobedience
     c. dishonesty
     d. cruelty

__c__ 8. "**unkempt,** dangerous, and dirty" (43)

     a. mean
     b. famous
     c. messy
     d. insane

__d__ 9. "liberation, and **defiance**" (43–44)

     a. devotion
     b. dedzz
     c. bravery
     d. rebelliousness

__b__ 10. "**enhance** values" (46–47)

     a. complicate
     b. strengthen
     c. imitate
     d. ignore

ASSESS YOUR LEARNING

Review confusing questions, seek clarification, and make notes in your text to help you remember new information and vocabulary.

Copyright ©1999 by Addison-Wesley Educational Publishers Inc.

EXPLORE THE NET

- What is the connection between the Rastafarians and Ethiopia?
- Where in the United States could you meet with other Rastafarians for religious services?

For additional readings and exercises, visit the Longman English Skills Web page at:

http://longman.awl.com/englishpages

For a user name and password, please see your instructor.

Vocabulary

◆ *What are context clues?*
◆ *What are roots, prefixes, and suffixes?*
◆ *How do you use the dictionary?*
◆ *Do words have "families"?*
◆ *What is a glossary?*
◆ *Why use a thesaurus?*
◆ *What comparisons form analogies?*

—*Library II*, 1960, Jacob Lawrence, Courtesy of the artist
and Francine Seders Gallery, Seattle, Washington

Copyright ©1999 by Addison-Wesley Educational Publishers Inc.

Learning New Words ◆◆◆◆◆◆◆◆◆◆

Recognizing the meaning of words is essential to understanding what you read. If you have a weak vocabulary and stumble over unknown words when you read, you will lose your train of thought and end up concentrating on words rather than on meaning. A poor vocabulary severely limits your reading comprehension and speed.

Research tells us that you are already phenomenally successful at vocabulary acquisition. On the average, you have learned 3,000 to 5,000 words each year from kindergarten through twelfth grade. Since experts estimate that only 300 new words are systematically taught each year by a teacher, congratulate yourself that independently you have learned approximately 2,700 words every year! Were you afraid of new words? Apparently not, because during each of those years, you encountered 15,000 to 30,000 unknown words and you survived. That makes you a very efficient vocabulary builder. Continue to expand your vocabulary knowledge using those skills that have already made you an expert.

To the college reader, being able to recognize a large number of words is more important than being able to use each one of them. Studies show that we use only about 20 percent of the words we know. The average high school graduate recognizes about 50,000 words and uses only 10,000, whereas the average college graduate recognizes around 70,000 words and uses approximately 15,000. This means that during your years in college you probably will learn about 20,000 new words.

The English language contains about one million words. This number includes technical words in all disciplines, many of which the average person would never use. As a college student, however, you are becoming an expert in a particular field and a mini-expert in several areas. Each time you take a course in a new discipline, you are faced with a vocabulary unique to that subject. It takes a little time and a lot of effort to master these new words. After overcoming this initial shock of vocabulary adjustment for each new course, the reading becomes easier and comprehension improves.

PERSONAL FEEDBACK 1

Name_____

1. What is your present system for remembering new words?

   _____

   _____

   _____

2. For the ten vocabulary items following the selections in Chapter 2 on hypnosis, Squanto, and dress codes, why do you think the line numbers were given for the words? _____

   _____

   _____

3. Why do instructors say that studying Latin is a useful way to increase your vocabulary? _____

   _____

4. What is the last new word you can remember learning? _____
_____

5. What is a word that you frequently encounter, but do not completely understand? _____
_____

6. On a scale of one to ten, with ten meaning *excellent at the college level,* how would you rate your vocabulary at present? _____
_____
_____

7. What do you feel are the benefits of having a large vocabulary? _____
_____
_____

8. List ten adjectives that describe you. Stretch your vocabulary and go beyond simple one- and two-syllable words. _____
_____
_____
_____

Remembering New Words ◆◆◆◆◆◆◆◆◆◆◆

Use Association

Certain new words, especially "college-level" words, are hard to remember because you don't hear them every day and can't easily work them into a typical conversation. To latch on to a new word, form an association with it. Try to remember the word in the context in which it was used. Visualize the word or a situation pertaining to the word. Always try to think of a new word in a phrase, rather than in isolation. For example, do you know the word *surrogate?* Perhaps you encountered the word in psychology class when studying Harlow's experiments on the need for love in infants. The surrogates were wire models substituted for real monkey mothers to test the infant monkey's attraction. To remember the word *surrogate,* think of it in the phrase *surrogate mother* and visualize the infant monkey cuddling up to a wire, artificial mother for love and affection. This association leaves an indelible picture in your mind.

Use Concept Cards

You can also use concept cards to help you remember vocabulary. *Concept* means idea. On a concept card you expand the definition of a single word into a fully developed idea. You are creating an episode for the new word by providing a sentence, a picture, and a source reference.

Copyright ©1999 by Addison-Wesley Educational Publishers Inc.

FRONT

surrogate mother

The baby monkey preferred
the terry cloth surrogate mother

Passage text on love

BACK

Def: substitute, as in the wire
mothers in the monkey love
experiments

Keep a concept card file of new words. Include more than the usual "mystery word" on the front of the card and the definition on the back. Use the technique of association, and on the front of the card write the word within a meaningful phrase or sentence, or both. Also on the front, note where you encountered the new word. On the back of the card, write the definition and, to add a further memory link, draw a picture that illustrates the way you are using the word in your phrase or sentence.

Practice Your New Words

Review your concept cards regularly. Look at the word on the front and quiz yourself on the definition. When you feel you have a clear understanding of the meaning, use your new word in writing or in conversation.

Notice the words around you. As you begin to pay attention to unfamiliar terms in print and in conversations, you will more than likely discover that you encounter more interesting words.

Unlocking the Meaning of New Words ◆◆◆◆◆◆◆◆◆◆◆

Use Context Clues

To figure out the meaning of a new word, do not immediately go charging off to the dictionary and record a definition as if it were one more addition to a giant notebook list of words. Contrary to what you may have heard, the dictionary is a *last* resort. Instead, first try to figure out the meaning from the context, the way the word is used in the sentence, or other clues within the paragraph.

Use Knowledge of Word Parts

Another way to discover the meaning of a word is to examine its parts. Do you recognize any prefixes, suffixes, or roots, such as *pseudo*, meaning *false*, or *nym*, meaning *name*, in *pseudonym?* If you know these word parts, you can easily figure out that *pseudonym* means a false name rather than a real one. Samuel Clemens' use of the name Mark Twain is an example of a pseudonym.

Use the Glossary and the Dictionary

If a word is unique to a subject area, such as the marketing term *promotional mix*, refer to the glossary in the back of the textbook for a definition that pertains specifically to that field. If all else fails and you can't understand what you are reading without a definition of the word, then go to the dictionary. But if the word is not essential to your general comprehension, skip it entirely or come back to it later. Your purpose for reading is to get meaning, not to collect vocabulary words. As you read more and encounter more new words, your vocabulary will naturally expand. Make a habit of noticing new words and try to remember them by association.

Types of Context Clues ◆◆◆◆◆◆◆◆◆◆◆

The first line of attack on a new word is to try to figure out the meaning from its context, or the way it is used in the sentence or paragraph. There are several types of context clues. The following examples show how each type can be used to figure out word meaning.

DEFINITION

The unknown word is defined within the sentence or paragraph.

EXAMPLE

The explorers landed in an *alien* environment, a place both foreign and strange to their beloved homeland.

EXPLANATION

The definition is set off by a comma following the phrase in which the word appears. *Alien* means *strange* or *foreign*.

EXERCISE 1

For each of the context clue exercises in this section, mark *a, b, c,* or *d* for the meaning closest to that of the boldface word. Do not use your dictionary.

_____d_____ 1. The CIA was engaged in **covert** activities in South America that were not made public.

    a. foreign
    b. dishonest
    c. dangerous
    d. hidden

FRONT

BACK

covert operations in South America

CIA activities

hidden or secret

Copyright ©1999 by Addison-Wesley Educational Publishers Inc.

_____c_____ 2. The meeting was brief, and the message was **concise** and to the point.

      a. laborious
      b. lengthy
      c. short
      d. important

_____a_____ 3. If we have to have a pet around the house, get one that is **docile** and easy to manage.

      a. gentle
      b. short
      c. sick
      d. young

_____a_____ 4. He talked so loudly that it became the **dominant** characteristic of his personality, the one you remembered.

      a. outstanding
      b. laudable
      c. negative
      d. diminished

_____a_____ 5. The student was accused of **plagiarism** because the term paper contained the exact words of an author without giving a reference.

      a. stealing words
      b. false handwriting
      c. counterfeiting
      d. sin

ELABORATING DETAILS

Descriptive details that suggest the meaning of the unknown word.

EXAMPLE

The natives were *hostile* when the settlers approached their village. They lined up across the road and drew their weapons. The settlers were afraid to go farther.

EXPLANATION

As described in the sentences after the word, *hostile* must mean *unfriendly.*

EXERCISE 2

_____b_____ 1. Since she had only a few minutes to spare, the professor gave the paper a **cursory** reading.

      a. careful
      b. hasty
      c. thoughtful
      d. modest

_____a_____ 2. No one was completely sure of the politician's position on the tax cut question because the answer was so **ambiguous.**

      a. confusing
      b. silly
      c. late
      d. incomplete

_____c_____ 3. Eating lunch on the edge of a dangerous precipice is a **precarious** position for a summertime picnic.

    a. exciting
    b. lovely
    c. risky
    d. scenic

_____c_____ 4. The winds and thunder **foreshadowed** the terrible storm that was to come.

    a. stalled
    b. intercepted
    c. foretold
    d. lessened

_____c_____ 5. Many years ago, when the king was in power, the country was a **monarchy.**

    a. democracy
    b. nation ruled by the few
    c. nation ruled by one
    d. nation with no ruler(s)

ELABORATING EXAMPLES

An anecdote or example before or after the word suggests the meaning.

EXAMPLE

The bird's appetite is *voracious*. In one day he ate enough worms to equal three times his body weight.

EXPLANATION

Because the bird ate an extraordinary amount, *voracious* means extremely *hungry* or *greedy*.

EXERCISE 3

_____c_____ 1. The dancer's movements were not rehearsed, but were a **spontaneous** response to the music.

    a. planned
    b. simple
    c. unpremeditated
    d. smooth

_____d_____ 2. The embargo will **restrict** previously flourishing trade with the country and stop the goods from entering at the seaport.

    a. promote
    b. enlist
    c. renew
    d. confine

_____b_____ 3. The **affluent** members of the community live in big homes with swimming pools.

    a. powerful
    b. wealthy
    c. athletic
    d. political

Copyright ©1999 by Addison-Wesley Educational Publishers Inc.

FRONT

BACK

affluent people

_____ b _____ 4. Both parents have blue eyes, so it must be a natural family **trait.**

    a. manner
    b. characteristic
    c. style
    d. color

_____ b _____ 5. In order to **divest** herself of properties that need management, she sold an apartment building and a shopping center.

    a. insure
    b. rid
    c. profit
    d. leverage

COMPARISON

A similar situation suggests the meaning of the unknown word.

EXAMPLE

The smell of the flower was as *compelling* as a magnet's pull on a paper clip.

EXPLANATION

Since a magnet will pull a paper clip to it, the comparison suggests that the smell of the flower had an attraction. *Compelling* means *attracting.*

EXERCISE 4 _____ a _____ 1. Since I have never heard the plan discussed or known anyone who used it, I am **skeptical** about its chances of success.

    a. doubtful
    b. confident
    c. remorseful
    d. hopeful

_____ b _____ 2. When good citizens are no longer watchful and shut their eyes to the warning signs of **corruption,** politicians can manipulate the rules of government for illegal self-gain.

    a. business
    b. dishonesty
    c. confusion
    d. money

_____a_____ 3. Because of what he had heard about his future from the prophets as a young boy, the leader thought it was his **destiny** to conquer the barbarous tribes.

    a. fate
    b. desire
    c. will
    d. power

_____d_____ 4. Since there is always a first time for everything, each of us is a **novice** at some point in our lives.

    a. fool
    b. master
    c. manager
    d. beginner

_____d_____ 5. If the climber is actually a circus performer, it is **plausible** that he attempted such a dangerous feat on the tall building.

    a. doubtful
    b. impossible
    c. terrible
    d. believable

CONTRAST

An opposite situation suggests the meaning of the unknown word.

EXAMPLE

In America, she is an *eminent* scientist, even though she is virtually unknown in England.

EXPLANATION

Even though are signal words indicating that an opposite is coming. Thus *eminent* means the opposite of *unknown;* it means *well known* or *famous.*

EXERCISE 5

_____a_____ 1. Unlike **introverted** people, very talkative folks love crowds and conversation.

    a. quiet
    b. loud
    c. friendly
    d. hostile

_____b_____ 2. His favorites were not the old stories of days gone by, but the works of more **contemporary** authors.

    a. intelligent
    b. recent
    c. revolutionary
    d. meaningful

_____c_____ 3. He did not mean to cause the problem. While looking for his hat, the young man **inadvertently** knocked over the lamp.

    a. purposely
    b. knowingly
    c. unintentionally
    d. suddenly

Copyright ©1999 by Addison-Wesley Educational Publishers Inc.

___a___ 4. Even though the athlete lost the last two matches, he has the **potential** to be a world champion.

      a. undeveloped ability
      b. need
      c. connections
      d. training

___b___ 5. I cannot even **conjecture** what interest rates will be by next year.

      a. calculate
      b. guess
      c. admit
      d. wish

EXERCISE 6   Use context clues to write the meanings of the following words that are frequently used in business textbooks.

1. In a university, the president is at the top of the administrative **hierarchy.**
   <u>ranking or order</u>

2. When you buy stocks, a fee for the **broker** is added to the cost. <u>agent making</u>
   <u>the sale</u>

3. **Consumers** today are demanding better quality from manufacturers.
   <u>customers</u>

4. **Competition** in the marketplace tends to bring prices down. <u>business rivalry</u>

5. Advertisers rely heavily on implied meaning as one of their **tactics.**
   <u>strategies</u>

6. In government, the **fiscal** year ends on June 30. <u>financial</u>

7. Fads run in **cycles,** so frequently an old fad is repeated. <u>recurring period</u>

8. He went from mowing lawns and selling newspapers to becoming a successful **entrepreneur** as an adult. <u>person who organizes and manages several</u>
   <u>businesses</u>

9. If you know who to contact, you can save money by buying goods **wholesale.** <u>sale in large quantities at lower prices</u>

10. During periods of high **inflation,** people are not rewarded for saving money.
    <u>fall in value of money and rise in prices</u>

Multiple Meanings of a Word ◆◆◆◆◆◆◆◆◆◆◆

Some words are confusing because they have several different meanings. For example, the dictionary lists over 30 meanings for the word *run*. To determine the proper meaning, you must use the context of the sentence and paragraph in which the word occurs. Many of the multiple-meaning words are simple words that are used frequently. If you are puzzling over an unusual use of a common word, consider the context and be aware that the word may have a new meaning.

EXERCISE 7　The boldface words in the following sentences have multiple meanings. Write a sentence in which the word is used differently than in the example.

1. Sally cannot **bear** to be in the house alone at night.
   <u>The bear approaches our campsite.</u>

2. Johnny fished from the **bank** of the river.
   <u>Don't bank on winning the lottery.</u>

3. The water in the mountain **spring** was cool and clean.
   <u>Spring forward and fall backward.</u>

4. Joyce showed **industry** and perseverance in doing her work.
   <u>Joyce worked in the computer industry.</u>

5. Mr. Robinson served on the **board** of directors for the school.
   <u>Put the extra board in the truck.</u>

6. The new principal will get to the **root** of the problem.
   <u>Root plants in water.</u>

7. Our **school** started in August rather than September.
   <u>School your children in proper manners.</u>

8. If we **pool** our money, we can afford the sofa.
   <u>Dive into the pool.</u>

9. The red pen had a **fine** point.
   <u>Park illegally and you'll pay a fine.</u>

10. Her loud sneeze was the first sign of a **cold.**
    <u>Add cold water to the mixture.</u>

Word Parts ◆◆◆◆◆◆◆◆◆◆

Many words that at first may seem totally foreign to you are actually made up of words that you already know. One authority claims that learning approximately 30 key word parts will help you unlock the meaning of about 14,000 words. Although this claim may be exaggerated, it emphasizes the importance of roots, prefixes, and suffixes. Word parts are clues to the meaning of new words.

Look at the following family of words. Some may be familiar, and some may be new to you. You probably know the meaning of the first two words and thus can deduce that *cide* means to *kill*. Try to figure out the meaning of the other *cide* words by applying your knowledge of closely related words.

suicide (*sui:* self) to kill oneself
homicide (*homo* man, as in human) to kill another person

What do these words mean? Use the clues to write the definitions.

fratricide: <u>killing a brother</u>　(Hint: fraternity party?)

matricide: <u>killing your mother</u>　(Hint: maternity dress?)

sororicide: <u>killing a sister</u>　(Hint: sorority house?)

Copyright ©1999 by Addison-Wesley Educational Publishers Inc.

patricide: <u>killing your father</u> (Hint: paternity suit?)

pesticide (*Easy one!*) <u>killing a pest or insect</u>

Roots

The root is the stem or basic part of the word. The roots that we use are derived primarily from Latin and Greek. For example, *port* is a root derived from Latin meaning *to carry*, as in the word *porter*. *Thermo* is a Greek word meaning *heat*, as in *thermometer*. In both cases, additional letters have been added to the word, but the meaning of the word has not changed. Knowing the definition of the root helps unlock the meaning of each word.

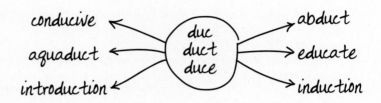

EXAMPLE   The root forms *duc*, *duct*, and *duce* mean *to lead*. This root branches out into a large word family. Use the root to supply appropriate words to complete the following three sentences.

1. If the factory is ready, the new line of furniture will go into <u>production</u> in September.

2. The company is trying to cut down overhead in order to <u>reduce</u> expenses.

3. Legitimate business expenses can be <u>deducted</u> from your taxes if you keep the proper receipts.

EXPLANATION   The correct answers are *production*, *reduce*, and *deducted*.

EXERCISE 8

The following exercises include frequently used roots. Use the root to supply an appropriate word to complete the sentences in each group.

cede, ceed, cess: go, yield, move

1. To <u>succeed</u> in a difficult job requires knowledge and hard work.

2. As he got older, his hairline began to <u>recede</u>.

3. Before <u>proceeding</u> to the next step, make sure the first two requirements have been satisfactorily completed.

port: carry

4. If we could <u>import</u> fewer goods into this country, our balance of payments would improve.

5. He wanted a <u>portable</u> radio so that he could listen to the game while riding in the boat on the lake.

6. Private contributions and volunteers ____support____ the efforts of the Salvation Army.

7. The organized ____transportation____ to and from the game will be by bus.

cred: believe

8. We could not believe what we saw: the feat was ____incredible____.

9. Some law schools in the country are not fully ____accredited____ by the state, and their courses will not transfer.

10. Derogatory remarks were made about his performance in an effort to ____discredit____ him.

Prefixes

A prefix is a group of letters with a special meaning that are added to the beginning of a word. For example, *ex* means *out of* and *im* means *into*. Adding these two prefixes to *port* gives two words that are opposite in meaning. *Export* means to send something out of the country, whereas *import* means to bring something in. Again, knowing the prefixes can help you identify the meaning.

EXAMPLE   The prefix *trans* means *across, over,* and *beyond*. Write a word beginning with *trans* to complete each of the following three sentences.

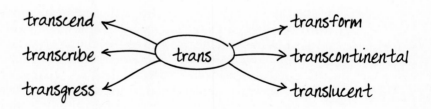

1. The radio station can now ____transmit____ programs to a wider audience.

2. Since she did not speak French, he acted as a ____translator____ while she conducted business in Paris.

3. When the business ____transaction____ was completed, the two executives shook hands.

EXPLANATION   The correct answers are *transmit, translator,* and *transaction.*

EXERCISE 9

The following exercises include frequently used prefixes. Use the prefix to supply an appropriate word to complete the sentences in each group.

re: back, again

1. If you want to back up, put the car in ____reverse____.

2. Most term papers need to be ____rewritten____ before the final draft is submitted.

Copyright © 1999 by Addison-Wesley Educational Publishers Inc.

3. When you take out a mortgage, the lender usually gives you 30 years to _____repay_____ the loan.

mis: wrong, bad

4. Because the child ____misbehaved____ in the restaurant, he was not allowed to go again.

5. The answer was not a lie, but it did ____misrepresent____ the truth.

6. Because of the lawyer's error, the judge declared a ____mistrial____ and court was adjourned.

pre: before

7. Even a fortune teller could not have ____predicted____ the fun we had scuba diving.

8. Police recommend alarm systems as a type of crime ____prevention____.

9. The student was so ____preoccupied____ with her mathematics assignment that she did not hear the doorbell ring.

10. If you order by phone, you will need a credit card to ____prepay____ for the concert tickets.

Suffixes

A suffix is a group of letters with a special meaning that are added to the end of a word. A suffix can alter the meaning of a word as well as the way the word can be used in the sentence. For example, the *er* in *porter* means the *person who* and makes the word into the name of a person. On the other hand, adding *able*, which means *capable of*, to *port*, does not change the meaning as much as it changes the way the word can be used in the sentence. Some suffixes, therefore, have more meaning than others, but all alter the way the word can be used in a sentence.

EXAMPLE   The suffix *ist* means *one who* or *that which*. Write a word ending with *ist* to complete each of the following three sentences.

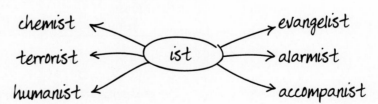

1. If you have a toothache, go to your ____dentist____ immediately.

2. The ____pianist____ played the piano with such force that the floorboards shook.

3. The picture was painted by a well-known American ____artist____.

EXPLANATION   The correct answers are *dentist*, *pianist*, and *artist*.

EXERCISE 10

The following exercises include frequently used suffixes. Use the suffix to supply an appropriate word to complete the sentences in each group.

ion, sion, tion: act of, state of, result of

1. To honor his birthday, we invited his friends to a party and had a big ___celebration___.

2. If you don't clean out the wound and use a bandage, you are likely to get an ___infection___.

3. The ___suspension___ bridge was held in the air by cables descending from two towers on either side of the river.

4. Use your ___imagination___ to visualize the festive atmosphere of music and outdoor dining.

ful: full of

5. Since we knew a few people who could not attend, we were still ___hopeful___ of getting tickets.

6. The surgeon was ___careful___ not to sever a nerve during the delicate operation.

7. Since the future is so uncertain, it is ___doubtful___ that we will be hiring any new employees in the next two months.

less: without

8. Because the show was boring, I became ___restless___ and could not sit still.

9. A baby lamb is ___helpless___ against fierce and determined predators.

10. He suffered from insomnia and spent many ___sleepless___ nights walking the halls.

The Dictionary ◆◆◆◆◆◆◆◆◆◆◆◆

Use the dictionary as a last resort for finding the definition of a word while you are reading, unless the word is crucial to your understanding. Remember, stopping in the middle of a paragraph breaks your concentration and causes you to forget what you were reading. Mark unknown words with a dot in the margin, and then, when you have finished reading, look the words up in the dictionary.

Dictionaries contain more than just the definition of a word. They contain the pronunciation, the spelling, the derivation or history, the parts of speech, and the many different meanings a word may have. An entry may also include an illustration, or give context examples of the use of the word in a phrase. Consider the entry on the next page.

Copyright ©1999 by Addison-Wesley Educational Publishers Inc.

doctrine ● doggerel

do·do \'dō-(,)dō\ *n, pl* **dodoes** *or* **dodos** [Pg *doudo,* fr. *doudo* silly, stupid] (1628)   **1   a :** an extinct heavy flightless bird (*Raphus cucullatus,* syn *Didus ineptus*) of the island of Mauritius that is related to the pigeon and larger than a turkey   **b :** an extinct bird of the island of Réunion similar to and apparently closely related to the dodo   **2   a :** one hopelessly behind the times   **b :** a stupid person

Source: By permission from *Merriam-Webster's Collegiate Dictionary Tenth Edition* © 1997 by Merriam-Webster, Incorporated.

Guide Words

The two words at the top of each dictionary page are guide words. They represent the first and last word on the page. Since the words in the dictionary are in alphabetical order, you can use the guide words to determine quickly if the word you are looking for is on that particular page. The guide words for the sample entry are *doctrine* and *doggerel*.

Pronunciation

Each word is divided into sounds after the boldface main entry. Letters and symbols are used to indicate special sounds. A key to understanding the special sounds appears at the bottom of one of the two pages open to you.

Spelling

Spellings are given for the plural form of the word (if the spelling changes) and for any special endings. This is particularly helpful when letters are dropped or added to form the new word. In the sample entry, the plural of *dodo* can be spelled correctly in two ways, either *dodoes* or *dodos*. The first spelling is usually the preferred one.

Word Meaning

Frequently, a word has many meanings. For example, *car* means automobile as well as the cargo part of an airship. In such a case, the dictionary uses a number to indicate each new meaning. In the sample entry, notice that a dodo can be a bird or a person.

Parts of Speech

For each meaning of a word, the part of speech is given in abbreviated form. For example, *n* means *noun, adj* means *adjective, adv* means *adverb,* and *vi* or *vt* means *verb.* Other abbreviations are listed in the section in the front of your dictionary. In the example, a dodo is only a noun.

Word History

The original language in which the word appeared is listed after the pronunciation or at the end of the entry. For example, *L* stands for Latin and *Gk* stands for Greek. Usually, the original meaning is also listed. *Dodo* is derived from the Portuguese *(Pg)* word *doudo,* which means silly or stupid.

Use the dictionary page that follows to label the statements below as either *T* (true) or *F* (false).

_____T_____   1. The *manual alphabet* for the deaf was created in 1864.

_____T_____   2. A *mantra* is used in Hinduism.

cloth or blanket used in southwestern U.S. and Latin America usu. as a cloak or shawl **2** [AmerSp, fr. Sp; fr. its shape] : DEVILFISH 1
man–tai·lored \'man-,tā-lərd\ *adj* (1922) : made with the severe simplicity associated with men's coats and suits
manta ray *n* (1936) : DEVILFISH 1
man·teau \man-'tō, 'man-,\ *n* [F, fr. OF *mantel*] (1671) : a loose cloak, coat, or robe
man·tel \'man-t³l\ *n* [ME, fr. MF, fr. OF, mantle] (15c) **1 a** : a beam, stone, or arch serving as a lintel to support the masonry above a fireplace **b** : the finish around a fireplace **2** : a shelf above a fireplace
man·tel·et \'mant-lət, 'man-t³l-ət, ,man-t³l-'et\ *n* [ME, fr. MF *mantlet*, dim. of *mantel*] (14c) **1** : a very short cape or cloak **2** *or* **mant·let** \'mant-lət\ : a movable shelter formerly used by besiegers as a protection when attacking
man·tel·piece \'man-t³l-,pēs\ *n* (1686) **1** : a mantel with its side elements **2** : MANTEL 2
man·tel·shelf \-,shelf\ *n* (ca. 1828) : MANTEL 2
man·tic \'man-tik\ *adj* [Gk *mantikos*, fr. *mantis*] (1850) : of or relating to the faculty of divination : PROPHETIC
man·ti·core \'man-ti-,kōr, -,kȯr\ *n* [ME, fr. L *mantichora*, fr. Gk *mantichōras*] (14c) : a legendary animal with the head of a man, the body of a lion, and the tail of a dragon or scorpion
man·tid \'man-təd\ *n* [NL *Mantidae*, group name, fr. *Mantis*, genus name] (1895) : MANTIS
man·til·la \man-'tē-yə, -'ti-lə\ *n* [Sp, dim. of *manta*] (1717) **1** : a light scarf worn over the head and shoulders esp. by Spanish and Latin≠ American women **2** : a short light cape or cloak
man·tis \'man-təs\ *n, pl* **man·tis·es** *or* **man·tes** \'man-,tēz\ [NL, fr. Gk, lit., diviner, prophet; akin to Gk *mainesthai* to be mad — more at MANIA] (1658) : any of an order or suborder (Mantodea and esp. family Mantidae) of large usu. green insects that feed on other insects and clasp their prey in forelimbs held up as if in prayer
man·tis·sa \man-'ti-sə\ *n* [L *mantisa, mantissa* makeweight, fr. Etruscan] (ca. 1847) : the part of a logarithm to the right of the decimal point
¹**man·tle** \'man-t³l\ *n* [ME *mantel*, fr. OF, fr. L *mantellum*] (13c) **1 a** : a loose sleeveless garment worn over other clothes : CLOAK **b** : a mantle regarded as a symbol of preeminence or authority ⟨invested his people with the ~ of universal champions of justice —Denis Goulet⟩ **2 a** : something that covers, enfolds, or envelops **b** (1) : a fold or lobe or pair of lobes of the body wall of a mollusk or brachiopod that in shell-bearing forms lines the shell and bears shell-secreting glands — see CLAM illustration (2) : the soft external body wall that lines the test or shell of a tunicate or barnacle **c** : the outer wall and casing of a blast furnace above the hearth; *broadly* : an insulated support or casing in which something is heated **3** : the back, scapulars, and wings of a bird **4** : a lacy hood or sheath of some refractory material that gives light by incandescence when placed over a flame **5 a** : REGOLITH **b** : the part of the interior of a terrestrial planet and esp. the earth that lies beneath the lithosphere and above the central core **6** : MANTEL
²**mantle** *vb* **man·tled; man·tling** \'mant-liŋ, 'man-t³l-iŋ\ *vt* (13c) : to cover with or as if with a mantle : CLOAK ⟨the encroaching jungle growth that *mantled* the building —Sanka Knox⟩ ~ *vi* **1** : to become covered with a coating **2** : to spread over a surface **3** : BLUSH ⟨her rich face *mantling* with emotion —Benjamin Disraeli⟩
man–to–man \'man-tə-'man\ *adj* (1902) **1** : characterized by frankness and honesty ⟨a ~ talk⟩ **2** : of, relating to, or being a system of defense (as in football or basketball) in which each defensive player guards a specified opponent
Man·toux test \,man-'tü-, ,mäⁿ-\ *n* [Charles *Mantoux* †1947 Fr. physician] (ca. 1923) : an intracutaneous test for hypersensitivity to tuberculin that indicates past or present infection with tubercle bacilli
man·tra \'män-trə *also* 'man- *or* 'mən-\ *n* [Skt, sacred counsel, formula, fr. *manyate* he thinks; akin to L *mens* mind — more at MIND] (1808) : a mystical formula of invocation or incantation (as in Hinduism); *also* : WATCHWORD 2 — **man·tric** \-trik\ *adj*
man·trap \'man-,trap\ *n* (1788) : a trap for catching humans : SNARE
man·tua \'man(t)-sh(ə-)wə, 'man-tə-wə\ *n* [modif. of F *manteau* mantle] (1678) : a usu. loose-fitting gown worn esp. in the 17th and 18th centuries
Manu \'ma-(,)nü\ *n* [Skt] : the progenitor of the human race and giver of the religious laws of Manu according to Hindu mythology
¹**man·u·al** \'man-yə-wəl, -yəl\ *adj* [ME *manuel*, fr. MF, fr. L *manualis*, fr. *manus* hand; akin to OE *mund* hand and perh. to Gk *marē* hand] (15c) **1 a** : of, relating to, or involving the hands ⟨~ dexterity⟩ **b** : worked or done by hand and not by machine ⟨~ a transmission⟩ ⟨~ computation⟩ ⟨~ indexing⟩ **2** : requiring or using physical skill and energy ⟨~ labor⟩ ⟨~ workers⟩ — **man·u·al·ly** *adv*
²**manual** *n* (15c) **1** : a book that is conveniently handled; *esp* : HANDBOOK **2** : the prescribed movements in the handling of a weapon or other military item during a drill or ceremony ⟨the ~ of arms⟩ **3 a** : a keyboard for the hands; *specif* : one of the several keyboards of an organ or harpsichord that controls a separate division of the instrument **b** : a device or apparatus intended for manual operation
manual alphabet *n* (ca. 1864) : an alphabet esp. for the deaf in which the letters are represented by finger positions
manual training *n* (1880) : a course of training to develop skill in using the hands and to teach practical arts (as woodworking and metalworking)
ma·nu·bri·um \mə-'nü-brē-əm, -'nyü-\ *n, pl* **-bria** \-brē-ə\ *also* **-briums** [NL, fr. L, handle, fr. *manus*] (ca. 1848) : an anatomical process or part shaped like a handle: as **a** : the cephalic segment of the sternum of humans and many other mammals **b** : the process that bears the mouth of a hydrozoan : HYPOSTOME
man·u·fac·to·ry \,man-yə-'fak-t(ə-)rē, ,ma-nə-\ *n* (1647) : FACTORY 2a
¹**man·u·fac·ture** \,man-yə-'fak-chər, ,ma-nə-\ *n* [MF, fr. ML *manufactura*, fr. L *manu factus*, lit., made by hand] (1567) **1** : something made from raw materials by hand or by machinery **2 a** : the process of making wares by hand or by machinery esp. when carried on systematically with division of labor **b** : a productive industry using mechanical power and machinery **3** : the act or process of producing something
²**manufacture** *vb* **-tured; -tur·ing** \-'fak-chə-riŋ, -'fak-shriŋ\ *vt* (1683) **1** : to make into a product suitable for use **2 a** : to make from raw

Copyright ©1999 by Addison-Wesley Educational Publishers Inc.

manual alphabet

materials by hand or by machinery **b** : to produce according to an organized plan and with division of labor **3** : INVENT, FABRICATE **4** : to produce as if by manufacturing : CREATE ⟨writers who ~ stories for television⟩ ~ *vi* : to engage in manufacture — **manufacturing** *n*
man·u·fac·tur·er \-'fak-chər-ər, -'fak-shrər\ *n* (1719) : one that manufactures; *esp* : an employer of workers in manufacturing
man·u·mis·sion \,man-yə-'mi-shən\ *n* [ME, fr. MF, fr. L *manumission-, manumissio*, fr. *manumittere*] (15c) : the act or process of manumitting; *esp* : formal emancipation from slavery
man·u·mit \,man-yə-'mit\ *vt* **-mit·ted; -mit·ting** [ME, fr. MF *manumitter*, fr. L *manumittere*, fr. *manus* hand + *mittere* to let go, send] (15c) : to release from slavery *syn* see FREE
¹**ma·nure** \mə-'nur, -'nyur\ *vt* **ma·nured; ma·nur·ing** [ME *manouren*, fr. MF *manouvrer*, lit., to do work by hand, fr. L *manu operare*] (15c) **1** *obs* : CULTIVATE **2** : to enrich (land) by the application of manure — **ma·nur·er** *n*
²**manure** *n* (1549) : material that fertilizes land; *esp* : refuse of stables and barnyards consisting of livestock excreta with or without litter — **ma·nu·ri·al** \-'n(y)ur-ē-əl\ *adj*
ma·nus \'mā-nəs, 'mä-\ *n, pl* **ma·nus** \-nəs, -,nüs\ [NL, fr. L, hand] (1826) : the distal segment of the vertebrate forelimb from carpus to terminus
¹**man·u·script** \'man-yə-,skript\ *adj* [L *manu scriptus*] (1597) : written by hand or typed ⟨~ letters⟩
²**manuscript** *n* (1600) **1** : a written or typewritten composition or document as distinguished from a printed copy; *also* : a document submitted for publication **2** : writing as opposed to print
¹**Manx** \'man(k)s\ *adj* [alter. of *Maniske*, fr. (assumed) ON *manskr*, fr. *Mana* Isle of Man] (1630) : of, relating to, or characteristic of the Isle of Man, its people, or the Manx language
²**Manx** *n* (1672) **1** : the Celtic language of the Manx people almost completely displaced by English **2** *pl in constr* : the people of the Isle of Man **3** : MANX CAT
Manx cat *n* (1859) : any of a breed of shorthaired tailless domestic cats
¹**many** \'me-nē\ *adj* **more** \'mȯr, 'mȯr\; **most** \'mōst\ [ME, fr. OE *manig*; akin to OHG *manag* many, OCS *munogŭ* much] (bef. 12c) **1** : consisting of or amounting to a large but indefinite number ⟨worked for ~ years⟩ **2** : being one of a large but indefinite number ⟨a man⟩ ⟨~ another student⟩ — **as many** : the same in number ⟨saw three plays in *as many* days⟩
²**many** *pron, pl in constr* (bef. 12c) : a large number of persons or things ⟨~ are called⟩
³**many** *n, pl in constr* (12c) **1** : a large but indefinite number ⟨a good ~ of them⟩ **2** : the great majority of people ⟨the ~⟩
man–year \'man-'yir\ *n* (1916) : a unit of the work done by one person in a year composed of a standard number of working days
many·fold \,me-nē-'fōld\ *adv* (14c) : by many times ⟨aid to research has increased ~⟩
many–sid·ed \,me-nē-'sī-dəd\ *adj* (1570) **1** : having many sides or aspects **2** : having many interests or aptitudes — **many–sid·ed·ness** *n*
many–val·ued \,me-nē-'val-(,)yüd, -yəd\ *adj* (1934) **1** : possessing more than the customary two truth-values of truth and falsehood **2** : MULTIPLE-VALUED
Man·za·nil·la \,man-zə-'nē-yə, -'ni-lə\ *n* [Sp, dim. of *manzana* apple] (1843) : a pale very dry Spanish sherry
man·za·ni·ta \,man-zə-'nē-tə\ *n* [AmerSp, dim. of Sp *manzana* apple] (1846) : any of various western No. American evergreen shrubs (genus *Arctostaphylos*) of the heath family with alternate leaves
Mao·ism \'mau̇-,i-zəm\ *n* (1950) : the theory and practice of Marxism≠ Leninism developed in China chiefly by Mao Tse-tung — **Mao·ist** \'mau̇-ist\ *n or adj*
Mao·ri \'mau̇(ə)r-ē\ *n, pl* **Maori** *or* **Maoris** (1843) **1** : a member of a Polynesian people native to New Zealand **2** : the Austronesian language of the Maori

---

\ə\ abut \ᵊ\ kitten, F table \ər\ further \a\ ash \ā\ ace \ä\ mop, mar
\au̇\ out \ch\ chin \e\ bet \ē\ easy \g\ go \i\ hit \ī\ ice \j\ job
\ŋ\ sing \ō\ go \ȯ\ law \ȯi\ boy \th\ thin \th\ the \ü\ loot \u̇\ foot
\y\ yet \zh\ vision \ä, k̲, ⁿ, œ, œ̄, ᵾ, ᵡ, ꞓ\ see Guide to Pronunciation

Source: By permission from *Merriam-Webster's Collegiate Dictionary Tenth Edition* © 1997 by Merriam-Webster, Incorporated.

_____F_____ 3. A *manticore* has the head of a man and the body of a bull.

_____T_____ 4. A devilfish can be called a *manta ray*.

_____T_____ 5. The word *manure* can be either a noun or a verb.

_____T_____ 6. The *Mantoux test* was named for a French physician.

_____F_____ 7. The *mantis* is a divine insect used by religious cults.

_____T_____ 8. A hearing-impaired person would probably know that pointing only the index finger upward represents the letter Z.

_____T_____ 9. The word *mantilla* has a Spanish derivation.

Word Origins ◆◆◆◆◆◆◆◆◆◆

Words have ancestors. Some of the ancestors are words that were borrowed from other languages. *Shampoo,* for example, comes from a Hindi word meaning *to press,* and *moccasin* comes from the Algonquian Indian word for shoe. Other word ancestors include mythology, literature, people, places, and customs. The origin of the word *sadist,* which refers to a person who enjoys inflicting pain on others, is attributed to the Marquis de Sade, an eighteenth-century French author who wrote with pleasure about such cruelty.

Etymology

The study of word origins is called **etymology.** An etymologist traces the development of a word back to its earliest recorded appearance. In dictionaries, the etymology of a word is usually given in brackets. The extent to which the word origin is explained varies from one dictionary to another. Note the information on the etymology of *mentor* in the following dictionaries:

The small paperback edition of the *American Heritage Dictionary:*

men·tor (mĕn′tôr′, -tər) *n.* A wise and trusted counselor or teacher. [< Gk. *Mentōr,* counselor of Odysseus. See men-·.]

The textbook-size edition of *Webster's New Collegiate Dictionary:*

·tor \'men-ˌtòr, -tər\ *n* [L, fr. Gk *Mentōr*] **1** *cap* : a frie͏ sseus entrusted with the education of Odysseus' son Telem͏ : a trusted counselor or guide **b** : TUTOR, COACH — me͏ \-ˌship\ *n*
tor *vt* (1983) : to serve as a mentor for

Source: By permission from *Merriam-Webster's Collegiate Dictionary Tenth Edition* © 1997 by Merriam-Webster, Incorporated.

In both cases, the entries give information on the origin, but the second explains the mythological background more clearly. Both of these dictionaries are abridged, which means that information has been condensed. An abridged dictionary is adequate for most college use. In special cases, however, you may desire information more on the origin or the past use of a word. If so, an unabridged, or unshortened, dictionary is necessary, but its large size dictates that you must go to it rather than carry it around with you. Note the entry for *mentor* in the unabridged *Webster's Third New International Dictionary:*

men·tor \'men·ˌtȯ(ə)r, -ȯ(ə), -ntə(r)\ *n* -s [after *Mentor*, tutor of Telemachus in the Odyssey of Homer, fr. L, fr. Gk *Mentōr*] **1 :** a close, trusted, and experienced counselor or guide ⟨every one of us needs a ~ who, because he is detached and disinterested, can hold up a mirror to us —P.W.Keve⟩ ⟨was much more than a ~; he supplied decisions —Hilaire Belloc⟩ ⟨has been my ~ since 1946 —Lalia P. Boone⟩ ⟨regarded by patrons ... as a personal friend as well as fashion ~ —*N. Y. State Legislative Committee on Problems of the Aging*⟩ **2 :** TEACHER, TUTOR, COACH ⟨a writer of monographs, and a ~ of seminars —*Atlantic*⟩ ⟨although he had never accepted a pupil ... she persuaded him to become her ~ —*Current Biog.*⟩ ⟨one of the game's most successful young ~s —*Official Basketball Guide*⟩

Source: By permission from *Webster's Third New International® Dictionary*, Unabridged © 1993 by Merriam-Webster, Inc.

Your college library probably has several unabridged dictionaries in the reference room. Other excellent choices for etymological research include the *Random House Dictionary of the English Language* and the *American Heritage Dictionary of the English Language*.

Why Study Etymology? The more you know about a word, the easier it is to remember. The etymology gives you the history of a word, which can help you establish new relationships on your "computer chip," or schema, for that word. "Meeting the ancestors" can also help you create a rich visual image of the word by using the background information. For example, the word *trivial* means "of little worth or importance." It comes from the Latin words *tri* for *three* and *via* for *way*, which combine to mean "the crossing of three roads" in Latin. The Romans knew that people would stand and talk at such an intersection. Since many strangers would be listening to the conversations, it was advisable to talk only of small, or trivial, matters. This history of *trivial* can increase your enjoyment of the word while enhancing your ability to remember the definition.

EXERCISE 12

Many English words have their roots in the names of characters in Greek mythology. The words represent a particular characteristic or predicament of the mythological person or creature. Read the entries below to discover their mythological origins, and answer the questions that follow.

tan·ta·lize \'tan-tᵊl-ˌīz\ *vb* **-lized; -liz·ing** [*Tantalus*] *vt* (1597) : to tease or torment by or as if by presenting something desirable to the view but continually keeping it out of reach ~ *vi* : to cause one to be tantalized — **tan·ta·liz·er** *n*
Source: By permission from *Merriam-Webster's Collegiate Dictionary Tenth Edition* © 1997 by Merriam-Webster, Incorporated.

tan·ta·lum \'tan-tᵊl-əm\ *n* [NL, fr. L *Tantalus*; fr. its inability to absorb acid] (1802) : a hard ductile gray-white acid-resisting metallic element of the vanadium family found combined in rare minerals (as tantalite and columbite) — see ELEMENT table
Source: By permission from *Merriam-Webster's Collegiate Dictionary Tenth Edition* © 1997 by Merriam-Webster, Incorporated.

1. *Tantalize* means ___to tease___

2. Explain the myth. ___Tantalus was teased with water and fruit that he could not reach.___

nar·cis·sism \'när-sə-ˌsi-zəm\ *n* [G *Narzissismus*, fr. *Narziss* Narcissus, fr. L *Narcissus*] (1822) **1 :** EGOISM, EGOCENTRISM **2 :** love of or sexual desire for one's own body — **nar·cis·sist** \'när-sə-sist\ *n or adj* — **nar·cis·sis·tic** \ˌnär-sə-'sis-tik\ *adj*
Source: By permission from *Merriam-Webster's Collegiate Dictionary Tenth Edition* © 1997 by Merriam-Webster, Incorporated.

nar·cis·sus \när-'si-səs\ *n* [L, fr. Gk *Narkissos*] **1** *cap* : a beautiful youth in Greek mythology who pines away for love of his own reflection and is then turned into the narcissus flower **2** *pl* **nar·cis·si** \-'si-ˌsī, -(ˌ)sē\ *or* **nar·cis·sus·es** *or* **narcissus** [NL, genus name, fr. L, narcissus, fr. Gk *narkissos*]: DAFFODIL; *esp* : one whose flowers have a short corona and are usu. borne separately
Source: By permission from *Merriam-Webster's Collegiate Dictionary Tenth Edition* © 1997 by Merriam-Webster, Incorporated.

Copyright ©1999 by Addison-Wesley Educational Publishers Inc.

3. *Narcissism* means ___excessive love of self___

4. Explain the myth. ___Narcissus was a youth who fell in love with his own___ ___image.___

Textbook Glossary ◆◆◆◆◆◆◆◆◆◆

Textbooks use words that are not found in the dictionary. This may sound strange, but it is true. For example, what does *loss leader* mean? Each word is listed separately in the dictionary, but the two words are not listed together and defined. Looking up *loss* and then looking up *leader* will not give you a correct definition of the term as it is used in the field of marketing. However, the glossary in the back of the marketing textbook will define the term as "a product whose price has been cut below cost to attract customers to a store." The textbook glossary defines words and phrases as they apply to particular fields of study. Consult it before using the dictionary for words that seem to be part of the terminology of the discipline.

The following exercise will give you an idea of the types of words and the amount of information presented in a glossary. In doing the exercise, notice that many of the words take on a special meaning within the particular field of study. Use the marketing glossary on the next page to answer the questions below with *T* (true) or *F* (false).

___T___ 1. Being upset after deciding to buy a Toyota rather than a BMW is called *cognitive dissonance*.

___F___ 2. A *brokerage allowance* is a marked-up price.

___T___ 3. In *cannibalization*, a new product outsells a similar existing product in the same company.

___F___ 4. A *buyer's market* is an advantageous time to sell a house.

___T___ 5. *Cartels* are illegal in the United States.

___T___ 6. In *comparative advertising*, rivals are mentioned.

___T___ 7. In a sales presentation, the *close* asks for action.

___T___ 8. Both a *cash discount* and *cash rebate* save the customer money.

___F___ 9. A *break-even analysis* shows the profit made on an item.

___F___ 10. The *business cycle* is the calendar year.

Thesaurus ◆◆◆◆◆◆◆◆◆◆

Dr. Peter Mark Roget, an English physician, collected lists of related words as a hobby and in 1852 the lists were published in a *thesaurus*, or treasury of words. In the book, he related words because they were synonyms such as *illegal* and *unlawful*, as well as antonyms such as *peaceful* and *warlike*. This book, still called *Roget's Thesaurus* because of the man who first had the idea, has been frequently revised by adding new words and deleting obsolete ones.

Roget's Thesaurus is not a dictionary. In fact, you would probably not use it while reading. Instead, it is a valuable source for writers who are stuck on using a particular word again and again and want a substitute. For example, if you are writing a history term paper and have already used the word *cause* twice in one paragraph and hesitate to use it again, consult *Roget's Thesaurus* for other

Copyright ©1999 by Addison-Wesley Educational Publishers Inc.

brand name   The pronounceable part of the brand. **(322)**

breakdown approach   An approach to estimating sales potential that assumes a product's sales potential varies with the country's general level of business activity. **(255)**

breakeven analysis   A method used to determine the level of sales at which total revenue will equal total cost, given the product's per-unit selling price. **(616)**

broadcast media   The communications channels that sell advertising time to marketers; radio and television. **(529)**

brokerage allowance   A reduction from list price granted to brokers for the marketing functions they perform. **(633)**

build-up approach   An approach to estimating sales potential that begins with an estimate of the number of units of the product category a typical buyer in a typical sales territory will buy, then multiplying that number by the number of potential buyers in the territory, and doing the same for all the other territories; adding the figures provides an estimate of market potential; estimating the share of that market potential the firm will capture at a given level of marketing effort provides an estimate of sales potential. **(255)**

business cycle   The sequence of changes that occur in an economy's overall level of business activity—prosperity, recession, depression, and recovery. **(33)**

buyclasses   The three basic types of industrial buying: new task buying, modified rebuy buying, and straight rebuy buying. **(184)**

buyer's market   An environment in which supply is greater than demand. **(18)**

buying center   The people who determine what will be purchased to fill an organization's needs and from whom the products will be purchased. **(188)**

buyphases   The problem-solving steps used by industrial buyers primarily in new task buying: recognizing a need; specifying the need; searching for potential suppliers; inviting, acquiring, and analyzing vendor proposals; selecting the vendor and placing the order; and following up. **(185)**

cannibalization   The situation that exists when a firm's new product experiences increased sales mainly due to the decreasing sales of its established product or products. **(298)**

cartel   A group of firms in different countries (or a group of countries) that agrees to share markets, limit output, and set prices; illegal in the United States. **(707)**

cash discount   A reduction in a product's list price that rewards customers for paying their bills promptly. **(632)**

cash rebate   A type of manufacturer's couponing effort in which the buyer requests a return of a portion of the price directly from the manufacturer. **(637)**

catalog retailing   A type of nonstore retailing in which the retailer offers its merchandise in a catalog that includes ordering instructions, and the customer orders by mail or phone or at a catalog counter in a retail store. **(408)**

catalog showroom   A discount retail facility whose customers preshop by catalog and then select merchandise from samples displayed in the showroom. **(406)**

channel conflict   Disagreement among members of a marketing channel as to their respective roles and functions; horizontal conflict occurs between members at the same level, and vertical conflict occurs between members at different levels. **(378)**

channel leader   The marketing channel member in an administered VMS who exerts power over the other channel members and can influence their decisions and actions. **(382)**

close   The point in a sales presentation at which the salesperson attempts to clinch the sale, to get action by asking the prospect for the order. **(566)**

cognitive dissonance   A state of psychological tension or postpurchase doubt that a consumer experiences after making a difficult purchasing choice. **(140)**

combination export manager   A domestic agent middleman that serves as the export department for several noncompeting manufacturers, contacting foreign customers and negotiating sales for manufacturer-clients for a commission. Similar to a selling agent in domestic commerce. **(721)**

combination store   A retail store that is larger than a superstore and offers even more diversified merchandise and services; a combination food and drugstore with roughly half the selling space devoted to nonfood items. **(404)**

communication   The process of influencing others' behavior by sharing ideas, information, or feelings with them; occurs when a sender transmits a message, a receiver receives it, and the sender and receiver have a shared meaning. **(480)**

comparative advertising   Advertising in which the marketer compares its brand to rival brands identified by brand name. **(519)**

competitive bidding   The practice of prospective sellers competing by submitting their prices for goods or services to an industrial buyer who is shopping around. **(645)**

options. You will find noun alternatives such as *origin, basis, foundation, genesis,* and *root.* If you need a verb for *cause,* you will find synonyms that include *originate, give rise to, bring about, produce, create, evoke,* and many others. Probably over a hundred words are listed as relating to *cause,* but not all of them are synonymous. Select the one that fits your need in the sentence, adds variety to your writing, and maintains the same shade of meaning that you desire. The words in a thesaurus are listed in alphabetical order and familiar dictionary abbreviations are used for parts of speech. The following is an example from *Roget's Thesaurus* showing the entry for the word *influence.*

> **influence,** *n. & v.* —*n.* influentialness; IMPORTANCE, POWER, mastery, sway, dominance, AUTHORITY, control, ascendancy, persuasiveness, ability to affect; reputation, weight; magnetism, spell; conduciveness; pressure. *Slang,* drag, pull. —*v.t.* affect; move, induce, persuade; sway, control, lead, actuate; modify; arouse, incite; prevail upon, impel; set the pace, pull the strings; tell, weigh. *Ant.,* see IMPOTENCE.

If a word is printed in small capitals such as IMPORTANCE, POWER, and AUTHORITY, it means that you can find additional synonyms by looking that particular word up in its alphabetical order. Explanations sometimes appear in brackets and not every word in the dictionary is listed.

◆◆◆ READER'S TIP

USING AN ELECTRONIC THESAURUS

Your word-processing program probably has a thesaurus. In *Word Perfect,* for example, the thesaurus is found in *Tools,* directly under *Spell Check.* To use this, select the word for which you want alternatives by dragging the cursor and then clicking on the thesaurus. An array of words will appear from which you can choose an option that fits the context of your sentence.

EXERCISE 14   Use the following entry for *right* in *Roget's Thesaurus* to select an alternate word that fits the meaning of *right* in the sentences.

> **RIGHT, RIGHTNESS [922]**
> *Nouns*—**1,** rightness, right, what ought to be, what should be, fitness, propriety; JUSTICE, morality, PROBITY, honor, virtue, lawfulness.
> **2,** privilege, prerogative, title, claim, grant, POWER, franchise, license.
> **3,** rightness, correctness, accuracy, precision; exactness; TRUTH.
> *Verbs*—**1,** be right, be just, stand to reason.
> **3,** right, make right, correct, remedy, see justice done, play fair, do justice to, recompense, hold the scales even, give every one his due.
> *Adjectives*—**1,** right, upright, good, just (see JUSTICE); reasonable, suitable, becoming.
> **2,** right, correct, proper, precise, exact, accurate, true.
> *Adverbs*—rightly, justly, fairly, correctly; in justice, in equity, in reason, without distinction of persons, on even terms.
> *Antonym,* see WRONG.

1. The first amendment gives every American the *right* of free speech. <u>privilege</u>

2. It was not *right* for the government to force the Indians out of the Southeast in the Trail of Tears. <u>just, correct, proper</u>

3. Can government payments help *right* some of the social wrongs of the past? <u>correct</u>

4. Do revolutionaries ignore the difference between *right* and wrong? <u>rightness, what ought to be</u>

5. Employers want to make the *right* fit between employee skills and job demands. <u>suitable</u>

Analogies ◆◆◆◆◆◆◆◆◆◆◆◆

An analogy is a comparison that mimics a previously stated relationship. Perhaps an example is the best explanation. Study the following:

Apple is to *fruit* as *potato* is to _____<u>vegetable</u>_____.

The first step in solving an analogy is to pinpoint the initial relationship. What is the relationship between *apple* and *fruit*? Since an apple is a member of the fruit group, you might say that it is one part of a larger whole. To complete the analogy, you must establish a similar relationship for *potato*. In what larger group does a potato belong? You've guessed it! *Vegetable* is the answer.

Analogies are challenging and can be very difficult. They test logical thinking as well as vocabulary. Working through analogies is an experience in problem solving.

The following list explains the many different relationships that can be expressed in analogy. Study both the list and the examples.

◆◆ **READER'S TIP**

CATEGORIES OF RELATIONSHIPS FOR ANALOGIES

Synonyms: Similar in meaning

Start is to *begin* as *end* is to *finish*.

Antonyms: Opposite in meaning

Retreat is to *advance* as *tall* is to *short*.

Function, use or purpose: Identifies what something does. Watch for the object (noun) and then the action (verb).

Car is to *drive* as *towel* is to *absorb*.

Classification: Identifies the larger group association

Mosquito is to *insect* as *gasoline* is to *fuel*.

Characteristics and descriptions: Shows qualities or traits

Sour is to *lemon* as *sweet* is to *sugar*.

Degree: Shows variations of intensity

Walking is to *running* as *cool* is to *frozen*.

Part to whole: Shows the larger group

Pupil is to *school* as *sailor* is to *navy*.

Cause and effect: Shows the reason (cause) and the result (effect)

Work is to *success* as *virus* is to *illness*.

Copyright ©1999 by Addison-Wesley Educational Publishers Inc.

EXERCISE 15 Study the following analogies to establish the relationship of the first two words. Record that relationship, using the categories outlined above. Then choose the word that duplicates that relationship to finish the analogy.

___b___ 1. *Wing* is to *bird* as *webfoot* is to _____duck_____.

Relationship? ___part to whole___

    a. pedal
    b. duck
    c. bottom
    d. head

___d___ 2. *Clear* is to *confusing* as *shallow* is to _____deep_____.

Relationship? ___antonyms___

    a. personality
    b. conversation
    c. water
    d. deep

___a___ 3. *Turnip* is to *vegetable* as *walnut* is to _____wood_____.

Relationship? ___classification___

    a. wood
    b. fuel
    c. house
    d. glass

___d___ 4. *Selling* is to *profit* as *germ* is to _____disease_____.

Relationship? ___cause and effect___

    a. vaccination
    b. carelessness
    c. wealth
    d. disease

___b___ 5. *Kind* is to *considerate* as *courage* is to _____bravery_____.

Relationship? ___synonyms___

    a. soldier
    b. bravery
    c. fear
    d. fighting

___c___ 6. *Towel* is to *absorb* as *oven* is to _____cook_____.

Relationship? ___function___

    a. safety
    b. speed
    c. cook
    d. kitchen

___b___ 7. *Tiny* is to small as *happy* is to _____exhilarating_____.

Relationship? ___degree___

    a. good
    b. exhilarating
    c. peace
    d. emotion

___a___ 8. *Soft* is to *pillow* as *humid* is to ___swamp___.

   Relationship? ___characteristics___

    a. swamp
    b. trip
    c. camp
    d. trees

___b___ 9. *Work* is to *success* as *study* is to ___knowledge___.

   Relationship? ___cause and effect___

    a. history
    b. knowledge
    c. professor
    d. college

___b___ 10. *Needle* is to *sew* as *bulb* is to ___illuminate___.

   Relationship? ___function___

    a. lamp
    b. illuminate
    c. electricity
    d. table

Easily Confused Words ◆◆◆◆◆◆◆◆◆◆◆

Many pairs of words cause confusion because they sound exactly alike or almost alike, but are spelled and used differently. *Principal* and *principle* are examples of this confusion. A common error is to write, "The new school principle is Mrs. Thompson." Remember, the *al* word is the person, or "pal," and the *le* word is the rule. To keep most of these words straight, you must memorize and associate. Study the following words that sound similar and learn their differences.

◆◆ READER'S TIP

EASILY CONFUSED WORDS

capital: city
capitol: building

cereal: breakfast food
serial: episode

cite: quote
sight: vision
site: place

aisle: row
isle: island

accept: receive
except: all but

angle: in math
angel: in heaven

birth: have a baby
berth: bed

stationary: fixed position
stationery: paper

vain: conceited
vein: blood vessel

your: ownership
you're: contraction of *you are*

Copyright © 1999 by Addison-Wesley Educational Publishers Inc.

EXERCISE 16   Circle the correct boldface word to fit the context of each sentence.

1. The letter was written on official university (**stationary**, **stationery**).
2. The geometry problem involved one right (**angle**, **angel**).
3. Atlanta is the (**capital**, **capitol**) of Georgia.
4. The cheapest room on the ship contains only one tiny (**birth**, **berth**).
5. Eat a bowl of (**cereal**, **serial**) in the morning.
6. Look for your friend in the second (**aisle**, **isle**) of the lecture hall.
7. The professor told the students to (**cite**, **sight**, **site**) the author's exact words in the paper.
8. Read all of the chapters (**accept**, **except**) the last two.
9. The swim coach wants to know when (**your**, **you're**) ready.
10. To draw blood, she stuck the needle in my (**vain**, **vein**).

PERSONAL FEEDBACK 2

Name_____

1. After reading this chapter, how will you change your system for remembering new words? _____
_____
_____

2. Why do you enjoy or dislike studying words? _____
_____

3. Some graduate schools use a test of analogies as part of their admissions criteria. What skills, other than identifying word meanings, would be used on such a test? _____
_____

4. Why is it not recommended that you look up unknown words as you read? _____
_____

5. What is one word that your instructor uses frequently that you were not previously accustomed to hearing? _____

6. What word does your instructor use that you do not completely understand? _____

7. List ten adjectives to describe characteristics that you would like in a spouse. Again, stretch your vocabulary beyond easy words. _____
_____

8. How do these adjectives compare to the adjectives that you use to describe yourself? What are the similarities and differences? _____

_____

_____

Vocabulary Enrichment ◆◆◆◆◆◆◆◆◆◆◆

Most of the longer textbook reading selections in this text will be followed by a *Vocabulary Enrichment* section with additional practice for the strategies presented in this vocabulary chapter. Expanding and enriching your vocabulary goes beyond one lesson and a single chapter. It is an exciting, lifelong activity.

POINTS TO PONDER

▲ Use context clues from a passage to figure out the meaning of new words.
▲ Visualize associations to remember new words.
▲ Put the word, the definition, a sentence, a picture, and the source on concept cards.
▲ Consider the context to figure out the correct meaning of multiple-meaning words.
▲ Word parts such as roots, prefixes, and suffixes can help unlock the meaning of new words.
▲ The dictionary contains much more than just the definitions of words.
▲ Words have families.
▲ The textbook glossary contains words that are part of the terminology of the discipline.
▲ The thesaurus suggests alternate word options for writers.
▲ Analogies are comparisons based on categories of relationships.

EXPLORE THE NET

● What general vocabulary-building tips can you find on the Internet that you would add to the information in this chapter?
● Describe any vocabulary-building programs that are for sale that relate to a specific area of interest for you.

For additional readings and exercises, visit the Longman English Skills Web page at:

http://longman.awl.com/englishpages

For a user name and password, please see your instructor.

Copyright ©1999 by Addison-Wesley Educational Publishers Inc.

Main Idea

◆ *What is a main idea?*

◆ *What is a topic?*

◆ *How do you recognize the difference between general and specific ideas?*

◆ *What is a stated main idea?*

◆ *What is an unstated main idea?*

Copyright ©1999 by Addison-Wesley Educational Publishers Inc.

What Is a Main Idea? ◆◆◆◆◆◆◆◆◆◆

The main idea of a passage is the core of the material. It is the particular point that the author is trying to convey about the material. The main idea of a passage can be stated in one sentence that condenses specific ideas or details in the passage into a general, all-inclusive statement of the author's message. In classroom discussions, all of the following words are sometimes used to help students understand the meaning of the main idea:

thesis
main point
central focus
gist
controlling idea
central thought

Whether you read a single paragraph, a chapter, or an entire book, many experts agree that your most important single task is to understand the main idea of what you read.

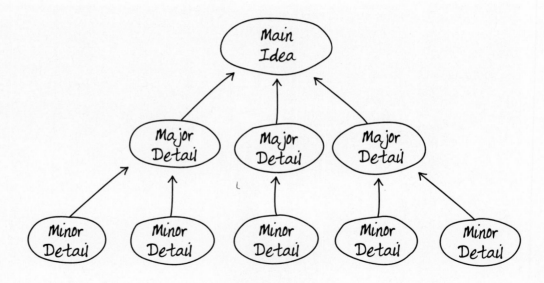

Recognize General and Specific Words

The first step in determining the main idea of a selection is to look at the specific ideas presented in the sentences and try to decide on a general topic or subject under which these ideas can be grouped. Before tackling sentences, begin with words. Pretend that the sentence ideas in a selection have been reduced to a short list of key words. Pretend also that within the list is a general term that expresses an overall subject for the key words. The general term encompasses or categorizes the key ideas and is considered the topic of the list.

EXAMPLE   The following list contains three specific ideas with a related general topic. Circle the general term that could be considered the subject of the list.

satin
wool
(fabric)
silk

EXPLANATION Satin, wool, and silk are different types of fabric. Thus, *fabric* is the general term or classification that could be considered the subject or topic.

EXERCISE 1

Circle the general term or subject for each of the following related groups of ideas.

1. chimpanzees
   orangutans
   (apes)
   gorillas

2. cirrus
   (clouds)
   cumulus
   stratus

3. oats
   wheat
   corn
   (grain)

4. Alps
   Appalachians
   (mountains)
   Rockies

5. shrimp
   (crustacean)
   crab
   lobster

Recognize General and Specific Phrases

Since topics of passages are more often stated as phrases rather than single words, the following list contains a phrase that is a general topic and three specific ideas related to the topic. Circle the general topic that could be the subject.

EXAMPLE

Turn on the ignition.

Press the accelerator.

Insert the key.

(Start the car.)

EXPLANATION The first three details are involved in starting a car. The last phrase is the general subject or topic.

EXERCISE 2

Circle the phrase that could be the topic for each list below.

1. totaling yearly income
   subtracting for dependents
   (filing an income tax return)
   mailing a 1040 form

2. paying fees
   buying books
   (starting college)
   going to class

3. picking up seashells
   (vacationing at the beach)
   walking in the surf
   riding the waves

4. pushing paper under sticks
   piling the logs
   (building a fire)
   striking a match

EXERCISE 3

Read the lists of specific details and write a general phrase that could be the subject or topic for each group below.

1. separate the white and dark clothes
   add one cup of detergent
   insert quarters into the machine
   General topic? _doing the laundry_____

Copyright ©1999 by Addison-Wesley Educational Publishers Inc.

  2. dribble the ball

     pass ball down court

     shoot a basket

     General topic? playing basketball

  3. release the break

     turn key in ignition

     press on gas pedal

     General topic? starting a car

  4. switch on power

     select a program

     load a disk into the drive

     General topic? working at the computer

  5. boil water in a large pot

     add salt and oil

     empty noodles into water

     General topic? cooking pasta

Recognize the General Topic for Sentences

Paragraphs are composed of sentences that develop a single general topic. The next practice exercises contain groups in which the sentences of a paragraph are numerically listed. After reading the sentences, circle the phrase that best expresses the topic or general subject of the sentences.

EXAMPLE

  1. The law of demand is illustrated in an experiment conducted by the makers of M&M candy.
  2. For a twelve-month period, the price of M&Ms remained the same in 150 stores, but the number of M&Ms in a package increased, which dropped the price per ounce.
  3. In these stores, sales immediately rose by 20 to 30 percent.

     Candy Maker's Experiment

     M&Ms Drop in Price

     ⟨M&Ms Prove the Law of Demand⟩

EXPLANATION The first phrase is too broad. The second relates a detail that is an important part of the experiment. The third links the candy with the purpose of the experiment and thus most accurately states the subject of the sentences.

EXERCISE 4

Circle the phrase that best describes the topic or subject for each group of sentences.

GROUP 1

  1. To provide a favorable climate for growing grapes, the winter temperature should not go below 15 degrees, and the summers should be long.
  2. During the growing season, rainfall should be light.

3. A gentle movement of air is required to dry the vines after rains, dispel fog, and protect the vines from fungus disease.

Protecting Grapes from Disease

Appropriate Temperatures for Growing Grapes

(Appropriate Climates for Growing Grapes)

GROUP 2

1. The spiritual stimulus that Mohammed provided united and mobilized the Arab world.
2. Mohammed received a series of revelations from Allah in Mecca, a city 45 miles from the Red Sea.
3. Mohammed fled to the safer haven of Medina, and he and his followers quickly spread the Islamic religion throughout North Africa and Southwest Asia.

The Arab Empire

(The Rise of Islam)

Mohammed's Revelations

GROUP 3

1. After accidents, suicide is the second leading cause of death among adolescents.
2. In a national survey, 42% of the 8th–10th grade girls reported contemplating suicide sometime in their lives.
3. In the last 40 years, the suicide rate among young men 15–19 years of age has quadrupled.

Prevention of Suicides

(Increase of Adolescent Suicides)

Reasons for Teen Suicides

GROUP 4

1. Some scientists believe that the vestigial diving response offers proof that humans evolved from aquatic animals.
2. If you submerge your face in water, your pulse rate is likely to drop and your metabolic rate decreases.
3. This slowdown suggests a vestigial diving response that would allow humans to remain submerged longer.

Human Science

(Vestigial Linkage to Aquatics)

Lowering the Metabolic Rate

GROUP 5

1. Simply drinking water is the best way to prevent dehydration from sweating.
2. Taking salt tablets before drinking water can dehydrate the body even more by extracting water from body tissue.
3. Plain water is better than beverages containing sugar or electrolytes because it is absorbed faster.

Salt Tablets versus Water

Value in Plain Water

(Preventing Dehydration)

Copyright ©1999 by Addison-Wesley Educational Publishers Inc.

Read the following groups of three sentences and then write a phrase that best states the subject or general topic for the sentences.

GROUP 1

1. The albatross is one of the few birds that is designed to live at sea and it seldom visits land.
2. Because it has special glands that excrete salt, it can drink sea water and eat salty fish.
3. The albatross's unusually long wings provide the lift for it to glide almost endlessly in high winds over rough seas.

General topic? <u>Designed for Sea Life or The Albatross's Unique Design</u>

GROUP 2

1. Once children begin to speak and understand words, their progress is remarkably fast.
2. Most children begin speaking at one year of age and speak only two to three words.
3. By age two, they speak about fifty words and understand two hundred to three hundred words.

General topic? <u>Early Word Knowledge or A Child's Understanding of Words</u>

GROUP 3

1. Dr. Sylvia Castillo of Stanford University founded the National Network of Hispanic Women.
2. This organization publishes a national newsletter that focuses on the successes of Hispanic women in academia and business.
3. The organization has become an important voice for Hispanic issues relating to gender.

General topic? <u>National Network of Hispanic Women or An Organization for Hispanic Women</u>

Recognize General and Supporting Sentences

Read the sentences in each of the following groups. The sentences are related to a single subject with two of the sentences expressing specific support and one sentence expressing the general idea about the subject. Circle the number of the sentence that best expresses the general subject. Then read the three topic phrases and circle the phrase that best describes the subject of the sentences.

EXAMPLE

1. If you had wisely purchased $1,000 of Rubbermaid stock in the 1980s, your stock would have been worth over $10,000 in seven years.
2. Rubbermaid tries as many as one hundred new products a year, and 90 percent are successful.
3. Rubbermaid listens to consumers, plans carefully, and has been enjoying the increased profits of a successful company.

New Products from Rubbermaid

The Success of Rubbermaid

Profits in the Stock Market

EXPLANATION The third sentence best expresses the general subject. The other two sentences offer specific supporting ideas. The second phrase, "The Success of Rubbermaid," best describes the general subject of the material. The first phrase is an important detail that is mentioned, and the last phrase relates to the entire stock market, not specifically to Rubbermaid.

EXERCISE 6 Circle the number of the sentence that best expresses the general subject. Then read the three topic phrases and circle the phrase that best describes the subject of the sentences.

GROUP 1

(1.) Although newborn infants seem unresponsive, new research has shown that they sense more of the environment than was previously thought.

2. Infants only one or two days of age show preferences to sweet-tasting liquids as opposed to those with salty, bitter, or bland tastes.

3. At one week of age, an infant can pick out its mother's voice from a group of female voices.

Infant Taste Preferences

(Early Infant Responsiveness)

Mother's Sweet Voice

GROUP 2

(1.) Berry Gordy, an ex-boxer and Ford auto worker, borrowed $700 from his family and successfully began to manufacture and sell his own records on the Hitsville USA (later called, "Motown," for "motor town") label.

2. The next year Smokey Robinson and the Miracles recorded "Shop Around," which was Gordy's first big million-copy hit.

3. Gordy signed an eleven-year-old boy to record for him under the name of Stevie Wonder.

(Gordy's Success)

Stevie Wonder at Motown

The Recording Artists at Motown

GROUP 3

1. The Czarina believed that the devious and politically corrupt Rasputin, known as the "mad monk," was the only one who could save her son.

2. The son of Nicholas II was afflicted with hemophilia, a condition in which the blood does not clot properly.

(3.) In Russia during the reign of Nicholas II, hemophilia played an important historical role.

Rasputin's Charm

Hemophilia

(Influence of Hemophilia on Russia)

GROUP 4

(1.) The success of Norman Rockwell's illustrations is based on the simple formula of drawing ordinary people doing ordinary things that make us laugh at ourselves.

Copyright ©1999 by Addison-Wesley Educational Publishers Inc.

2. Rockwell used humor to poke fun at situations but never at people.
3. Rockwell painted the people and children in the neighborhood, first from real life and, in later years, from photographs.

Rockwell's Neighborhood

(Rockwell's People Formula)

Art from Photographs

GROUP 5

(1.) In 1993, the population of deer mice, a common carrier of hantavirus, exploded in the southwestern United States after an unusually wet season.
2. New viral diseases, such as hantavirus, spread from one host species to another.
3. Humans then acquired hantavirus by inhaling dust containing traces of urine and feces from infected mice.

(Spread of New Viruses)

Deer Mice

Inhaling Dust

EXERCISE 7

For each group of sentences, write a phrase that states the topic, and then circle the number of the sentence that best expresses the main idea.

GROUP 1

1. Four hundred Navajos were recruited as Marine radio operators, and the codes based on the Navajo language were never broken by the enemy.
(2.) During World War II, over twenty-five thousand Native Americans served in the armed forces and made amazing contributions toward the war effort.
3. The most famous Indian GI was a Pima Indian, the Marine Ira Hayes, who helped plant the American flag on Iwo Jima.

General topic? <u>Contribution of Native Americans in WWII</u>

GROUP 2

(1.) One of the earliest and most lasting attempts to explain dreams was Freud's theory that they are products of the mind that can be interpreted and understood.
2. More specifically, Freud believed that dreams are disguised attempts at the fulfillment of wishes that the individual finds unacceptable at the conscious level.
3. While modern cognitive psychologists reject many of Freud's ideas, they still note that aspects of his dream theory have cognitive validity.

General topic? <u>Freud's Theory of Dreams</u>

GROUP 3

1. To prevent thawing, special insulation was developed to cool the hot pipelines carrying oil from Prudhoe Bay to Valdez.
2. Permafrost covers more than 80 percent of Alaska and 50 percent of Canada.
(3.) Maintaining the delicate thermal balance is vital to Alaska and Canada because the thawing of permafrost can cause destructive slides, slumps, and frost heaves.

General topic? <u>Maintaining Alaska's Thermal Balance</u>

Each of the following sentence groups contains three specific supporting sentences. Write a general sentence that states the overall message for each group. In addition, write a phrase that briefly states the general topic of the sentence.

GROUP 1

1. The battered woman does not want to believe the man she loves is actually violent in nature.
2. She doesn't want to face the possibility that he may be violent for the rest of their lives together.
3. She wants to hold onto the hope that someday he will quit drinking and the relationship will change.

—Marriages and Families in a Diverse Society by Robin Wolf

General sentence stating the main idea? <u>The battered woman does not want to face the reality of abuse.</u>

General topic? <u>The Battered Woman's Denial</u>

GROUP 2

1. Soon after being bitten by an infected flea, they developed high fever, began coughing, and suffered excruciatingly painful swellings in the lymph nodes of the groin or armpits.
2. In the final stages the victims began to vomit blood.
3. The bubonic form of the disease usually killed within five days, whereas people infected by the airborne pneumonic form usually died in less than three days.

—The Unfinished Legacy by Mark Kislansky et al.

General sentence stating the main idea? <u>Bubonic plague victims died quickly and painfully.</u>

General topic? <u>Death from Bubonic Plague</u>

GROUP 3

1. A colleague of mine gave a lecture in Beijing, China, to a group of Chinese college students.
2. The students listened politely but made no comments and asked no questions after her lecture.
3. Later, she learned that Chinese students show respect by being quiet and seemingly passive.

—Messages by Joseph DeVito

General sentence stating the main idea? <u>In China, students show respect through quiet rather than questions.</u>

General topic? <u>Student Response in China</u>

Differentiate Topic, Main Idea, and Supporting Details

A topic is a word or phrase that describes the subject or general category of a group of specific ideas. Frequently, the topic is stated as the title of a passage. The main idea, on the other hand, is a complete sentence that states the topic

Copyright © 1999 by Addison-Wesley Educational Publishers Inc.

and adds the writer's position or focus on the topic. The supporting details are the specifics that develop the topic and main idea.

Read the following example from a textbook paragraph and label the topic, the main idea, and a supporting detail.

EXAMPLE

Topic   The Body Signaling Feeling

Main Idea   Some signals of body language, like some facial expressions, seem to be "spoken" universally.

Detail   When people are depressed, it shows in their walk, stance, and head position.

—Psychology by Carole Wade and Carol Tavris

Compare the items within each group and indicate which is the topic (T), the main idea (MI), and the specific supporting detail (D).

GROUP 1

___D___   1. Much in this American document comes from England's Magna Carta, which was signed in 1215.

___T___   2. British Roots in American Government

___MI___   3. The American Constitution has its roots in the power of past documents.

GROUP 2

___D___   1. Like Latinos, African Americans view "children as wealth," believing that children are important in adding enjoyment and fulfillment to life.

___T___   2. Valuing Children.

___MI___   3. Children are highly valued in African-American families.

—Marriage and Families in a Diverse Society by Robin Wolf

GROUP 3

___D___   1. Some welcomed the Americans; many others, recognizing the futility of resistance, responded to the American conquest with ambivalence.

___T___   2. The Fate of Mexican Americans

___MI___   3. The 80,000 Mexicans who lived in the Southwest did not respond to the Mexican War with a single voice.

—America and Its People by James Martin et al.

GROUP 4

___D___   1. Her early research led to an understanding of how viruses infect the plant and destroy its tissues.

___T___   2. Esau's Early Career with Beets

___MI___   3. Sugar beets played a major role in the career of Dr. Katherine Esau, one of this century's most prolific plant scientists.

—Biology: Concepts and Connections by Neil Campbell et al.

GROUP 5

___T___ 1. Discrimination Against Women in Higher Education.

___D___ 2. Harvard, for example, was one of the last to give up sex discrimination and began admitting women to its graduate business program only in 1963.

___MI___ 3. In general, the more prestigious the educational institutions, the more strongly they discriminated against women.

—*Sociology* by Alex Thio

Questioning for the Main Idea ◆◆◆◆◆◆◆◆◆◆◆

To determine the main idea of a body of material, ask questions in the following three basic areas. The order may vary according to how much you already know about the subject. Usually, the general topic is determined first, sometimes from the title and sometimes by considering the details. If you are familiar with the material, constructing a main idea may seem almost automatic. If the material is unfamiliar, however, you may need to connect the key thoughts to formulate a topic and then create your main idea statement.

1. Establish the Topic

Question: Who or what is this about?

What general word or phrase identifies the subject? The topic should be broad enough to include all the ideas, but narrow enough to focus on the direction of the details. For example, identifying the topic of an article as "College Costs," "Change in College," or "Changing to Cut College Costs," might all be correct, but the last may be the most pointed and descriptive for the article.

2. Identify the Key Supporting Terms

Question: What are the important details?

Look at the details that seem to be significant to see if they point in a particular direction. What aspect of the subject do they address? What seems to be the common message? In a passage on college costs, the details might describe benefits of larger classes, telecommunication networks, and video instruction. A common thread is that each idea relates to changes targeted at cutting the costs of college instruction.

3. Focus on the Message of the Topic

Question: What is the main idea the author is trying to convey about the topic?

This statement should be:

  a. A complete sentence,
  b. Broad enough to include the important details, and
  c. Focused enough to describe the author's slant.

In the example about cutting college costs, the main idea might be "Several colleges experiment with ways to cut college costs."

Copyright ©1999 by Addison-Wesley Educational Publishers Inc.

Stated Main Ideas

Research shows that students comprehend better when the main idea is directly stated, particularly when it is stated at the beginning of a passage. Such an initial main idea statement, or thesis statement, is a signpost for the reader, briefing him or her on what to expect. This thesis or main idea statement overviews the author's message and connects the supporting details. Read the following example and use the three-step method to determine the main idea.

EXAMPLE

In Virginia, men got elected to office by plying the freeholders with bumbo—in the vernacular of the day. <u>Rum punch</u> was preferred, accompanied by <u>cookies</u> and ginger <u>cake</u> and occasionally a <u>barbecued bullock</u> or a hog. For one election in 1758, George Washington supplied <u>160 gallons of liquor</u> to <u>391 voters</u>—a stiff one and a half quarts per voter.

—*American Politics* by Gary Wasserman

1. Who or what is the topic of this passage? <u>Buying Votes with Rum</u>
2. Underline the key terms.
3. What point is the author trying to make? <u>In Virginia, men got elected to</u> <u>office by entertaining voters.</u>

EXPLANATION The topic of this passage is "Buying Votes with Rum." The details give specifics such as rum punch, cookies, barbecue, and 160 gallons of liquor for 391 voters. The author states the main idea in the first sentence, although the details do expand the bribery to both food and drink.

Textbook authors do not always state the main idea in the first sentence. Stated main ideas may be the beginning, middle, or concluding sentence of a passage. Therefore, you should not think of stating the main idea only as a search for a particular sentence. Instead, rely on your own skill in answering the three questions about topic, details, and focus. Connect the details to form your own concept of the main idea and, if a specific sentence in the paragraph restates it, you will recognize it as the main idea.

EXERCISE 10

Apply the three-question technique to identify the topic, key terms, and main idea of the following passages, all of which have stated main ideas.

PASSAGE 1

One of the most popular legends of all time concerns the disappearance of the so-called continent of Atlantis. According to the accounts provided by Plato, an island empire named *Atlantis* <u>disappeared beneath the sea in a single day and night</u>. This event, which reportedly took place between 1500 B.C. and 1400 B.C. and caused the collapse of the Minoan civilization, is thought by many to have been the result of a <u>cataclysmic volcanic eruption</u>.

—*The Earth* by Edward Tarbuck and Frederick Lutgens

1. Who or what is the topic of this passage? <u>The Disappearance of Atlantis</u>
2. Underline the key terms.

3. What point is the author trying to make? <u>The legendary disappearance of Atlantis is thought to have been caused by a volcanic eruption.</u>

PASSAGE 2

Henry Dreyfuss, in his *Symbol Sourcebook,* points out some of the positive and negative meanings associated with various colors and some cultural comparisons. For example, <u>red</u> in <u>China</u> is used for <u>joyous</u> and <u>festive occasions</u>, whereas in <u>Japan</u> it signifies <u>anger</u> and <u>danger</u>. <u>Blue</u> signifies <u>defeat</u> for the <u>Cherokee</u> Indian, but <u>virtue</u> and <u>truth</u> for the <u>Egyptian</u>. In the <u>Japanese</u> theater, <u>blue</u> is the color for <u>villains</u>. <u>Yellow</u> signifies <u>happiness</u> and <u>prosperity</u> in <u>Egypt</u>, but in tenth-century <u>France</u> yellow colored the doors of <u>criminals</u>. <u>Green</u> communicates <u>femininity</u> to certain American <u>Indians</u>, <u>fertility</u> and <u>strength</u> to <u>Egyptians</u>, and <u>youth</u> and <u>energy</u> to the <u>Japanese</u>. <u>Purple</u> signifies <u>virtue</u> and <u>faith</u> in Egypt, <u>grace</u> and <u>nobility</u> in Japan.

—*Essentials of Human Communication* by Joseph DeVito

1. Who or what is the topic of this passage? <u>Meaning Associated with Colors</u>
2. Underline the key terms.
3. What point is the author trying to make? <u>The positive or negative meanings associated with colors vary according to different cultures.</u>

PASSAGE 3

The study of circadian rhythms has produced information that can help in the scheduling of shift rotations for the 20–30 million people in the United States who work at such jobs. For example, it is easier to <u>reset</u> the internal clock to a <u>later</u> time <u>than</u> to an <u>earlier</u> time. This explains why we adjust more easily to travel from east to west than in the opposite direction. It also suggests that rotating shifts should be scheduled so that <u>people work the day, evening, and night shifts in that order</u>, rather than switching to nights and then evenings after the day shift. Furthermore, since it takes up to a week for a person to adjust to the new schedule, workers should be <u>left on each shift for as long as possible</u>. Workers at a mineral mine in Utah were switched from spending a week on each shift and then rotating to an earlier one, to a new schedule, on which they worked three weeks at each shift and then rotated to a later one. They <u>reported increased job satisfaction</u> and better health on the new schedule, and not one fell asleep during work hours anymore. The employer gained, too, in <u>less employee turnover</u> and in <u>increased output.</u>

—*A Journey into Life* by Karen Arms and Pamela Camp

1. Who or what is the topic of this passage? <u>Using Circadian Rhythms in Scheduling Shift Rotations</u>
2. Underline the key terms.
3. What point is the author trying to make? <u>Information from the study of circadian rhythms can be used to increase the output of shift workers.</u>

Copyright ©1999 by Addison-Wesley Educational Publishers Inc.

PASSAGE 4

Many people wonder how they can tell whether or not someone else is sexually attracted to them. Shotland and Craig discovered that when people first meet a person in whom they are sexually interested, they exhibit a particular pattern of behavior. In their study, pairs of male and female college students who had just met were videotaped having a conversation. Afterward, the researchers asked the subjects whether their interest in the other person had been sexual or just friendly. The researchers then matched reports of sexual interest to specific behaviors in the videotapes. They found that behaviors that exhibit sexual interest include long eye contact; playing with inanimate objects; asking questions; giving long answers; discontinuing eating, drinking, or reading; being the first to speak after a pause; doing most of the talking; and, especially, mentioning that one has noticed the other person before this meeting. Although these behaviors, such as asking questions, also tend to occur when a person has only a friendly interest in the partner, they occur to a greater degree when sexual interest is present. When the interest is simply friendly rather than sexual, eye contact is briefer; fidgeting is less; answers to questions tend to be shorter; and the person tends to continue eating, drinking, or even reading when the other person is present. However, because friendly and sexually interested behavior fall at two ends of a continuum and the difference between them is a matter of degree, interpreting behaviors can be difficult.

—*Marriage and Families in a Diverse Society* by Robin Wolf

1. Who or what is the topic of this passage? Behaviors of the Sexually Attracted
2. Underline the key terms.
3. What point is the author trying to make? Persons who are sexually
   interested in each other exhibit particular patterns of behavior.

PASSAGE 5

Alcoholism has an impact that extends beyond the chemically dependent family member. The other family members become caught up in the addiction process in their attempt to cope with the chaotic family life that alcoholism produces. The alcoholic is known as the "dependent" because he or she is dependent on a chemical substance. The spouse typically takes on the role of the "enabler" (sometimes called "co-dependent") who tries to help the alcoholic and thereby unwittingly engages in behavior that allows the alcoholic to continue drinking. The enabler attempts to save the alcoholic from experiencing the consequences of addictive behavior. For example, if the alcoholic is drunk or hung over and does not show up at a family barbecue attended by extended kin, the enabler will make excuses for the alcoholic and might say that the alcoholic has the flu. Thus the alcoholism is kept secret and the alcoholic is protected from the anger of relatives.

—*Marriages and Families in a Diverse Society* by Robin Wolf

1. Who or what is the topic of this passage? <u>The Family Impact of Alcoholism</u>

2. Underline the key terms.

3. What point is the author trying to make? <u>Family members typically engage in enabling behavior to protect the alcoholic member.</u>

Unstated Main Ideas

Research shows that only about half of the paragraphs in textbooks have directly stated main ideas. This should not be a problem if you understand the three-question technique for locating the main idea. The questions guide you in forming your own statement so that you are not dependent on finding a line in the text.

When the main idea is not directly stated, it is said to be *implied*, which means that it is suggested from the thoughts that are revealed.

In this case, the author has presented a complete idea, but for reasons of style and impact has not chosen to express it concisely in one sentence. As a reader, it is your job to systematically connect the details and focus the message.

In the passage below, the main idea is not stated, but it may be determined by answering the three questions that follow.

EXAMPLE

"I'll scratch your back if you'll scratch mine." That is the essence of reciprocity. Assume that a paper manufacturing firm supplies most of the pre-printed office forms and other paper goods to your company, an office equipment manufacturer. As marketing manager you would ensure that the paper goods manufacturer received a call about buying your office machinery and equipment. That your company buys most of its paper products from the paper goods firm would, of course, be noted. When agreements are informal, cancellation of reciprocal purchases by one firm may trigger the other to transfer its business to companies willing to reciprocate.

—*Modern Marketing* by Edward Fox and Edward Wheatley

1. Who or what is the topic of this passage?
   The passage is about reciprocity. (This gives you the general topic or heading.)

2. What are the key terms or details?
   You buy paper goods and printed forms from a company and they buy office equipment from you

3. What idea is the author trying to convey about reciprocity?
   Reciprocity sales are made by trying to sell your product to someone from whom you already buy a product. (This is the main idea the author is trying to communicate.)

EXPLANATION The sentence stating the main idea might very well have been the first, middle, or last sentence of the paragraph. Having it stated, however, was not necessary for understanding the passage. In many cases, readers spend time searching for a single sentence that encapsulates the meaning rather than digesting the information and forming ideas. Instead, answer the three questions: "Who or what is this about?" "What are the key terms?" and "What point is the author trying to make?"

Copyright ©1999 by Addison-Wesley Educational Publishers Inc.

EXERCISE 11

PASSAGE 1

In Chicago, only half the viewers watch network news. In San Francisco, <u>more people</u> <u>watch *Wheel of Fortune* than watch the two competing CBS and ABC nightly news pro-</u> <u>grams *combined*.</u> Just as bad is that the game show <u>attracts younger people, especially</u> <u>women,</u> that advertisers want to reach, while people 50 and older watch the news. In addition, <u>local stations' news programs are muscling out network</u> news with earlier head- lines and larger audiences. The networks also have a <u>problem attracting an audience that</u> <u>seems to prefer "soft" news</u> shows like *A Current Affair* and *Hard Copy,* stressing crime and scandals.

—*American Politics* by Gary Wasserman

1. Who or what is the topic of this passage?   Declining Network News Audiences
2. Underline the key terms.
3. What point is the author trying to make?   Network news shows are losing the
young audiences.

PASSAGE 2

A young woman named Edith finished grammar school in four years, skipped high school, and went straight to college. She graduated from college at age 15 and obtained her <u>doctorate before she was 18.</u> Was she born a genius? Not at all. Ever since she had stopped playing with dolls, her <u>father had seen to it that her days were filled with read-</u> <u>ing, mathematics, classical music, intellectual discussions and debates,</u> and whatever learning her father could derive from the world's literature. When she felt like playing, her father told her to <u>play chess</u> with someone like himself, who would be a challenge to her.

—*Sociology* by Alex Thio

1. Who or what is the topic of this passage?   Creating Genius
2. Underline the key terms.
3. What point is the author trying to make?   Edith's genius was not innate, but
was fostered by the intellectual nurturing of her father.

PASSAGE 3

If the person is extremely important, you had better be there early just in case he or she is able to see you ahead of schedule. As the individual's status decreases, it is less important for you to be on time. <u>Students,</u> for example, <u>must be on time for conferences</u> with teachers, but it is <u>more important to be on time for deans</u> and still <u>more important</u> to be on <u>time for the president</u> of the college. <u>Teachers,</u> on the other hand, may be <u>late for</u> <u>conferences</u> with <u>students</u> but not for conferences with <u>deans or the president.</u> Deans, in turn, may be late for teachers but not for the president. Business organizations and other

Copyright ©1999 by Addison-Wesley Educational Publishers Inc.

hierarchies have similar rules. Even the time of dinner and the time from the arrival of guests to eating varies on the basis of status. Among <u>lower-status individuals, dinner is served relatively early</u>. If there are guests, they eat soon after they arrive. For <u>higher-status people, dinner is relatively late</u>, and a longer time elapses between arrival and eating.

—*Human Communication* by Joseph DeVito

1. Who or what is the topic of this passage? <u>The Relationship of Time and Status</u>

2. Underline the key terms.

3. What point is the author trying to make? <u>Time functions as a symbol of status in social and business situations.</u>

PASSAGE 4

Try as she might, Marie Antoinette (1755–1793) found insufficient diversion in her life at the great court of Versailles. When she was fourteen, she had married the heir to the French throne, the future Louis XVI. By the age of nineteen she was queen of the most prosperous state in continental Europe. Still she was bored. Unpopular as a foreigner from the time she arrived in France, Marie Antoinette suffered a further decline in her reputation as gossip spread about <u>her gambling and affairs at court</u>. The public heard exaggerated accounts of the fortunes she <u>spent on clothing</u> and <u>jewelry</u>. In 1785 she was linked to a cardinal in a nasty scandal over a <u>gift of a diamond necklace.</u>

This Austrian-born queen may not have been more shallow or spendthrift than other queens, but it <u>mattered that people came to see her that way.</u> The queen's reputation sank to the nadir when it was reported that she dismissed the suffering of her starving subjects with the haughty retort that if <u>they had no bread,</u> "Let them eat cake."

—*The Unfinished Legacy* by Mark Kishlansky et al.

1. Who or what is the topic of this passage? <u>Marie Antoinette's Reputation</u>
2. Underline the key terms.
3. What point is the author trying to make? <u>Marie Antoinette's reputation for haughtiness and waste was both deserved and exaggerated.</u>

PASSAGE 5

A mother had a son who threw temper tantrums: lying on the floor, pounding his fists, kicking his legs, and whining for whatever he wanted. One day while in a supermarket he threw one of his temper tantrums. In a moment of desperation, <u>the mother dropped to the floor, pounded her fists, kicked her feet, and whined, "I wish you'd</u> stop throwing temper tantrums! I can't stand it when you throw temper tantrums!" By this time, the son had stood up. He said in a hushed tone, "Mom, there are people watching! <u>You're embarrassing me!</u>" The mother calmly stood up, brushed off the dust, and said in a clear, calm voice. "That's what you look like when you're throwing a temper tantrum." Sometimes, traditional approaches such as bribing, threatening, ignoring, or giving in seem so natural that we overlook the possibility that something different, such as embarrassment, might work too.

—*The Creative Problem Solver's Toolbox* by Richard Fobes

1. Who or what is the topic of this passage? <u>A Temper Tantrum Reversal</u>
2. Underline the key terms.
3. What point is the author trying to make? <u>The mother used an unexpected solution to influence her son's temper tantrum behavior.</u>

Differentiating Distractors

To gain insight into recognizing a correctly stated main idea, categorizing incorrect responses can be helpful. When stating the topic or main idea of a passage, it is easy to make the mistake of creating a phrase or a sentence that is either too broad or too narrow. The same two types of errors occur when students are answering main idea questions on standardized tests. A phrase that is too broad is too general and thus would suggest the inclusion of much more than is actually stated in the passage. A phrase that is too narrow is a detail within the passage. It may be an interesting and eye-catching detail, but it is not the subject of the passage.

EXAMPLE   After reading the following passage, decide which of the suggested titles is correct (C), too broad (TB), or a detail within the passage (D).

> One interesting research finding shows that listeners can accurately judge the socioeconomic status (whether high, middle, or low) of speakers from 60-second voice samples. In fact, many listeners reported that they made their judgments in fewer than 15 seconds. Speakers judged to be of high status were also rated as being of higher credibility than speakers rated middle and low in status. Listeners can also judge with considerable accuracy the emotional states of speakers from vocal expressions.
>
> —*Human Communication* by Joseph DeVito

____TB____ 1. Importance of Voice

____TB____ 2. Speaking

____C____   3. Making Judgments by Voice

____D____   4. Emotional States of Speakers

EXPLANATION   The third response most accurately describes the topic of the passage. The first two are too broad and would include much more than is in the paragraph. The last response is a detail that is part of one of the experiments with listeners.

EXERCISE 12   Read the following passage and label the suggested titles as correct (C), too broad (TB), or as a detail within the passage (D).

PASSAGE 1

> In California, Mexican Americans were outnumbered and vulnerable to discrimination. During the early years of the Gold Rush, Mexican Americans were robbed, beaten, and lynched with impunity. The 1850 Foreign Miners' Tax imposed a $20 a month tax on Mexican American miners, even though the Treaty of Guadalupe Hidalgo had granted them citizenship. Many Mexicans were forced to sell land to pay onerous taxes that fell heaviest on the Spanish speakers.
>
> —*America and Its People* by James Martin et al.

____D____   1. Treaty of Guadalupe Hidalgo

____TB____ 2. Discrimination

____D____   3. Foreign Miners' Tax during the Gold Rush

____C____   4. Discrimination against Mexican Americans in California

PASSAGE 2

> Humpback whales strain their food from seawater. Instead of teeth, these giants have an array of brushlike plates called baleen on each side of their upper jaw. The baleen is used to sift food from the ocean. To start feeding, a humpback whale opens its mouth, expands its throat, and takes a huge gulp of seawater. When its mouth closes, the water squeezes out through spaces in the baleen, and a mass of food is trapped in the mouth. The food is then swallowed whole, passing into the stomach, where digestion begins. The humpback's stomach can hold about half a ton of food at a time, and in a typical day, the animal's digestive system will process as much as 2 tons of krill and fish.
>
> —*Biology: Concepts and Connections* by Neil Campbell et al.

Copyright ©1999 by Addison-Wesley Educational Publishers Inc.

___TB___ 1. Humpback Whales

___D___ 2. Baleen for Teeth

___TB___ 3. The Digestive System of the Humpback Whale

___C___ 4. How Whales Filter Food

PASSAGE 3

Knowledge about AIDS does not seem to deter high-risk sexual behavior. However, AIDS *worry* appears to be an important factor in changing sexual behavior in a more cautious direction. College students who report that they spend some time worrying about AIDS are far more likely than others to use condoms and avoid multiple partners. There is probably a generalized tendency for people to be risk takers or risk avoiders. People who regularly wear car seat belts are also likely to avoid casual sex and to use condoms consistently.

—*Marriages and Families in a Diverse Society* by Robin Wolf

___TB___ 1. Changing Sexual Behavior

___C___ 2. Linking Safe Sex and Risk Tendency

___TB___ 3. AIDS Prevention

___TB___ 4. College Students and Sex

Getting the Main Idea of Longer Selections

Because of the bulk of material, understanding the main idea of longer selections such as chapters and articles seems more difficult than understanding a single paragraph. Longer selections have several major ideas contributing to the main point and many paragraphs of supporting details. To pull the ideas together under one central theme, an additional step is necessary: The reader needs to simplify the material by organizing paragraphs or pages into manageable subsections and then deciding how each subsection contributes to the whole.

The following questions can help you determine the central theme for a longer selection:

1. What is the significance of the title? What does the title suggest about the topic?
2. Do the first paragraphs suggest the topic or thesis?
3. Under what subsection can these paragraphs and ideas be grouped?
4. How do these subsections support the whole?
5. What is the overall topic?
6. What point is the author trying to convey?

PERSONAL FEEDBACK 1

Name_____

1. Describe the theme or main idea of a movie that you have seen recently, one that you liked, and give reasons for your positive evaluation.

Movie Title: _____

Theme or Main Idea: _____

_____

Reasons for Positive Evaluation:_____

_____

2. What do you not understand about getting the main idea?

   _____

3. Approximately how many hours of sleep do you get each night?_____

   _____

4. What time do you usually go to bed?_____

5. What time do you get up?_____

6. When do you eat breakfast?_____

   What do you eat for breakfast? _____

   _____

7. Typically what, when, and where do you eat the other meals of the day?

   _____

   Lunch: _____

   _____

   Dinner:_____

8. What exercise do you get on a regular basis, and when do you do it?

   _____

   _____

9. Do you typically go out on weeknights? If so, typically when and where

   do you go? _____

   _____

10. Evaluate your energy level and concentration ability._____

    _____

    _____

POINTS TO PONDER

▲ Getting the main idea is the most important skill in reading.
▲ The main idea may be stated directly within a passage or it may be implied.
▲ To find the topic of a passage ask, "Who or what is the subject?"
▲ To find the main idea of a passage ask, "What point is the author trying to make?"
▲ The main idea of a passage should always be stated by the reader in a complete sentence.
▲ To get the main idea of longer selections, break the material into subsections and determine how they support the whole.

Copyright ©1999 by Addison-Wesley Educational Publishers Inc.

Psychology

THINKING BEFORE READING

Preview for content, activate your schema, and anticipate what you will learn.

Did you dream last night?

What dream or dreams have you had recently?

Can you explain the meaning of any of your dreams?

I think this will tell me _____.

VOCABULARY PREVIEW

Are you familiar with these words?

unconscious	paradox	convenient	symbolizes	bullied
idling	depriving	ascribed	critical	synchronized

Which word has the same root as *chronological*?

What is the definition of the prefix in *unconscious*?

Is the phrase *jumbo shrimp* a paradox?

Your instructor may give a true-false vocabulary review before or after reading.

THINKING DURING READING

As you read, use the five thinking strategies of a good reader: predict, picture, relate, monitor, and correct.

SLEEPING AND DREAMING

The time when we are most obviously unconscious is when we are asleep. Yet we have dreams during that time. This implies that something is going on in our brain.

Is all sleep the same? Are there stages in sleep? When do humans dream? How can you tell if a person is dreaming? Why do people have dreams, anyway? These are the
5   questions to be answered in this section.

Researchers have learned more about sleep and dreaming in the past twenty-five years than in all of history up to that time. One major reason for this is the discovery that when people are asleep there are changes in the activity of their brain and eyes. These changes can be recorded.

10   Beth Smith lies down to sleep after a hard day. She drifts off. At first she is in a light kind of sleep. Her brain waves, if recorded on a brain-wave machine, show a pattern that is definitely different than when she is awake. After less than an hour, two things happen to Beth. Her brain waves change, so that they now look pretty much the way they do when she is awake. Yet she is still asleep. Also, although her eyelids are closed, her eyes
15   begin to move about rapidly under the lids. This lasts for twenty minutes. Then Beth returns to the sleep of easy brain waves and no eye movement.

Basically, there are two kinds of sleep. One is Rapid Eye Movement (REM) sleep. In this, the brain waves are similar to those of a waking person, and the eyes move about

rapidly under the closed lids. The other kind of sleep is Non-Rapid Eye Movement sleep.
20   You can guess what that's like, right? Stop for a moment and describe REM and non-REM sleep to yourself.

REM sleep is also called *paradoxical sleep.* A paradox is something that seems contradictory within itself. What is the paradox about REM sleep? That the sleeper's brain waves would lead you to believe the person is awake, but in fact the person is asleep.

25   Now, the interesting thing is this. Suppose Beth is showing non-REM sleep. We wake her up and say: "Wake up, Beth! What are you dreaming?"

"Uh . . . nothing," Beth mumbles.

Disappointed, we let her go back to sleep. Later on, Beth begins to show REM sleep. Again, we wake her up. "What are you dreaming, Beth?"

30   "Uh . . . this man has ridden a camel into Mom's office. It's too big. The camel fills up the whole office. The man riding him is an Arab." She goes on with her dream.

Dreaming happens mainly in REM sleep. This is very convenient for researchers. They get volunteers to sleep in a bed in the laboratory. An electronic sensing device that registers eye movement is placed on the eyelids of the volunteers. Thus the researcher can tell
35   exactly when the volunteer is showing REM sleep.

"Wake up, volunteer! What are you dreaming?"

WHAT HAS BEEN LEARNED ABOUT DREAMING?

Everyone dreams about 20 percent of the time they are sleeping—that is, they show REM sleep about that much. Even people who say they never dream show about 20 percent REM sleep. If these "nondreamers" do their sleeping in a laboratory where the researcher
40   can wake them up, it turns out that they dream as much as others. They just don't remember the dreams in the morning, perhaps because memories for dreams fade fast and they are slow waking up.

People go back and forth between REM and non-REM sleep during the night. If something happens in their environment while they are sleeping, people may fit this into

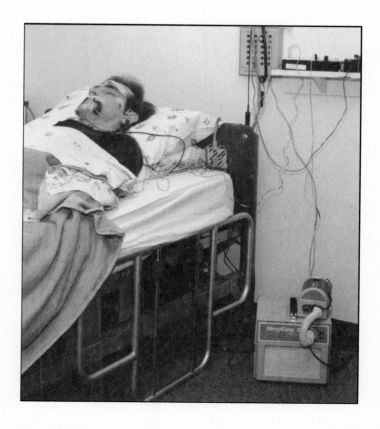

Copyright ©1999 by Addison-Wesley Educational Publishers Inc.

45 the dream. Did you ever have the experience of someone calling you in the morning, but at first you thought it was part of a dream?

Events in daily life sometimes occur in symbolic form in dreams. For example, a boy was having a lot of difficulty on the school playground because a bigger boy kept bully-ing him. That night the smaller boy dreamed of being alone and unarmed in the African

50 grass country, facing a lion. The lion symbolizes the bully. At other times the dreaded event from daily life simply occurs in a dream in its real-life form—the boy dreams of being bullied by the bigger boy. How and when dream symbols are used is not yet understood.

WHY DO WE DREAM?

Do people actually need to dream? Or is it just the brain "idling its motor"? It's possible

55 that dreams are unimportant, just an accidental part of REM sleep.

One experimenter waked volunteers each time they started REM sleep. This meant that he was also depriving them of their dreams. When they showed non-REM sleep, he let them sleep on. Notice that by itself this experiment wouldn't prove much, even if effects did occur. Why? Because the effects might result from just being waked up all the

60 time, rather than from just not being allowed to dream. The experimenters realized this, so they used a second group of volunteers. These were waked exactly as much as the first group, but no attention was paid to whether it was REM or non-REM sleep. Thus any dif-ferences could be ascribed to lack of REM sleep periods in the one group.

There were differences. People who were deprived of most of their REM sleep for

65 three nights in a row became irritable and somewhat disrupted in their actions. When on the fourth night they were allowed to sleep on, so they could have REM sleep, they had it about 30 percent of the time instead of the usual 20 percent. Apparently they were "catching up" on their REM sleep. It looks as though people do, indeed, need REM sleep. The critical question is: Is it the REM sleep that they need or the dreams? Do we have

70 REM sleep because it brings dreaming, or is dreaming just an accidental aspect of the needed REM sleep? We don't know.

Why do people dream, then? We don't know that either. It does seem that REM sleep is necessary. But are dreams? What do they accomplish? Some theorists have sug-gested that we use dreaming to solve emotional problems, some have suggested that

75 memories are stored in the brain during sleep time and dream time. Some even suggest this is a way of keeping our two eyes synchronized. Tomorrow we may know the answer. The discovery of rapid eye movements during dreaming has opened up the world of dreams for research. Notice that the researchers here do something interesting. They go from an observable behavior—the eye movements—to an internal condition—the

80 dream. The discovery of REM sleep helps bridge the gap between mental processes and the outside world.

(1,124 words)

—Psychology: What It Is/How to Use It by David Watson

THINKING AFTER READING

RECALL: Self-test your understanding. Your instructor may choose to give you a true-false review.

REACT: Why are sleep and dreaming important research topics for psycholo-gists? _____

_____

REFLECT: Describe and try to interpret one of your recent or recurring dreams. _____

_____

THINK CRITICALLY: Would you predict that there is any correlation between a good night's sleep and a good quality of life? Why or why not? Write your answer on a separate sheet of paper.

MAIN IDEA

Answer the following questions concerning the selection.

1. Who or what is the topic of the selection? <u>Sleeping and Dreaming</u>
2. What point is the author trying to make? <u>Everyone dreams about 20 percent of the time and this dreaming occurs during REM sleep.</u>

Copyright ©1999 by Addison-Wesley Educational Publishers Inc.

Name _____

Date_____

COMPREHENSION QUESTIONS

Answer the following with *a, b, c,* or *d,* or fill in the blank. In order to help analyze your strengths and weaknesses, the question types are indicated.

Main Idea   __b__   1. The best statement of the main idea of this selection is:

    a. People become irritable when they do not have an adequate amount of dreaming.
    b. Through the discovery of REM, researchers have begun to learn about sleeping and dreaming, but many questions remain unanswered.
    c. Sleep is an observable behavior, whereas dreaming is an internal condition reflecting the mental processes.
    d. Dreams follow an irregular pattern, with people moving back and forth between REM and non-REM sleep all during the night.

Detail   __d__   2. During REM sleep a person experiences

    a. different brain waves than when awake.
    b. the same brain waves as when awake.
    c. eye movement under closed lids.
    d. both *b* and *c.*

Inference   3. REM sleep is called paradoxical sleep because <u>the brain waves signal the opposite of sleep.</u>

Detail   __b__   4. Dreaming occurs

    a. during REM and non-REM sleep.
    b. mainly during REM sleep.
    c. only during non-REM sleep.
    d. as people go back and forth between REM and non-REM sleep.

Detail   __d__   5. Some people probably cannot remember dreams because

    a. they awaken in the middle of a dream.
    b. they are nondreamers.
    c. they experience only 20 percent REM sleep.
    d. they are slow waking up.

Inference   __d__   6. The author implies that dreams do all of the following *except*

    a. symbolically reflect real-life problems.
    b. include experiences in the environment.
    c. relieve tension and irritability.
    d. normally occur in the last two hours of sleep.

Detail   __b__   7. According to the passage, after several nights of interrupted REM sleep, people need to

    a. sleep longer.
    b. dream a greater percentage of the next sleeping time.
    c. have a higher percentage of non-REM sleep.
    d. sleep more frequently for brief periods of time.

Answer the following with *T* (true), *F* (false), or *CT* (can't tell).

Inference   <u> F </u> 8. Research shows that dreams are unimportant and just an accidental part of REM sleep.

Inference   <u> T </u> 9. The author feels that the discovery of rapid eye movement is the most significant finding thus far in dream research.

Inference   <u> CT </u> 10. Dreams help people store memories.

VOCABULARY

Answer the following with *a, b, c,* or *d* for the word or phrase that best defines the boldface word as used in the selection. The number in parentheses indicates the line of the passage in which the word is located.

<u>d</u> 1. "most obviously **unconscious**" (1)

    a. alert
    b. daydreaming
    c. half-knowing
    d. not aware

<u>c</u> 2. "the **paradox** about REM" (23)

    a. mystery
    b. error
    c. contradictory truth
    d. reasoning

<u>b</u> 3. "**convenient** for researchers" (32)

    a. logical
    b. easy to use
    c. necessary
    d. cooperative

<u>c</u> 4. "**symbolizes** the bully" (50)

    a. warns
    b. summarizes
    c. represents
    d. suspects

<u>a</u> 5. "**bullied** by the bigger boy" (52)

    a. intimidated
    b. befriended
    c. joined
    d. recognized

<u>b</u> 6. "**idling** its motor" (54)

    a. exhausting
    b. running without power
    c. withdrawing
    d. renewing

<u>d</u> 7. "**depriving** them of" (57)

    a. irritating
    b. educating
    c. encouraging
    d. preventing

<u>c</u> 8. "**ascribed** to lack of" (63)

    a. convened
    b. remembered
    c. attributed
    d. returned

<u>c</u> 9. "The **critical** question is" (69)

    a. first
    b. general
    c. crucial
    d. most frequent

<u>a</u> 10. "keeping our two eyes **synchronized**" (76)

    a. working simultaneously
    b. working vigorously
    c. focused
    d. slightly crossed

VOCABULARY ENRICHMENT

A. An acronym is an invented word formed by the initial letters of a compound term. REM, for example, is pronounced as a word that rhymes with *them,* rather than pronouncing the three letters separately to indicate rapid eye movement. Write an A beside the following letters that are pronounced as words and thus are acronyms.

<u>A</u> 1. HUD   <u>No</u> 3. FBI   <u>A</u> 5. NAFTA

<u>A</u> 2. UNICEF   <u>No</u> 4. CIA   <u>A</u> 6. radar

Copyright ©1999 by Addison-Wesley Educational Publishers Inc.

B. Study the following easily confused words, and circle the one that is correct in each sentence.

conscience: sense of right or wrong
conscious: awareness of self

7. Let your (conscience, conscious) be your guide when faced with temptation.

    its: ownership or possessive
    it's: contraction of *it is*

8. Don't tell me (its, it's) already the end of the month.

    to: toward
    too: more than enough
    two: the number 2

9. Many professors assign (to, too, two) much homework for one night.

C. Use the context clues in the following sentences to write the meaning of the boldface psychology terms.

10. Relaxation exercises can be used to reduce test **anxiety.** Fear; worry

11. After years of practice, we **condition** ourselves to always wash our hands before meals. develop a behavioral pattern

12. With the birth of the second child, the first child's desire for a bottle was a sign of **regression.** reversion to earlier behavior patterns

13. Saying that you are too busy to call a sick friend is only **rationalizing.** attempting to explain failure by protecting self-esteem

14. Television has become more **permissive** in treating sexual topics openly during prime time. less restrictive

15. Compliments can be effective in **reinforcing** desired behaviors. rewarding

EXPLORE THE NET

- What are some of the recommended techniques for overcoming insomnia?
- Describe several different forms of sleep disorders other than insomnia.

For additional readings and exercises, visit the Longman English Skills Web page at:

http://longman.awl.com/englishpages

For a user name and password, please see your instructor.

ASSESS YOUR LEARNING

Review confusing questions, seek clarification, and make notes in your text to help you remember new information and vocabulary.

 **Essay**

SELECTION 2

THINKING BEFORE READING

Preview the selection for clues to content. Activate your schema and anticipate what you will learn.

When have you experienced the effects of economic prejudice?

When have you felt economic prejudice toward someone else?

I'll read this to find out _____.

VOCABULARY PREVIEW

Are you familiar with these words?

agile	despaired	absentmindedly	coincidence	fidgeted
dismay	muster	gaunt	vile	crumpled

What is the opposite of gaunt?

Where do you find crumpled paper?

Your instructor may give a true-false vocabulary review before or after reading.

THINKING DURING READING

As you read, use the five thinking strategies of a good reader: predict, picture, relate, monitor, and correct.

THE SCHOLARSHIP JACKET

The small Texas school that I attended carried out a tradition every year during the eighth grade graduation: a beautiful gold and green jacket, the school colors, was awarded to the class valedictorian, the student who had maintained the highest grades for eight years. The scholarship jacket had a big gold S on the left front side, and the winner's
5   name was written in gold letters on the pocket.

My oldest sister Rosie had won the jacket a few years back, and I fully expected to win also. I was fourteen and in the eighth grade. I had been a straight A student since the first grade, and the last year I had looked forward to owning that jacket. My father was a farm laborer who couldn't earn enough money to feed eight children, so when I was six I
10   was given to my grandparents to raise. We couldn't participate in sports at school because there were registration fees, uniform costs, and trips out of town; so even though we were quite agile and athletic, there would never be a sports school jacket for us. This one, the scholarship jacket, was our only chance.

In May, close to graduation, spring fever struck, and no one paid any attention in
15   class; instead we stared out the windows and at each other, wanting to speed up the last few weeks of school. I despaired every time I looked in the mirror. Pencil thin, not a curve

Copyright ©1999 by Addison-Wesley Educational Publishers Inc.

anywhere, I was called ''Beanpole'' and ''String Bean,'' and I knew that's what I looked like. A flat chest, no hips, and a brain, that's what I had. That really isn't much for a four-teen-year-old to work with, I thought, as I absentmindedly wandered from my history

20 class to the gym. Another hour of sweating in basketball and displaying my toothpick legs was coming up. Then I remembered my P.E. shorts were still in a bag under my desk where I'd forgotten them. I had to walk all the way back and get them. Coach Thompson was a real bear if anyone wasn't dressed for P.E. She had said I was a good forward and once she even tried to talk Grandma into letting me join the team. Grandma, of course,

25 said no.

I was almost back at my classroom door when I heard angry voices and arguing. I stopped. I didn't mean to eavesdrop; I just hesitated, not knowing what to do. I needed those shorts and I was going to be late, but I didn't want to interrupt an argument between my teachers. I recognized the voices: Mr. Schmidt, my history teacher, and Mr.

30 Boone, my math teacher. They seemed to be arguing about me. I couldn't believe it. I still remember the shock that rooted me flat against the wall as if I were trying to blend in with the graffiti written there.

''I refuse to do it! I don't care who her father is, her grades don't even begin to com-pare to Martha's. I won't lie or falsify records. Martha has a straight A plus average and

35 you know it.'' That was Mr. Schmidt and he sounded very angry. Mr. Boone's voice sounded calm and quiet.

''Look, Joann's father is not only on the Board, he owns the only store in town; we could say it was a close tie and—''

The pounding in my ears drowned out the rest of the words, only a word here and

40 there filtered through. ''. . . Martha is Mexican. . . . resign. . . . won't do it. . . .'' Mr. Schmidt came rushing out, and luckily for me went down the opposite way toward the auditorium, so he didn't see me. Shaking, I waited a few minutes and then went in and grabbed my bag and fled from the room. Mr. Boone looked up when I came in but didn't say anything. To this day I don't remember if I got in trouble in P.E. for being late or how

45 I made it through the rest of the afternoon. I went home very sad and cried into my pil-low that night so Grandmother wouldn't hear me. It seemed a cruel coincidence that I had overheard that conversation.

The next day when the principal called me into his office, I knew what it would be about. He looked uncomfortable and unhappy. I decided I wasn't going to make it any

50 easier for him so I looked him straight in the eye. He looked away and fidgeted with the papers on his desk.

''Martha,'' he said, ''there's been a change in policy this year regarding the scholar-ship jacket. As you know, it has always been free.'' He cleared his throat and continued. ''This year the Board decided to charge fifteen dollars—which still won't cover the com-

55 plete cost of the jacket.''

I started at him in shock and a small sound of dismay escaped my throat. I hadn't expected this. He still avoided looking in my eyes.

''So if you are unable to pay the fifteen dollars for the jacket, it will be given to the next one in line.''

60 Standing with all the dignity I could muster, I said, ''I'll speak to my grandfather about it, sir, and let you know tomorrow.'' I cried on the walk home from the bus stop. The dirt road was a quarter of a mile from the highway, so by the time I got home, my eyes were red and puffy.

''Where's Grandpa?'' I asked Grandma, looking down at the floor so she wouldn't

65 ask me why I'd been crying. She was sewing on a quilt and didn't look up.

''I think he's out back working in the bean field.''

I went outside and looked out at the fields. There he was. I could see him walking between the rows, his body bent over the little plants, hoe in hand. I walked slowly out to him, trying to think how I could best ask him for the money. There was a cool breeze

70 blowing and a sweet smell of mesquite in the air, but I didn't appreciate it. I kicked at a dirt clod. I wanted that jacket so much. It was more than just being a valedictorian and giving a little thank you speech for the jacket on graduation night. It represented eight

—*Cortador de Caña*, Rafael Tufiño. From the collection of
the Museum of History, Anthropology and Art of the University of Puerto Rico

years of hard work and expectation. I knew I had to be honest with Grandpa; it was my
only chance. He saw me and looked up.

75   He waited for me to speak. I cleared my throat nervously and clasped my hands
behind my back so he wouldn't see them shaking. "Grandpa, I have a big favor to ask
you," I said in Spanish, the only language he knew. He still waited silently. I tried again.
"Grandpa, this year the principal said the scholarship jacket is not going to be free. It's
going to cost fifteen dollars and I have to take the money in tomorrow, otherwise it'll be
80 given to someone else." The last words came out in an eager rush. Grandpa straightened
up tiredly and leaned his chin on the hoe handle. He looked out over the field that was
filled with the tiny green bean plants. I waited, desperately hoping he'd say I could have
the money.

    He turned to me and asked quietly, "What does a scholarship jacket mean?"

85   I answered quickly; maybe there was a chance. "It means you've earned it by having
the highest grades for eight years and that's why they're giving it to you." Too late I realized the significance of my words. Grandpa knew that I understood it was not a matter of
money. It wasn't that. He went back to hoeing the weeds that sprang up between the
delicate little bean plants. It was a time-consuming job; sometimes the small shoots were
90 right next to each other. Finally he spoke again.

    "Then if you pay for it, Marta, it's not a scholarship jacket, is it? Tell your principal I
will not pay the fifteen dollars."

    I walked back to the house and locked myself in the bathroom for a long time. I was
angry with Grandfather even though I knew he was right, and I was angry with the
95 Board, whoever they were. Why did they have to change the rules just when it was my
turn to win the jacket?

    It was a very sad and withdrawn girl who dragged into the principal's office the next
day. This time he did look me in the eyes.

Copyright ©1999 by Addison-Wesley Educational Publishers Inc.

"What did your grandfather say?"

100 I sat very straight in my chair.

"He said to tell you he won't pay the fifteen dollars."

The principal muttered something I couldn't understand under his breath, and walked over to the window. He stood looking out at something outside. He looked bigger than usual when he stood up; he was a tall gaunt man with gray hair, and I watched

105 the back of his head while I waited for him to speak.

"Why?" he finally asked. "Your grandfather has the money. Doesn't he own a small bean farm?"

I looked at him, forcing my eyes to stay dry. "He said if I had to pay for it, then it wouldn't be a scholarship jacket," I said and stood up to leave. "I guess you'll just have to

110 give it to Joann." I hadn't meant to say that; it had just slipped out. I was almost to the door when he stopped me.

"Martha—wait."

I turned and looked at him, waiting. What did he want now? I could feel my heart pounding. Something bitter and vile tasting was coming up in my mouth; I was afraid I

115 was going to be sick. I didn't need any sympathy speeches. He sighed loudly and went back to his big desk. He looked at me, biting his lip, as if thinking.

"Okay, damn it. We'll make an exception in your case. I'll tell the Board, you'll get your jacket."

I could hardly believe it. I spoke in a trembling rush. "Oh, thank you, sir!" Suddenly I

120 felt great. I didn't know about adrenaline in those days, but I knew something was pumping through me, making me feel as tall as the sky. I wanted to yell, jump, run the mile, do something. I ran out so I could cry in the hall where there was no one to see me. At the end of the day. Mr. Schmidt winked at me and said, "I hear you're getting a scholarship jacket this year."

125 His face looked as happy and innocent as a baby's, but I knew better. Without answering I gave him a quick hug and ran to the bus. I cried on the walk home again, but this time because I was so happy. I couldn't wait to tell Grandpa and ran straight to the field. I joined him in the row where he was working and without saying anything I crouched down and started pulling up the weeds with my hands. Grandpa worked

130 alongside me for a few minutes, but he didn't ask what had happened. After I had a little pile of weeds between the rows, I stood up and faced him.

"The principal said he's making an exception for me, Grandpa, and I'm getting the jacket after all. That's after I told him what you said."

Grandpa didn't say anything, he just gave me a pat on the shoulder and a smile. He

135 pulled out the crumpled red handkerchief that he always carried in his back pocket and wiped the sweat off his forehead.

"Better go see if your grandmother needs any help with supper."

I gave him a big grin. He didn't fool me. I skipped and ran back to the house whistling some silly tune.

(1,952 words)

—*Growing Up Chicana/o: An Anthology* by Marta Salinas

THINKING AFTER READING

RECALL: Self-test your understanding. Your instructor may choose to give you a true-false review.

REACT: What was so forceful about Grandpa's argument, "If you have to pay for it, it's not a scholarship jacket"?

REFLECT: Why is earning the scholarship jacket not only a personal goal, but also a symbol of achievement for Martha and her family?

THINK CRITICALLY: Express your opinion on the statement, "The rich and poor are treated differently," and give specific examples in the areas of education, business, medicine, and law. Organize your response into five paragraphs and write on a separate sheet of paper.

MAIN IDEA

What is the principal issue that concerns the author in this story?

The family held firm against discrimination and forced the school officials into
an ethnic decision.

Copyright ©1999 by Addison-Wesley Educational Publishers Inc.

Name _____

Date_____

COMPREHENSION QUESTIONS

Answer the following with *a*, *b*, *c*, and *d*, or fill in the blank. In order to help you analyze your strengths and weaknesses, the question types are indicated.

Main Idea ___d___ 1. The best statement of the main idea of this selection is:

  a. Martha won the scholarship jacket because of her high grades.
  b. The Board acted without prejudice in awarding the scholarship jacket.
  c. Mr. Schmidt felt that Martha deserved the jacket.
  d. Despite prejudice, Martha's hard work and her grandfather's thoughtful response won her the scholarship jacket.

Detail ___c___ 2. Martha did not participate in sports at school because

  a. she was not good at athletics.
  b. she did not like athletics.
  c. sports at school cost too much money.
  d. she was too busy studying.

Inference ___a___ 3. The Board decided to charge $15 for the scholarship jacket because

  a. they wanted Joann to have it.
  b. the cost of the jacket had gone up.
  c. they wanted to give more than one.
  d. the school was establishing a new scholarship.

Inference ___d___ 4. Mr. Boone wanted to keep Martha from winning the jacket because

  a. Joann was the best student in his class.
  b. she did not deserve the jacket.
  c. she was Mexican and from a poor family.
  d. Joann's family had more status than Martha's.

Detail ___c___ 5. The scholarship jacket was all of the following except

  a. awarded each year.
  b. given to the valedictorian.
  c. a gold and black jacket.
  d. similar to the athletic jackets.

Inference ___d___ 6. All of the following are true about Mr. Schmidt except

  a. he got angry when Mr. Boone suggested the jacket go to Joann.
  b. he felt that Martha deserved the jacket because she had the best grades.
  c. he was happy when Martha got the jacket.
  d. he resigned over the conflict.

Inference ___c___ 7. Martha's grandfather would not pay the $15 for the jacket because

  a. he did not want Martha to wear a jacket from such a school.
  b. he could not get $15.
  c. he felt that Martha had already earned the jacket.
  d. he thought the jacket was too expensive.

Answer the following with *T* (true) or *F* (false).

Detail   ___T___   8. Martha's real name was Marta.

Inference   ___T___   9. The principal and Mr. Schmidt demonstrated higher ethical standards than Mr. Boone and the Board.

Inference   ___T___ 10. The reader can conclude that the principal made an exception for Martha because he felt she was treated unfairly.

VOCABULARY

Answer the following with *a, b, c,* or *d* for the word or phrase that best defines the boldface word used in the selection. The number in parentheses indicates the line of the passage in which the word is located.

___c___ 1. "quite **agile** and athletic" (12)

    a. awkward
    b. quick
    c. nimble
    d. clumsy

___a___ 2. "**despaired** every time" (16)

    a. gave up hope
    b. yelled
    c. felt good
    d. laughed

___a___ 3. "**absentmindedly** wandered" (19)

    a. preoccupied
    b. purposely
    c. carefully
    d. intentionally

___c___ 4. "a cruel **coincidence**" (46)

    a. joke
    b. planned meeting
    c. accident
    d. remark

___b___ 5. "**fidgeted** with the papers" (50–51)

    a. worked
    b. nervously moved
    c. wrote notes
    d. filed

___c___ 6. "sound of **dismay**" (56)

    a. laughter
    b. joy
    c. fear
    d. hope

___b___ 7. "could **muster**" (60)

    a. face
    b. gather
    c. fake
    d. confront

___d___ 8. "a tall **gaunt** man" (104)

    a. attractive
    b. heavy
    c. evil
    d. thin

___b___ 9. "**vile** tasting" (114)

    a. sweet
    b. unpleasant
    c. salty
    d. sour

___a___ 10. "**crumpled** red handkerchief" (135)

    a. wrinkled
    b. old
    c. unusual
    d. ordinary

VOCABULARY ENRICHMENT

A. Use the indicated prefix to write words that complete each sentence in the groups.

dis: not, take away, deprive of

    1. Since the daughter would not finish college, the family threatened to ___disinherit___ her in the will.

Copyright ©1999 by Addison-Wesley Educational Publishers Inc.

2. The soldier's cowardice brought ____disrespect____ on the whole regiment.

3. Because of the severe injury to his spinal cord, the man is now completely ____disabled____ and cannot work.

con, com, co: with, together

4. The minister looked out at the ____congregation____ and asked them to stand and sing a hymn.

5. Our plane was late arriving in Atlanta, and thus we were unable to make our scheduled ____connection____ to Miami.

6. If all members would ____consolidate____ their efforts and lend a hand, the job could be finished in half the time.

ad: to, toward

7. If the tape is no longer ____adhesive____, it will not stick to the package.

8. To gain public recognition for the new product, the company had to ____advertise____ on the radio.

9. Some people say they are ____addicted____ to chocolate chip cookies because they can't stop eating them.

B. Use the context clues in the sentence to write the meaning of the boldface words.

10. **Narratives** never preach, but rather deliver a message to our emotions, senses, and imagination through a powerful shared experience.
A narrative tells a true or fictional story through characters and carries a message.

11. The **theme** of the story about a college tennis champion might be that the journey to the top, including the hard work and discipline, was more meaningful than the final victory. The theme of a narrative is the main idea, controlling point, or central insight.

12. Poisoned apples and talking mirrors may not seem realistic in a modern telephone conversation, however, in the context of the Snow White, we easily find both **plausible.** Plausibility is the sense of believability or reality within the realm of the story.

13. E. M. Forster said that "The king died, and the queen died," is a narrative, but changing this to "The king died, and the queen died of grief," creates a **plot.** The plot is the sequence of events in the story, which build to a climax as conflict intensifies.

14. The **suspense** of a narrative is based on conflict, which perhaps starts out as mild and intensifies as each incident occurs. <u>Suspense is the</u> <u>eagerness to know what is going to happen next and is based on the</u> <u>conflict of the story and concern for the character.</u>

15. Good writers select incidents and details that give **unity** to the story and advance the central theme. <u>Unity means that every event and detail is</u> <u>relevant to the central theme.</u>

ASSESS YOUR LEARNING

Review confusing questions, seek clarification, and make notes in your text to help you remember new information and vocabulary.

EXPLORE THE NET

- Describe the variety of scholarship services available to students.
- Find a scholarship that applies to you.

For additional readings and exercises, visit the Longman English Skills Web page at:

http://longman.awl.com/englishpages

For a user name and password, please see your instructor.

SELECTION 3 *History*

THINKING BEFORE READING

Preview for clues to the content. Activate your prior knowledge. Anticipate what is coming and think about your purpose for reading.

What recent western movies have included African Americans in major roles?

Name a famous African American military general.

Why were soldiers fighting the Native Americans?

I want to learn _____.

VOCABULARY PREVIEW

Are you familiar with these words?

distinction	stamina	closed	raided	restless
plundered	desolate	grueling	ironic	pacify

Copyright ©1999 by Addison-Wesley Educational Publishers Inc.

What factors help create a closed society?

How do parents pacify crying children?

What makes students restless in class?

Your instructor may give a true-false vocabulary review before or after reading.

THINKING DURING READING

As you read, use the five thinking strategies of a good reader: predict, picture, relate, monitor, and correct.

BLACKS IN BLUE: THE BUFFALO SOLDIERS IN THE WEST

On Saturday afternoons youngsters used to sit in darkened movie theaters and cheer the victories of the United States cavalry over the Indians. Typically, the Indians were about to capture a wagon train, when army bugles suddenly sounded. Then the blue-coated cavalry charged over the hill. Few in the theaters cheered for the Indians; fewer still noticed
5 the absence of black faces among the on-charging cavalry. But in fact, more than 2000 black cavalrymen served on the western frontier between 1867 and 1890. Known as the "buffalo soldiers," they made up a fifth of the U.S. cavalry.

Black troops were first used on a large scale during the Civil War. Organized in segregated units, with white officers, they fought with distinction. Nearly 180,000 blacks
10 served in the Union army; 34,000 of them died. When the war ended in 1865, Congress for the first time authorized black troops to serve in the regular peacetime army. In addition to infantry, it created two cavalry regiments—the Ninth and Tenth, which became known as the famous buffalo soldiers.

Like other black regiments, the Ninth and Tenth Cavalry had white officers who took
15 special examinations before they could serve. The chaplains were assigned not only to preach but to teach reading, writing, and arithmetic. The food was poor; racism was widespread. The army stocked the first black units with worn-out horses, a serious matter to men whose lives depended on the speed and stamina of their mounts. "Since our first mount in 1867 this regiment has received nothing but broken down horses and repaired
20 equipment," an officer said in 1870.

Many white officers refused to serve with black troops. George A. Custer, the handsome "boy general," turned down a position in the Ninth and joined the new Seventh Cavalry, headed for disaster at Little Bighorn. The *Army and Navy Journal* carried ads that told similar story:

**A FIRST LIEUTENANT
OF INFANTRY**
(*white*)
stationed at a
very desirable post
in the Department of the South
desires a transfer with
an officer of the same grade
on equal terms
if in a white regiment
but if in a colored regiment
a reasonable bonus
would be expected.

---

25   There was no shortage of black troops for the officers to lead. Blacks enlisted because the army offered some advancement in a closed society. It also paid $13 a month, plus room and board.

In 1867 the Ninth and Tenth Cavalry were posted to the West, where they remained for two decades. Under Colonel Benjamin H. Grierson, a Civil War hero, the Tenth went
30   to Fort Riley, Kansas; the regiment arrived in the midst of a great Indian war. Kiowas, Comanches, Cheyennes, Arapahos, and Sioux were on the warpath. Troopers of the Tenth defended farms, stages, trains, and work crews building railroad tracks to the West. Cornered by a band of Cheyennes, they beat back the attack and won a new name. Earlier known as the "brunettes" or "Africans," the Cheyenne now called them the buffalo
35   soldiers, a name that soon applied to all black soldiers in the West (some of the "buffalo soldiers" of the Tenth Cavalry are shown in the photo below and on page 122).

From 1868 to 1874 the Tenth served on the Kansas frontier. The dull winter days were filled with drills and scouting parties outside the post. In spring and summer the good weather brought forth new forays. Indian bands raided farms and ranches and
40   stampeded cattle herds on the way north from Texas. They struck and then melted back into the reservations.

The Ninth Cavalry also had a difficult job. Commanded by Colonel Edward Hatch, who had served with Grierson in the Civil War, it was stationed in West Texas and along the Rio Grande. The summers were so hot that men collapsed with sunstroke, the winters
45   were so cold that water froze in the canteens. Indians from outside the area frequently raided it. From the north Kiowa and Comanche warriors rode down the Great Comanche War Trail; Kickapoos crossed the Rio Grande from Mexico. Gangs of Mexican bandits and restless Civil War veterans roamed and plundered at will.

In 1874–1875 the Ninth fought in the great Red River War, in which the Kiowas and
50   Comanches, fed up with conditions on the reservations, revolted against Grant's peace policy. Marching, fighting, then marching again, the soldiers harried and wore out the Indians, who finally surrendered in the spring of 1875. Herded into a new and desolate reservation, the Mescalero Apaches of New Mexico took to the warpath in 1877 and again in 1879. Each time it took a year of grueling warfare to effect their surrender. In

Copyright ©1999 by Addison-Wesley Educational Publishers Inc.

55 1886 black cavalrymen surrounded and captured the famous Apache chief Geronimo. In that and other campaigns, several buffalo soldiers won the Congressional Medal of Honor.

Black troops hunted Big Foot and his band before the slaughter at Wounded Knee in 1890 and they served in many of the West's most famous Indian battles. While a third 60 of all army recruits deserted between 1865 and 1890, the Ninth and Tenth Cavalry had few desertions. In 1880 the Tenth had the fewest desertions of any regiment in the country.

It was ironic that in the West black men fought red men to benefit white men. Once the Indian wars ended, the buffalo soldiers worked to keep illegal settlers out of Indian or 65 government land; much of this land was later opened to settlement. Both regiments saw action in the Spanish-American War, the Ninth at San Juan Hill, the Tenth in the fighting around Santiago. The old buffalo soldiers were forgotten in retirement, although some of them had the satisfaction of settling on the western lands they had done so much to pacify.

(900 words)

—America: Past and Present by Robert Divine et al.

THINKING AFTER READING

RECALL: Self-test your understanding. Your instructor may choose to give a true-false review.

REACT: Were African American soldiers treated fairly? Were the Native Americans treated fairly? _____

REFLECT: Why would you think that the black cavalry liked the name "buffalo soldiers"? _____

 THINK CRITICALLY: Reacting to the passage: a college student in Tacoma, Washington, wrote, "My ancestors raided most of the time out of anger, loss, retaliation, and defense of their nations. All of these places were in their country, so therefore they were reclaiming what belonged to them." Why did this student react in this manner?

MAIN IDEA

Write a sentence that states what you think is most important about the Buffalo Soldiers. More than 2,000 black cavalrymen known as the "buffalo soldiers" served bravely on the western frontier between 1867 and 1890, and they made up a fifth of the U.S. cavalry.

Copyright ©1999 by Addison-Wesley Educational Publishers Inc.

Name _____

Date _____

COMPREHENSION QUESTIONS

Answer the following with *a, b, c,* or *d,* or fill in the blank. In order to help you analyze your strengths and weaknesses, the question types are indicated.

Main Idea ___b___ 1. The main idea of this selection is:

    a. Black troops conquered the Indians.
    b. Black cavalrymen fought hard on the western frontier with little recognition.
    c. Black cavalrymen were discriminated against in the West.
    d. Black soldiers should have been fighting on the side of the Indians rather than against them.

Detail ___c___ 2. According to the passage, the primary reason blacks enlisted in the army was

    a. to travel in the West.
    b. to fight Indians.
    c. to seek opportunity.
    d. to escape racism.

Inference ___a___ 3. The author implies that the name *buffalo soldier* was

    a. complimentary.
    b. derogatory.
    c. racist.
    d. ironic.

Inference 4. The advertisement from the *Army and Navy Journal* shows __racial__ prejudice in the army. _____

Detail ___a___ 5. The Ninth and Tenth Cavalry were noted for all of the following *except*

    a. serving in the Civil War under Colonel Grierson.
    b. the capture of Geronimo.
    c. a year with the fewest desertions of any regiment.
    d. defending farms, trains, and railroad crews in Kansas.

Inference ___b___ 6. The primary purpose of this selection is to explain

    a. why blacks are not shown in western movies.
    b. the contribution of blacks to the conquest of the western frontier.
    c. the importance of the wars against the Indians.
    d. how blacks migrated from the South to the West.

Inference ___c___ 7. The author implies that

    a. the buffalo soldiers were responsible for Wounded Knee.
    b. the black soldiers received pensions after the Indian wars.
    c. the black soldiers who settled in the West probably had realized an opportunity.
    d. the buffalo soldiers were the only black military men to win the Congressional Medal of Honor.

Answer the following with *T* (true), *F* (false), or *CT* (can't tell).

Inference   __F__ 8. The author implies that the buffalo soldiers received special treatment and quality supplies because of their bravery.

Detail   __T__ 9. At one point in the 1800s, 20 percent of the soldiers in the U.S. cavalry were black.

Inference   __CT__ 10. The cavalry defeat at Little Bighorn would have been avoided if Custer had taken command of the Ninth.

VOCABULARY

Answer the following with *a, b, c,* or *d* for the word or phrase that best defines the boldface word as used in the selection. The number in parentheses indicates the line of the passage in which the word is located.

__d__ 1. "fought with **distinction**" (9)

    a. fierceness
    b. drive
    c. ambition
    d. honor

__b__ 2. "**stamina** of their mounts" (18)

    a. size
    b. endurance
    c. source
    d. breed

__c__ 3. "advancement in a **closed** society" (26)

    a. rural
    b. lonely
    c. nonmobile
    d. economic

__d__ 4. "bands **raided** farms" (39)

    a. burned
    b. ruled
    c. visited
    d. attacked

__a__ 5. "**restless** Civil War veterans" (48)

    a. discontented
    b. angry
    c. moody
    d. dishonest

__d__ 6. "**plundered** at will" (48)

    a. fought
    b. slaughtered
    c. killed
    d. looted

__c__ 7. "new and **desolate** reservation" (52–53)

    a. disorganized
    b. remote
    c. forlorn
    d. damp

__b__ 8. "a year of **grueling** warfare" (54)

    a. distant
    b. exhausting
    c. prolonged
    d. conclusive

__a__ 9. "It was **ironic**" (63)

    a. unexpected
    b. suspicious
    c. unfair
    d. discouraging

__c__ 10. "done so much to **pacify**" (68–69)

    a. settle
    b. mold
    c. make peaceful
    d. harm

VOCABULARY ENRICHMENT

A. Use the indicated root to write words to complete each sentence in the groups.

Copyright ©1999 by Addison-Wesley Educational Publishers Inc.

voc, vok: voice, call

1. His remarks angered her, and it seemed that, despite our mediation, further conversation would only ___provoke___ an argument.

2. The opera star did not appear in the third act because of damage to her ___vocal___ cords.

3. To increase his ___vocabulary___, the student learned a new word each day.

gress, grad, gred: step, degree

4. If he can take one additional night course this year, he hopes to ___graduate___ from college by June.

5. The company was looking for ___aggressive___ young employees rather than meek applicants.

6. The progress was so ___gradual___ that we could hardly see any success on a daily basis.

spec, spect: see, watch

7. The grand finale of the fireworks display was quite a ___spectacle___.

8. With the growing audiences, tennis has become a profitable ___spectator___ sport.

9. When buying cuts of meat at the grocery store, look for the government ___inspection___ sticker.

B. Use context clues and mark *a, b, c,* or *d* for the meaning closest to that of the boldface word.

___a___ 10. High blood pressure and shortness of breath can **signify** danger to a person with heart disease.

    a. indicate
    b. simplify
    c. curtail
    d. admonish

___b___ 11. To complete the work on schedule, the committee needs more **diligent** members like you.

    a. convincing
    b. hard-working
    c. older
    d. talkative

___c___ 12. The criminal cannot be convicted on accusation alone. We need **tangible** evidence of his guilt that can be presented in court.

    a. sizable
    b. tremendous
    c. actual
    d. movable

C. Study the following easily confused words, and circle the one that is correct in each sentence.

thorough: careful
threw: tossed
through: by means of

13. Do a (**thorough**, threw, through) job on your term paper if you want to make a good grade.

straight: not curving
strait: narrow passage of water

14. Rush (**straight**, strait) from here to the library.

loose: not tight
lose: misplace

15. My tooth is (**loose**, lose).

ASSESS YOUR LEARNING

Review confusing questions, seek clarification, and make notes in your text to help you remember new information and vocabulary.

Connect

Read the following passage about the death of the last of the buffalo soldiers. If you had been a student at one of the Virginia schools he visited, what five questions would you have asked him? List them.

JONES MORGAN, 110, THOUGHT TO BE LAST OF BUFFALO SOLDIERS

Jones Morgan, thought to be the last surviving member of the Buffalo Soldiers—the famous black calvary unit that fought in the Spanish-American War—has died at age 110.

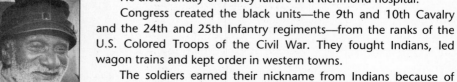

He died Sunday of kidney failure in a Richmond hospital.

Congress created the black units—the 9th and 10th Cavalry and the 24th and 25th Infantry regiments—from the ranks of the U.S. Colored Troops of the Civil War. They fought Indians, led wagon trains and kept order in western towns.

The soldiers earned their nickname from Indians because of their big coats, curly hair and fierce fighting style, said Bill Hunter, historian of the 24th Regiment Association. Black troops carried on the tradition of the Buffalo Soldiers. The 92nd Airborne took up the nickname during the Korean War.

Mr. Morgan was born to freed slaves on a Newberry County, S.C., farm on Oct. 23, 1882, the 14th of 15 children.

When he was 15, he ran off and joined the 9th Cavalry and spent two years with the unit. He watched as Buffalo Soldiers joined the Rough Riders in their famous charge on July 1, 1898.

"They used me for domestic stuff. Anything they needed fixing in the place, they sent me," Mr. Morgan said in a 1991 interview.

Mr. Morgan became known as a living legend to thousands of Virginia students who often invited him to visit their schools.

"I always said let my last days be my best days," Mr. Morgan said at his 108th birthday party thrown by students at Armstrong High School in Richmond. "And it's come true."

August 30, 1993
—*The Atlanta Journal/The Atlanta Constitution*

Copyright ©1999 by Addison-Wesley Educational Publishers Inc.

EXPLORE THE NET

- Find out additional information on how several of the Buffalo Soldiers won the Congressional Medal of Honor.
- Why and how was Geronimo captured?

For additional readings and exercises, visit the Longman English Skills Web page at:

http://longman.awl.com/englishpages

For a user name and password, please see your instructor.

PERSONAL FEEDBACK 2

Name_____

1. Review your responses on the three longer reading selections. Summarize and comment on your error patterns. _____
_____
_____

2. What selection, short or long, has held your attention the best? Why do you think it did so? _____
_____

3. What are your major responsibilities other than going to college?
_____

4. Did you receive any scholarships for college? If so, describe how you qualified for them. _____
_____

5. Describe your mode of transportation and your average traveling time to class. _____
_____

6. What unforeseen difficulties have you already encountered this term that have interfered with your ability to study? _____
_____
_____

Supporting Details and Organizational Patterns

◆ *What is a detail?*
◆ *How do you recognize levels of importance?*
◆ *What is a major detail?*
◆ *What is a minor detail?*
◆ *What organizational patterns are used in textbooks?*
◆ *How do transitional words signal organization?*

Copyright ©1999 by Addison-Wesley Educational Publishers Inc.

What Is a Detail? ◆◆◆◆◆◆◆◆◆◆◆

Details develop, explain, and prove the main idea. They are the facts, descriptions, and reasons that convince the reader and make the material interesting. Details answer questions and paint visual images so that the reader has an experience with the author and sees what the author sees and understands. For example, in a passage on the validity of movie reviews, the supporting details might include information on the rating scale, the qualifications of the raters, and the influence of the production companies on the eventual reviews.

Details can be ranked by their level of importance in supporting a topic. Some details offer major support and elaboration, while others merely provide illustrations to relate the material to the reader's prior knowledge and make visualizing easier. All details play a part in our enjoyment of reading, but it is necessary to recognize their varying levels of importance.

Recognize Levels of Importance

To organize related words or ideas into levels of importance, the general topic is stated first, followed by subcategories of details, which may be further subdivided into specific examples. Either an outline or a diagram can be used to organize information into levels of importance.

EXAMPLE   Notice that by using an outline and a diagram, the following list of words can be unscrambled to show relationships and levels of importance:

Words

horses	grass	botany
zoology	cows	ants
bees	rabbits	entomology
branches of biology	flowers	mosquitoes
trees		

EXERCISE 1

Major ideas and supporting details have been mixed together in the following lists of words. Think about how the ideas should be organized, and insert them in the outline or diagram form provided. The main idea or topic of each list appears either on the line above the outline or in the top box of the diagram.

LIST 1

elm, pine, conifers, maple, oak, deciduous, types of trees, spruce

Types of Trees

I. Conifers

    A. Pine

    B. Spruce

II. Deciduous

    A. Elm

    B. Maple

    C. Oak

LIST 2

Maine, North Carolina, Southeastern, states in regions of the U.S., Oregon, Northwestern, Washington, Rhode Island, Georgia, Connecticut, Florida, Northeastern

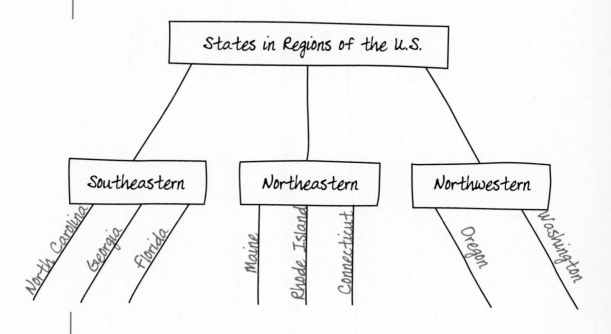

LIST 3

honest, personality, appearance, description of a person, shy, well-dressed, blond, straightforward, tall

Copyright ©1999 by Addison-Wesley Educational Publishers Inc.

Description of a Person

I. Personality

   A. Shy

   B. Honest

   C. Straightforward

II. Appearance

   A. Well-dressed

   B. Blond

   C. Tall

LIST 4

Himmler, Eisenhower, United States, Patton, leaders of World War II, Rommel, Germany, MacArthur, Göring

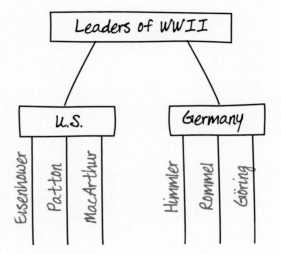

LIST 5

speeding, misdemeanor, felony, types of crime, murder, disorderly conduct, rape, gambling, armed robbery

Types of Crime

I. Misdemeanor

   A. Speeding

   B. Disorderly conduct

   C. Gambling

II. Felony

   A. Murder

   B. Rape

   C. Armed robbery

LIST 6

mayor, local, governor, president, state, senator, representative, federal, senator, representative, elected government officials, city council members, representative

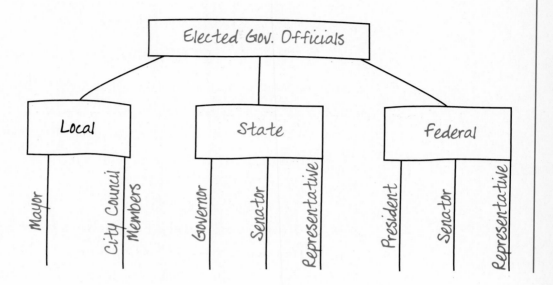

Distinguish Major and Minor Details

As demonstrated by the previous outlines and diagrams, all details are not of equal importance. In textbooks, students receive an overload of details. Not only is it impossible to remember all of them, it can be a waste of time. With practice, students learn that some details are major and should be remembered, while others are of only minor significance in support of the main idea. The importance of a particular detail depends on what point the author is making, and what information is essential to develop, explain, or prove that point. For example, in a passage about communication by sound, the reason a bird sings would be of major significance, whereas the particular species of a bird would be a minor detail the author included for interest rather than for essential support. In a passage on the limitations of acupuncture, the origin of the technique would most likely be a minor detail. If the focus of the passage, however, were on the history of acupuncture, the date of origin would be a major detail.

To determine which details are of major or minor significance, first identify the author's main point and then ask the following questions:

1. What details are needed to explain or prove the main idea? (These are major details.)
2. What details are included just to make the passage more interesting? (These are minor details.)

Minor details add interest and generally "fill out" a passage, but are not essential in the logical development of the point. They are incidental to the passage, and the point could be made without them. Major details, however, directly support the main idea, regardless of whether it is directly or indirectly stated, and are vital to understanding the passage.

EXAMPLE   Read the following paragraph, and first determine the main point and then which details are major and which are minor.

Copyright ©1999 by Addison-Wesley Educational Publishers Inc.

John Quincy Adams was a chip off the old family glacier. Short (5 feet 7 inches; 1.7 meters), thickset, and billiard-bald, he was even more frigidly austere than his presidential father, John Adams. Shunning people, he often went for early morning swims, sometimes stark naked, in the then pure Potomac River. Essentially a closeted thinker rather than a politician, he was irritable, sarcastic, and tactless. Yet few men have ever come to the presidency with a more brilliant record in statecraft, especially in foreign affairs. He ranks as one of the most successful secretaries of state, yet one of the least successful presidents.

—*The American Pageant* by Thomas Bailey and David Kennedy

1. What is the point the author is trying to make? <u>Adams had been a brilliant</u> <u>secretary of state but was socially inept.</u>

2. Are the following details major or minor in their support of the author's point?

<u>minor</u> a. He was 5 feet 7 inches tall.

<u>minor</u> b. He was thickset and bald.

<u>major</u> c. He was a closeted thinker rather than a politician.

<u>minor</u> d. He swam naked in the Potomac River.

<u>major</u> e. He came to the presidency with a brilliant record in statecraft.

EXPLANATION The author's main point is that John Quincy Adams had been a brilliant secretary of state but was a socially inept politician and thus one of the least successful presidents. Items *a* and *b* on appearance are minor details that add interest. Item *c* is a major detail because it shows his isolation as a socially inept politician. Swimming naked (*d*) is an interesting minor detail, and the last item (*e*) is a major detail because it develops the main point.

Transitional Words to Signal Levels of Importance. Sometimes the following connecting words signal the importance of details:

Major: first   second   last   in addition
Minor: for example   to illustrate

EXERCISE 2   For each of the following topics, three details are given. Determine whether the details offer major or minor support to the development of the topic, and write the appropriate word in the blanks.

1. Silence as a Weapon

<u>major</u> a. Giving someone "the silent treatment" can be a method used to hurt others.

<u>major</u> b. After a disagreement, silence is used as a kind of punishment to demonstrate the total indifference one person feels toward another.

<u>minor</u> c. Silence can express shyness or can be used as a time to cool off before expressing hatred.

2. Humanitarian Reform by Dorothea Dix

<u>major</u> a. After visiting a jail to teach a Sunday school class to the female inmates and finding female patients in a mental hospital freezing in unheated, filthy cells, Dix started a lifelong campaign to improve conditions in such institutions.

<u>major</u> b. From 1845 to 1885 she was directly responsible for establishing thirty-three mental hospitals at home and abroad.

<u>minor</u> c. Dix was born in Maine but moved to Boston at the age of twelve to live with her grandmother.

3. Diet of an Armadillo

<u>major</u> a. The armadillo enjoys scorpions, tarantulas, and grasshoppers, but its favorite food is ants, including the eggs and larvae.

<u>minor</u> b. If pursued, the armadillo can outrun a human and quickly dig itself into the ground.

<u>major</u> c. Sometimes it will eat fungus and wild berries or catch a lazy lizard, but the belief that the armadillo raids henhouses is unfounded.

EXERCISE 3

Create your own list of details for the following topics. Write two major details that provide support or elaboration for the development of the topic and one minor detail that adds interest but does not add essential support.

EXAMPLE

Topic: Profit in Fitness

Major: *Popular fitness centers charge a stiff fee for the initial enrollment.*

Major: *Sports stores feature specialty clothing and shoes for aerobics, jogging, and biking.*

Minor: *Jogging strengthens leg muscles but not the upper body muscles.*

EXPLANATION The enrollment fee and expensive gear support the profit notion, whereas muscle strengthening is merely an interesting added detail.

For each topic below, write two major details and one minor detail.

1. **Topic:** Mind Control in Religious Cults

Major: Members meet each night for a ritual chant of the doctrine of the cult.

Major: New inductees are not allowed to use the telephone to call friends or relatives.

Minor: Members wear dark clothing and do not cut their hair.

2. **Topic:** Mandating Volunteer Hours for College Graduation

Major: College students who do volunteer work have a better sense of ethical and moral responsibility.

Major: The enthusiasm of the college volunteers is uplifting to the needy whom they help.

Minor: Working on a house at Habitat for Humanity usually takes at least six hours.

Copyright ©1999 by Addison-Wesley Educational Publishers Inc.

Distinguishing between major and minor details is important, whether you are studying a single paragraph, a chapter, or a whole book. After reading each of the following passages, first identify the author's main point. Then determine which of the details listed are major and which are minor in supporting that point. The skills you will use apply equally to these short readings and to the larger units that you will be studying in college textbooks.

PASSAGE 1

PRICE SETTING

The DeBeers Company of South Africa, a syndicate that controls most of the sales of raw diamonds, maximizes profits by determining what quantity of raw diamonds to offer on the world raw-diamond market. DeBeers markets diamonds through an unusual marketing procedure called a sight. About three weeks before each sight, DeBeers sends notices to the 300 largest diamond purchasers, who are asked to send in requests in carats for the amount of diamonds they wish to buy. Two days before the sight (held in London, Luzerne, and Kimberley, South Africa), the buyers are informed how many carats they have been allocated—an amount often below the quantity requested. At the sight each buyer is handed a container of raw diamonds. Buyers who refuse to purchase would run the risk of not being invited back. The market price of diamonds is regulated by the number of diamonds offered in each sight.

—*Essentials of Economics* by Paul Gregory

1. What point is the author trying to make? The DeBeers Company maximizes the price of diamonds by regulating the number available for sale.

2. Which details are major and which are minor in supporting the author's point?

   minor a. The sight is held in London, Luzerne, and Kimberley.

   major b. DeBeers invites the 300 largest diamond buyers to the sight.

   major c. The buyers are offered fewer diamonds than the quantity requested.

PASSAGE 2

COMPLEXITY OF THE BRAIN

The human brain possesses the basic characteristics of any vertebrate brain. But it is unique in the high degree to which some of its essential parts are developed. In sheer complexity it does not appear to be matched by any other known structure. Each of its more than 15 billion neurons carries information of only a simple type. Yet this information is sorted out, classified, and interpreted in a constant process of feedback between knowledge already present and knowledge newly acquired. The brain of an individual contains the physical foundation of that individual's memory, reason, thought, and probably most of the attributes of his or her personality. Actually, there is more material available in the human brain than we can hope to use during a normal lifetime. This has led some people to speculate that our life expectancy should be much longer than it is today.

—*Biology: The Science of Life* by Victor Greulach and Vincent Chiappetta

1. What point is the author trying to make? The complexity of the human brain cannot be matched by any other known structure.

2. Which details are major and which are minor in supporting the author's point?

<u>minor</u> a. Our life expectancy should be much longer than it is today.

<u>major</u> b. The brain constantly sorts, classifies, and interprets newly acquired and old knowledge.

<u>major</u> c. The brain contains the physical foundation of an individual's memory, reason, and thought.

PASSAGE 3

MARKET RESEARCH

Big companies figure out all sorts of stuff about us we don't even know ourselves—from how many headaches we get to how much dust we vacuum up. They know how many times we change our babies' diapers, how often we lose the cap to our toothpaste tube, and what we think about our local car dealer.

Of all businesses, the prize for research thoroughness may go to toothpaste makers. Among other things, they know that our favorite color for a toothbrush is blue and that only 37 percent of us are using one that is more than six months old. They know that 47 percent of us put water on our brush before we apply the paste, that 15 percent of us put water on after the paste, and that 24 percent of us do both. They also know that 14 percent of us don't wet the brush.

But that, of course, isn't all they know. They have also figured out that 21 percent of Americans have some difficulty handling one of their tubes, complaining of such problems as "trouble squeezing the last toothpaste out" (16 percent) and "tube breaks" (7 percent).

—You Aren't Paranoid If You Think Someone Eyes Your Every Move by John Koten

1. What point is the author trying to make? <u>Big companies know details about us by examining our habits for marketing information.</u>

2. Which details are major and which are minor in supporting the author's point?

<u>major</u> a. Big companies know how many headaches we get.

<u>major</u> b. Toothpaste takes the prize for thoroughness in research.

<u>minor</u> c. The toothpaste tube breaks on 7 percent of us.

PASSAGE 4

VACCINATION

Vaccination against a specific disease works by inducing the immune system to mount a primary immune response and to produce memory cells, ready to trigger a secondary response at the body's first real battle against the disease antigen. The practice of vaccination, however, began long before people understood how it works. Arabic and Chinese manuscripts more than a thousand years old refer to vaccination against smallpox. Lady Mary Wortley Montagu, wife of the British ambassador to Turkey, introduced this ancient custom into England in 1718. She had her children vaccinated by rubbing part of the scab from a healed smallpox sore into a small wound in the skin. This introduced a few live smallpox viruses into the body, stimulating a primary immune response and thereby

Copyright ©1999 by Addison-Wesley Educational Publishers Inc.

conferring immunity to smallpox in later life. The snag was that vaccination with even a small amount of live virus sometimes caused a case of smallpox, which could be fatal.

—*A Journey into Life* by Karen Arms and Pamela Camp

1. What point is the author trying to make? <u>Vaccinations against disease</u>
<u>introduce a live virus in order to build up an immune response.</u>

2. Which details are major and which are minor in supporting the author's point?

   <u>minor</u> a. Lady Mary Wortley Montagu was the wife of the British ambassador.

   <u>major</u> b. Lady Montagu rubbed the scab of a healed smallpox sore on her children's skin to immunize them.

   <u>major</u> c. Live virus can sometimes cause a case of fatal smallpox.

PASSAGE 5

DIFFERENT BY CHOICE

We wear our Indian dress because of our culture, and because we are proud of it. But there are people who say, "This is like a curtain." They embarrass us. "You are wrapped around a curtain?" They don't even know the value. They don't know the culture. They don't know that we want to cover up our bodies, that we don't show our bodies to people, to have them look at us, to give us remarks. In India, we don't use the clothes people in this country use, like bikinis or shorts or clothes that show the body. We cover it up. Pants suits and long skirts aren't bad because you can't see the legs. But if anyone sits and shows her legs, that is not good. It is not right to show a man my legs. We don't like it because we were raised like that. The whole country is like that, not just myself. That's why these people shout their remarks but we don't care. We don't say anything about their dress. My dress is mine, yours is yours. I don't care.

—"Different by Choice," by Sundershan Chawla, from *Asian Americans* by Joann Faung Jean Lee

1. What point is the author trying to make? <u>It is offensive to remark negatively</u>
<u>about the cultural dress of others.</u>

2. Which details are major and which are minor in supporting the author's point?

   <u>major</u> a. People say, "You are wrapped around a curtain."

   <u>major</u> b. In India, we cover our bodies.

   <u>minor</u> c. Americans wear bikinis and shorts.

Patterns of Organization ◆◆◆◆◆◆◆◆◆◆

The logical presentation of details in textbooks tends to form several identifiable patterns. For example, introductory psychology texts tend to list many definitions and examples, whereas history texts present events in time order with numerous cause-and-effect conclusions. Recognizing these patterns helps you to read more efficiently and take notes for later study.

The primary organizational patterns used in textbooks are:

◆ Listings
◆ Definition with examples
◆ Time order or sequence
◆ Comparison or contrast
◆ Cause and effect

Each organizational pattern can be predicted by key terms that signal the structure. Learn to use the patterns to mark your text and take notes for later study. Your markings and your notes are an organization of main ideas and major supporting details.

Listing

To organize and condense material for the reader, introductory texts often enumerate key ideas. The listing technique may be used within one paragraph, or it may be used over three or four pages to pull material together. The alert reader recognizes the organizational pattern and uses it as a convenient aid in organizing relevant details for future learning.

Transitional Words to Signal Listing.   Listed items usually begin with general phrases, such as:

Many of the items included were . . .
A number of factors were . . .

Actual numbers or terms are then used to enumerate, including:

| first | furthermore | third | also |
| next | last | finally | in addition |

Mark Your Text.   After reading a listing, circle the topic of the list, that is, the words that best describe what the list contains. Next, insert numbers for each item and underline any key words that help explain the details listed. The following is an example of this technique.

EXAMPLE

THE POST–CIVIL WAR BOOM

A number of (factors were responsible for the post–Civil War industrial boom.) The United States possessed ¹bountiful raw materials, and the government was willing to turn them over to industry for little or no money. Coupled with the abundance of natural resources was a ²home market steadily expanding through immigration and a high birth rate. Both ³capital and ⁴labor were plentiful. The increase in trade and manufacturing in the Northeast in the years before the war produced an accumulation of savings, while additional

Copyright ©1999 by Addison-Wesley Educational Publishers Inc.

millions of dollars came from <u>European investors</u>. Unbroken waves of European <u>immigration</u> provided American industry with workers as well as with customers. From 1860 to 1900 about 14 million immigrants came to the United States, most of whom settled in cities and became industrial workers.

—The Democratic Experience by Carl Degler et al.

Take Notes. To show relationships and levels of importance, as well as to help you remember the material, take notes on what you have read. Jot down the topic and, under that, number the items that are relevant. If an item needs explanation, put the necessary key words in parentheses beside it.

Your Notes on "The Post–Civil War Boom" would be as follows:

EXAMPLE

Topic: Factors responsible for post–Civil War industrial boom
1. Bountiful raw material (gov. made cheap)
2. Expanding home market
3. Plentiful capital (savings and European investors)
4. Plentiful labor (immigration)

EXERCISE 5 For each of the following paragraphs, mark your text by writing a topic at the beginning of the passage, numbering the items in the list, and underlining key words. Take notes by first recording the topic and then listing the items. If more explanation is needed for recall, record a few key notes in parentheses. Respond with *T* (true) or *F* (false) to the comprehension items.

PASSAGE 1

Predation

But why does <u>predation not wipe out the prey species entirely?</u> Why did the wolves not kill off all the Isle Royale moose? One reason is that [1] <u>large prey</u>, such as moose and deer, <u>are hard to capture.</u> Even several wolves together have trouble bringing down a healthy adult moose. They would probably use up more energy in chasing and killing it than they would get back by feeding on it. Some of them might even be killed in the battle. So the <u>predators are limited mostly to taking old, sick, or very young prey.</u> This not only ensures that some prey animals will survive and reproduce. It also means that the ones that survive will probably be the strongest and healthiest. Thus predation not only keeps the prey population stable; it also <u>keeps it healthy.</u>

Another reason prey species survive is that as their [2] <u>numbers fall, they become harder to find.</u> One or two rabbits in a field are harder for a prowling fox to locate than are a large population of rabbits. And if the fox fails to find rabbits in that field for awhile, it may be attracted by some tender, juicy field mice instead. The few rabbits that are left will then have a better chance to survive, mate, and raise their young.

—Biology: The Science of Life by Victor Greulach and Vincent Chiappetta

1. Mark your text and then take notes.

Topic: Predation

(1) Large prey are hard to capture.

(2) As numbers fall, they become harder to find.

_____T_____ 2. Wolves prefer to prey on sick rather than healthy deer.

_____T_____ 3. Lone rabbits have a better chance of survival against a fox.

PASSAGE 2

Advantages of Incumbency

During elections to Congress the advantages of incumbency (being currently in office) are considerable. The incumbent is well known, and by issuing "official" statements or making "official" trips to his district, he can get a lot of free publicity[1] that his opponents would have to pay for. Members of the House have office and staff budgets of approxi-[2]mately $350,000 a year; senators are given at least that and often considerably more if their states are large. Both receive 32 government-paid round trips to their districts each year. Facilities for making television or radio tapes[3] are available in Washington at a low cost. And there is the frank,[4] the privilege of free official mailing enjoyed by Congress. Two hundred million pieces of mail, much of it quite partisan, are sent free under the frank every year.

—*The Basics of American Politics* by Gary Wasserman

1. Mark your text and then take notes.

Topic: Advantages of Incumbency

(1) Free publicity

(2) Office and staff budgets

(3) Taping facilities available

(4) Free franking for mail

_____F_____ 2. A *frank* privilege is a government-paid trip home.

_____T_____ 3. Incumbents receive publicity paid for by taxpayers.

Definitions with Examples

In each freshman course, you enter a completely new field with its own unique concepts and ideas. Introductory courses frequently seem to be the hardest because of the overload of information presented. In a single beginning course, you are expected to survey the field from beginning to end. Beyond simply learning vocabulary, you must learn the terminology for major ideas that create a framework for the entire course. You must create a new schema. For example, in an introductory psychology textbook, several paragraphs might be devoted to

Copyright ©1999 by Addison-Wesley Educational Publishers Inc.

describing *schizophrenia, paranoia,* or a *manic-depressive cycle.* To remember these terms you would mark your text and take notes defining the conditions. You would also include examples to help you visualize the terms.

Transitional Words to Signal Definition and Examples. The new terms or concepts may appear as headings or they may appear in quotation marks, boldface, or italics. Connecting words include:

for example	in this case	to illustrate
more specifically	in more precise terms	in one instance

Term

Def

Characteristics

Example

Mark Your Text. After reading the definition of a new term, circle the term and then underline the *key words.* A word of caution here: only underline *key* words. Refrain from underlining sentence after sentence, which leaves you with too much highlighted material for later reference. Mark *Ex.* by the example that best helps you remember the term. The following paragraph illustrates this technique.

EXAMPLE

DISPLACEMENT

Father spanks son, who kicks the dog, who chases the cat. Displacement is the shifting of response from one object to another. The boss has yelled at the father, the father is angry at the boss but can't express it safely, so he displaces his anger to his son and spanks him. The son is angry at his father, but can't express it safely, so he displaces his anger to the dog and kicks it. [Ex.] The dog is "angry" at the son but can't express it safely, so he displaces his "anger" to the cat and chases it. In the mechanism of displacement, a feeling is displaced to a safer substitute.

—*Introductory Psychology* by Morris Holland

Take Notes. For your study notes, jot down the term, define it in your own words, and list an example. Frequently, you will need to condense several sentences into a short phrase for your notes. If you think the text uses a clear and concise definition, it is permissible to use the same words, but don't let yourself fall into the "delayed learning" trap. If you simply copy textbook words that you do not understand, you won't be any better off weeks later when you study your notes for a midterm or final exam. The appropriate time to understand the term is when you first study and take notes on it.

Your notes on displacement might look like this:

Displacement: shifting the expression of a feeling from one object to another safe substitute

Example: Son angry at father, so kicks dog

EXERCISE 6 Read the paragraphs below, and write a topic for the beginning of each passage. Circle the terms being defined, underline key phrases, and then write notes for later study. Respond to the comprehension items with *T* (true) or *F* (false).

PASSAGE 1

Adolescent's Imaginary Audience

Thoughts and behavior during adolescence may appear to be egocentric. The (imaginary audience) refers to the adolescent's feeling of being onstage, that all eyes are focused on him or her. Much of the adolescent's time, then, is spent constructing, or reacting to, the imaginary audience. This audience is called imaginary because in reality the adolescent is not the object of such attention. In David Elkind's view, the construction of imaginary audiences helps account for a variety of adolescent behaviors and experiences, including the adolescent's sometimes ^{Ex.} excruciating self-consciousness. It is a minor tragedy of adolescent life that when these young people actually meet, each is likely to be more preoccupied with himself or herself than with observing the other.

—*Adolescence and Youth* by John Conger and Nancy Galambos

1. Mark your text and then take notes.

Imaginary audience: Adolescent's feeling of being onstage

Example: Self-conscious when meeting because preoccupied with self.

___F___ 2. The author feels that when adolescents meet, each is usually focused on the other person.

___F___ 3. The imaginary audience gives the adolescent a sense of security.

PASSAGE 2

Hidden Agenda

Suppose you have just opened a quick copy-printing service in a new town, and you need contacts to develop your clientele. You might join a civic or social group with the ^{Ex.} sole purpose of meeting businesspeople and office personnel to whom you can sell your service. You are more interested in this unstated goal than in the goals or activities of the group itself.

When an individual conceals personal goals or needs in hopes of satisfying them through a group's interaction, the individual has a (hidden agenda.) A member with a hidden agenda can detract from a group's effectiveness because he or she will waste the group's time and energy for personal gain.

—*Effective Speech Communication* by John Masterson et al.

Copyright ©1999 by Addison-Wesley Educational Publishers Inc.

1. Mark your text and then take notes.

   Hidden agenda: <u>a concealed personal goal</u>

   Example: <u>joining a civic organization to find customers</u>

____T____ 2. Seeking customers can be a hidden agenda for joining a club.

____F____ 3. The author suggests that members with hidden agendas tend to be positive for a club.

Time Order and Sequence

Items in time order or sequence are listed in the order in which they occurred or in a specifically planned order in which they must develop. Changing the order would change the results. For example, events in history are typically organized in time order, and complicated processes in science are explained in a sequence of steps or in order of importance.

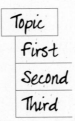

Transitional Words to Signal Time Order or Sequence. Signal words often used for time order or sequence include:

first	second	afterward	after	before	when
until	at last	next	most important	finally	

Mark Your Text. After reading a time-ordered or sequenced section, first circle the topic and then decide on the significant events or steps and number them. Insert numbers for each important stage and underline key words that explain each one. History is, by its nature, full of time-ordered or chronological events. Readers should be aware that every event is not of equal significance. History textbooks also include many details that help you visualize but do not need to be remembered. Use the subheadings in the text to help you judge the importance of events.

EXAMPLE   As if you didn't have enough to worry about, now there's (Lyme disease.) What it is, is a disease *caused by a spirochaete,* a corkscrew-shaped bacterium, *Borrelia burgdorferi,* and carried by a tick, *Ixodes dammini* (at least in the Northeast and Midwest). The (tick has three stages in its life cycle.) In its ¹larval stage, it mainly infects the white-footed mouse. In its ²nymph stage, it infects a range of mammals, including dogs, raccoons, and humans. In its ³adult stage, it mainly infects white-tailed deer. The problem is, in the nymph stage, it is very small, about the size of a comma. (It may look like a tiny moving freckle.) Thus, it is easy to overlook.

—Biology: The World of Life by Robert Wallace

Take Notes. After marking your text, jot down the topic and number the items that are relevant. Be brief. If these items need explanation, put key words underneath the item or in parentheses beside it. Your notes on the previous paragraph would be as follows:

Life Cycle of Lyme Disease Tick

1. Larval → *infects white-footed mice*

2. Nymph (very small) → *infects dogs, raccoons, and humans*

3. Adult → *infects white-tailed deer*

EXERCISE 7

Read the paragraphs below, and mark your text by writing a topic at the beginning of the passage, circling or numbering listed items, and underlining key phrases. Then write notes for later study. Respond to the comprehension items with *T* (true) or *F* (false).

PASSAGE 1

Mexican Americans Voting

On election day, 1963, hundreds of Mexican Americans in Crystal City, Texas, the "spinach capital of the world," gathered near a statue of Popeye the Sailor to do something that most had never done before: vote. Although Mexican Americans outnumbered whites two to one, whites controlled all five seats on the Crystal City council. For three years, organizers struggled to register Mexican-American voters. When the election was over, Mexican Americans had won control of the city council. "We have done the impossible," declared Albert Fuentes, who led the voter-registration campaign. "If we can do it in Crystal City, we can do it all over Texas. We can awaken the sleeping giant."

Since 1960 Mexican Americans have made impressive political gains. During the 1960's four Mexican Americans—Senator Joseph Montoya of New Mexico and representatives Eligio de la Garza and Henry B. Gonzales of Texas and Edward R. Roybal of California—were elected to Congress. In 1974, two Chicanos were elected governors—Jerry Apodaca in New Mexico and Raul Castro in Arizona—becoming the first Mexican-American governors since early in this century. In 1981 Henry Cisneros of San Antonio, Texas, became the first Mexican-American mayor of a large city.

—*America and Its People* by James Martin et al.

1. Mark your text and take notes.

Topic? Mexican Americans Voting

1960	Four Mexican Americans elected to Congress
1963	Won control of Crystal City council
1974	Two Chicanos elected as governors
1981	First Mexican-American mayor of large city

___F___ 2. Albert Fuentes was elected governor of California.

___T___ 3. The voting area in Crystal City was located near a statue of Popeye.

Copyright ©1999 by Addison-Wesley Educational Publishers Inc.

PASSAGE 2

Discovering the DNA Fingerprint

Criminals now have to worry about their own (very unique DNA.) Any cells will do, whether from blood, semen, teeth, hair follicle, or saliva. Samples are collected from the crime scene and suspect. The DNA is extracted, concentrated, and subjected to restriction enzymes, which chop the DNA into fragments. The fragments are then separated by gel electrophoresis. There are far too many different fragments in the gel to be of use, so the next step is critical. The gel layer is transferred to a sheet impregnated with nitrocellulose, which opens the strands up. Then radioactive DNA probe is added. The probe consists of short, single strands of radioactive DNA, whose sequence will match and join highly selected known human DNA sequences somewhere in the fragments. The selected fragments will form the fingerprint. To make the selected radioactive fragments visible, the nitrocellulose sheet is laid over X-ray film, and the desired pattern emerges. Since each person's DNA differs from all others (except for identical twins), the pattern becomes the "fingerprint." The odds of misidentification have been estimated one in a million and one in 70 billion.

—*Biology: The World of Life* by Robert Wallace

1. Mark the text and take notes.
   Topic? Discovering the DNA Fingerprint
   (1) Collect samples at crime scene
   (2) DNA extracted and fragmented
   (3) Gel layer transferred and strands open
   (4) Radioactive probe added
   (5) Human DNA join radioactive DNA
   (6) Laid over X-ray film to see

___F___ 2. The odds of making an error in DNA identification are one in a hundred.

___T___ 3. The DNA pattern usually emerges on X-ray film.

Comparison and Contrast

The fourth pattern that you will find in introductory texts is one that relates items according to existing comparisons and contrasts. To enrich your understanding of a topic, items are paired and then similarities or differences are listed.

Transitional Words to Signal Comparison and Contrast. Signal words that are often used for comparison or contrast include:

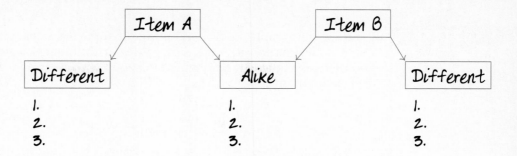

Comparison: similar   like   in the same way   likewise
Contrast: different   on the other hand   but   nevertheless   however
  although   instead   conversely

Mark Your Text. After reading the passage, record the topic and then write an abbreviation for similarities or differences in the margin. Underline key words. The following paragraph illustrates the technique.

EXAMPLE

Diff.

Sim.

Sim.

Diff.

CHICAGO AND CLEVELAND

Chicago, at the southern tip of Lake Michigan, is a port city and an important commercial and industrial center of the Middle West. It is also an important educational, cultural, and recreational center, drawing thousands to its concert halls, art museum, and sports arenas. Cleveland, on the south shore of Lake Erie, is also a port city and a commercial and industrial center important to its area. Like Chicago, it has several important colleges and universities, a distinguished symphony orchestra, one of the fine art museums of the world, and many recreational centers. The location of the two cities undoubtedly contributed to their growth, but this similarity is not sufficient to explain their wide social diversity.

—*Short Essays* ed. by Gerald Levin

Take Notes. First jot down the topics, and then write a heading for similarities or differences. Some passages will be mostly comparisons and some will be mostly contrasts. List how the topics are alike or different. Add key words needed for explanation. The following is an example.

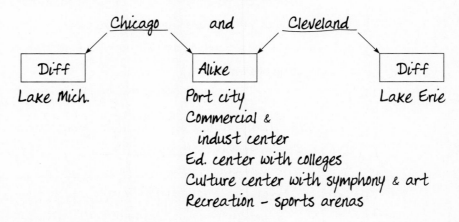

Copyright ©1999 by Addison-Wesley Educational Publishers Inc.

EXERCISE 8

Read the paragraphs below, and write the topic at the beginning of the passage. Use an abbreviation to mark similarities or differences, underline key phrases, and then take notes for later study. Respond with *T* (true) or *F* (false) to the comprehension items.

PASSAGE 1

Political Labels

I devoutly wish we could get rid of two words in the popular lexicon: *liberal* and *conservative.* Both are beautiful and useful words in their origins, but now each is used (and misused) as an epithet by its political enemies.

Diff. (Liberal) means liberating—it implies more freedom, more openness, more flexibility, more humaneness, more willingness to change when change is called for.

Diff. (Conservative) means conserving—it implies preserving what is best and most valuable from the past, a decent respect for tradition, a reluctance to change merely for its own sake.

Diff. Both attributes, in fruitful tension, are necessary for the welfare of any social order. Liberalism alone can degenerate into mere permissiveness and anarchy. Conservatism alone is prone to harden into reaction and repression. As Lord Acton brilliantly put it: "Every institution tends to fail by an excess of its own basic principle."

Sim. Yet, in the rhetoric of their opponents, both *liberal* and *conservative* have turned into dirty words. Liberals become "bleeding hearts"; conservatives want "to turn the clock back." But sometimes hearts *should* bleed; sometimes it would profit us to run the clock back if it is spinning too fast. (Radical,) of course, has become the dirtiest of words, flung around carelessly and sometimes maliciously. Today it is usually applied to the left by the right—but the right is often as "radical" in its own way.

The word originally meant "going to the roots" and was a metaphor drawn from the radish, which grows underground. We still speak of "radical surgery," which is undertaken when lesser measures seem futile. The American Revolution, indeed, was a radical step taken to ensure a conservative government, when every other effort had failed.

Dorothy Thompson was right on target when she remarked that her ideal was to be "a radical as a thinker, a conservative as to program and a liberal as to temper." In this way she hoped to combine the best and most productive in each attitude, while avoiding the pitfalls of each.

—"Opposing Principles Help Balance Society" by Sidney Harris in *Short Essays* ed. by Gerald Levin

1. Mark your text and take notes. Describe each of the political labels.

Conservative: traditionalists who want to keep things as they are and not change

Liberal: humanists who want change

Radical: extremists who turn to the far left or right

_____ T _____ 2. The author believes that liberals can become too permissive.

_____ F _____ 3. The author believes that conservatives should lead the government.

PASSAGE 2

Changing the Marlboro Image

In the minds of many consumers, the (Marlboro Man) was the essence of masculinity, and the advertising image itself became an icon. The history of the Marlboro Man, however, suggests just how potent images of the West are. In 1954, Marlboro was the name brand of a filtered cigarette produced by Philip Morris and sold primarily to women. The ciga-

Old   rettes came in a white soft pack, had a red "beauty tip" filter to camouflage lipstick, and sold under the slogan, "Mild as May." Considered effeminate cigarettes, Marlboros had less than one-quarter of one percent market share. "Men will never smoke cigarettes with filters," was the common advertising wisdom.

Then Chicago advertiser Leo Burnett took over the Marlboro account. He changed the woman's cigarette into a man's cigarette, in fact a man's man's cigarette. The white

New   soft pack become a strong red and white hard, flip-top pack. The "beauty tip" bit the dust, as did the "Mild as May" slogan, replaced by the image of a cowboy with a tattoo on the back of one hand. The original photographer of the series later recalled, however, that he used pilots, not cowboys, for models "because pilots seem to have little wrinkles around the eyes." The combination of rustic masculinity and a western setting—Marlboro Man and Marlboro Country—had an immediate appeal, and Burnett's campaign became the most financially successful in advertising history.

—*America and Its People* by James Martin et al.

1. Mark the text and take notes.

   Topic? Changing the Marlboro Image _____

   Old image white soft pack, red tip, "Mild as May," effeminate

   New image red and white flip-top pack, cowboy with tatoo, masculinity

_____ T _____ 2. The original Marlboro package was soft.

_____ T _____ 3. The filter for the cigarette was later dropped.

Cause and Effect

In this pattern, one of several factors, or causes, is shown to lead to or result in certain events, or effects. Cause-and-effect patterns can be complex, since a single effect can have multiple causes and vice versa.

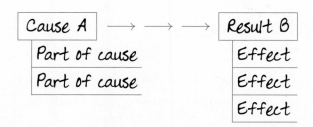

Copyright ©1999 by Addison-Wesley Educational Publishers Inc.

Transitional Words to Signal Cause and Effect. Signal words often used to indicate cause and effect include:

for this reason	consequently	on that account	thus
hence	because	made	therefore

Mark Your Text. Circle the topic and then remember that there can be many causes and many effects. Therefore, you should give both labels and numbers to the causes and effects, as well as underlining key words to explain the items. The following paragraph illustrates the technique.

EXAMPLE

The cause: (1) summer and (2) after-school jobs

Effects:
1. Money management
2. Skills
3. Belief in work
   a. Anxiety over free time
   b. Guilt over nonwork activity

EARLY JOBS

Aside from ¹ basic money management, *Eff.* what did I actually learn from all my summer and *Cause* after-school jobs? Each one may have given me some ² small skills *Eff.* but the cumulative effect was to deepen my belief that ³ work was the essential *Eff.* aspect of grown-up life. Even now, I am sometimes filled with anxieties at the prospect of stretches of *free time.* When I do not immediately rush to fill that time with work, I have to fight off *guilt, Eff.* struggling mentally against a picture of a Real Grown-up shaking a finger at me, someone with the droning voice of our high school career counselor, but with firm overtones of former employers, teachers, even my mother. "This," the voice beats relentlessly into my ear, "is your preparation for life."

—"Blooming: A Small-Town Girlhood" by Susan Allen Toth in *The Compact Reader*
ed. by Jane Aaron

Take Notes. Write the topic and then write headings to label causes and effects. List and number the causes and effects and add key words that are needed to explain. Here is an example.

Results of Early Jobs

Causes ⟶ ⟶	Results
Summer jobs	1. Money mgt.
After-school jobs	2. Skills
	3. Belief in work
	Anxiety over fun time
	Guilt over non-work

EXERCISE 9

Read the paragraphs below, and write the topic at the beginning of the passage, label the causes and effects, underline key terms, and then take notes for later study. Respond with *T* (true) or *F* (false) to the comprehension items.

PASSAGE 1

Insects in the Environment

Insects perform many roles vital to human life. Without bees and other insects, *Cause* for instance, many *Eff.* flowering plants would never be pollinated—a prerequisite to producing

Cause

crops such as apples, citrus fruits, berries, and cucumbers. Many <u>beetles, ants,</u> and <u>flies</u>

Eff.

are important <u>decomposers,</u> breaking down the dead bodies of plants and animals.

Nevertheless, people have devoted more time to killing insects than to praising them. It is perhaps unduly gloomy to conclude that we are losing the battle against insects, who will one day inherit the earth, but those who believe this have good reason for their opinion.

Eff.

<u>Insects destroy more than 10% of all crops</u> in the United States, but the damage is even worse in the tropics, where hot weather throughout the year permits insects to grow and reproduce faster. In Kenya, officials estimate that <u>insects destroy 75% of the</u>

Eff.

<u>nation's crops.</u> A locust swarm in Africa may be 30 meters deep along a front 1500 meters long, and will consume every fragment of plant material in its path, leaving hundreds of square kilometers of country devastated.

Pesticides have not solved the insect problem. This is partly because pesticides act as

Eff.

selective pressures for <u>the evolution of resistant strains of insects,</u> which evolve too fast for expensive pesticide research to keep up.

—*A Journey into Life* by Karen Arms and Pamela Camp

1. Mark your text and take notes.

Topic? Insects in the Environment

Causes ⟶	Effects
Bees and others	Pollinate crops
Beetles, ants, and flies	Decomposers
Pests	Damage crops and evolve to resist pesticides

_____ F _____ 2. Bees are considered decomposers.

_____ F _____ 3. Locusts can probably be eradicated in Africa with pesticides.

PASSAGE 2

Eating Healthier Foods

Cause

Americans are also more conscious of what they are eating. The <u>desire to reduce choles-</u>

Eff.

<u>terol</u> intake has caused a <u>shift away from red meat and dairy products.</u> The trend was substantial enough to cause beef producers to band together and mount an educational campaign to convince consumers that beef is healthful. The trend to healthier foods has primarily affected product rather than promotional strategies. Producers of dairy foods

Eff.   Eff.

are coming out with lines of <u>low-cholesterol products,</u> cereal companies with <u>high-fiber</u>

Eff.

<u>products,</u> and liquor manufacturers with <u>lower-alcohol</u> lines to reflect the trend away from hard liquor.

The combined effects of better medical care and greater health awareness have resulted in increased longevity in the past twenty years. From 1970 to 1990, <u>life</u>

Copyright ©1999 by Addison-Wesley Educational Publishers Inc.

Eff.   Eff.
expectancy of the average American went from 70 to 76 years and should reach 80 by

the turn of the century.

—*Consumer Behavior and Marketing Action,* 4th ed., by Henry Assael

_____ 1. Mark your text and take notes.

Topic? Eating Healthier Foods _____

Causes	Results
Desire to reduce cholestrol	Less red meat and dairy products
	Low-cholesterol products
	Lower alcoholic content in drinks
	Longer life expectancy

___T___ 2. Americans are eating fewer dairy products.

___F___ 3. Eating beef tends to lower cholesterol levels.

POINTS TO PONDER

▲ All details are not of equal importance.
▲ Major details are needed to explain or prove the main idea.
▲ Minor details are included to make the passage more interesting.
▲ A common organizational pattern in textbooks is to list ideas.
▲ Another common pattern is to define an idea and give several examples.
▲ Events listed in the order in which they occur are in a chronological pattern or a sequence.
▲ A comparison or contrast pattern shows how items are alike or different.
▲ A cause-and-effect pattern shows how one event stimulated a particular result or results.

PERSONAL FEEDBACK 1

Name_____

1. Describe a poster, painting, or photograph that you particularly like. What is the theme? How do the details support the theme? Why do you like it?

_____

_____

_____

2. So far this term, have you collaborated on homework or products with other classmates? _____ If so, describe your work.

_____

_____

3. In this class, who would you feel comfortable calling for assignment information? _____

_____

4. What organizations have you joined? _____

_____

5. What campus events or social functions have you attended?

_____

6. When you have a break at school, where do you "hang out"?

_____

7. What volunteer work have you recently done on or off campus?

_____

8. What do you think "bonded to the college" means?

_____

9. What would make you feel bonded to your college?

_____

Copyright ©1999 by Addison-Wesley Educational Publishers Inc.

SELECTION 1   *Psychology*

THINKING BEFORE READING

Preview for content and organizational clues. Activate your schema and anticipate what you will learn.

What is the happiest part of your day?

Why do you like hugs?

I think this will say that _____.

VOCABULARY PREVIEW

Are you familiar with these words?

pervasive	encounters	excessive	timidity	frailties
chronic	perspective	profoundly	competence	self-transcendence

What does the prefix *per* in *pervasive* and *perspective* mean?

How long does a chronic illness last?

Do you suffer from timidity?

Your instructor may give a true-false vocabulary review before or after reading.

THINKING DURING READING

As you read, use the five thinking strategies of a good reader: predict, picture, relate, monitor, and correct.

BECOMING HEALTHY

How can you grow and eventually become fully functioning? How can you achieve that ideal stage of psychological health? You cannot be healthy simply by trying to be healthy; you cannot be happy simply by deciding to be happy.

5   Pleasure, happiness, and self-actualization cannot be effectively pursued; instead, they ensue, or automatically result, from your having satisfied a need, attained a goal, or grown toward health. Your deciding to be happy will not make you happy; happiness follows from what you *do*.

THREE THINGS TO AVOID

You have unpleasant feelings sometimes and this is quite natural. But if your unpleasant feelings are pervasive, unending, and tend to color your whole emotional life, then you
10 want to stop feeling so bad. We are all sometimes blue, but if you are blue most of the time, then you want to change. As you grow toward health, you tend to experience fewer and fewer persistent unpleasant feelings. Three of these unpleasant feelings are doubt, dread, and depression.

    Doubt. Self-doubt makes you feel worthless, stupid, and dull. Many persons have exces-
15 sive doubts about their physical appearance; they consider themselves unattractive, ugly, and unlovable. They then retreat from dating and other interpersonal encounters and remain highly self-conscious about their appearance. Other persons have excessive doubts about their intelligence; they consider themselves uninteresting, ordinary, and dull. They act with great shyness and timidity when among other people, believing that
20 no one would want to listen to their ideas. Excessive self-doubt, in general, comes from a feeling that other people will not find you acceptable in some way; this feeling leads you not to accept yourself. Understanding yourself and others is one way to avoid self-doubt; you will discover that your frailties and fears are not unique. Being loved and prized by someone is another way to escape excessive self-doubt; to be wholly accepted by some-
25 one else makes it easier for you to accept yourself.

    Dread. Dread is a feeling of anxiety or worry. You feel afraid, but you are not sure why. Dread makes you feel nervous, high-strung, restless, and irritable. The tension that you feel may show up physically in nail-biting, in crying spells, in chain-smoking, in frequent headaches or neck aches, or in chronic fatigue. The persistent feeling of dread is a mes-
30 sage, and the message is this: Relax, reduce the pressures in your life, and try to resolve some of your conflicts.

    Relaxing is something you may have to practice and learn how to do. Here is something for you to try: Go to a quiet darkened room. Sit or lie in a comfortable position. Begin breathing deeply and slowly while you try to empty your mind of thoughts. Begin-
35 ning with your feet, tighten and then relax your muscles one by one, until all of the muscles of your body are relatively relaxed. Then close your eyes and imagine yourself floating in a tub of warm water. The pressures of your life can sometimes be reduced by getting away from them for a while—take a break and change your scene. For a change of pace take a walk every day or do some light reading. You can sometimes be helped in
40 working out your problems and conflicts by talking to other people about them. As you listen to yourself, you may gain some insights. The feedback of other people may also give you a new perspective. Expressing your feelings to other people often in itself reduces the tension that you feel.

    Depression. When you are depressed, you feel profoundly unhappy, blue, and sad. You
45 are moody and pessimistic; you don't feel that things will get better in the near future.

You tend not to do things; your energy level is low. Things that once were significant now seem rather pointless. The persistent feeling of depression is a message, and the message is this: Become active, get to work, begin to be involved. Get a part-time job, start a project, volunteer as a helper in a clinic or community agency, join a club—do
50 something. Depression is the opposite of involvement.

THREE THINGS TO DO

What you do and what happens to you are under your control. You are in charge. And what you do will determine whether you grow toward health or whether you stay as you are now. While you cannot attain psychological health by pursuing it directly, you can grow in the direction of health through certain kinds of experiences and these experi-
55 ences are under your control. Some experiences move you toward health; some move you away from health. To learn about yourself and others, to love and to be loved, and to live actively and productively—all are growth-producing.

Learn. To learn about others you must be involved with them. You must have a relationship with them of mutual trust. For how can I learn about you unless you trust me enough
60 to disclose your "inner self" to me? And how can you trust me unless I am willing to reveal myself to you? You can help me understand myself, if I trust what you say about me.

Self-understanding cannot easily be achieved in isolation; other people help us to define who we are. Our impression of ourselves depends upon how other people consistently react to us. My self-understanding and my knowledge of you thus depend upon
65 our relationship. If we do not have a trustful relationship, you may hide yourself from me. You may "mystify" me by trying to create an impression that you are different from what you really are. But if you allow me to know you, then you help me understand myself. Knowing others and understanding yourself leads to self-acceptance. You discover that the qualities in yourself that you have rejected are not unique to yourself; others are very
70 similar to you. And as you are accepted by others, you are led to accept yourself. Self-understanding and self-acceptance are experiences of growth that make possible a state of self-actualization.

Copyright ©1999 by Addison-Wesley Educational Publishers Inc.

Love. Experiences that confirm or validate who you are are health-producing experiences. Being loved by another is the most profound validation of your self; for to be loved
75 means that someone knows you, that they accept the way you are, and that they value and prize you. To be loved, and therefore validated, is health-producing because it leads you to know, accept, and value yourself. And if you can do this, you are better able to function in life and more likely to experience a continual feeling of well-being.

The capacity for love is a symptom of health. The ability to love depends upon the
80 extent to which you value yourself, have faith in your own powers, and are not afraid of giving yourself.

Live. Living fully implies involvement with the world. When you actively do things, you experience your self, your power, and your capacity. When you become intensely involved in a job, hobby, cause, or other person, you tend to lose self-consciousness,
85 develop feelings of competence, and invest yourself in something "outside your own skin." You have feelings of purpose and meaningfulness and may taste the satisfaction of what has been called "meaning fulfillment." When you become absorbed in something outside yourself, you begin to experience a kind of self-transcendence, accompanied by a feeling of well-being. Thus the experience of active involvement is a growth experience.

(1,225 words)

—*Psychology: Introduction to Human Behavior* by Morris Holland

THINKING AFTER READING

RECALL: Self-test your understanding. Your instructor may choose to give you a true-false review.

REACT: How does someone you know well create unhappiness? _____

_____

REFLECT: What makes you depressed? _____

THINK CRITICALLY: Discuss how learning can help you achieve good health. Write your answer on a separate sheet of paper.

DETAILS AND ORGANIZATIONAL PATTERNS: Mark the following as major (M) or minor (m) details in support of the author's main point.

___M___ 1. Self-doubt makes you feel worthless, stupid, and dull.

___m___ 2. Tension may show up physically in nail-biting or headaches.

___M___ 3. Learn about others.

___m___ 4. Join a club to beat depression.

___M___ 5. Live fully and be involved with the world.

6. What is the purpose of the first paragraph? To get the reader's
attention by asking questions.

7. What is the pattern of organization of the section entitled *Three Things to Avoid?* Listing

8. What is the pattern of organization of the section entitled *Three Things to Do?* Listing

Name _____

Date_____

COMPREHENSION QUESTIONS

Answer the following with *a*, *b*, *c*, or *d*, or fill in the blank. In order to help you analyze your strengths and weaknesses, the question types are indicated.

Main Idea ___b___ 1. The best statement of the main idea of this selection is:

    a. Negative and unpleasant feelings are natural but tend to ruin your emotional life.
    b. You can achieve health and happiness by avoiding negative feelings and focusing on certain positive experiences.
    c. In achieving good health, love and learning are more important than money.
    d. Pleasure, happiness, and self-actualization result as you grow toward health.

Inference ___a___ 2. The author's attitude toward becoming healthy is

    a. optimistic.
    b. pessimistic.
    c. sarcastic.
    d. sympathetic.

Inference ___b___ 3. The author believes that

    a. happiness can be pursued.
    b. happiness follows positive action.
    c. deciding to be happy can make you happy.
    d. setting realistic goals brings happiness.

Inference ___b___ 4. The author suggests that relaxation is a cure for

    a. self-doubt.
    b. anxiety.
    c. depression.
    d. timidity.

Inference 5. The author suggests that shyness is primarily a reflection of
self-doubt. _____

Detail ___c___ 6. The author views learning as

    a. getting a college degree.
    b. becoming involved in new hobbies.
    c. learning about yourself and others.
    d. always actively pursuing knowledge.

Inference ___d___ 7. The author feels that being loved

    a. is more important than loving.
    b. is not as important as involvement with the world.
    c. is the single key to good health.
    d. gives a feeling of self-worth.

Answer the following with *T* (true), *F* (False), or *CT* (can't tell).

Inference ___T___ 8. The author is more concerned with the psychological than the physiological contributions to health.

Copyright ©1999 by Addison-Wesley Educational Publishers Inc.

Inference   __T__   9. According to the author, involvement and activity help to prevent depression.

Detail   __CT__ 10. Shy people can benefit from associating with self-confident, aggressive friends.

VOCABULARY

Answer the following with *a*, *b*, *c*, or *d* for the word or phrase that best defines the boldface word as used in the selection. The number in parentheses indicates the line of the passage in which the word is located.

__d__ 1. "unpleasant feelings are **pervasive**" (8–9)

    a. upsetting
    b. uncharacteristic
    c. surprising
    d. prevalent

__a__ 2. "other interpersonal **encounters**" (16)

    a. meetings
    b. groups
    c. friendships
    d. circumstances

__c__ 3. "have **excessive** doubts" (17–18)

    a. endless
    b. needless
    c. more than usual
    d. inferior

__b__ 4. "shyness and **timidity**" (19)

    a. nervousness
    b. meekness
    c. unreasonableness
    d. inconsistency

__d__ 5. "your **frailties** and fears" (23)

    a. expectations
    b. unusual features
    c. hopes
    d. weaknesses

__a__ 6. "**chronic** fatigue" (29)

    a. habitual
    b. unwanted
    c. difficult
    d. nervous

__b__ 7. "give you a new **perspective**" (42)

    a. interest
    b. view
    c. tension
    d. desire

__c__ 8. "feel **profoundly** unhappy" (44)

    a. slightly
    b. briefly
    c. deeply
    d. frankly

__b__ 9. "feelings of **competence**" (85)

    a. love
    b. ability
    c. belonging
    d. need

__a__10. "a kind of **self-transcendence**" (88)

    a. excelling
    b. rejection
    c. inner analysis
    d. admiration

VOCABULARY ENRICHMENT

A. Invented Words

The purpose of many invented words is to form shorter expressions that carry the same meaning. Write the definitions and elongated forms of the following words:

Acronyms are words made from the initial letters of other words.

scu·ba \\'skü-bə\ *n, often attrib* [self-contained underwater breathing apparatus] (1952) : an apparatus utilizing a portable supply of compressed gas (as air) supplied at a regulated pressure and used for breathing while swimming underwater

1. *Scuba* means a device for breathing under water.

2. It comes from self-contained underwater breathing apparatus.

Blends are words formed by combining parts of other words.

> **medi·care** \'me-di-ˌker, -ˌkar\ *n, often cap* [blend of *medical* and *care*]
> (1955) : a government program of medical care esp. for the aged

3. *Medicare* means government insurance for the elderly.

4. It comes from Medi (cal) care.

Abbreviations are shortened forms of longer words.

> ¹**ad** \'ad\ *n, often attrib* (1841) **1 :** ADVERTISEMENT 2 **2 :** ADVERTISING
> ²**ad** *n* (1947) : ADVANTAGE 4

5. *Ad* means advertisement.

6. It comes from the first two letters of the word.

B. Use an unabridged dictionary in your college library to find the definitions
and origins of the following words.

Achilles heel

7. Definition: a vulnerable point

8. Origin: Achilles, the giant Greek warrior who had a weak spot only at his
heel.

maudlin

9. Definition: overly sentimental

10. Origin: The practice of depicting Mary Magdalene as a weeping sinner.

babel

11. Definition: a confusion of voices

12. Origin: The city of Babel, or Babylon, where a tower was built amid a
confusion of languages.

C. Circle the similar-sounding word that is correct in each sentence.

anecdote: story
antidote: medicine

13. The professor told an amusing (**anecdote,** antidote) about Queen Elizabeth.

access: entrance
excess: more than needed

14. The new key will give you easy (**access,** excess) to the computer room.

moral: honorable
morale: spirit

15. After the test grades were announced, the class (**moral,** **morale**) was
high.

Copyright ©1999 by Addison-Wesley Educational Publishers Inc.

ASSESS YOUR LEARNING

Review confusing questions, seek clarification, and make notes in your text to help you remember new information and vocabulary.

EXPLORE THE NET

- Evaluate the information that is available in advice columns on health, nutrition, and fitness.
- What are some of the most frequently asked questions of doctors? Will doctors reply to individual medical questions?

For additional readings and exercises, visit the Longman English Skills Web page at:

http://longman.awl.com/englishpages

For a user name and password, please see your instructor.

SELECTION 2 | *History*

THINKING BEFORE READING

Preview for content and organizational clues. Activate your schema and anticipate what you will learn.

If you were a reformer today, what would you fight for?

What roles have women had in national reform movements?

I think this will say that _____.

VOCABULARY PREVIEW

Are you familiar with these words?

inevitability	alleviate	devoutly	zeal	denounced
subordinate	acquitted	orator	emancipation	eloquent

What does the prefix *sub* mean in subordinate?
Would you rather be acquitted or convicted?

Your instructor may give a true-false vocabulary review before or after reading.

THINKING DURING READING

As you read, use the five thinking strategies of a good reader: predict, picture, relate, monitor, and correct.

AMERICA'S FIRST AGE OF REFORM

SOURCES OF THE REFORM IMPULSE

What factors gave rise to the reform impulse and why was it unleashed with such vigor in pre–Civil War America? Reformers had many different reasons for wanting to change American society. Some hoped to remedy the distresses created by social disorder, violence, and widening class divisions. Others found motivation in a religious vision of a
5   godly society on earth.

A NEW MORAL SENSIBILITY

The philosophy of the Enlightenment, with its belief in the people's innate goodness and with its rejection of the inevitability of poverty and ignorance, was another important source of the reform impulse. Those who espoused Enlightenment philosophy argued that the creation of a more favorable moral and physical environment could alleviate
10   social problems. Religion further strengthened the reform impulse. Almost all the leading reformers were devoutly religious men and women who wanted to deepen the nation's commitment to Christian principles. Two trends in religious thought, religious liberalism and evangelical revivalism, strengthened reformers' zeal. Religious liberalism was an emerging form of humanitarianism that rejected the harsh Calvinist doctrines of original
15   sin and predestination. Its preachers stressed the basic goodness of human nature and each individual's capacity to follow the example of Christ.

THE RISE OF ABOLITIONIST SENTIMENT IN THE NORTH

Initially, free blacks led the movement condemning colonization and northern discrimination against African Americans. As early as 1817, more than 3000 members of Philadelphia's black community staged a protest against colonization, at which they denounced
20   the policy as "little more merciful than death." In 1829 David Walker (1785–1830), the free black owner of a second-hand clothing store in Boston, issued the militant *Appeal to the Colored Citizens of the World.* The appeal threatened insurrections and violence if calls for the abolition of slavery and improved conditions for free blacks were ignored. The next year, some 40 black delegates from eight states held the first of a series of annual
25   conventions denouncing slavery and calling for an end to discriminatory laws in the northern states.

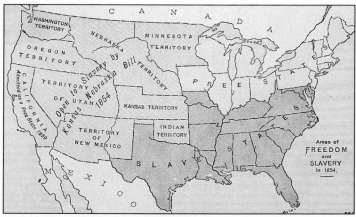

Areas of Freedom and Slavery in 1854.

Copyright ©1999 by Addison-Wesley Educational Publishers Inc.

SOJOURNER TRUTH

She was born into slavery around 1797 in New York State's Hudson River Valley, 80 miles from New York City. As a slave, she was known simply as "Isabella." But a decade and a half after escaping from bondage, she adopted a new name. As Sojourner Truth, she
30 became a legend in the struggle to abolish slavery and extend equal rights to women.

The youngest of some ten or twelve children, she grew up in a single room in a dark and damp cellar, sleeping on straw on top of loose boards. For sixteen years, from 1810 to 1826, she served as a household slave in upstate New York, and was sold five times. One owner beat her so savagely that her arms and shoulders bore scars for the rest of her
35 life. She bore a fellow slave five children, only to see at least three of her offspring sold away. In 1826, just a year before slavery was finally abolished in the state, she fled after her owner broke a promise to free her and her husband. She took refuge with a farm family that later bought her freedom.

Isabella then moved to New York City, carrying only a bag of clothing and twenty-
40 five cents. There she supported herself as a domestic servant. It was a period of intense religious excitement, and, although she lacked formal schooling, Isabella began to preach at camp meetings and on street corners. In the early 1830s, she found herself caught up in one of the major sensations of the day. Briefly, she resided with a religious sect led by Robert Matthews, a former carpenter and self-declared savior who called himself
45 Matthias, the last of the Apostles. Matthias, who had shoulder-length hair and a long beard, denounced alcohol, called ministers devils, demanded that women subordinate themselves to men, and proclaimed that marriage vows were not binding. In the fall of 1834, national attention focused on Matthias; he was arrested, tried, and ultimately acquitted of embezzlement and murder.

50 In succeeding years, Isabella became involved in many of the reform activities of the time, including temperance (the movement to curb drinking) and antislavery. For a short time, she joined a utopian community in Massachusetts that had been founded by abolitionists.

In 1843, Isabella took on the name Sojourner Truth, convinced that God had called
55 on her to wander the country and boldly speak out the truth. Her fame as a preacher,

singer, and orator for abolition and women's rights spread quickly and three incidents became the stuff of legend. During the late 1840s, when the black abolitionist Frederick Douglass expressed doubt about the possibility of ending slavery peacefully, she replied forcefully: "Frederick, is God dead?" Several years later, in a speech before a woman's
60   rights convention in Akron, Ohio, in 1851, she demanded that Americans recognize that impoverished African-American women were women too, reportedly saying: "I could work as much and eat as much as a man—when I could get it—and bear de lash as well! And ain't I a woman?" And in 1858, when a hostile audience insisted that the six-foot tall orator spoke too powerfully to be a woman, she reportedly bared her breasts before
65   them.

During the Civil War, she took an active role promoting the Union cause, collecting food and supplies for black troops and struggling to make emancipation a war aim. When the war was over, she traveled across the North, collecting signatures on petitions calling on Congress to set aside western land for former slaves. At her death in 1883, she
70   could rightly be remembered as one of the nation's most eloquent opponents of discrimination in all forms.

The decades before the Civil War saw the birth of the American reform tradition. Reformers launched unprecedented campaigns to educate the deaf and the blind, rehabilitate criminals, extend equal rights to women, and abolish slavery. Our modern sys-
75   tems of free public schools, prisons, and hospitals for the infirm and the mentally ill are all legacies of this first generation of American reform.

(1,110 words)

—*America and Its People* by James Martin et al.

THINKING AFTER READING

RECALL: Self-test your understanding. Your instructor may choose to give you a true-false review.

REACT: Why should Sojourner Truth join a religious cult led by Matthias?

_____

REFLECT: Why are the new philosophies important in a discussion of Sojourner

Truth? _____

 THINK CRITICALLY: According to the author, the legend of Sojourner Truth evolved from three incidents. What did each incident say about the character and beliefs of the woman? Write your answer on a separate sheet of paper.

DETAILS AND ORGANIZATIONAL PATTERNS

1. What is the purpose of the first paragraph? <u>To introduce larger reform issues of which Sojourner Truth was a part.</u>

2. What is the organizational pattern of the section entitled *A New Moral Sensibility?* <u>Cause and effect</u>

3. What is the organizational pattern of the section entitled *Sojourner Truth?* <u>Time order</u>

4. What is the purpose of the last paragraph? <u>To summarize accomplishments of the reformers.</u>

Copyright ©1999 by Addison-Wesley Educational Publishers Inc.

Mark the following as major (M) or (m) details in support of the author's main point.

___M___ 5. The philosophy of the Enlightenment rejected the inevitability of poverty and ignorance.

___m___ 6. Sojourner Truth was born in the Hudson River Valley in New York.

___M___ 7. Sojourner Truth became a legend in the fight for the abolition of slavery and equal rights for women.

___m___ 8. Sojourner Truth was one of ten or twelve children.

Name _____

Date _____

COMPREHENSION QUESTIONS

Answer the following with *a*, *b*, *c*, or *d*, or fill in the blank. In order to help you analyze your strengths and weaknesses, the question types are indicated.

Main Idea ___a___ 1. The best statement of the main idea of the selection is:

    a. a new moral sense and religious trend led the way for the work of reformers like Sojourner Truth.
    b. Sojourner Truth promoted the Union cause during the Civil War.
    c. abolitionist sentiment began in the North and spread to the South.
    d. the Civil War changed society.

Inference ___b___ 2. It can be concluded that Calvinist doctrines

    a. stressed the basic goodness of human nature.
    b. were not easily forgiving and optimistic about human nature.
    c. were evangelical.
    d. say that everyone can be as good as Christ.

Detail ___d___ 3. The chronological order for the following important events in the reform movement against slavery and discriminatory laws is

    a. Truth's escape, Philadelphia protest, Walker's appeal, series of Conventions.
    b. Philadelphia protest, Walker's appeal, series of Conventions, Truth's escape.
    c. series of Conventions, Philadelphia protest, Truth's escape, Walker's appeal.
    d. Philadelphia protest, Walker's appeal, Truth's escape, series of Conventions.

Inference ___b___ 4. It can be concluded that Sojourner Truth

    a. was freed during emancipation.
    b. was deceived by her owner.
    c. escaped immediately after a beating.
    d. took her five children with her when she escaped.

Inference 5. Isabella probably changed her name to Sojourner Truth because she felt it symbolically described her mission of traveling to speak the truth.

Detail ___d___ 6. The author suggests that Matthias was all of the following *except*

    a. an accused murderer.
    b. a religious fanatic.
    c. narrow minded toward women.
    d. founder of a mainstream religion.

Inference ___c___ 7. The author includes the three incidents that created the legend of Sojourner Truth in order to show

    a. examples of the Calvinist doctrine.
    b. opposition to Frederick Douglass.
    c. her strength and evangelical zeal.
    d. her resentment and intolerance of men.

Copyright ©1999 by Addison-Wesley Educational Publishers Inc.

Answer the following with *T* (true), *F* (false), or *CT* (can't tell).

Detail   __F__   8. A belief of the Enlightenment was that some people in society are meant to be rich, and thus, others should be poor.

Detail   __F__   9. David Walker issued his militant appeal as a result of an annual convention of 40 black delegates.

Inference   __T__ 10. The legend of Sojourner Truth suggests that her beliefs about women were not the same as those of Matthias.

VOCABULARY

Answer the following with *a, b, c,* or *d* for the word or phrase that best defines the boldface word as used in the selection. The number in parentheses indicates the line of the passage in which the word is located.

__a__   1. "**inevitability** of poverty" (7)

     a. unavoidable nature
     b. extinction
     c. wastefulness
     d. sorrow

__b__   2. "**alleviate** social problems" (9–10)

     a. ignore
     b. relieve
     c. restrain
     d. finance

__c__   3. "**devoutly** religious men and women" (11)

     a. disagreeably
     b. slightly
     c. sincerely
     d. distractingly

__a__   4. "strengthened reformers' **zeal**" (13)

     a. enthusiasm
     b. need
     c. anger
     d. hatred

__d__   5. "**denounced** the policy" (19–20)

     a. renamed
     b. warned
     c. predicted
     d. condemned

__d__   6. "**subordinate** themselves" (46–47)

     a. associate
     b. connect
     c. unite
     d. make secondary

__b__   7. "ultimately **acquitted**" (49–50)

     a. fined
     b. cleared
     c. accused
     d. charged

__a__   8. "**orator** for abolition" (56)

     a. speaker
     b. scholar
     c. soldier
     d. leader

__d__   9. "make **emancipation** a war aim" (67)

     a. religion
     b. voting
     c. discrimination
     d. liberation

__b__ 10. "most **eloquent** opponents" (70)

     a. loud
     b. well-spoken
     c. forceful
     d. meaningful

VOCABULARY ENRICHMENT

TRANSITIONAL WORDS

Transitions are signal words that connect parts of sentences and lead readers to anticipate a continuation or a change in the writer's thoughts. They are the same signal words that suggest patterns of organization and are categorized as follows:

Signal Addition: in addition   furthermore   moreover
Signal Examples: for example   for instance   to illustrate   such as
Signal Time: first   secondly   finally   last   afterward
Signal Comparison: similarly   likewise   in the same manner
Signal Contrast: however   but   nevertheless   whereas   on the contrary
conversely   in contrast
Signal Cause and Effect: thus   consequently   therefore   as a result

---

Choose a signal word from the boxed lists to complete the sentences.

---

however   consequently   for example   likewise   furthermore

---

1. Betty Shabazz, the widow of Malcolm X, recognized the value of a college education; and _____consequently_____, she returned to college to earn a doctorate and become a college teacher and administrator.

2. Anthropologists must be persistent. _____For example_____, Louis and Mary Leakey initially found primitive tools in Olduvai Gorge, but it was 28 years later that Mary discovered the first skull.

3. His real name was Samuel Longhorne Clemens; _____however_____, millions know him as Mark Twain.

4. Plant hormones that regulate growth include auxins and gibberellins. _____Likewise_____, humans have important growth hormones.

5. People enjoy eating steaks rare. _____Furthermore_____, some people use raw steak to cover an open wound as did the ancient Egyptians.

---

nevertheless   therefore   in this case   similarly   moreover

---

6. Some vitamins act as antioxidants, which means they neutralize free radicals and _____therefore_____ reduce the risk of cancer.

7. Despite the benefits of antioxidants, new research _____nevertheless_____ shows a danger because some minerals in multivitamins cause vitamin C to be released as a free radical.

8. More research on vitamins should be done. _____Moreover_____, doctors should be cautious in recommending vitamins that may not be needed.

9. At least five people were dead from botulism. _____In this case_____, the poison could be traced to a swollen can of food that should have been discarded.

10. Hornwort is a bryophyta. _____Similarly_____, liverwort is also a bryophyta.

11. A cut in the skin breaks the protective covering around the body and _____for this reason_____ can be dangerous.

Copyright ©1999 by Addison-Wesley Educational Publishers Inc.

> on the contrary   for this reason   secondly   as an illustration
> by the same token

12. To give CPR, first lift the neck and tilt the chin upward to open the airway. _____Secondly_____, check for breathing by holding your ear to the victim's mouth.

13. Dogs can be conditioned to respond to smell. __By the same token__, humans will sometimes salivate when smelling cookies baking.

14. Abnormal pituitary secretions can cause sudden increases in hormone production. Acromegaly, __as an illustration__, is a condition known as dwarfism.

15. Plants store glucose in starch granules. Animals, __on the contrary__, store glucose in glycogen molecules.

ASSESS YOUR LEARNING

Review confusing questions, seek clarification, and make notes in your text to help you remember new information and vocabulary.

EXPLORE THE NET

- What additional information can you find on Sojourner Truth's speeches?
- Describe the writings of Frederick Douglass.

For additional readings and exercises, visit the Longman English Skills Web page at:

http://longman.awl.com/englishpages

For a user name and password, please see your instructor.

SELECTION 3   *Psychology*

THINKING BEFORE READING

Preview for content and organizational clues. Activate your schema and anticipate what you will learn.

Do fraternity and sorority members engage in group activities that they would not participate in as individuals?

Did German citizens know about Nazi death camps?

What happened at Jonestown?

I think this will say that _____.

VOCABULARY PREVIEW

Are you familiar with these words?

underlings	adjacent	ominous	legitimate	anguish
vividly	communal	incomprehensible	mock	solitary

What is the root of *communal*?
Is breaking a mirror considered an ominous sign?
What is real about a mock trial?

Your instructor may choose to give a true-false vocabulary review before or after reading.

THINKING DURING READING

As you read, use the five thinking strategies of a good reader: predict, picture, relate, monitor, and correct.

OBEDIENCE

Although it's possible to get a group of high school students to conform to Nazi-like values and beliefs, it's still a long way from there to the death camps and the murder of millions of people. Or is it? During the Nuremberg trials, in which the Nazi war criminals were brought to account, one phrase was heard so often that it has come to be associ-
5   ated with the German underlings even by people who are not old enough to remember World War II. The phrase is, ''I was just following orders.'' As the court records show, this excuse was not well-received. The lowest-ranking officers, it was conceded, might possibly use such an excuse. But certainly the higher-ranking officers had a choice.

THE MILGRAM EXPERIMENT

In 1961 social psychologist Stanley Milgram investigated **obedience** in a study that is
10   now considered a classic. Milgram began by using students from Yale University as sub-

jects and later expanded his research to include a cross section of people of different ages, occupations, and educational levels.

15   Two subjects were ushered into an experimental room and were told that they were part of an investigation to test the effects of punishment, in the form of an electric shock, on memory. An experimenter, dressed in a white lab coat, would oversee the experiment. The subjects would draw lots to find out who would be the "learner" and who would be the "teacher." Unknown to the real subject, the other subject, "Mr. Wallace," a gentle-looking, friendly 50-year-old man, was really an actor working for Milgram. The lots were rigged so that the real subject would be assigned the role of teacher.

20   The teacher was given a sample shock of 45 volts to find out what it would feel like— it stung. The learner, Mr. Wallace, was then strapped into the electric chair as the subject chosen to be the teacher watched. The teacher-subject was then taken into an adjacent room and put in front of an array of switches ranging from "Slight shock, 15 volts," to "Danger: severe shock, 450 volts." The learner was instructed to repeat a list of words.
25   Every time he made an error, the teacher was to administer a shock, starting with the lowest level and gradually increasing. The actor playing the role of learner had been given a script to follow for each voltage level, since the teacher would be able to hear him from the next room. As the shock level rose, the learner would begin to protest. The stronger the shock, the louder he was to protest. At 75 volts he would moan; at 150 volts
30   he would demand to be released from the chair. At 180 volts he would yell that he could no longer stand the pain. At 300 volts he would protest that he had a heart condition and begin to scream. If the teacher complained at any time, the experimenter would say, "Teacher, you have no other choice; you must go on!" (Milgram, 1963, p. 374). After the 300-volt level, it was planned that there would be an ominous silence from the
35   learner's room, as though he were unconscious or even dead. Unknown to the teacher, the learner received no real shocks.

Milgram's aim was to find out how much pressure to obey would be created by the experimenter in the lab coat when he said, "Teacher, you have no other choice; you must go on!" How far would subjects go under these circumstances? Before conducting
40   the experiment, Milgram interviewed 40 psychiatrists, describing the procedure you have just read. He asked them to estimate the behavior of most subjects. The psychiatrists agreed that the majority would not go beyond 150 volts, and that perhaps only one in a thousand, those who were very deviant or sadistic, would go all the way to 450 volts. How far would you have gone?

45   To everyone's horror, when the experiment was conducted, 62 percent of the teacher-subjects went all the way to 450 volts! None of them seemed to enjoy it. For example, after delivering 180 volts, one subject said,

He can't stand it! I'm not going to kill that man in there. You hear him hollering?
He's hollering. He can't stand it. What if something happens to him? . . . I mean,
50   who is going to take the responsibility if anything happens to that gentleman?

At that point the experimenter said that he would take responsibility. The subject replied, "All right," and continued delivering shocks.

Of the 38 percent of the subjects who were not willing to go to 450 volts, many went to high levels (see graph on page 171). All who refused to continue simply walked
55   out of the experiment. Not one of them tried to see how Mr. Wallace was. Interestingly, the personality tests that were administered to the subjects failed to reveal any differences between the subjects who obeyed and those who refused.

Variables Influencing Obedience. Social psychologists have identified at least three variables in this experiment that may help to explain the high rate of obedience. First, a
60   legitimate authority, the experimenter, was present and was willing to take responsibility. Second, the victim was in another room, and this distance may have lessened the teacher's stress by eliminating the need to see the learner's anguish. Third, the teacher-subject accepted the subordinate role, applying all the rules the subject had ever learned

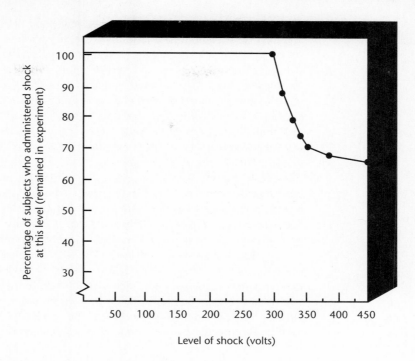

Percentage of subjects who administered shock at this level (remained in experiment)

Level of shock (volts)

about being a good follower. Perhaps, as social psychologist Philip Zimbardo has sug-
65   gested, such follower training in public situations begins on the first day of school, when
the teacher says, "Stay in your seat no matter what."

It should be stressed that obedience does not happen only under these select conditions. Even if the learner is directly in front of the teacher-subject, the latter may still obey.
In a variation of the Milgram experiment, the teacher-subject actually had to force the
70   learner's hand down onto an electric shock plate. Obedience under these conditions,
although less frequent, was still much higher than anyone had predicted.

By today's standards, the Milgram experiment may not be considered ethical
because of the stress placed on the teacher-subject. Some of the subjects were shaking
and weeping as they pressed the 450-volt lever. How do you debrief such a subject after
75   the experiment? Do you say, "Don't feel bad—the learner is only an actor. I just wanted
to see if you would electrocute a stranger just because I told you to." No serious after-
effects were observed among the teacher-subjects, but even after a careful debriefing
many felt that they had discovered an evil side of themselves. Some of the volunteer
experimenters who helped Milgram to conduct the research were called to account by
80   university authorities, who asked why they had continued the experiment when they
could plainly see that the teacher-subjects were under stress. The frightening answer:
"Milgram told us to!"

The Milgram findings are not specific to the United States. Similar results have been
obtained in many other countries, including Germany and Australia. The same results
85   even were found among three groups of children, aged 7, 11, and 15 years, who were
ordered to shock an innocent victim.

The Jonestown tragedy vividly demonstrated the potential consequences of conformity and blind obedience to authority. In 1978 almost 900 members of the California-
based People's Temple died in a ritual mass suicide in Jonestown, Guyana, at the com-
90   mand of their leader, Reverend Jim Jones. Jones believed that his communal group was
under attack from the outside by forces bent on destroying it. (This outside force was, in
reality, nothing more than one congressman, Leo Ryan, who had come to Guyana to
check on people from his district and who was leaving there with 14 of them.) After
Jones's men had murdered the congressman and several of his party, Jones ordered his
95   followers to kill themselves by taking cyanide. The mass death shocked the world and left
people wondering how such a thing could have happened.

Copyright ©1999 by Addison-Wesley Educational Publishers Inc.

Although a few members disobeyed Jones and ran into the jungle, most complied. The final tape recordings of Jonestown are horrifying to hear. The people went to their self-administered deaths crying and screaming for help. Most were not happy to die,
100   which makes their deaths even more incomprehensible.

Now that you have learned something about conformity and obedience, you may begin to appreciate the powerful influences that were in effect that day in Jonestown. The people in Jones's community were followers; they had learned through much practice and training to obey their leader, even carrying out mock suicides. Like Milgram's
105   teacher-subjects, many of them cried and were under great stress at the end, but they obeyed. Social comparison certainly had an effect. We would predict that a person surrounded by hundreds of other people committing suicide would be much more likely to do the same than would a solitary person ordered to kill himself. By their actions, the people in Jonestown were also complying with reference group norms. Jones's followers
110   had no other group to which they could refer. They were not only completely dependent on the group, but also isolated in a dense South American jungle, far from their homes.

Would you have been one of the few who escaped? It's easy to feel invulnerable to social forces when they aren't directly working on you. Most people believe that, in all except extreme circumstances, such as a gun held to their head, their own internal values
115   and belief systems would override external social forces. But social psychologists are finding that this is in fact a rarity. More often the opposite is true; the social forces turn out to be stronger than our personal values, beliefs, and feelings.

(1,603 words)

—*Psychology* by John Dworetzky

THINKING AFTER READING

RECALL: Self-test your understanding. Your instructor may choose to give you a true-false review.

REACT: Do you consider the Milgram experiment ethical? _____

REFLECT: How do colleges protect the rights of students who volunteer to participate in experiments? _____

 THINK CRITICALLY: Explain how the research studies prove that the Nazi officers' behavior in the death camps was not a fluke. Write your answer on a separate sheet of paper.

DETAILS AND PATTERNS OF ORGANIZATION

1. What is the overall pattern of organization for the logic and thought of this selection? <u>Cause and effect</u>

Mark the following as major (M) or minor (m) details in support of the author's main point.

__m__   2. A 450-volt lever can inflict pain.

__m__   3. Milgram's research began by using students from Yale University.

__M__   4. Subjects were willing to obey when a legitimate authority took responsibility.

__m__   5. Jonestown was located in the dense South American jungle.

Name _____

Date_____

COMPREHENSION QUESTIONS

Answer the following with *a, b, c,* or *d,* or fill in the blank. In order to help you analyze your strengths and weaknesses, the question types are indicated.

Main Idea ___b___ 1. The best statement of the main idea of this selection is:

    a. Research shows that many variables influence obedience.
    b. Research shows a high rate of obedience to commands that result in harm to others.
    c. Research indicates that Nazi officers were not responsible for their action in the death camps.
    d. Milgram's research shows that people are basically evil.

Detail ___a___ 2. Milgram's subjects were told that the experiment was investigating

    a. punishment.
    b. obedience.
    c. electric shock.
    d. memory.

Detail ___b___ 3. The forty psychiatrists who were asked to predict the results of the experiment

    a. overestimated the power of obedience.
    b. underestimated the power of obedience.
    c. gave answers that closely resembled the actual findings.
    d. portrayed a more negative view of human nature than the research itself.

Inference _____ 4. The major objection of the subject who said, "He can't stand it!" seems to have been _over who would take responsibility if anything_ _happened to the victim._

Inference ___a___ 5. Today the Milgram experiment might be considered inhumane or unethical because

    a. the subjects were upset by their own actions.
    b. the learner could have been injured.
    c. experimenters cannot make subjects perform.
    d. it investigates the dark side of human nature.

Inference _____ 6. The answer, "Milgram told us to!" shows that the volunteer experimenters _responded obediently to an authority despite their_ _understanding of conformity._

Detail ___d___ 7. In the Jonestown tragedy, the religious followers

    a. killed each other.
    b. fought Jim Jones.
    c. were tricked by Leo Ryan.
    d. poisoned themselves.

Copyright © 1999 by Addison-Wesley Educational Publishers Inc.

Answer the following with *T* (true) or *F* (false).

Inference _____T_____ 8. Although two subjects entered the experimental room, only one was an actual subject.

Detail _____T_____ 9. In experiments similar to Milgram's, the level of obedience drops when the teacher is in close physical contact with the learner.

Inference _____F_____10. The community in Jonestown was a satanic cult that believed in evil deeds.

VOCABULARY

Answer the following with *a, b, c,* or *d* for the word or phrase that best defines the boldface word as used in the selection. The number in parentheses indicates the line of the passage in which the word is located.

__b__1. "German **underlings**" (5)

    a. children
    b. persons of lesser rank
    c. enemies
    d. citizens

__a__ 2. "into an **adjacent** room" (22–23)

    a. adjoining
    b. convenient
    c. soundproof
    d. comfortable

__d__ 3. "an **ominous** silence" (34)

    a. oppressive
    b. sudden
    c. painful
    d. foreboding

__b__ 4. "a **legitimate** authority" (59–60)

    a. university
    b. lawful
    c. convincing
    d. diplomatic

__c__ 5. "the learner's **anguish**" (62)

    a. desire
    b. objections
    c. distress
    d. protests

__a__ 6. "**vividly** demonstrated" (87)

    a. clearly
    b. hopelessly
    c. sadly
    d. carefully

__c__ 7. "his **communal** group" (90)

    a. religious
    b. hard-working
    c. collective
    d. fanatic

__b__ 8. "even more **incomprehensible**" (100)

    a. tragic
    b. unintelligible
    c. cruel
    d. ruthless

__d__ 9. "**mock** suicides" (104)

    a. multiple
    b. recent
    c. illegal
    d. fake

__c__10. "a **solitary** person" (108)

    a. simple
    b. brave
    c. single
    d. trusting

VOCABULARY ENRICHMENT

A. Context Clues

Select the word from the list below that completes the sentences.

| underlings | adjacent | ominous | legitimate | anguish |
| vividly | communal | incomprehensible | mock | solitary |

It was Maria's first day in her new job. She entered the room and walked beyond the large desk. In her own mind she believed that she was the _____solitary_____ person who could turn this company from debt to profit. On her new desk was an __incomprehensible__, poorly written letter from the manager before her. He had made mistakes. Rather than treat the employees like associates, he had treated them like mere _____underlings_____ who were there to serve him. His antics and temper tantrums had been _____vividly_____ described to her on the day that she interviewed for the job. The secretary, who was located in the _____adjacent_____ office, said his harsh criticism caused her great _____anguish_____ and unhappiness. He had even refused to use the _____communal_____ coffee pot, insisting instead on having his own. She recognized this refusal as an _____ominous_____ sign of events to come. Because of his personality, most of the employees did not respect him. After discovering that he was the son of the president's new spouse, the sales staff would _____mock_____ his credentials, saying he had no _____legitimate_____ right to be there.

B. Thesaurus

Use a thesaurus, either the computer or book version, to find four alternative words for each of the following:

1. indication mark, display, evidence, exhibit

2. habit custom, practice, tendency, addiction

3. beginning origin, start, dawn, inauguration

4. agreement accord, consensus, harmony, unanimity

5. respect admiration, consideration, esteem, regard

ASSESS YOUR LEARNING

Review confusing questions, seek clarification, and make notes in your text to help you remember new information and vocabulary.

EXPLORE THE NET

- What organizations are particularly concerned with ethics in research?
- What are the ethical guidelines for research using human subjects?

For additional readings and exercises, visit the Longman English Skills Web page at:

http://longman.awl.com/englishpages

For a user name and password, please see your instructor.

Copyright ©1999 by Addison-Wesley Educational Publishers Inc.

Connect

Read the following reaction to the Milgram experiment. How would you have felt if you had taken part in the experiment? In most colleges, professors conduct experiments on human research subjects. What are the rules in your college on such experiments? How are students protected? Collaborate in groups to find out about the procedures and policies regarding human research subjects. Ask group members to report those policies to the class. If possible, find out and report on current research being conducted at your college. Describe to the class any research project in which you have participated and evaluate its effects on you.

CRITICISMS OF THE MILGRAM EXPERIMENT

In reading about Milgram's research, it should have occurred to you that putting subjects in such a stressful experience might be considered morally and ethically objectionable. Milgram himself was quite concerned with the welfare of his subjects. He took great care to debrief them fully after each session had been completed. He told them that they had not really administered any shocks and explained why deception had been necessary.

Milgram reported that the people in his studies were not upset over having been deceived and that their principal reaction was one of relief when they learned that no electric shock had in fact been used. Milgram also indicated that a follow-up study performed a year later with some of the same subjects showed that no long-term adverse effects had been created by his procedure.

Despite these precautions, Milgram was severely criticized for placing people in such an extremely stressful situation. Indeed, one of the effects of this research was to establish in the scientific community a higher level of awareness of the need to protect the well-being of human research subjects. It is probably safe to say that because of the nature of Milgram's experience, no one would be allowed to perform such experiments today.

—*Essentials of Psychology* by Josh Gerow

PERSONAL FEEDBACK 2

Name_____

1. Approximately how much time do you spend each day studying for this class? _____

2. Where do you typically study? _____
_____

3. How do you manage telephone calls during your scheduled study time?
_____

4. Describe a time this week that you have procrastinated. _____
_____

5. What were the consequences of your procrastination? _____
_____

Textbook Learning

◆ *What is annotating?*
◆ *What is the Cornell Method of notetaking?*
◆ *How do you write a summary?*
◆ *How can you use outlining?*
◆ *What is mapping?*

Copyright ©1999 by Addison-Wesley Educational Publishers Inc.

Expect Knowledge to Exist ◆◆◆◆◆◆◆◆◆◆

Watching the words go by for an hour or two while reading is not good enough. Expect to know something after you have read a textbook assignment. Use strategies to select key elements and to prepare for remembering. In the previous chapter, two such strategies, marking the text and taking notes, were introduced. In this chapter our discussion of these strategies will continue and summarizing, outlining, and mapping will be introduced.

The process of reading, marking, and organizing textbook information takes time. Many students ask, "How much do I need to do?" The answer to that is, "Typically, the more you do, the more you learn." In other words, it is better to read the text than not to read the text. What's more, it is better to read and mark, than only to read. Finally, it is better to read, mark, and take notes in some form (summary, Cornell notes, outline, or map), than just to read and mark. Your choices depend on the amount of time that you can dedicate to learning. "Time on task" is a critical element in college success.

Annotating ◆◆◆◆◆◆◆◆◆◆◆

Annotating is a system of marking that includes underlining and highlighting. It is the first and basic step for all of the other organizing strategies.

When to Annotate

Annotating should be done after a complete thought is presented. When you mark as you read, there is a tendency to mark too much, and overmarking will waste valuable review time. Wait until a complete thought has been presented to separate the most important ideas from the least important ones. Such a thought unit may be as short as one paragraph or as long as an entire section under a subheading.

How to Annotate

The word *annotate* is used to suggest a notation system for selecting important ideas that goes beyond straight lines and includes numbers, circles, stars, and written comments. With practice, students tend to form their own notation systems, which may include a variation of the following examples:

══════	Main idea (or write the topic in the margin beside the paragraph)	{ }	Section of material to reread for review
─────	Supporting material	(1), (2), (3)	Numbering of important details under a major issue
✭	Major trend or possible essay exam question	?	Didn't understand and must seek advice
✓	Important smaller point to know for multiple-choice item	Topic, Def. or Ex.	Notes in the margin
⬭	Word that you must be able to define	How does it operate?	Questions in the margin
▭	A key issue to remember	⤳	Indicating relationships

Unless you are reading a library book, always use some form of annotation for study reading. For example, hopefully you have been annotating throughout this text as you have been reading. If your instructor were to say at this moment, "Take 15 minutes to review what we have covered in this text for a quiz," would you be ready to study? Could you quickly review your annotations? Remember, it is a waste of time to read for the purpose of learning and not to annotate.

EXAMPLE   The following passage represents information typically found in college psychology books. Notice a mixture of two organizational patterns: (1) definitions with examples and (2) listing. Do you recognize signals that predict those patterns? Do the reader's markings help organize the material for later study?

Personality Types

According to Jung, Plato and Aristotle represent two fundamentally different tendencies in the human personality. Plato, concerned with the inner world, was an introvert and Aristotle, focusing his energies on the outer world, was an extrovert.

Introverts

Extroverts

[1] (**Introverts**) turn inward, seek isolation, and tend to withdraw from social engagements. They are reflective and introspective, absorbed with self-searching thoughts. They are self-critical and self-controlled, giving an outwardly cold appearance. They prefer to change the world rather than to adjust to it. [2] (**Extroverts**) seek social contacts and are outgoing and accommodating. They appear friendly and outspoken and make friends easily. They are tolerant of others but relatively insensitive to the motivations and moods of their friends. They prefer to experience things rather than to read about them. Can you apply one of Jung's two personality types to yourself? How do you appear to others, as an introvert or an extrovert?

Most people are a mixture of introvert and extrovert, being neither wholly one nor the other. This is one of the problems of classifying people into types. Unlike rocks, few people can be easily sorted into boxes according to type. We are just not that simple; each of us has the potential for behaving in different ways in different circumstances.

—*Introductory Psychology* by Morris Holland

The learner's task is not just to read but also to earmark relevant ideas for future study. To be an efficient learner, do not waste time.

Read the following passage and use the suggested notations to organize the material and mark key ideas for later study.

Copyright ©1999 by Addison-Wesley Educational Publishers Inc.

FEEDBACK

Throughout the listening process, listeners give the speaker (feedback)—the messages we send back to the speaker concerning our reactions to what is said. On the basis of this feedback, the speaker may adjust the message's content or form.

Ex.　What is and is not appropriate feedback will depend in large part on the culture you are in. For example, a friend of mine gave a lecture in Beijing. No one asked any questions, either during or after the lecture. My friend was sure the lack of feedback meant that what she said was unclear or irrelevant. Later she learned that in China, it is considered impolite to ask questions; it would imply that the speaker was not clear and would therefore be insulting.

The following suggestions for giving and receiving feedback will prove useful in most contexts. Like all suggestions offered, these should be modified on the basis of the specific culture and its norms and rules.

GIVING FEEDBACK EFFECTIVELY

Effective feedback is immediate, honest, and appropriate. The most effective feedback is *immediate.*[1] Ideally, feedback is sent immediately after you receive the message. It loses its effectiveness with time. The longer you wait to praise or punish, for example, the less effect it will have.

Feedback should be an *honest* reaction[2] to communication. But feedback should not be merely a series of messages to build up the speaker's ego. Feedback about your understanding of and agreement with the message should be honest. Do not be afraid to admit you did not understand a message. Nor should you hesitate to disagree.

Feedback should be *appropriate*[3] to the communication situation. Remember, however, that appropriateness is a learned concept. So, what is appropriate in your culture is

Ex.　not necessarily appropriate in another. In the United States, for example, it is considered appropriate to signal interest in a public speaker by maintaining focused eye contact with the speaker throughout the speech. In Japan, that same interest is signaled by closing one's eyes to aid concentration.

Further, distinguish between feedback to the *message* and feedback to the *speaker.* Make clear when disagreeing with speakers, for example, that you are disagreeing with what they say, not rejecting them as people.

—*Essentials of Human Communication* by Joseph DeVito

Check your annotations with a "study buddy." Could you study from the annotations without rereading the passage?

Notetaking ◆◆◆◆◆◆◆◆◆◆◆

Notetaking involves using your own words and a separate notebook to condense the key ideas that you have marked in your text while annotating. Simply jotting these ideas down on paper is notetaking. In more elaborate systems, important ideas are written in sentences, and then notes are inserted in the left margin for a quick topic reference.

When to Take Notes

Notetaking is useful for textbook study and class lectures. The marginal topic notes placed on the left are particularly helpful in organizing the study of a large body of material for a midterm or final exam.

How to Take Notes

The Cornell Method, one of the most popular systems of notetaking, includes the following steps:

1. Draw a line down your paper two and one-half inches from the left edge to create a margin for noting key words and a wider area on the right for sentence summaries.
2. After reading a section, review your thoughts and write sentence summaries on the right side of your paper. Include the main ideas and key supporting details. Be brief and concise.
3. Review your summary sentences and underline key words. Write these key words in the column on the left side of your paper. These words can be used to stimulate your memory of the material for later study.

Abbreviations. Use short cuts. Develop your own system of abbreviations for notetaking, both for textbook and lecture notes. Some students mix shorthand symbols with their regular writing. Brainstorm with a "study buddy" and list abbreviations and symbols that can help you save time.

EXAMPLE The following is an example of how the Cornell Method might be used to organize notes on the passage about Jung's theories for future study.

	Jung's Personality Types
2 Types	Jung believed in two types of personality and most people are a <u>mixture of</u> each.
Introverts	<u>Introverts</u> turn inward, seek isolation, are reflective, self-critical, and want to change the outside world.
Ex.	<u>Plato</u> is an example.
Extroverts	<u>Extroverts</u> are outgoing, friendly, tolerant of others, and prefer to experience things rather than to read about them.
Ex.	<u>Aristotle</u> is an example.

Copyright ©1999 by Addison-Wesley Educational Publishers Inc.

EXERCISE 2 Read the following passage, and then use the Cornell Method to take notes for future use. Write your notes in the box that follows the selection.

THE USE OF POWER IS SEEN IN OUR VERBAL AND NONVERBAL BEHAVIORS

Demanding that someone do something, shouting at a subordinate, or shaking your fist at someone are rather obvious expressions of power. Yet there are also a number of more subtle ways that power is expressed in our interactions with others. In a review of the literature, Nancy Henley (1977) reports several ways that this occurs.

Posture. People who perceive themselves as equal in power and status tend to assume postures when talking. If equal, both may sit in a relaxed position or stand together while casually discussing something. When there are power differences, the person with less power often has to stand, or if sitting, is in a much less relaxed posture.

Height. Judges, police desk sergeants, and the rabbi, priest, or minister all tell us what to do from several feet over our heads. In business organizations, the heads of the organization are typically on an upper floor while subordinates occupy the lower floors.

Space. Individuals with more power tend to occupy more space. Key managers in an organization have more office space than do their subordinates. The rich and powerful typically have bigger homes and yards than do the poor and less powerful. In most homes, adults tend to have larger territory claims than do children. Not only do more powerful people have more space, but they are generally freer to enter the space of those with less power. A guard can enter the cell of a prisoner anytime. A boss can typically enter the office of a subordinate unannounced, but the opposite is not generally true.

Time. The use of time reflects the amount of power people have. People with less power are often asked to wait to see those with more. Patients wait to see a doctor and subordinates must wait to see their boss. Poorer and less powerful individuals in fact spend more time waiting than do the more powerful. Their lives are filled with waiting in hospital emergency rooms and clinics, for unemployment or welfare benefits, for food stamps, in courts, and for other services.

People with less power are often treated as if their time is unimportant. "They can afford to wait" is a comment sometimes heard. Yet people with more power treat their time as a precious commodity. They account for every minute and may even take time management seminars to see how to use it better. They may make those with less power feel guilty for taking some of it. Students, for example, are sometimes apologetic because they took some of a faculty member's time outside of class. I have noticed that the faculty members involved send verbal and nonverbal messages that suggest they are busy and do not have much time to be bothered. It is also not unusual for people with more power to sell their time as consultants. Expertise is an important source of influence, and people are willing to pay for it.

Style of Speech. People who are dominant and have more power are much more confident and precise when they speak. Individuals with less power tend to have more hesitancy and self-doubt in their expressions. They use many more qualifying phrases and tend to put themselves down somewhat. They might say, "I may not know anything about this and probably should not say anything, but I think the solution may be . . ."

Interruptions. Individuals with more power and status typically interrupt those with less power more often. Teachers interrupt students more often, and within an academic setting, instructors with a higher academic rank interrupt those with a lower academic rank. In male-female conversations, Henley argues that men tend to have more power. This gets reflected in the pattern of interruptions. Some studies have shown that as many as 96 percent of the interruptions and 100 percent of the overlaps in conversation were made by men.

Touch. People with more power and status tend to touch those with less more often. In conversations, bosses touch their subordinates more, physicians touch their patients, and men touch women more than they do other men.

—*Practical Applications of Psychology* by Anthony Grasha

	Subtle Ways Power Expressed
Posture	If unequal, person with less power may stand.
Height	Executives on upper floors, rather than lower.
Space	More power equals more space and more freedom to enter space of lessers.
Time	People with less power are asked to wait.
Speech	Dominant people are confident and precise in speaking.
Interruptions	People with power interrupt those with less power more often.
Touch	People with power touch those with less power more often.

Copyright ©1999 by Addison-Wesley Educational Publishers Inc.

Summarizing ◆◆◆◆◆◆◆◆◆◆

The summary is a short, concise method of stating the main idea and significant supporting details of the material. It can be thought of as the key words and phrases linked by complete sentences and presented in paragraphs.

When to Summarize

Professors frequently ask students to take notes in the form of a summary on assigned readings. Such readings, which are usually in the library, might include chapters from related texts, research articles from periodicals, or scholarly essays from books or periodicals. The preparation of a written summary can demonstrate to the professor that the student has a clear understanding of the main points of the assignment. For the student, a summary provides reference notes for later study, and can be used in compiling information from several sources for a long research paper.

How to Summarize

When you write a summary, put the ideas into your own words. If you need to quote an author directly, place quotation marks around the *exact* wording to avoid plagiarism. Keep in mind the purpose of your summary. The way in which the information will be used will influence the number of details you include. Generally, be brief but make your point. A summary should never be as long as the piece that it is summarizing!

◆◆ **READER'S TIP**

HOW TO WRITE A SUMMARY

1. Remember your purpose; be brief.
2. Underline the key ideas in the text that you want to include.
3. Begin your summary with a general statement that unites the key ideas.
4. Include the key ideas that support the general statement. Link these ideas in sentences, and show their significance.
5. Delete irrelevant or trivial information.
6. Delete redundant information.
7. Use your own words to show your understanding of the material. Don't try to camouflage a lack of comprehension.

EXAMPLE

The following is a summary of the passage on Jung's personality types. Notice that the first sentence states the main ideas and the others concisely state the major supporting details.

> Jung believed in two types of personality and that most people are a mixture of each. Introverts turn inward, seek isolation, are reflective, self-critical, and want to change the outside world. Plato is an example.
>
> Extroverts, on the other hand, are friendly, tolerant of others, and prefer to experience things rather than to read about them. Aristotle is an example.

Annotate the following passage and then write a summary. Do not include irrelevant details in your summary. For example, the first paragraph is an anecdote that dramatizes the problems of schizophrenia, but does the information belong in the summary?

PSYCHOSIS: LOSS OF CONTACT WITH REALITY

Jess was fired from his job in October. His parents told him he could move in with them till he found a new job. Jess moved in, but he didn't do anything about getting a new job. He sat around the house all day in his pajamas, smoking and watching TV. Both his parents worked, so it took them a while to notice that something was seriously wrong. Once his father became suspicious, he stayed home to see what was happening.

Jess didn't come out of his room that day, but his father could hear him talking. "No, that would be wrong," Jess said several times. "You don't know that's true!" he shouted. "How do you expect me to help it?" he cried out. Again, "No, no. That's all wrong. That's bad." There was no one in the room with Jess, but Jess wasn't talking to himself. He thought there was a Presence in the room with him.

SCHIZOPHRENIA

Jess's parents took him to the family doctor, who sent him to a psychiatrist. He placed Jess in a hospital, in the mental wing. Jess was diagnosed as suffering from *schizophrenia.* Schizophrenia is a whole group of mental disorders—*disorders of thinking, activity, feelings, and perceptions.* It is a *psychosis,* a word that means the *person is out of touch with reality.* Psychosis is a *distortion of thinking and feeling* that puts the person out of touch.

In the hospital, Jess seemed very excited and agitated. He paced around quite a bit and yelled at people. He talked to the voices he heard more and more. In psychological testing his thinking was distorted and unrealistic. For example, when the psychiatrist said: "Here's a proverb: New brooms sweep clean. Tell me what that means, please." Jess replied: "That's the trouble, always changing things. The weak get pushed around. You can't help it. It's wrong."

Jess was showing several typical symptoms of the group of disorders known as schizophrenia. What are they?

SYMPTOMS OF SCHIZOPHRENIA

Traditionally, psychiatry put people into different *categories* of schizophrenia, depending on the symptoms of psychosis they showed. An entire classification system was worked out, and is still in use. Unfortunately, it is almost totally useless. The old divisions into types of schizophrenia are *worthless* for two reasons. First, there is very *little agreement* among psychiatrists as to what category a particular person falls into. Second, the various

Copyright ©1999 by Addison-Wesley Educational Publishers Inc.

categories *overlap* so much that research often can't find differences among them. Instead of asking: "What are the different kinds of schizophrenia?" let's ask: What kinds of thoughts or behaviors are called schizophrenic?"

—*Psychology* by David Watson

WRITTEN SUMMARY

Schizophrenia is a group of mental disorders involving thinking, activity, feelings, and perceptions. It is a psychosis that puts the person out of touch with reality. Old classification systems are not useful because there is little agreement among psychiatrists on categories and categories overlap.

EXERCISE 4   Annotate the following passage and write a summary.

ENCOURAGING CHILDREN TO SOLVE PROBLEMS CREATIVELY

Whenever the opportunity arises, encourage children to solve problems creatively.

Young children don't need to be taught how to *think* creatively. They're naturally creative. Watch kids of about two to seven years of age at play and you'll see them imagining an airplane where you see only boxes, and they'll play "school" using an imaginary blackboard and imaginary desks. Creativity and imagination come naturally. But children are soon taught to stop thinking creatively. They hear, "Now that's a silly idea" or "But that wouldn't work." Adults judge kids' ideas according to adult standards and the kids' ideas are usually flawed.

If a young boy comes up with the idea of using a laser beam to zap mosquitoes he can't know that such an idea is impractical due to the difficulty of detecting mosquitoes and accurately aiming a laser beam, not to mention the high cost of the electric bill. Yet, the underlying idea is creative (if he didn't learn it from somewhere else). When you hear children's creative ideas, you can encourage their creative thinking by saying something like, "That's a clever idea" or "I like the basic idea, but it has some disadvantages." Such comments separate the creative part from the impracticality and make it clear that creative thinking is valued. However, don't mistake this recommendation to mean that lots of praise is needed; undeserved praise undermines the value of deserved praise.

Looking back on my own experiences, I now see that I preserved my creative thinking by keeping my ideas to myself. I quickly learned that sharing a creative idea led to criticism. Fortunately I realized I didn't have to stop thinking creatively, I only had to stop revealing my creative ideas. As my understanding of the world improved, my ideas became more practical.

In addition to encouragement, kids need more opportunities to practice solving *real* problems. It might seem that homework problems provide children with lots of problem solving practice, but most school problems have already been solved countless times using well-established techniques.

—*The Creative Problem Solver's Toolbox* by Richard Fobes

WRITTEN SUMMARY

Begin by writing a general statement about encouraging creativity in children. Link the key ideas and delete irrelevant information.

Children should be encouraged to solve problems creatively. Both creativity and imagination come naturally to kids. Adults should praise children for creative ideas and be careful not to be overly critical. Children need practice solving real problems.

Outlining ◆◆◆◆◆◆◆◆◆◆◆

Outlining is a form of notetaking that gives a quick display of key issues and essential supporting details. Outlining uses indentations, numbers, and letters to show levels of importance. The outline forces you to sort out significant details and decide on levels of importance. Being able to outline shows that you understand main ideas and can distinguish between major and minor supporting details.

When to Outline

Outlining can be used to take notes on a textbook chapter or a class lecture or for brainstorming the answer for a possible essay question.

How to Outline

Letters, numbers, and indentations are used in an outline to show levels of importance. In a perfect outline, Roman numerals mark items of greatest importance and letters indicate supporting details. The greater distance from the left margin an item is listed, the less significance it is afforded. Your outline need not be "picture-perfect," but you should use indentation and some form of enumeration. Always remember that you are outlining to save time for later study and review. Don't cram all your facts on half a sheet of paper when you should use several sheets. Give yourself plenty of room to write. You want to be able to look back quickly to get a clear picture of what is important and what supports it.

When taking notes in outline form, be brief and to the point. Use phrases rather than sentences. Record the main points, including key explanatory words, but leave out the insignificant details or "fillers."

The following is the format for a "perfect" outline. Notice how the numbers, letters, and indentations show the importance of an idea.

Main Point or Topic

I. First major point

    A. Supporting detail

    B. Supporting detail

    C. Supporting detail

Copyright ©1999 by Addison-Wesley Educational Publishers Inc.

II. Second major point

    A. Supporting detail

    B. Supporting detail

        1. Minor supporting detail or example

        2. Minor supporting detail or example

III. Third major point

    A. Supporting detail

    B. Supporting detail

Remember, making a picture-perfect outline is not critical; the important thing is to distinguish between the major ideas and the supporting details. In an informal study outline, you could show the same levels of importance with indentations and bullets.

EXAMPLE The following example shows how the passage on Jung's theories (see page 179) might be outlined for future study.

> *Jung's Personality Types*
>
> I. Introverts
>
>   A. turn inward, seek isolation
>
>   B. reflective and introspective (self-searching)
>
>   C. self-critical and self-controlled
>
>   D. wish to change world rather than adjust
>
>   E. ex. Plato
>
> II. Extroverts
>
>   A. seek social contacts, outgoing
>
>   B. friendly and outspoken
>
>   C. tolerant of others
>
>   D. prefer to experience than read about
>
>   E. ex. Aristotle

EXPLANATION Notice that even though Plato and Aristotle are mentioned in the first paragraph, they fit logically as examples of each personality type. The "filler," such as the details in the last paragraph, is left out of the outline, but enough information is included so that rereading the passage won't be necessary.

EXERCISE 5

Make a study outline for the following material. Annotate first and then organize your notes into an informal outline with numbers or bullets.

THE SIX TYPES OF LOVE

EROS: BEAUTY AND SENSUALITY

1

Erotic love focuses on beauty and physical attractiveness, sometimes to the exclusion of qualities you might consider more important and more lasting. The erotic lover has an idealized image of beauty that is unattainable in reality. Consequently, the erotic lover often feels unfulfilled. In defense of eros, however, it should be noted that both male and female eros lovers have the highest levels of reward and satisfaction when compared with all other types of lovers (Morrow, Clark, & Brock 1995).

LUDUS: ENTERTAINMENT AND EXCITEMENT

2

Ludus love is seen as fun, a game to be played. To the ludic lover, love is not to be taken too seriously; emotions are to be held in check lest they get out of hand and make trouble. Passions never rise to the point at which they get out of control. A ludic lover is self-controlled and consciously aware of the need to manage love rather than to allow it to control him or her. The ludic lover is manipulative and the extent of one's ludic tendencies has been found to correlate with the use of verbal sexual coercion (Sarwer, Kalichman, Johnson, Early, et al. 1993). Ludic-oriented sexually coercive men also experience less happiness, friendship, and trust in their relationships than do noncoercive men (Kalichman, Sarwer, Johnson, & Ali 1993). Ludic lover tendencies in women are likewise related to a dissatisfaction with life (Yancey & Berglass 1991).

STORGE LOVE: PEACEFUL AND SLOW

3

Like ludus love, **storge love** lacks passion and intensity. Storgic lovers do not set out to find lovers but to establish a companion-like relationship with someone they know and with whom they can share interests and activities. Storgic love develops over a period of time rather than in one mad burst of passion. Sex in storgic relationships comes late, and when it comes it assumes no great importance. Storgic love is sometimes difficult to separate from friendship; it is often characterized by the same qualities that characterize friendship: mutual caring, compassion, respect, and concern for the other person.

PRAGMA: PRACTICAL AND TRADITIONAL

4

The **pragma lover** is practical and wants compatibility and a relationship in which important needs and desires will be satisfied. In its extreme, pragma may be seen in the person who writes down the qualities wanted in a mate and actively goes about seeking someone who matches up. The pragma lover is concerned with the social qualifications of a potential mate even more than personal qualities; family and background are extremely important to the pragma lover, who relies not so much on feelings as on logic. The pragma lover views love as a necessity—or as a useful relationship—that makes the rest of life easier. The pragma lover therefore asks such questions about a potential mate as, "Will this person earn a good living?" "Can this person cook?" and "Will this person help me advance in my career?"

MANIC LOVE: ELATION AND DEPRESSION

5

The quality of mania that separates it from other types of love is the extremes of its highs and lows, its ups and downs. The **manic lover** loves intensely and at the same time worries intensely about and fears the loss of the love. With little provocation, for example, the

Copyright ©1999 by Addison-Wesley Educational Publishers Inc.

manic lover may experience extreme jealousy. Manic love is obsessive; the manic lover has to possess the beloved completely—in all ways, at all times. In return, the manic lover wishes to be possessed, to be loved intensely. It seems almost as if the manic lover is driven to these extremes by some outside force or perhaps by some inner obsession that cannot be controlled.

AGAPE: COMPASSIONATE AND SELFLESS

6

Agape is a compassionate, egoless, self-giving love. Agape is nonrational and nondiscriminative. Agape creates value and virtue through love rather than bestowing love only on that which is valuable and virtuous. The agapic lover loves even people with whom he or she has no close ties. This lover loves the stranger on the road, and the fact that they will probably never meet again has nothing to do with it. Jesus, Buddha, and Gandhi practiced and preached this unqualified love. Agape is a spiritual love, offered without concern for personal reward or gain. The agapic lover loves without expecting that the love will be returned or reciprocated. For women, agape is the only love style positively related to their own life satisfaction (Yancy & Berglass 1991).

—*Human Communication* by Joseph DeVito

Six Types of Love

I. Eros: Beauty and Sensuality
    A. Focus: physical attractiveness
    B. Idealized and unattainable image of beauty
    C. Often unfulfilled
    D. Report highest levels of satisfied lovers

II. Ludus: Entertainment and Excitement
    A. Focus: fun, a game
    B. Emotions and passion held in control
    C. Self-controlled and manipulative
    D. Report dissatisfaction; less happiness, friendship, and trust

III. Storge: Peaceful and Slow
    A. Focus: companion relationship with shared interests
    B. Lacks passion and intensity
    C. Develops over time and sex is late
    D. Mutual caring and respect

IV. Pragma: Practical and Traditional
    A. Focus: meet needs for a good life
    B. Concern over social qualifications
    C. Family, background, and job important
    D. Relies on logic rather than feelings

V. Manic: Elation and Depression

    A. Focus: <u>has to possess the beloved completely</u>

    B. Loves, worries, and fears intensely

    C. Obsessive and driven

    D. Wishes to be possessed

VI. Agape: Compassionate and Selfless

    A. Focus: <u>self-giving love</u>

    B. Love for strangers

    C. Spiritual love offered without gain

    D. Related to female life satisfaction

Mapping ◆◆◆◆◆◆◆◆◆◆

Mapping visually condenses material to show relationships. A map is a diagram that places important topics in a central location and connects major points and supporting details in a visual display that shows degrees of importance. The previous study methods are linear in nature, whereas mapping uses space in a free and graphic manner.

When to Map

A map provides a quick reference for overviewing a chapter to stimulate prior knowledge, emphasize relationships, and aid recall. College students use maps or charts to reduce information for memorizing from lecture notes and the text.

How to Map

To prepare a map, do the following:

1. Draw a circle or a box in the middle of a page, and in it write the subject or topic of the material.
2. Determine the main ideas that support the subject, and write them on lines radiating from the central circle or box.
3. Determine the significant details and write them on lines attached to each main idea. The number of details you include will depend on the material and your purpose.

Maps are not restricted to any one pattern but can be formed in a variety of creative shapes, as the following diagrams illustrate:

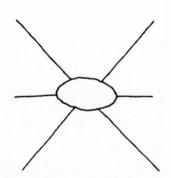 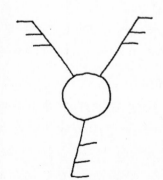 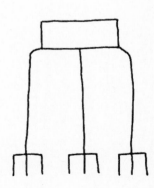

Copyright ©1999 by Addison-Wesley Educational Publishers Inc.

The following is an example of how the passage on Jung's theories might be mapped for future study:

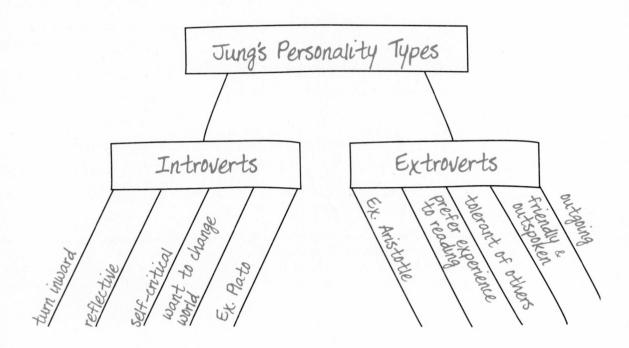

EXERCISE 6

Read the following passage and map the key ideas for each. The structure of the maps is already provided. Insert the main idea first and arrange the supporting ideas to radiate appropriately.

RELIEF FOR INJURIES

For the past several hundred years many injuries were treated with heat—steaming baths where leisurely soaking was encouraged, hot water bottles, or electric heating pads or wraps. It was assumed that since heat speeded up metabolism, it would also speed the healing process. Today's researchers have proved that just the opposite is true. . . . Heat does speed up body processes but it also stimulates injured tissue and dilates blood vessels. In turn, this causes swelling to increase and enlarges the pools of blood and fluid, actually slowing healing. Even if there is no injury, heat after exercising can cause aches and pains. A quick, cool shower is recommended after your jog rather than a hot tub.

Four basic first aid procedures are used in treating the majority of runners' injuries.

1 STOP ACTIVITY

The first and most critical is to stop jogging as soon as the symptom appears. About the only pain you can run through is a side stitch. Joggers who insist on running with pain or walking off an injury usually incur further harm. Even though the pain does not become more intense, continuing the activity may aggravate the injury and prolong healing.

2
APPLY COLD

Cold packs are now universally accepted as the best first aid for virtually any jogging injury and constitute the second step in treatment. Chilling numbs the pain and minimizes swelling and inflammation by constricting blood and lymph vessels. Apply cold packs at least twice a day until the swelling and tenderness disappear. The ice pack should not be left in place longer than 30 minutes at one time. Muscle cramps are one of the few conditions associated with jogging where heat instead of cold should be applied.

3   4
IMMOBILIZE AND ELEVATE

Injuries that would benefit from being immobilized and/or given additional support should be wrapped with an elastic Ace-type bandage. This wrapping should be snug, but not tight enough to inhibit blood circulation. This third step should be taken before the final step of elevating the injured body part. Elevation not only helps drain fluid from the area, but also prevents blood and fluid from rushing to the area, thereby causing further swelling.

—Jogging Everyone by Charles Williams and Clancy Moore

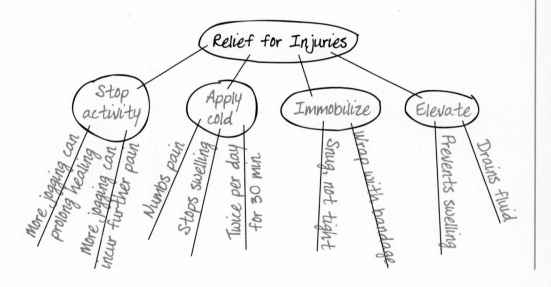

EXERCISE 7   Make a study map or chart to diagram the essential information in the previous passage entitled *The Six Types of Love* (see Exercise 5).

Take Organized Lecture Notes ◆◆◆◆◆◆◆◆◆◆

Develop an efficient system for organizing class lectures. Professors speak rapidly, yet expect students to remember important information. The Cornell system uses marginal notes to emphasize main points, while the outline format shows importance through indentation. Whichever system you use, allow yourself plenty of room to write. Considering your investment in college, paper is

Copyright ©1999 by Addison-Wesley Educational Publishers Inc.

inexpensive. Use a pen to avoid smudges. Try writing on only one side of the paper so that you can backtrack to add information when the professor summarizes. Compare your lecture notes with those of other students. Why would some professors say, "I can tell how much a student understood by looking at his or her lecture notes"?

EXERCISE 8

Choose a "study buddy" and divide the work in order to compare the two notetaking systems, the Cornell Method and the modified outline format. Ask permission and, if possible, both go visit a regular history, psychology, sociology, or political science class. One of you should take notes using the Cornell Method and the other using an informal version of the outline format. After class, compare notes and decide which method works better for you.

POINTS TO PONDER

▲ Use a system of notations to annotate your text for future study.
▲ The Cornell Method of notetaking includes writing summaries and marginal notes.
▲ The summary is a short, concise method of stating the main idea and significant supporting details.
▲ Outlining gives a quick graphic display of key issues and can be used to brainstorm answers to essay exam questions.
▲ Mapping visually condenses material to show relationships.

PERSONAL FEEDBACK 1

Name_____

1. What format do you prefer for notetaking? Why?
   _____

2. What has been your experience with highlighting? How would you evaluate your own highlighting as compared with other methods of annotating? _____
   _____

3. Why should you take lecture notes only on one side of a notebook page?
   _____

4. How do you reward yourself during study breaks?
   _____

5. What is the most useful thing you have learned from this chapter?
   _____

6. What is the most interesting thing you have learned so far from your instructor? _____

7. What do you feel are the five major differences in academic expectations between high school and college?

_____

_____

_____

_____

_____

| SELECTION 1 | *History* |

THINKING BEFORE READING

Preview for content and organizational clues. Activate your schema and anticipate what you will learn.

What were the early centers of African culture?

In what part of Africa is the Sudan?

How did African traders get rich?

After reading this I will probably know _____.

VOCABULARY PREVIEW

Are you familiar with these words?

debatable	detest	savannah	tether	caparisoned
zealots	bungled	engrosses	curb	dissolution

What is the meaning of the prefix and root in *dissolution*?

Why should you be cautious of religious zealots?

Your instructor may give a true-false vocabulary review before or after reading.

THINKING DURING READING

As you read, use the five thinking strategies of a good reader: predict, picture, relate, monitor, and correct.

OUTLINING

Make an informal study outline to answer the following essay exam question: Describe the life and significance of the three most powerful states of the Sudan.

Copyright ©1999 by Addison-Wesley Educational Publishers Inc.

TIMBUKTU

In the same period three powerful states—Ghana, Mali, and Songhay—emerged in the western Sudan, a broad belt of open country, sandwiched between the Sahara in the north and the rain forests of the Guinea Coast in the south. At one time the peoples and rulers of these countries were classified out of the Negro race. It is now known that they
5   were blacks, some of whom were converted to Islam in the eleventh century. The extent of Moslem influence is debatable, but it seems probable that the upper classes and leaders, especially in the large cities, were black Moslems.

As political entities, Ghana, Mali and Songhay do not suffer in comparison with their European contemporaries. In several areas, in fact, the Sudanese empires were clearly
10   superior. "It would be interesting to know," Basil Davidson wrote, "what the Normans might have thought of Ghana. Anglo-Saxon England could easily have seemed a poor and lowly place beside it."

The economic life of these states revolved around agriculture, manufacturing and international trade. Rulers wielded power through provincial governors and viceroys and
15   maintained large standing armies. Chain-mailed cavalry, armed with shields, swords and lances, formed the shock troops of the armies. Ibn-Batuta, an Arab traveler who visited Mali in the fourteenth century, was impressed by the flow of life in these states. "Of

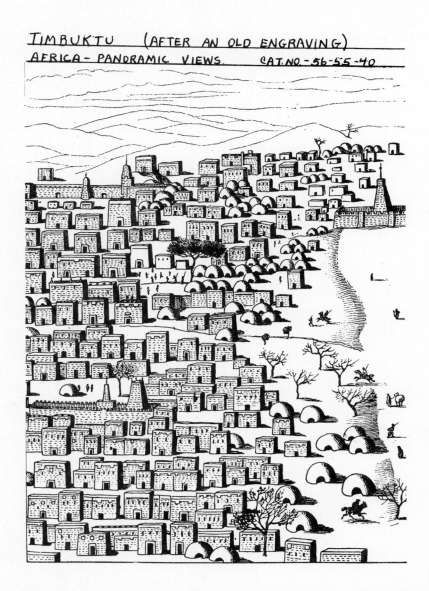

TIMBUKTU (AFTER AN OLD ENGRAVING)
AFRICA – PANORAMIC VIEWS.   CAT. NO. – 56-55-40

all people," he said, "the blacks are those who most detest injustice. Their Sultan never forgives anyone who has been guilty of it."

20   Trade and commerce flourished in the great cities that sprang up in the Sudanese savannah, and the intellectual life was brisk and stimulating. Jenn and Timbuktu were known throughout the Moslem world as centers of culture and learning. Ibn-Batuta said the black women of these cities were "of surpassing beauty." They were neither down-trodden nor meek, these women. Ibn-Batuta said they were "shown more respect than
25 the men," adding: "Their men show no signs of jealousy whatever" and the women "show no bashfulness before men and do not veil themselves."

    The power and wealth of Ghana, Mali and Songhay stemmed from the trans-Saharan trade, which exerted a profound influence on Sudanese civilization. The basis of this trade was gold. From the north came caravans of twelve thousand or more camels,
30 laden with wheat, sugar, fruit, salt and textiles, which were exchanged in the Sudan for gold and other products. In the power politics of that day, the country that controlled this trade controlled the Sudan.

THE GOLD OF GHANA

Ghana, which was old when the Arabs first mentioned it in A.D. 800, dominated the Sudan for almost three hundred years, flourishing in the ninth and tenth centuries and
35 reaching the peak of its power in the early part of the eleventh century. The rulers of Ghana, which was one of the main suppliers of gold for North Africa and Europe, were fabulously wealthy. Al-Bakri, an Arab geographer who wrote in 1067, said the king owned a nugget of gold so large that he could tether his horse to it.

    Tenkamenin, who ruled Ghana in the middle of the eleventh century, had an army of
40 two hundred thousand men and lived in a castle decorated with sculpture and painted windows. "When he gives audience to his people," Al-Bakri said, "to listen to their complaints . . . he sits in a pavilion around which stand his horses caparisoned in cloth of gold; behind him stand ten pages holding shields and gold-mounted swords; and on his right hand are the sons of the princes of his empire, splendidly clad and with gold plaited
45 into their hair. The governor of the city is seated on the ground in front of the king, and all around him are his vizirs in the same position. The gate of the chamber is guarded by dogs of an excellent breed, who never leave the king's seat, they wear collars of gold and silver."

MALI BECOMES AN EMPIRE

In the eleventh century Ghana fell to a band of Moslem zealots, and the torch of
50 Sudanese civilization passed to Mali, which began as a small Mandingo state on the left bank of the upper Niger River. Although the history of this country goes back to the seventh century, it owes its fame to two men—Sundiata Keita and Mansa Musa. Keita transformed the small state into a great empire. Musa, the most celebrated ruler of the ancient Sudan, came to power in 1307 and put together one of the greatest countries of the
55 medieval world. Musa is best known for a pilgrimage he made to Mecca in 1324. He went in regal splendor with an entourage of sixty thousand persons, including twelve thousand servants. Five hundred servants, each of whom carried a staff of pure gold weighing some six pounds, marched on before him. Eighty camels bore twenty-four thousand pounds of gold, which the black monarchs distributed as alms and gifts. Musa
60 returned to his kingdom with an architect who designed imposing buildings in Timbuktu and other cities of the Sudan.

ASKIA BRINGS PEACE AND WEALTH

Mali declined in importance in the fifteenth century and its place was taken by Songhay, whose greatest king was Askia Mohammed. Askia, a general who had served as prime minister, seized power in 1493, a year after the European discovery of America. He
65 reigned for nineteen years and built the largest and most powerful of the Sudan states.

Copyright ©1999 by Addison-Wesley Educational Publishers Inc.

His realm was larger than all Europe and included most of West Africa. "He was obeyed," a Sudanese writer said, "with as much docility on the farther limits of the empire as he was in his own palace, and there reigned everywhere great plenty and absolute peace."

A brilliant administrator and an enlightened legislator, Askia recognized the army, improved the banking and credit systems and made Gao, Walata, Timbuktu and Jenn intellectual centers. Certain scholars, Alexander Chamberlain in particular, believe he was one of the greatest monarchs of this period. "In personal character, in administrative ability, in devotion to the welfare of his subjects, in open-mindedness towards foreign influences, and in wisdom in the adoption of non-Negro ideas and institutions," Chamberlain said "King Askia . . . was certainly the equal of the average European monarch of the time and superior to many of them."

Timbuktu, during Askia's reign, was a city of some one hundred thousand people, filled with gold and dazzling women. One of the most fabled and exotic cities in the medieval world, the Sudanese metropolis was celebrated for its luxury and gaiety. The towering minarets of two great mosques dominated the face of the city. From the Great Mosque, flat-roofed houses (of wood and plaster) radiated in all directions. The older Sankore Mosque, to which was attached the University of Sankore, was the center of intellectual life. The mosque and the university were of cut stone and lime. Other buildings fronted the narrow streets: factories and shops where one could buy exotic goods from North Africa and faraway Europe. Leo Africanus, a Christianized Moor who visited the city in the sixteenth century, said it "is a wonder to see what plentie of Merchandize is daily brought hither and how costly and sumptuous all things be. . . . Here are many shops of . . . merchants and especially of such as weave linnen."

In the narrow streets of this Sudanese metropolis, scholars mingled with rich black merchants and young boys sat in the shade, reciting the Koran. Visiting Arab businessmen wandered the streets, looking, no doubt, for the excitement for which the city was famed. Youths from all over the Moslem world came to Timbuktu to study law and surgery at the University of Sankore; scholars came from North Africa and Europe to confer with the learned historians and writers of the black empire. Es Sadi, a Timbuktu intellectual who wrote a history of the Sudan, said his brother came from Jenn for a successful cataract operation at the hands of a distinguished surgeon. Es Sadi, incidentally, had a private library of sixteen hundred volumes.

TIMBUKTU'S INTELLECTUAL VITALITY

If we can credit contemporary reports, Timbuktu, during the reign of Askia the Great, was an intellectual's paradise. A Sudanese literature developed and Es Sadi, Ahmed Baba and other intellectuals wrote books.

"In Timbuktu," Leo Africanus said, "there are numerous judges, doctors, and clerics, all receiving good salaries from the king. He pays great respect to men of learning. There is a big demand for books in manuscript, imported from Barbary. More profit is made from the book trade than from any other line of business." Since man first learned to write, few cities have been able to make such a claim.

The University of Sankore and other intellectual centers in Timbuktu had large and valuable collections of manuscripts in several languages, and scholars came from faraway places to check their Greek and Latin manuscripts. The seeds scattered here put down deep roots. Hundreds of years later Heinrich Barth met an old blind man in the Sudan. "This," he reported, "was the first conversation I had with this man. . . . I could scarcely have expected to find in this out of the way place a man not only versed in all the branches of Arabic literature, but who had even read, nay, possessed a manuscript of those portions of Aristotle and Plato which had been translated into Arabic."

How did the people of Timbuktu amuse themselves? If the writers of Songhay can be believed, Timbukto was Paris, Chicago and New York blended into an African setting. Shocked Songhay historians said most of the people amused themselves with parties, love and the pleasures of the cup. Music was the rage (orchestras with both male and female singers were preferred) and midnight revels were common. The dress of the

120 women was extravagantly luxurious. Men and women were fond of jewels, and the
women dressed their hair with bands of gold.

Dramatic displays, including dancing, fencing, gymnastics and poetry recitations,
were popular. So was chess. The story is told of a Songhay general who bungled a military campaign and explained that he became so engrossed in a chess game that he paid
no attention to the reports of his scouts. Askia—a liberal man who had several wives and
125 one hundred sons, the last of whom was born when he was ninety—was disturbed by the
free and easy life of Timbuktu and attempted, apparently without too much success, to
curb the social excesses.

SOCIAL DECLINE

Timbuktu and the civilization of which it was a flower declined in the seventeenth century
and the reign of the great West African states came to an end. Why did Sudanese civiliza-
130 tion collapse? W. E. B. Du Bois says it fell before the triphammer blows of two of the
world's great religions, Islam and Christianity. Other students cite the difficulties of
defense in the open Sudanese savannah and the corrupting influence of the slave trade.
Es Sadi, who wrote the *Tarikh al-Sudan* in the dying days of the Songhay empire,
advanced another reason—social dissolution. The people, he said, had grown fat and soft
135 on luxury and good living.

(1,852 words)

—*Before the Mayflower* by Lerone Bennett, Jr.

THINKING AFTER READING

RECALL: Self-test your understanding. Your instructor may choose to give you a
true-false review.

REACT: What other cultures would you compare to Timbuktu?

REFLECT: What is the value of learning about Timbuktu?

 THINK CRITICALLY: Why was Askia Mohammed considered the greatest king of
Songhay? Write your answer on a separate sheet of paper.

TEXTBOOK LEARNING: Compare your study outline for the essay question with
the outlines of other students. Change your outline, if appropriate.

Copyright ©1999 by Addison-Wesley Educational Publishers Inc.

Name _____

Date _____

COMPREHENSION QUESTIONS

Answer the following with *a, b, c,* or *d,* or fill in the blank. In order to help you analyze your strengths and weaknesses, the question types are indicated.

Main Idea   __d__ 1. The best statement of the main idea of this selection is:

    a. Timbuktu declined in the seventeenth century.
    b. Timbuktu was a Moslem center of learning.
    c. The economic life of Africa was centered in the Sudan.
    d. The Sudan was an early center of culture, learning, and wealth.

Detail   __b__ 2. In the trans-Saharan trade, the caravans from the north

    a. brought gold to the Sudan for agricultural products.
    b. brought wheat, sugar, and fruit to exchange for gold.
    c. primarily traded camels for gold.
    d. brought agricultural products to exchange for textiles.

Inference   3. The author implies that the most important "cash crop" of Ghana was _____gold_____.

Inference   __a__ 4. According to the periods of history described in the selection, the chronological order of the emergence of political importance of the states of the Sudan was

    a. Ghana, Mali, and Songhay.
    b. Songhay, Mali, and Ghana.
    c. Ghana, Songhay, and Mali.
    d. Mali, Ghana, and Songhay.

Detail   __d__ 5. According to the author, the largest and most powerful of the Sudan states was ruled by

    a. Tenkamenin.
    b. Keita.
    c. Musa.
    d. Askia.

Detail   __b__ 6. Important firsthand accounts of Timbuktu during its glory days were contributed by

    a. Alexander Chamberlain.
    b. Es Sadi.
    c. Heinrich Barth.
    d. Al-Bakri.

Detail   __a__ 7. Before the fall of Timbuktu, Askia

    a. warned his people of their excesses.
    b. converted from Islam to Christianity.
    c. curbed social excesses in the state.
    d. sold people into slavery.

Answer the following with *T* (true), *F* (false), or *CT* (can't tell).

Detail   __F__ 8. The intellectual height of the Sudan, as measured by profits in the book trade, was during the rule of Musa.

Inference ___F___ 9. In Timbuktu, women were considered socially inferior to men.

Detail ___F___ 10. Ghana was overtaken by Christians in the eleventh century.

VOCABULARY

Answer the following with *a, b, c,* or *d* for the word or phrase that best defines the boldface word as used in the selection. The number in parentheses indicates the line of the passage in which the word is located.

___b___ 1. "influence is **debatable**" (6)

    a. final
    b. questionable
    c. acceptable
    d. rejected

___a___ 2. "who most **detest** injustice" (18)

    a. despise
    b. disallow
    c. damage
    d. fight

___d___ 3. "in the Sudanese **savannah**" (20–21)

    a. desert
    b. plains
    c. swamp
    d. grassland

___b___ 4. "**tether** his horse to it" (38)

    a. confront
    b. tie
    c. flatten
    d. charm

___d___ 5. "horses **caparisoned** in . . . gold" (42–43)

    a. resting
    b. united
    c. strutting
    d. decorated

___c___ 6. "Moslem **zealots**" (49)

    a. soldiers
    b. spies
    c. extremists
    d. leaders

___b___ 7. "**bungled** a military campaign" (122–123)

    a. deserted
    b. mismanaged
    c. manipulated
    d. defended

___a___ 8. "**engrossed** in a chess game" (123)

    a. captivated
    b. frightened
    c. overshadowed
    d. beaten

___d___ 9. "**curb** the social excesses" (127)

    a. outlaw
    b. expose
    c. avoid
    d. restrain

___b___ 10. "social **dissolution**" (134)

    a. renewal
    b. degeneration
    c. adjustment
    d. frustration

VOCABULARY ENRICHMENT

A. Words from Literature

The names of certain characters in literature have dropped their capital letters and taken on special meaning in the English language. The following are from Spanish and English literature, respectively. Read the entries to determine their definitions and origins:

> **qui·xote** \\'kwik-sət, kē-'hō-tē, -'ō-\\ *n, often cap* [Don *Quixote*, hero of the novel *Don Quixote de la Mancha* (1605, 1615) by Cervantes] (1648) : a quixotic person — **quix·o·tism** \\'kwik-sə-,ti-zəm\\ *n* — **quix·o·try** \\-sə-trē\\ *n*
> **quix·ot·ic** \\kwik-'sä-tik\\ *adj* [Don *Quixote*] (1815) **1** : foolishly impractical esp. in the pursuit of ideals; *esp* : marked by rash lofty romantic ideas or extravagantly chivalrous action **2** : CAPRICIOUS, UNPREDICTABLE *syn* see IMAGINARY — **quix·ot·i·cal** \\-ti-kəl\\ *adj* — **quix·ot·i·cal·ly** \\-ti-k(ə-)lē\\ *adv*

Copyright © 1999 by Addison-Wesley Educational Publishers Inc.

1. *Quixotic* means ___impractical or impulsive___

2. It comes from ___the name Don Quixote___

> **Lil·li·put** \ˈli-li-(ˌ)pət\ *n* : an island in Swift's *Gulliver's Travels* where the inhabitants are six inches tall
> **lil·li·pu·tian** \ˌli-lə-ˈpyü-shən\ *adj, often cap* (1726) **1** : of, relating to, or characteristic of the Lilliputians or the island of Lilliput **2 a** : SMALL, MINIATURE **b** : PETTY
> **Lilliputian** *n* **1** : an inhabitant of Lilliput **2** *often not cap* : one resembling a Lilliputian; *esp* : an undersized individual

3. *Lilliputian* means ___small___

4. It comes from ___the name of small people in *Gulliver's Travels*.___

B. Analogies

5. *Knife* is to *cut* as *gun* is to ___shoot___.
   Relationship? ___function___

6. *Old* is to *ancient* as *recent* is to ___new___.
   Relationship? ___degree___

7. *Eye* is to *see* as *ear* is to ___hear___.
   Relationship? ___function___

8. *Go* is to *come* as *sell* is to ___buy___.
   Relationship? ___antonyms___

9. *State* is to *governor* as *city* is to ___mayor___
   Relationship? ___function___

10. *Skin* is to *person* as *fur* is to ___animal___.
    Relationship? ___part to whole___

11. *Smart* is to *intelligent* as *chilly* is to ___cool___.
    Relationship? ___synonyms___

12. *Razor* is to *sharp* as *cement* is to ___hard___.
    Relationship? ___characteristic___

13. *Winter* is to *summer* as *wet* is to ___dry___.
    Relationship? ___antonyms___

C. Circle the similar-sounding word that is correct in each sentence.

> **consul:** foreign representative
> **council:** elected officials
> **counsel:** give advice

14. Many professors are willing to (**consul, council, (counsel)**) students with study problems.

> **personal:** private
> **personnel:** employees

15. Take your job application to the (**personal, (personnel)**) office.

ASSESS YOUR LEARNING

Review confusing questions, seek clarification, and make notes in your text to help you remember new information and vocabulary.

- Print a current map of the area that was Timbuktu.
- What is the current economic situation of the area known as Timbuktu?

For additional readings and exercises, visit the Longman English Skills Web page at:

http://longman.awl.com/englishpages

For a user name and password, please see your instructor.

SELECTION 2   *Biology*

THINKING BEFORE READING

Preview the selection for clues to content. Activate your schema and anticipate what you will learn.

Why are people afraid of bats?

Are porpoises and dolphins the same?

How can bats see in the dark?

I'll read this to find out _____.

VOCABULARY PREVIEW

Are you familiar with these words?

| belfry | roost | impeded | baffled | emitted |
| phenomenon | detect | unerring | feats | din |

What is the meaning of the phrase, "You have bats in your belfry"?

Where do chickens roost?

Which word has a homonym, a word that sounds alike but is spelled differently?

Your instructor may give a true-false vocabulary review before or after reading.

Copyright ©1999 by Addison-Wesley Educational Publishers Inc.

THINKING DURING READING

As you read, use the five thinking strategies of a good reader: predict, picture, relate, monitor, and correct.

ANNOTATE

As you read the following selection, use a variety of annotations to highlight information for later study. When you have finished the selection, make a brief study outline.

ECHOLOCATION: SEEING IN THE DARK

For hundreds of years, naturalists have wondered how bats are able to fly through caves in total darkness or through wooded fields at night, capturing fast-flying insects they can't possibly see. Near the end of the eighteenth century, Lazarro Spallanzani, an Italian biologist, caught a number of bats in a cathedral belfry, impaired their vision, and let
5 them go. Returning to the belfry at a later time, Spallanzani found the bats back in their roost at the top of the cathedral. Not only did the bats return home, but their stomachs were full of insects, indicating that they had been able to capture food without their sense of sight. In contrast, bats whose ears had been plugged with wax were reluctant even to take flight and frequently collided into objects when they tried to fly. Hanging
10 objects in front of the bats' mouths also impeded the animals' flying abilities. Spallanzani was baffled: How could an animal's ears and mouth be of more importance than its eyes in guiding flight?

The question remained unanswered until 1938, at which time, Donald Griffin, an undergraduate at Harvard University, brought a cage of bats to one of his physics profes-
15 sors, George Pierce. Pierce had developed an apparatus for converting high-frequency sound waves into a form that could be heard by the human ear. After placing the cage of bats in front of the sound detector, Griffin and Pierce became the first people to "hear" the bursts of sounds emitted by bats. When the bats were set free in the physics laboratory, these same high-frequency sounds could be heard as a bat flew in a straight direc-
20 tion toward the microphone. For Griffin, this was the initial step in a long, illustrious career centered around studying the role of sound in animal navigation.

The mechanism bats use to fly through a pitch-black obstacle course relies on the same principles first employed by the Allied navy to hunt for German submarines during World War II. That mechanism is sonar. The basic principle of sonar is simple: Sound
25 waves are emitted from a transmitter; they bounce off objects in the environment; and the "echoes" are detected by an appropriate receiver. The elapsed time between the emission of the sound pulse and its return provides precise information about the loca-

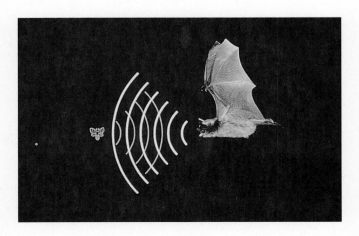

tion and shape of the objects. Most bats employ a remarkably compact and efficient sonar system to detect insect prey and to avoid colliding with objects during flight. High-
30 frequency sounds—those beyond the range of the human ear—are produced by the bat's larynx (voicebox), and the echoes are received by the animal's large ears. Impulses from the ears are then sent to the brain, where they are perceived as a detailed mental picture of the objects in the environment. Griffin coined the term "echolocation" to describe this phenomenon.

35   Echolocation by bats is an adaptation appropriate for their nocturnal (nighttime) peak of activity. Using echolocation, a bat flying at night can detect and avoid a wire as thin as 0.3 millimeters in diameter or can hone in on a tiny, moving insect with unerring accuracy. These feats become even more impressive when you realize that the echo returning to the bat from such objects is about 2,000 times less intense than is the sound
40 emitted. Moreover, a bat can pick out this faint echo in a crowd of other bats, each sending its own pulses of sound waves.

During the early 1950s, studies by Winthrop Kellogg, a marine biologist at Florida State University, and others, demonstrated that bats were not the only mammals capable of navigating by echolocation. One day, Kellogg and Robert Kohler, an electronics engi-
45 neer, were out in a boat in the Gulf of Mexico when they saw a school of porpoises swimming toward them. The scientists lowered a microphone connected to a speaker and tape recorder into the water. As the porpoises swam toward them, all that could be heard above water was the sound of the animals exhaling through their blowholes. ". . . but the underwater listening gear told a very different story." According to Kellogg, the animals
50 were emitting sequences of underwater clicks and clacks "such as might be produced by a rusty hinge if it were opened slowly. . . . By the time the group was about to make its final dive, the crescendo from the speaker in our boat had become a clattering din which almost drowned out the human voice."

To study the echolocating capabilities of these animals, Kellogg persuaded Florida
55 State University to build a special "porpoise laboratory" at its nearby marine station. There, investigators discovered that porpoises possessed a sophisticated sonar system they could use to distinguish between similarly shaped objects, to avoid invisible barriers (such as sheets of glass), to swim through an elaborate obstacle course, to locate food, and to pick up objects off the bottom of their enclosure.

60   It may surprise you to learn that you probably have some capability to echolocate as well. Over the past hundred years or so, many reports have been written about the remarkable ability of many blind people to detect the presence of obstacles in their path without the use of a cane. The first carefully controlled experiment on this subject was conducted in 1940 by Michael Supa and Milton Kotzin, a pair of graduate students at
65 Cornell University, one of whom was blind himself. Subjects that were either blind or sighted but blindfolded were asked to walk down a long wooden hallway. They were told that a large, fiberboard screen *might* be placed at some random site along their way and were asked to report when they detected the presence of the screen. The subjects were able to detect the screen within 1 to 5 meters of its presence. In those cases when the
70 screen was absent, none of the subjects reported its presence. In contrast, when the subjects' ears were tightly plugged, they collided with the screen in every trial. The authors of the experiment concluded that the echo of the sound emitted from the subjects' footsteps on the floor provided information about the location of the screen. A later report documented the case of a young blind boy who was able to avoid obstacles while riding
75 a bicycle by making clicking sounds and listening to the echoes.

(1,044 words)

—*Biology: Exploring Life* by Gil Brum, Larry McKane, and Gerry Karp

THINKING AFTER READING

RECALL: Self-test your understanding. Your instructor may choose to give you a true-false review.

Copyright ©1999 by Addison-Wesley Educational Publishers Inc.

REACT: Why would a university support research on echolocation and build a "porpoise laboratory"? _____

REFLECT: Why might a gardener both want and not want a bat house?

 THINK CRITICALLY: Compare the scientific research techniques in Spallanzani's experiment with bats and Supa and Kotzin's experiment with humans. Explain why the researchers used plugged and unplugged ears, sighted and unsighted subjects, and present and absent fiberboard screens.

Name _____

Date_____

COMPREHENSION QUESTIONS

Answer the following with *a, b, c,* and *d* or fill in the blank. In order to help you analyze your strengths and weaknesses, the question types are indicated.

Main Idea _____c_____ 1. The best statement of the main idea of this selection is:

      a. Echolocation is used by bats to navigate in the dark.
      b. Bats use sound waves to guide flight.
      c. Bats, porpoises, and even humans use echolocation to navigate.
      d. Echolocation allows bats and porpoises to see in the dark.

Detail _____d_____ 2. In the eighteenth century, Lazarro Spallanzani discovered that bats

      a. use sonar to navigate.
      b. were able to fly with wax in their ears.
      c. with impaired vision will not return home.
      d. use their ears and mouth more than their eyes in flight.

Inference _____ 3. The reader might assume that Donald Griffin suspected that bats use

    sonar because <u>he brought the bats to Pierce who had a high-</u>

    <u>frequency sound wave apparatus.</u>

Detail _____b_____ 4. A basic principle of sonar in bats is that

      a. the transmitter does not need a receiver.
      b. the transmitter and receiver are the same.
      c. the receiver does not require a transmitter.
      d. multiple transmitters are necessary for one receiver.

Detail _____c_____ 5. The author states that porpoises

      a. emit clicks that can be heard above the water.
      b. exhale water through their blowholes in order to navigate by sound.
      c. make noises that can be transmitted by an underwater microphone.
      d. use noises to frighten away divers.

Detail _____d_____ 6. The subjects in Supa and Kotzin's experiment were

      a. all blind from birth.
      b. riding bicycles and making noises.
      c. not told about the screen.
      d. both blind and sighted.

Inference _____d_____ 7. The author suggests that echolocation allows animals to do all of the following *except*

      a. find food.
      b. locate each other.
      c. return home.
      d. alert humans to their presence.

Answer the following with *T* (true) or *F* (false).

Detail _____F_____ 8. The echo that is returned to the bat is more intense than the sound emitted.

Copyright ©1999 by Addison-Wesley Educational Publishers Inc.

Detail _____F_____ 9. According to the article, Griffin was able to photograph the mental picture of environmental objects sent to the bat's brain.

Detail _____F_____ 10. According to the selections, bats and porpoises have large ears to receive echos.

VOCABULARY

Answer the following with *a, b, c,* or *d* for the word or phrase that best defines the boldface word as used in the selection. The number in parentheses indicates the line of the passage in which the word is located.

__c__ 1. "in a cathedral **belfry**" (4)

    a. ceiling
    b. attic
    c. bell tower
    d. choir loft

__a__ 2. "back in their **roost**" (5–6)

    a. perch
    b. tree
    c. nest
    d. traffic pattern

__c__ 3. "**impeded** the animals' flying abilities" (10)

    a. aided
    b. facilitated
    c. blocked
    d. lengthened

__a__ 4. "Spallanzani was **baffled**" (10–11)

    a. puzzled
    b. angry
    c. hurt
    d. embarrassed

__d__ 5. "**emitted** by bats" (18)

    a. received
    b. monitored
    c. heard
    d. given off

__c__ 6. "describe this **phenomenon**" (34)

    a. mistake
    b. mechanism
    c. curiosity
    d. secret

__b__ 7. "**detect** and avoid a wire" (36)

    a. move
    b. locate
    c. zigzag
    d. inspect

__c__ 8. "with **unerring** accuracy" (37–38)

    a. dangerous
    b. cruel
    c. faultless
    d. mysterious

__a__ 9. "**feats** become even more impressive" (38)

    a. accomplishments
    b. noises
    c. needs
    d. choices

__d__ 10. "become a clattering **din**" (52–53)

    a. distance
    b. music
    c. motion
    d. noise

VOCABULARY ENRICHMENT

A. Use context clues and word parts to write the meaning of the boldface words from a science text.

    1. Animals have an **instinct** to protect their young from danger.
      innate tendency

2. Some seeds need to be in the ground two weeks before they **germinate.**
   sprout and grow

3. If parts of a starfish are broken, it has the ability to **regenerate** itself.
   grow missing parts

4. Animals are **dependent** on the food supply for their livelihood.
   reliant on

5. The direction of the wind is a **variable** in determining future weather.
   fluctuating factor

6. Many tropical plants are **adaptable** to indoor gardening.
   suitable

7. By analyzing the supplied information, he solved the problem by **deduction.**
   reasoning from a known principle to an unknown

8. Fish and mammals fall into different categories in the animal **phylum.**
   basic division of animal kingdom

9. New concerns about pesticides indicate that they threaten our **ecological** balance.
   related to the relationship between living organisms and the environment

10. Physical activity can affect a person's **metabolism.**
    process of assimilating food and releasing energy

B. Analogies
   Supply a word that completes the following analogies, and then state the relationship that has been established.

11. *Music* is to *piano* as *explosion* is to ___dynamite or bomb___.
    Relationship? ___function___

12. *Whale* is to *mammal* as *ant* is to ___insect___.
    Relationship? ___classification___

13. *Bones* are to *leg* as *freckles* are to ___skin___.
    Relationship? ___part to whole___

14. *Attract* is to *repel* as *pretty* is to ___ugly___.
    Relationship? ___antonyms___

15. *Tiger* is to *meat* as *cow* is to ___hay, grass, or grain___.
    Relationship? ___function___

ASSESS YOUR LEARNING

Review confusing questions, seek clarification, and make notes in your text to help you remember new information and vocabulary.

Copyright ©1999 by Addison-Wesley Educational Publishers Inc.

EXPLORE THE NET

- ● What are the two major types of bats and how do they differ?
- ● What are some of the popular myths about bats?

For additional readings and exercises, visit the Longman English Skills Web page at:

http://longman.awl.com/englishpages

For a user name and password, please see your instructor.

SELECTION 3 ◆ *Communication*

THINKING BEFORE READING

Preview for clues to content. What do you already know about conflict resolution? Activate your schema and anticipate what you will learn.

How does your best friend react in an argument?

Why do you get angry with your parents?

Why would you say that a person doesn't fight fairly?

This selection will probably tell me _____.

VOCABULARY PREVIEW

Are you familiar with these words?

attaining	assumption	pettiness	reciprocal	legitimate
validate	feign	escalate	noncombative	contingent

Why is car pooling a reciprocal arrangement?

Describe a recent example of pettiness.

Are conclusions based on assumptions?

Your instructor may give a true-false vocabulary review before or after reading.

THINKING DURING READING

As you read, use the five thinking strategies of a good reader: predict, picture, relate, monitor, and correct.

ANNOTATING

As you read the following selection, use a variety of annotations to highlight information for later study. When you have finished the selection, make a brief study outline.

EFFECTIVENESS IN INTERPERSONAL CONFLICT

The principles of interpersonal effectiveness receive their toughest test in interpersonal conflict. During such a conflict you are least likely to be mindful, sensitive to cultural differences, flexible, or to want to talk about your talk. Let's look first at the nature of interpersonal conflict and then examine the various strategies we use when we fight.

WHAT IS INTERPERSONAL CONFLICT?

5   Tom wants to go to the movies and Sara wants to stay home. Tom's insisting on going to the movies interferes with Sara's staying home and Sara's determination to stay home interferes with Tom's going to the movies. Randy and Grace have been dating. Randy wants to get married; Grace wants to continue dating. Opposing goals interfere with each attaining his or her goals.

CONTENT AND RELATIONSHIP CONFLICTS

10   Using concepts developed earlier, we may distinguish between content conflict and relationship conflict. *Content conflict* centers on objects, events, and persons that are usually, but not always or entirely, external to the parties involved in the conflict. These include the millions of issues that we argue and fight about every day—the value of a particular movie, what to watch on television, the fairness of the last examination or job promotion,
15   and the way to spend our savings.

   Relationship conflicts are equally numerous and include such conflict situations as a younger brother who disobeys his older brother, two partners who want an equal say in making vacation plans, and the mother and daughter who each want to have the final

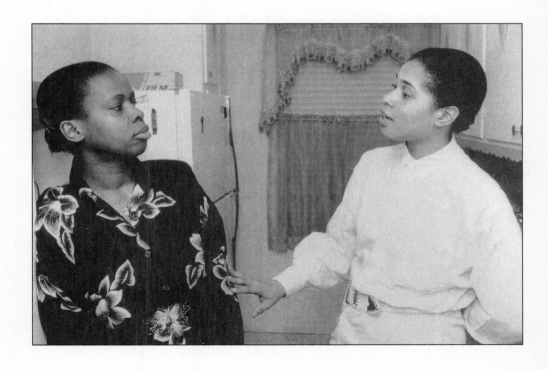

Copyright ©1999 by Addison-Wesley Educational Publishers Inc.

20 word concerning the daughter's life-style. Here the conflicts do not concern some external object as much as relationships between the individuals—issues such as who is in charge, the equality of a primary relationship, and who has the right to set down rules of behavior.

It is easier to separate content and relationship conflicts in a textbook than in real life, where many contain both elements. But if we can recognize which issues pertain to con-25 tent and which to relationship, we can understand the conflict well enough to manage it effectively and productively.

MYTHS ABOUT INTERPERSONAL CONFLICT

One of the problems in studying and dealing with interpersonal conflict is that we may have false assumptions about what conflict is and what it means. For example, do you think the following are true or false?

30 If two people in a relationship fight, it means their relationship is a bad one.
Fighting hurts an interpersonal relationship.
Fighting is bad because it reveals our negative selves, for example, our pettiness, our need to be in control, our unreasonable expectations.

As with many things, the easy answer is not always correct. The three assumptions above 35 may all be true or false. It depends. In and of itself, conflict is neither good nor bad. Conflict is a part of every interpersonal relationship, between parents and children, brothers and sisters, friends, lovers, co-workers. If it isn't, then the relationship is probably dull, irrelevant, or insignificant. Conflict is inevitable in any meaningful relationship.

It is not so much the conflict that creates the problem as the way in which the indi-40 viduals approach and deal with it. Some approaches can resolve difficulties and improve the relationship while others can do damage—destroy self-esteem, create bitterness, and foster suspicion. Our task is not to create conflict-free relationships but to learn appropriate and productive ways to manage conflict.

Similarly, it is not the conflict that will reveal our negative side but our fight strate-45 gies. We reveal our negative side when we personally attack the other person, use force, or personal rejection or manipulation. But, we can also reveal our positive selves—our willingness to listen to opposing points of view, to change unpleasant behaviors, and to accept imperfection in others.

When we attempt to resolve conflict within an interpersonal relationship, we are say-50 ing in effect that the relationship is worth the effort; otherwise we would walk away. Although there may be exceptions—as when we confront to save face or to gratify some ego need—usually confronting a conflict indicates concern, commitment, and a desire to preserve the relationship.

We need to learn not to avoid conflict but to engage in it with effective and produc-55 tive strategies that will address our problem and improve our relationship.

UNPRODUCTIVE CONFLICT MANAGEMENT

The major value in examining ineffective methods is to help us identify them in the behaviors of others and ultimately in our own behaviors. Once we can identify them, we can try to reduce them in our own communications.

Avoidance. *Avoidance* often takes the form of actual physical flight and the person may 60 leave the scene of the conflict, fall asleep, or blast the stereo.

At times the conflict is defined out of existence, as when someone says, "It was not a date—it was a business trip that we had to take together." At other times, the conflict may be redefined so that it becomes a totally different issue, as when someone says: "Your jealousy is getting out of hand. You really had better see a therapist about it."

65 Notice that with these types of behavior, the conflict source is never confronted. It is just pushed aside. You can be almost certain, however, that it will surface again.

Force. When confronted with conflict, many people prefer not to deal with the issues but rather to physically force their position on the other person. At times, the force used is more emotional than physical. In either case, however, the issues are avoided and the person who "wins" is the one who exerts the most force. This is the technique of warring nations, children, and even some normally sensible and mature adults.

More than 50 percent of couples, both single and married, reported that they had experienced physical violence in their relationship. If we add symbolic violence (for example, threatening to hit the other person or throwing something), the percentages are above 60 percent for singles and above 70 percent for marrieds. In another study, 47 percent of a sample of 410 college students reported some experience with violence in a dating relationship. In most cases the violence was reciprocal—each person in the relationship used violence.

One of the most puzzling findings is that many victims of violence interpret it as a sign of love. For some reason, they see being beaten, verbally abused, or raped as a sign that their partner is fully in love with them. Many victims, in fact, accept the blame for contributing to the violence instead of blaming their partners.

Minimization. Sometimes we deal with conflict by making light of it. We say and perhaps believe that the conflict, its causes, and its consequences are really not important. We use minimization when we make light of the other person's feelings. "What are you so angry about? I'm only forty minutes late." When you do this, you are in effect telling the other person that his or her feelings are not legitimate. Rather than minimize the other person's feelings, try to validate and acknowledge their legitimacy: "You have a right to be angry. I should have called when I knew I'd be late."

Blame. Most often conflict is caused by such a wide variety of factors that any attempt to single out one or two is doomed to failure. And yet, a frequently employed fight strategy is to avoid dealing with the conflict by blaming someone else. In some instances we blame ourselves, but more often, we blame the other person. For example, a couple has a conflict over a child's getting into trouble with the police. Instead of dealing with the conflict itself, the parents blame each other for the child's troubles. Such blaming does nothing to resolve the conflict or to help the child.

Silencers. *Silencers* include a wide array of fight techniques that literally silence the other individual. One frequently used silencer is crying. When unable to deal with a conflict or when winning seems unlikely, an individual may silence the other person by crying. Another silencer is to feign extreme emotionalism—to yell and scream and pretend to lose control. Still another is to develop some "physical" reaction—headaches and shortness of breath are probably the most popular.

One of the major problems with silencers is that you can never be certain if they are strategies to win the argument or real physical reactions that need attention. Regardless of what you do, the conflict remains unexamined and unresolved.

Gunnysacking. A gunnysack is a large bag, usually made of burlap. As a conflict strategy, *gunnysacking* refers to the practice of storing up grievances and then unloading them during a fight. The immediate occasion may be relatively simple (or so it might seem at first), such as coming home late without calling. Instead of arguing about this, the gunnysacker unloads all past grievances: the birthday you forgot, the time two months ago when you arrived late for an important dinner, the time last year when you delayed making hotel reservations until the rooms were all taken, and on and on. As can be expected, the original problem frequently does not get addressed. Instead, resentment and hostilities escalate. The true gunnysacker, even after unloading these grievances, will put them right back in the sack to be dumped out at some later date.

Manipulation. In *manipulation,* there is avoidance of open conflict. The individual tries to divert the conflict by being especially charming (disarming, actually). The objective is

Copyright ©1999 by Addison-Wesley Educational Publishers Inc.

120 to get the other person into a receptive and noncombative frame of mind before disagreeing. By so handling the conflict situation and the other person, the manipulating individual may eventually win the argument or disagreement.

Personal Rejection. In *personal rejection,* the individual withholds love and affection, seeking to win the argument by getting the other person to break down under this withdrawal. The individual acts cold and uncaring, trying to demoralize the other person. In withdrawing affection, the individual hopes to make the other person question his or her

125 self-worth. Once the other is demoralized and feels unworthy, it is relatively easy to get one's own way. The person simply makes the restitution of love and affection contingent upon resolving the conflict in his or her favor.

PRODUCTIVE CONFLICT MANAGEMENT

We approach effective conflict management by examining some of the insights provided by George Bach and Peter Wyden in their influential *Intimate Enemy.* Their simple but

130 powerful guides to fair fighting will go a long way toward making our interpersonal conflicts more productive.

Fight Above the Belt. Restrict your blows (in topic and intensity) to what the other person can absorb without severe emotional injury. Don't hit Jessica with her inability to have children or Michael with his failure to secure a permanent job. These attacks may

135 easily prevent continued communication and may encourage resentment and perhaps retaliation.

Fight Actively. Play an active role in your interpersonal conflicts. Don't close your ears (or mind), blast the television, or walk out of the house during an argument. This is not to say that a cooling-off period is not at times desirable. It is to say that if you are to resolve

140 conflicts, you need to confront them actively.

Take Responsibility for Your Thoughts and Feelings. When you disagree with your partner or find fault with her or his behavior, take responsibility for these feelings. Say, for example, "I disagree with . . ." or "I don't like it when you. . . ." Don't avoid responsibility by saying, for example, "Everybody thinks you're wrong about . . ." or "Chris thinks

145 you shouldn't. . . ." Own your own thoughts and feelings and make this ownership explicit with "I" messages.

Be Direct and Specific. Focus on the here-and-now rather than on issues that occurred two months ago (as in gunnysacking). Similarly, focus on the person with whom you are fighting, not on the person's mother, boss, child, or friends.

150 Focus your conflict on observable behaviors—on what the other person did that bothers you. Avoid *mind reading:* don't try to attribute motives to the person without first describing and understanding the behavior. Thus, if the person forgot your birthday and this disturbs you, fight about the forgetting of the birthday (the actual behavior). Try not to presuppose motives: "Well, it's obvious you just don't care about me. All you really

155 care about is yourself. If you really cared, you could never have forgotten my birthday!"

Use Humor for Relief, Never for Ridicule. In almost any conflict situation, humor will be used. Unfortunately, most often it is used sarcastically to ridicule or embarrass the other person—a use that aggravates and intensifies the conflict. Use humor to provide a momentary break in the tension. Avoid using it as a strategy to win the battle or put

160 down the other person.

(2,247 words)

—*Essentials of Human Communication* by Joseph DeVito

STUDY OUTLINE

Use your annotations to make a study outline for this selection.

THINKING AFTER READING

RECALL: Self-test your understanding. Your instructor may choose to give a true-false review.

REACT: Which unproductive conflict resolution methods do you tend to use?

_____

REFLECT: What do you think would be the value of teaching conflict resolution strategies in high school? How could they be taught?

_____

THINK CRITICALLY: What was your last big fight about? Describe your reactions and categorize your productive and unproductive behaviors. In addition, what strategies did the other person use? Write your answer on a separate sheet of paper.

Copyright ©1999 by Addison-Wesley Educational Publishers Inc.

Name _____

Date _____

COMPREHENSION QUESTIONS

Answer the following with *a, b, c,* or *d,* or fill in the blank. In order to help you analyze your strengths and weaknesses, the question types are indicated.

Main Idea   __c__   1. The best statement of the main idea of this selection is:

    a. Interpersonal conflict can and should be avoided.
    b. Fighting destroys self-esteem and hurts interpersonal relationships.
    c. Although conflict is inevitable, appropriate ways to manage conflict can be learned.
    d. Conflict and conflict strategies are predictable.

Inference   __d__   2. The author believes that conflict

    a. rarely occurs between caring people.
    b. inevitably fosters suspicion.
    c. happens repeatedly in insignificant relationships.
    d. usually occurs in meaningful relationships.

Inference   __b__   3. Louis and Tiffany had an argument over money and family budgeting. Louis left the house saying he wanted to drive around, calm down, and would probably not be back that night. Louis was engaging in

    a. force.
    b. avoidance.
    c. minimization.
    d. blame.

Inference   __c__   4. Whenever Maria failed to do a chore or came home late, her mother became angry and reminded Maria of her poor report card, her sloppy room, and her traffic ticket. Her mother was responding to conflict by

    a. force.
    b. avoidance.
    c. gunnysacking.
    d. minimization.

Detail   5. Responding to conflict by belittling the other person's anger is called __minimization__ .

Inference   __c__   6. The author implies that ironically many victims of violence

    a. face the problems openly.
    b. tend to fight back aggressively.
    c. cover up the problems.
    d. affix blame accurately.

Detail   __c__   7. The response tactic of personal rejection includes all of the following *except*

    a. demoralization.
    b. withdrawal of affection.
    c. honesty.
    d. selfishness.

Answer the following with *T* (true) or *F* (false).

Detail   _T_   8. According to the passage, Coleman and Ethel's argument over which stereo to buy would most likely be considered a content conflict.

Inference   _T_   9. The author believes that confronting a concern usually means that the relationship is worth the effort.

Inference   _F_   10. The author thinks that stating the perceptions of others regarding a particular behavior is productive in conflict resolution.

VOCABULARY

Answer the following with *a, b, c,* or *d* for the word or phrase that best defines the boldface word as used in the selection. The number in parentheses indicates the line of the passage in which the word is located.

_a_   1. "**attaining** his or her goals" (9)

a. achieving
b. desiring
c. accomplishing
d. dreaming

_c_   2. "false **assumptions**" (28)

a. hopes
b. fears
c. guesses
d. information

_d_   3. "our **pettiness**" (32)

a. anger
b. greed
c. insensitivity
d. narrow-mindedness

_b_   4. "violence was **reciprocal**" (77)

a. complex
b. shared
c. aggravated
d. triggered

_a_   5. "feelings are not **legitimate**" (87)

a. genuine
b. necessary
c. noticeable
d. accurate

_b_   6. "try to **validate**" (88)

a. diffuse
b. verify
c. force
d. sharpen

_d_   7. "**feign** extreme emotionalism" (100)

a. offer
b. suggest
c. prevent
d. pretend

_b_   8. "hostilities **escalate**" (114)

a. begin
b. rise
c. collide
d. interact

_b_   9. "**noncombative** frame of mind" (118)

a. disagreeable
b. friendly
c. aggressive
d. trusting

_d_ 10. "**contingent** upon resolving" (126–127)

a. acceptable
b. supportive
c. secure
d. conditional

VOCABULARY ENRICHMENT

A. Study the similar-sounding words, and then circle the one that is correct in each sentence.

alter: change
altar: platform in church

Copyright ©1999 by Addison-Wesley Educational Publishers Inc.

1. You must (**alter,** **altar**) your study habits to make better grades.

    coarse: not smooth
    course: studies or path

2. To change a (**coarse, course**), you must go through a drop-add procedure.

    dual: two
    duel: fight

3. The two senators fought a (**dual, duel**) at dawn.

B. Use context clues to mark *a, b, c,* or *d* for the meaning closest to that of the boldface word.

    ___d___ 4. From listening to her talk about the trip, I got **vicarious** pleasure and felt as if I had been there.

    a. selfish
    b. enormous
    c. secret
    d. secondhand

    ___d___ 5. The **cardiac** patient was waiting in surgery for a by-pass operation.

    a. rested
    b. cancer
    c. emotion
    d. heart

    ___b___ 6. Because of his **phobia,** he did not want to climb to the top of the tower and look down.

    a. rash
    b. fear
    c. disease
    d. mood

C. Use the indicated root to write words to complete each sentence in the groups.

    vis, vid: **see**

    7. When she plays tennis, she wears a _____visor_____ to keep the sun out of her eyes.

    8. From the description you have given me, I cannot _____visualize_____ the actor's face.

    9. The rip was so well-mended that the hole is now _____invisible_____.

    tin, ten, tent: **hold, hold together**

    10. We cannot _____continue_____ the trip without stopping for gas.

    11. The _____maintenance_____ crew cleans the floors at night when no one is in the building.

    12. She has been _____discontent_____ at her present job for a long time and is thus seeking other employment.

clud, clus: **shut**

13. She gradually became a _____recluse_____ by staying in the house and not receiving any visitors.

14. To _____conclude_____ the interview, the manager stood up and shook her hand.

15. A correct address should _____include_____ the zip code.

ASSESS YOUR LEARNING

Review confusing questions, seek clarification, and make notes in your text to help you remember new information and vocabulary.

EXPLORE THE NET

- What types of help lines are available for conflict, violence, and abuse prevention?
- What outstanding programs have been developed to teach alternatives to violence?

For additional readings and exercises, visit the Longman English Skills Web page at:

http://longman.awl.com/englishpages

For a user name and password, please see your instructor.

Connect

The following statements refer to ways in which you may communicate in an interpersonal conflict situation—one involving a disagreement between yourself and some other individual with whom you have an interpersonal relationship, such as a friend, lover, or family member. For each of the following statements indicate T (true) if the statement is a generally accurate description of your conflict behavior, and F (false) if the statement is a generally inaccurate description of your conflict behavior.

HOW DO YOU FIGHT?

_____ 1. I avoid conflict situations by physically leaving the situation.

_____ 2. I state any feelings and thoughts openly, directly, and honestly without any attempt to disguise the real object of my disagreement.

_____ 3. I try to force the other person to accept my way of thinking by physically overpowering the individual or by threatening to use physical force.

_____ 4. I take responsibility for my thoughts and feelings. I say "I feel hurt . . ." rather than "You hurt me . . ."

Copyright ©1999 by Addison-Wesley Educational Publishers Inc.

_____ 5. I use humor (especially sarcasm or ridicule) to minimize the conflict.

_____ 6. I try to feel what the other person is feeling and see the situation as the other person does.

_____ 7. I try to establish blame before attempting to resolve the conflict.

_____ 8. I validate the other person's feelings. I let the other person know that I think his or her feelings are legitimate and appropriate.

_____ 9. I cry and sometimes pretend to be extremely emotional in order to get my way or win the argument.

_____10. I concentrate on describing the behaviors with which I have difficulty rather than evaluating them.

_____11. I remember and store up grievances (for example, past indiscretions and mistakes) and bring them up when a conflict arises.

_____12. I state my position tentatively—provisionally—rather than as the final word. Further, I demonstrate flexibility and a willingness to change my opinion or position should appropriate reasons be given.

_____13. In an interpersonal conflict situation, I bring up the strongest arguments I can find, even if the other person cannot deal with them effectively or they may hurt the other person's ego or self-esteem.

_____14. I emphasize areas of agreement before approaching the disagreements.

_____15. I attempt to manipulate the other person by being especially charming (even disarming) and getting the other person into a receptive and noncombative frame of mind.

_____16. I express positive feelings for the other person and for the relationship between us even during the actual conflict exchange.

_____17. I withhold love and affection and attempt to win the argument by getting the other person to break down under this withdrawal.

_____18. I treat my combatant as an equal.

_____19. I sometimes refuse to discuss the conflict or disagreement and even to listen to the other person's argument or point of view.

_____20. I engage in conflict actively rather than passively as both speaker and listener.

Scoring: This conflict scale was developed to sensitize you to some of the conflict strategies to be discussed in this chapter rather than to provide you with a specific score. Generally, however, you would be following recommended conflict resolution procedures if you responded *T* to the even-numbered statements and *F* to the odd-numbered statements.

Some of the statements refer to general principles of effective interpersonal communication that we've covered. These are statements (2) openness, (4) openness, (6) empathy, (8) empathy, (10) supportiveness, (12) supportiveness, (14) positiveness, (18) equality, and (20) equality. The other statements refer to strategies and techniques covered in this chapter. These are statements (1) avoidance, (3) force, (5) using humor to ridicule, (7) blame, (9) silencers, (11) gunnysacking, (13) beltlining, (15) manipulation, (17) personal rejection, and (19) nonnegotiation.

—Essentials of Human Communication by Joseph DeVito

PERSONAL FEEDBACK 2

Name_____

1. Would you describe yourself as a spontaneous person or a person who plans?

   _____

   _____

2. What type of noise bothers you when you study? _____

   _____

3. Have you been generally happy or unhappy this week? Explain why.

   _____

4. What has happened this week to make you laugh at yourself?

   _____

5. List a few questions that you have asked in any of your classes during the past two weeks. _____

   _____

6. What routine do you usually follow at night to get ready for the next day at school? _____

   _____

7. What has pleasantly surprised you about your college experience?

   _____

   _____

8. How did you waste time this past week? _____

   _____

   _____

Copyright © 1999 by Addison-Wesley Educational Publishers Inc.

Copyright © 1999 by Addison-Wesley Educational Publishers Inc.

7

Test-Taking Strategies

◆ *Can your physical condition affect your test score?*
◆ *Are test questions predictable?*
◆ *How can you keep your mind on what you are reading?*
◆ *How are standardized test items made especially tricky?*
◆ *How do you organize an essay response?*

Achieve Your Highest Potential ◆◆◆◆◆◆◆◆◆◆◆◆

High test scores should reflect your knowledge and ability, not your use of tricks or gimmicks. Awareness of test-taking strategies, however, can help you achieve your highest potential.

In college you are basically faced with two types of tests, content exams and standardized tests. A content exam measures your knowledge on a subject that you have been studying. For example, the final exam in Psychology 101 measures your understanding and retention of what was taught throughout the course. The score becomes a major part of your final grade in the course. A standardized test, on the other hand, measures your mastery of a skill that has developed over a long period of time, such as reading or doing mathematics. The scores on standardized tests usually help you qualify for entering or exiting specific college programs that are important to your academic success.

The purpose of this chapter is to help you increase your test scores by being aware of what is expected in the test-taking situation. Many of the following suggestions are obvious, but it is surprising how frequently they are overlooked. Some relate to your physical and mental readiness for peak performance, whereas others explore means for coping with the challenging demands of the testing situation. Technical aspects of test construction are presented with opportunities for application and practice. Awareness and practice can indeed improve test scores and give you that winning edge!

Be Prepared ◆◆◆◆◆◆◆◆◆◆◆◆

Read the passage below, and then write *agree* or *disagree* for the statements that follow.

> Ed was earning money for college by working at a local convenience store in the late afternoon and early evening. On Wednesday night his boss asked him to work long past midnight for an employee who had called in sick. Since Ed needed money for his car payments, he agreed. He did not tell his boss that he had an important test early the next morning.
>
> Thursday morning Ed slept through the alarm but fortunately was awakened by the telephone a half-hour later. He arrived at the exam as the test booklets were being distributed, having missed the professor's introductory remarks and responses to students' questions. Ed spent the first part of the test settling down mentally and physically. He was surprised by some of the material on the test. As he began to read and answer questions, he worried that he would not do well.

<u>disagree</u> 1. Ed was mentally alert after a good night's sleep.

Ed made a poor decision in not telling his boss that he needed adequate sleep on the night before his big test. Being alert rather than drowsy can make the difference in answering correctly one item or more. That correct item, for example, could make the difference in a failing score of 68 or a passing score of 70. Don't take chances when the stakes are high. Being alert can make a difference. *Set yourself up for success, and get plenty of sleep the night before a test.*

<u>disagree</u> 2. Since Ed arrived while the test was being distributed, his lateness did not work against him.

Ed could not immediately begin to work on the test because he had to calm himself first. If you arrive late and flustered, you lose valuable time and begin at a disadvantage. Do your nerves a favor and avoid close calls. *Arrive five or ten minutes early for a test, and get settled.* Find a seat, greet your friends, and take out a pen or pencil.

disagree 3. Ed knew what to expect on the test.

Ed expressed surprise over some of the material on the test. Always check to be sure you know exactly what the test will cover. Know the format of the test. Will it be essay or multiple choice? Study with the format in mind. *Know what to expect on the test.*

disagree 4. Ed had probably asked how the test would be scored.

Since Ed arrived late and missed the professor's introductory remarks, he probably did not know about the scoring. Sometimes, but not very often, guessing is penalized in the scoring. When scores are based on answering all questions, you are better off guessing than leaving items blank. To be safe, ask if omitted items count against you. Also, sometimes some items are worth more points than others; this information is usually stated on the test itself. *Be aware of how the test will be scored.*

disagree 5. Ed approached the test with a positive mental attitude.

Ed had unnecessarily hurt himself and thus lost confidence. Preparation breeds self-confidence, and the lack of it breeds anxiety. Be prepared and plan for success. Give yourself good reasons to be optimistic. *Have confidence in your abilities.*

Stay Alert ◆◆◆◆◆◆◆◆◆◆

EXERCISE 2

Read the passage below, and then write *agree* or *disagree* for the statements that follow.

> After reading the first passage on the comprehension test, Julie realized that she had no idea what she had read. She had seen all the words, but her mind was not on the message. She was excited and wanted to do well, but was having trouble focusing on the material. She moved to the questions hoping—erroneously—that they would provide clues to the meaning. They did not, and so she began rereading the passage with greater determination.
>
> Julie finally gained control over the test and was doing fine until her classmates began to leave. She panicked. She was not finished, but saw others turning in their tests. She was stuck on an item that she had reread three times. She looked at her watch and saw that she had ten minutes left. That would be plenty of time to finish the last passage, if she could only regain her composure.

agree 1. Julie was unable to concentrate when she began the test.

Julie could not initially focus her attention and comprehend the material. She was anxious and excited. *Concentration is essential for comprehension.* If you are distracted, take a few deep breaths to relax and get your mind on track. Tune out internal and external distractions, and focus on the meaning. Visualize the mes-

Copyright ©1999 by Addison-Wesley Educational Publishers Inc.

sage and relate it to what you already know. *Follow directions,* and proceed with confidence. Use your pen as a pacer to concentrate on the passage. (This technique of rhythmically following the words is discussed further in Chapter 8.) If anxiety is a consistent problem, seek help from the campus counseling center.

agree 2. Julie was smart to wear a watch to the test.

Time is usually a major consideration on a test, so always wear *and use* a watch. *Size up the task and schedule your time.* Look over all parts of the test when you receive it. Determine the number of sections to be covered and allocate your time accordingly. Check periodically to see if you are meeting your time goals.

On teacher-made tests, the number of points for each item will sometimes vary. Spend the most time on the items that yield the most points.

disagree 3. Julie should be sure of her answer to each item before moving to another.

Do not waste time that you may need later by pondering an especially difficult question. Mark the item with a dot and move on to the rest of the test. If you have a few minutes at the end, return to the marked items. *On a test every minute counts, so work rapidly.* Be aggressive and alert in moving through the test.

disagree 4. Changing an answer usually makes it wrong.

If you have time at the end of the test, *go back to the items about which you were unsure.* If careful rethinking indicates another response, change your answer. Research shows that scores can be improved making such changes.[1]

disagree 5. Students who finish a test early make the best grades.

The evidence indicates that there is no correlation between high scores and the time taken to complete a test.[2] Speed does not always equal accuracy. *Don't be intimidated by students who finish early.* Schedule your time and meet your goals.

Seek Feedback ◆◆◆◆◆◆◆◆◆◆◆

After a test, investigate your errors, if possible. On many standardized tests, only the score is reported, so you are unable to review the test itself. But when feedback is available, take advantage of the opportunity. Analyze your mistakes so that you can learn from them and avoid repeating the same errors. Wrong answers give you valuable diagnostic information. If you do not understand the error in your thinking, seek advice from another student or the professor. Never merely look at your grade and forget the test if feedback is available.

---

[1]Marshal A. Geiger, "Changing Multiple-Choice Answers: Do Students Accurately Perceive Their Performance?" *Journal of Experimental Educating* 59 (1991): 250–257.

[2]Robert K. Bridges, "Order of Finish, Time to Completion, and Performance on Course-Based Objective Examinations: A Systematic Analysis of Their Relationship on Both Individual Exam Scores and Total Score Across Three Exams," Annual Meeting of the Eastern Psychological Association, Baltimore, MD, April, 1982.

PERSONAL FEEDBACK 1

Name_____

1. Depending on which test you were required to take, what were your scores on the SAT, the ACT, or a college placement test?

_____

2. How do you feel you could improve your scores if you took the test again?

_____

3. What state- or college-mandated tests will you need to take before college graduation?

_____

4. What skills are included in those mandated tests?

_____

_____

5. What class activities do you feel you need to help you improve your standardized test scores?

_____

_____

6. What individual assistance could your instructor offer to help you improve?

_____

_____

7. Review the comprehension questions that you have missed in previous chapters. What question types do you tend to miss most often? Why?

_____

_____

8. What do you feel is the biggest misconception about standardized tests?

_____

_____

Copyright ©1999 by Addison-Wesley Educational Publishers Inc.

Standardized Reading Tests ◆◆◆◆◆◆◆◆◆◆◆

Students are required to take standardized reading tests to show proficiency in reading comprehension for a variety of reasons. Tests such as the SAT or the ACT are required for admission to many colleges. Computerized tests such as the Compass are used by many colleges for placement. Some states require additional testing for entering students, such as the TASP in Texas and the CLAST in Florida. In Georgia, students must take a test with a reading component, the Regents Exam, before they are allowed to graduate. Thus, for college students, performing well on standardized tests can be critical to success.

Read to Comprehend

Read for the main idea of the passage. Don't fixate on details. Read to understand the author's message. Students ask, "Should I read the questions first and then the passage?" Experts differ in their opinions, but most advise reading the passage first and then answering the questions. If you read the questions first, you have five or six purposes for reading. Reading thus becomes fragmented and lacks focus. Read with one purpose: to understand the main idea. Avoid paying too much attention to detail.

Interact

Interact with the passage. Use the thinking strategies of good readers: Predict the topic and activate your schema. Visualize the message and relate it to what you already know. Monitor and self-correct. Apply what you already know about the reading process to each test passage.

Anticipate

Anticipate what is coming. Test passages are frequently untitled and thus offer no clue to content. To activate your schema before reading, glance at the passage for a repeated word, name, or date that might signal its subject.

Read the first sentence carefully. Reread if necessary. The first sentence usually sets the stage for what is to come. It sometimes states the central theme and sometimes simply stimulates your curiosity. In any case, the first sentence starts you thinking about what you will be reading. Continue to anticipate throughout the passage. Some of your guesses will be right and some will be wrong. Double-check information and self-monitor.

Relax

Don't allow yourself to feel rushed. Work with control and confidence. That anxious, pressured feeling tends to occur at the beginning, middle, and end of a test. In the beginning, you are worried about not being able to concentrate immediately and thus having to reread. In the middle, you may be upset because you are only half-finished, which actually is where you should be. When the first student finishes the test, you may again feel rushed and lose your concentration. To combat this feeling, use your pen as a pacer to focus your attention both mentally and physically on the printed page. Plan your time, relax, and concentrate.

Read to Learn

Test passages are not all that dull. They will never compete with steamy novels, but some are quite interesting and informative. Anticipate having fun. Rather than reading with the artificial purpose of answering questions, read to learn and enjoy. You may surprise yourself!

Recall

Pull the passage together before pulling it apart. Remind yourself of the author's main point, rather than waiting for questions to prod you. This final monitoring step in the reading process only takes a few seconds.

EXERCISE 3 Using the above suggestions, read the following passage as if it were part of a reading comprehension test. The handwritten side notes will help to make you aware of a few aspects of your thinking.

A what?
How could she get out of there?

Where?

Reread to get her straight
Evil?

Full Power

Puppets?'

Evil monks wanting power Manipulated scripture

Does the author think it's O.K.? Surprise!

Expanded empire Weaknesses?

Lover?

One too many Downfall

One of the most remarkable women in world history, famed for her vices as well as for her strong and able rule, governed China from about 660 to 705. The Empress Wu began her career as a concubine in the harem of the third T'ang emperor. When the emperor died, Wu and all the other concubines, according to custom, had their heads shaved and entered a Buddhist convent. Here they were expected to pass the remainder of their lives. Wu, however, was too intelligent and beautiful—as well as too unscrupulous—to accept such a fate. Within a year she had won the new emperor's heart and had become his concubine. According to a hostile tradition, she first met the new emperor in a lavatory when he was paying a ceremonial visit to the convent.

Wu rose steadily in the new emperor's favor until, after accusing the empress of engaging in sorcery, murdering her baby daughter, and plotting to poison her husband, she was herself installed as empress. According to the official history of the age, "The whole sovereign power passed into her hands. Life and death, reward and punishment, were determined by her word. The Son of Heaven merely sat upon his throne with hands folded."

After the death of the emperor twenty years later, Wu installed two of her sons as successive puppets. She ruthlessly employed secret police and informers to suppress conspiracies against her. Finally, in 690 at the age of sixty-two, she usurped the imperial title and became the only woman ever to rule China in name as well as in fact.

To legitimize her usurpation, the empress was aided by a group of unscrupulous Buddhist monks, one of whom is reputed to have been her lover. They discovered in Buddhist scriptures a prophecy that a pious woman was destined to be reborn as the ruler of an empire that would inaugurate a better age and to which all countries would be subject. Not only did he monks identify Wu as the woman in the prophecy, but they acclaimed her as a divine incarnation of the Buddha. The T'ang capital was renamed the Divine Capital, and Wu assumed a special title—"Holy Mother Divine Imperial One."

Despite her ruthlessness—understandable in the totally unprecedented situation of a woman seeking successfully to rule a great empire—the Empress Wu was an able ruler who consolidated the T'ang Dynasty. She not only avenged earlier Sui and T'ang defeats at the hands of the northern Koreans who had been subject to the Han, but she made all of Korea a loyal vassal state of China. Yet because she was a woman and a usurper, she found little favor with Chinese Confucian historians. They played up her vices, particularly her many favorites and lovers whom she rewarded with unprecedented honors.

Among those who gained great influence over the aging empress was a peddler of cosmetics, famous for his virility, who was first made abbot of a Buddhist monastery, then palace architect, and finally commander-in-chief of the armies on the northern frontier. At the age of seventy-two, her favorites—and reputed lovers—were two young brothers of a type known as "white faces" (men who were physically attractive but otherwise of no account), whose powdered and rouged faces were a common sight around the palace. When the empress appointed a younger brother of her two favorites to an important governorship, her leading ministers successfully conspired to put her son back on the throne. The two brothers were decapitated in the palace and the Empress Wu, the founder and only member of the Wu Dynasty, was forced to abdicate.

—*Civilization Past-and-Present* by Walter Wallbank et al.

Understand Major Question Types ◆◆◆◆◆◆◆◆◆◆◆

Test questions follow certain predictable patterns. For example, almost all passages are followed by one question on the main idea. Learn to recognize the types of questions and understand how they are constructed. What techniques does the test writer use when creating correct answers and incorrect distractors? Well-written distractors are tempting incorrect responses that draw attention, cause confusion, and thus force the test taker to use knowledge and logic. This

Copyright ©1999 by Addison-Wesley Educational Publishers Inc.

section will discuss each major question type, offer insight into their construction, and give you an opportunity to play the role of test writer.

Main Idea Questions

Main idea questions ask the reader to identify the author's main point. These questions are often stated in one of the following forms:

The best statement of the main idea is . . .

The best title for this passage is . . .

The author is primarily concerned with . . .

The central theme of the passage is . . .

Incorrect responses to main idea items fall into two categories: Some are too broad or general. They suggest that the passage includes much more than it actually does. For example, for a passage describing the hibernation of goldfish in a pond during the winter, the title "Fish" would be much too general to describe the specific topic. Other incorrect answers are too narrow. They focus on details within the passage that support the main idea. The details may be attention-getting and interesting, but they do not describe the central focus. They are tempting, however, because they are direct statements from within the passage.

If you have difficulty understanding the main idea of a passage, reread the first and last sentences. Sometimes, but not always, one of these sentences will give you an overview or focus.

EXAMPLE   Answer the following main idea items on the passage about Empress Wu. Then read the handwritten remarks describing the student's thinking involved in judging whether a response is correct.

____*d*____ 1. The best statement of the main idea of this passage is:

   a. Buddhist monks bring Wu to power.

   (Important detail, but the focus is on her.)

   b. Women in China were not equal to men.

   (Too broad and general, or not really covered.)

   c. Empress Wu's ambition for her young lovers leads to her downfall.

   (Very interesting, but a detail.)

   d. Empress Wu ruthlessly usurped power but became an able ruler of a great empire.

   (Yes, includes all and sounds great!)

____*c*____ 2. The best title for this passage is:

   a. Confucians Defeat Wu.

   (Detail.)

   b. Empress Wu and Her Lovers.

   (Very interesting, but a detail.)

   c. Empress Wu, Ruler of China.

   (Sounds best.)

   d. Rulers of China.

   (Too broad; this is about only one one woman.)

Create Test Items. Learn by doing. Learn about the thinking involved in answering main idea questions by constructing such items yourself. For Exercises 4 and 5, read the passages, and then create your own test questions, using the italicized hints as guidelines. Be clever. Be sure your correct answer is totally correct, without exception. Use tempting, not silly, distractors as the incorrect responses.

EXERCISE 4

From the time that batters first took to the baseball field, they have been told to keep their eyes on the ball. It now appears though, that this advice might better have been left unsaid. The reason? Computer tracking of baseball pitches has shown that the fastballs thrown in major-league baseball simply travel too fast for the eye to follow and if a batter tries to follow a ball from the moment it leaves a pitcher's hand, he will lose sight of it by the time it gets about five feet from the plate.

According to Dr. A. Terry Bahill of the University of Arizona, good hitters take their eyes off the ball during the middle of its trip to home plate, and shift their vision closer to the plate, waiting for its arrival and, they hope, impact with the bat. "The human eye simply is incapable of tracking a fastball over the entire path of 60 feet 6 inches. For one segment of its trajectory, the last 10 feet or so, the ball is going too fast," said Dr. Bahill. "We hypothesize that the best imaginable athlete could not track the ball closer than 5 feet from the plate, at which point it is moving three times faster than the fastest human could track it."

Bahill's advice to batters is to make an anticipatory visual leap, just after the ball is thrown by the pitcher, to where it ought to be when it arrives at the plate. Therefore, instead of relying on the raw sensory input from the traveling ball—the process of sensation—batters should use what they have learned to expect about the way balls travel, characteristic of the processes involved in perception. In the future, then, we should not be surprised if baseball coaches advise their batters to keep their eyes *off* the ball.

—*Understanding Psychology* by Robert Feldman

_____d_____ 1. The best title for this passage is

    a. Catching the Fast Ball

       (This is not about catching.)

    b. Computer Tracking

       (Write a phrase about a detail.)

    c. Baseball

       (Create a response that is too broad.)

    d. Eyes off the Ball

       (Write a correct title.)

_____c_____ 2. The best statement of the main idea of this passage is:

    a. The human eye cannot follow a fastball over a path of 60 feet, 6 inches.

       (This is an extremely important detail, but it needs more to it to describe the author's point.)

    b. Bahill gives advice to batters.

       (Write a detail that sounds tempting.)

    c. Batters cannot totally track a fastball and thus should predict its path.

       (Write a correct statement.)

    d. Computer tracking tells more about speed than the human eye.

       (Write a general statement that includes too much.)

Copyright ©1999 by Addison-Wesley Educational Publishers Inc.

Detail Questions

Detail questions check your ability to understand material that is directly stated in the passage. To find or double-check an answer, note a key word in the question, and then quickly glance at the passage for that word or synonym. When you locate the term, reread the sentence for clarification. Detail questions fall in the following patterns:

The author states that . . .

According to the author . . .

According to the passage . . .

All of the following are true except . . .

A person, term, or place is . . .

Incorrect answers to detail questions tend to be false statements. Test writers like to use pompous or catchy phrases stated directly from the passage as distractors. Such phrases may sound authoritative but mean nothing.

EXAMPLE Answer the following detail question on the passage about Empress Wu (see page 229). Then note the handwritten remarks reflecting the thinking involved in judging whether a response is correct.

  _____d_____ 1. Empress Wu did all the following except
        (Note the use of except; look for the only false item to be the correct answer.)

  a. consolidate the T'ang Dynasty.

    (True, this is stated in the fifth paragraph.)

  b. accuse the empress of sorcery.

    (True, this is stated in the second paragraph.)

  c. appoint the brother of a young favorite to an important governorship.

    (True, this is stated in the last paragraph.)

  d. poison her husband.

    (She did not do this, so this is the correct answer.)

 **EXERCISE 5** Read the following passage, and then write your own detail question, using the italicized hints as guidelines.

Van Gogh left Paris for the southern provincial city of Arles. There he was joined briefly by the painter Paul Gauguin, with whom Van Gogh hoped to work very closely, creating perfect art in a pure atmosphere of self-expression. However, the two artists quarreled, and, apparently in the aftermath of one intense argument, Van Gogh cut off a portion of his ear and had it delivered to a prostitute living in a brothel. Soon after, Van Gogh realized that his instability had gotten out of hand, and he committed himself to an asylum, where—true to form—he continued to work prolifically at his painting. Most of the work we admire so much was done in the last two years at Arles. Vincent (as he always signed himself) received much sympathetic encouragement during those years, both from his brother and from an unusually perceptive doctor and art connoisseur, Dr. Gachet, whom he painted several times. Nevertheless, his despair deepened, and in July of 1890 he shot himself to death.

—*Living with Art* by William McCarter and Rita Gilbert

_____<u>c</u>_____ 1. Van Gogh cut off his ear in

    a. Paris. *(No, he had left Paris.)*

    b. an asylum. *(No, after the incident, he went to the asylum.)*

    c. <u>Arles   </u>. *(Write the correct answer.)*

    d. <u>a brothel   </u>. *(Use another location mentioned in the pas-*

    sage as an incorrect response.)

Implied Meaning Questions

An implied meaning is suggested but not directly stated. Clues in the passage lead the reader to make assumptions and draw conclusions. Items testing implied meaning deal with the attitudes and feelings of the writer that emerge as if from behind or between words. Favorable and unfavorable descriptions suggest positive and negative opinions toward a subject. Sarcastic remarks indicate the motivation of characters. Look for clues that help you develop logical assumptions. Implied meaning questions may be stated in one of the following forms:

The author believes (or feels or implies) . . .

It can be inferred (deduced from clues) from the passage . . .

The passage (or author) suggests . . .

It can be concluded from the passage that . . .

    Base your conclusion on both what is known and what is suggested. Incorrect responses to implied meaning items tend to be false statements that lack logical support.

EXAMPLE   Answer the following implied meaning questions on the passage about Empress Wu. Then note the handwritten remarks reflecting the thinking involved in judging whether a response is correct.

_____<u>c</u>_____ 1. The author implies that Empress Wu

    a. was a devout Buddhist.

        (She was aided by them, but her religious zeal is not suggested.)

    b. killed the first empress's baby daughter.

        (No, she accused the former empress of doing this.)

    c. let her vices lead to her downfall.

        (True, rewarding her young lovers probably hurt the empire.)

    d. conquered Korea to satisfy the Confucian historians.

        (She did conquer Korea, but it is not suggested that she tried to satisfy the Confucian historians.)

EXERCISE 6   Read the following passage, and then write your own implied meaning question, using the italicized hints as guidelines.

In 1642 Rembrandt's fortunes again changed, this time, irrevocably, for the worse. Saskia died not long after giving birth to Titus. The artist's financial affairs were in great disarray,

Copyright ©1999 by Addison-Wesley Educational Publishers Inc.

no doubt partly because of his self-indulgence in buying art and precious objects. Although he continued to work and to earn money, Rembrandt showed little talent for money management. Ultimately he was forced into bankruptcy and had to sell not only his art collection but even Saskia's burial plot. About 1649 Hendrickje Stoffels came to live with Rembrandt, and she is thought of as his second wife, although they did not marry legally. She joined forces with Titus to form an art dealership in an attempt to protect the artist from his creditors. Capping the long series of tragedies that marked Rembrandt's later life, Hendrickje died in 1663 and Titus in 1668, a year before his father.

—*Living with Art* by William McCarter and Rita Gilbert

_____d_____ 1. The author implies that Saskia was Rembrandt's

    a. sister.

       (This is not suggested.)

    b. business partner
       (Write an incorrect response.)

    c. friend who was an artist
       (Write another incorrect response.)

    d. Wife
       (Supply the correct response, and underline the clues in the passage that suggest it.)

Purpose Questions

The purpose of a passage is not usually stated. Instead, it is implied and is related to the main idea. In responding to a purpose item, you are answering the question "What was the author's purpose in writing this material?" This question might be restated as, "What did the author do to or for me, the reader?"

EXAMPLE   Reading comprehension tests tend to include three basic types of passages, each of which suggests a separate set of purposes. Study the outline of the three types shown in the Reader's Tip box, and answer the question on the Empress Wu passage. Then note the handwritten remarks reflecting the thinking involved in judging whether an answer is correct.

◆◆ READER'S TIP

TYPES OF TEST PASSAGES

Factual Passages

What? Science or history articles
How to read? Read for the main idea, and do not get bogged down in details. Remember, you can look back.
Author's Purpose?

❖ To inform
❖ To explain
❖ To describe

Example: Textbooks

Opinion Passages

What? Articles with a particular point of view on a topic.

How to read? Read to determine the author's opinion on the subject. Then judge the value of the support included, and decide whether you agree or disagree.

Author's Purpose?

- ❖ To argue
- ❖ To persuade
- ❖ To condemn
- ❖ To ridicule

Examples: Newspaper editorials

Fiction Passages

What? Articles that tell a story

How to Read? Read to understand what the characters are thinking and why they act as they do.

Author's Purpose?

- ❖ To entertain
- ❖ To narrate
- ❖ To describe
- ❖ To shock

Examples: Novels and short stories

_____b_____ 1. The purpose of the passage on Empress Wu is

    a. to argue.

      (No side is taken.)

    b. to explain.

      (Yes, because the material is factual, like a textbook.)

    c. to condemn.

      (The reading is not judgmental.)

    d. to persuade

      (No point of view is argued.)

EXERCISE 7

Read the following passage, and then write your own purpose question, using the italicized hints as guidelines.

. . . [A]nyone who has had a reasonable amount of contact with the federal government has encountered people who should be fired. There are, of course, some superb civil servants—maybe ten per cent of the total—who have every right to become indignant at blanket criticism of government workers. There are another 50 to 60 percent who range from adequate to good. Unfortunately, that leaves 30 to 40 percent in the range downward from marginal to outright incompetent.

Copyright ©1999 by Addison-Wesley Educational Publishers Inc.

Yet fewer than one percent are fired each year. This is because 93 percent are under some form of civil service and are therefore virtually impossible to fire.

Being able to fire people is important for two reasons: 1) to permit you to hire the people you want and to get rid of those you don't want, and 2) to make it possible for you to attract the kind of risk-takers who are repelled by the safe civil service and the political emasculation it entails.

—*Points of View: Readings in American Government and Politics*
by Robert E. DiClerico and Allan S. Hammock

___b___ 1. The author's primary purpose in this passage is to

    a. narrate. *(The author is not telling a story.)*

    b. persuade, condemn, or argue
       (What is the author really trying to do?)

    c. entertain
       (Check the list of purposes in the Reader's Tip box and use one that is incorrect.)

    d. describe
       (Use another incorrect purpose from the Reader's Tip box.)

Vocabulary Questions

Vocabulary items test your general word knowledge as well as your ability to figure out meaning by using context clues. Vocabulary items are usually stated as follows:

As used in the passage, the best definition of _____ is . . .

Both word knowledge and context are necessary for a correct response. Go back and reread the sentence before the word, the sentence with the word, and the sentence after the word to be sure that you understand the context and are not mislead by unusual meanings. Be suspicious of common words such as *industry,* which seems simple on the surface but can have multiple meanings.

EXAMPLE   Answer the following vocabulary question on the passage about Empress Wu (see page 229). Then note the handwritten remarks reflecting the thinking involved in judging whether an answer is correct.

___d___ 1. As used in the third paragraph of the passage, the best definition of *usurped* is

    (Reread the sentence. Look also at the use of "usurpation" in the fourth paragraph.)

    a. earned.

       (This is too positive to describe her ruthless behavior.)

    b. won.

       (Again, this is too positive for her negative actions.)

    c. bought.

       (No pay-off is suggested.)

    d. seized.

       (Yes, she took control and then tried to make it legal.)

 **EXERCISE 8**

Read the following passage, and then write your own vocabulary question, using the italicized hints as guidelines.

Perhaps Mahatma Gandhi was one of the most aggressive men who ever lived, if one would wish to measure aggressiveness by motivation. This great chronicler of nonviolence aggressed against a social structure he believed was wrong and he won. Could a less aggressive, less assertive person have accomplished what he did? Yet his life is generally believed to be the antithesis of aggressiveness. The point is, aggression, especially among humans, may be hard to define, and thus the problem of investigating its motivation and historical origins becomes enormously complicated.

—*Animal Behavior* by Robert Wallace

____c____ 1. As used in the passage, the best definition of *antithesis* is

  a. denial.

  (Figure out the correct response, and you'll see that this doesn't fit.)

  b. dogma or doctrine_____.
  (Supply an authoritative-sounding wrong answer.)

  c. opposite_____.
  (Use the context and your dictionary to write a correct response.)

  d. culmination_____.
  (Write an incorrect response that sounds good.)

Hints for Taking Multiple-Choice and True-False Tests ◆◆◆◆◆◆◆◆◆◆◆

Study the following hints, and answer the items on the passage about Empress Wu with *a, b, c,* or *d,* or *T* (true) or *F* (false), before reading the explanation in italics.

READ ALL OPTIONS

Even if the first answer seems undisputedly correct, read all the options. Be careful, not careless, in considering each answer. Multiple-choice tests usually ask for the *best* answer, not for any one that is reasonable.

_____ 1. The author suggests that

  a. the empress wanted the emperor dead.
  b. the sons of the empress were disobedient.
  c. Wu's sons plotted against the emperor.
  d. the emperor gave the empress immense power.
  (Although the first option may be tempting, the last answer is implied by the quote describing her power and thus is correct.)

PREDICT THE CORRECT ANSWER

As you read the stem (or beginning) of a multiple-choice item, anticipate what you would write for a correct response. Develop an answer in your mind before you read the options, and then look for a choice that corresponds to your thinking.

Copyright ©1999 by Addison-Wesley Educational Publishers Inc.

_____ 2. At the end of her reign, the Empress Wu was

      a. decapitated.
      b. married.
      c. pushed from power.
      d. imprisoned.
        (It says in the last sentence that she "was forced to abdicate." The third option most closely matches this answer.)

AVOID ANSWERS WITH "100 PERCENT" WORDS

All and *never* mean 100 percent, without exception. In a true-false question, a response containing either word is seldom correct. Rarely can a statement be so definitely inclusive or exclusive. Other "100 percent" words to avoid are *no, none, only, every, always,* and *must.*

_____ 3. Empress Wu was hated by all the Chinese Confucian historians.
        (All means 100 percent, and thus is too inclusive. Surely one or two Confucians might not have felt so strongly against Wu.)

CONSIDER ANSWERS WITH QUALIFYING WORDS

Words such as *sometimes* and *seldom* suggest frequency, but do not go so far as to say *all* or *none.* Such qualifying words can mean more than none and less than all. By being so indefinite, they are difficult to dispute. Therefore, qualifiers are more likely to be included in a correct response to a true-false question. Other qualifiers are *few, much, often, may, many, some, perhaps,* and *generally.*

_____ 4. Empress Wu was hated by many of the Chinese Confucian historians.
        (The phrase "she found little favor" with Confucians and "They played up her vices" suggest dislike. The statement is true.)

DO NOT OVERANALYZE

Try to follow the thinking of the test writer rather than overanalyzing minute points. Don't make the question harder than it is. Use your common sense, and answer what you think was intended.

_____ 5. Empress Wu fought Korea and won.
        (Naturally Empress Wu was not standing on the front line of battle with a sword but, as the leader of China, she was ultimately responsible for the victory. Thus the answer is true.)

TRUE STATEMENTS MUST BE TRUE WITHOUT EXCEPTION

A statement is either totally true or it is incorrect. Adding an incorrect *and, but,* or *because* phrase to a true statement makes it false and thus an unacceptable answer. If a statement is half true and half false, mark it false.

_____ 6. The Chinese Confucian historians plotted against Empress Wu because they were concerned about the welfare of the poor people of China.
        (It is true that the Confucians plotted against Wu, but their reasons for doing so are not stated. The statement is half true and half false, so it is false.)

IF TWO OPTIONS ARE SYNONYMOUS, ELIMINATE BOTH

If two items say basically the same thing but only one answer is possible, then neither can be correct. Eliminate the two and spend your time on the others.

_____ 7. The purpose of this passage is

    a. to argue.
    b. to persuade.
    c. to inform.
    d. to entertain.
      (Since "argue" and "persuade" are basically synonyms, you can eliminate both and move on to other options.)

FIGURE OUT THE DIFFERENCE BETWEEN SIMILAR OPTIONS

If two similar options appear, frequently one of them will be correct. Study the choices to see the subtle difference intended by the test maker.

_____ 8. Empress Wu was

    a. supported by many Buddhists.
    b. supported by all the Buddhists.
    c. beloved by the poor.
    d. the greatest ruler of the T'ang Dynasty.
      (The last two answers are not suggested. Close inspection shows that the word all *is the only difference between the first and second answers and is the reason that the second is untrue. Thus the first answer, with the qualifying word, is correct.)*

USE LOGICAL REASONING IF TWO ANSWERS ARE CORRECT

Some tests include the option *all of the above* and *none of the above*. If you see that two of the answers are correct and are unsure about a third, then *all of the above* would be a logical response.

_____ 9. Empress Wu was a

    a. concubine.
    b. mother.
    c. wife.
    d. all of the above.
      (If you recall that Wu was a concubine and a mother but are not sure that she was a wife, "all of the above" would be your logical option because you know that two of the choices are correct.)

LOOK SUSPICIOUSLY AT DIRECTLY QUOTED POMPOUS PHRASES

In searching for distractors, test makers sometimes quote a pompous phrase from the passage that doesn't make much sense. Such a phrase may include lofty, ornate, and seemingly important language from the passage, yet still be incorrect. However, students read the phrase and think, "Oh yes, I saw that in the passage. It sounds good, so it must be right." Be sure authoritative phrases make sense before choosing them.

Copyright ©1999 by Addison-Wesley Educational Publishers Inc.

_____10. Wu was installed as empress because

    a. the Son of Heaven folded his hands.
    b. the imperial title was suppressed in conspiracy.
    c. the prophecy in Buddhist scriptures identified her by name.
    d. the brilliant conniving of an ambitious woman was successful.
    (The first two are pompous and do not make any sense. The third is false because of the phrase "by name." The last is the correct answer.)

SIMPLIFY DOUBLE NEGATIVES BY CANCELING OUT BOTH

Double negatives are confusing and time-consuming to unravel. Simplify a double-negative statement by first canceling out both negatives. Then reread the statement without the confusion of the two negatives, and decide on the accuracy of the statement.

_____11. Empress Wu was not unscrupulous.
    (Cancel out the two negatives, not *and* un. *Reread the sentence without the negatives: "Empress Wu was scrupulous!" This is a false statement).*

CERTAIN RESPONSES ARE NEITHER TRUE NOR FALSE

For some items, you are not given the clues necessary for judging their accuracy. There is not sufficient evidence to indicate whether they are true or false.

_____12. Empress Wu was loved by the Chinese people.
    (The passage does not provide any clues to indicate that she was loved or not loved by the Chinese people.)

VALIDATE TRUE RESPONSES

If you are told that all of the answers are correct except one, you must corroborate each response and, by the process of elimination, find the one that does not fit.

_____13. Empress Wu was all of the following *except*

    a. a scheming concubine.
    b. a ruthless woman.
    c. the first woman to rule China.
    d. the founder of the T'ang Dynasty.
    (Always note the "except" and look for the response that is false. The first three answers are true and the last is untrue, so it is the correct answer.)

RECOGNIZE FLAWS IN TEST-MAKING

Professionally developed reading tests are usually well-constructed and do not contain obvious clues to the correct answers. However, some teacher-made tests are hastily written and thus have errors in test-making that can help a student find the correct answer. Do not, however, rely on these flaws to make a big difference in your score, because such errors should not occur on a well-constructed test.

GRAMMAR. Eliminate responses that do not have subject–verb agreement. The tense of the verb as well as modifiers such as *a* or *an* can also give clues to the correct response.

_____14. Wu's ambition was to become an
      a. concubine.
      b. empress.
      c. lover.
      d. Buddhist.
        (The an *suggests an answer that starts with a vowel. Thus "empress" is the obvious answer.)*

CLUES FROM OTHER PARTS OF THE TEST. Information in one part of the test may help you with an uncertain answer in another section.

_____15. During Wu's reign, China defeated
      a. Vietnam.
      b. India.
      c. Russia.
      d. Korea.
        (A previous question has already included the conquest of Korea.)

LENGTH. On poorly constructed tests, longer answers are more frequently correct.

_____16. The author suggests that Wu promoted the cosmetics peddler to commander-in-chief because he

      a. was a good soldier.
      b. knew how to sell.
      c. had been a Buddhist monk.
      d. was her lover and she wanted to give him favors.
        (In an effort to be totally correct without question, the test maker has written the last—and longest—answer.)

ABSURD IDEAS AND EMOTIONAL WORDS. Avoid distractors that contain absurd ideas or emotional words. The test maker probably got tired of trying to think of distractors and in a moment of weakness included a nonsense answer.

_____17. As used in the passage, the best definition of *concubine* is

      a. wife.
      b. child.
      c. mistress.
      d. dog.
        (The last answer is totally absurd. The test maker should take a break.)

Hints for Taking Essay Exams ◆◆◆◆◆◆◆◆◆◆

In many ways, essay tests are more demanding than multiple-choice tests, for rather than simply recognizing correct answers, you must recall, create, and organize. You face a blank sheet of paper instead of a list of options, and, to write an appropriate response, you must remember ideas and present them in a logical and well-organized manner. The following suggestions can help you respond effectively.

Copyright © 1999 by Addison-Wesley Educational Publishers Inc.

Reword the Statement or Question

Sometimes the statement or question that you are asked to discuss is written in a confusing or pompous manner. Be sure that you understand the meaning, and then rephrase it in your own words. If it is a statement, put it in the form of a question. If it is a question, simplify it and, if possible, divide it into parts.

Decide on the approach you will use in making your response. Will you define, describe, explain, or compare? For example, suppose you were asked to support the following statement:

> Wu rose to power through unscrupulous deception, and fell through her own vice and weaknesses.

You should first rephrase the statement as a question, using words such as *why, what,* or *how:*

> *How did Wu rise to power through unscrupulous deception and fall through her own vice and weaknesses?*

The question really contains two parts, which can be listed separately:

1. *How did Wu rise to power through unscrupulous deception?*
2. *How did Wu fall from power through her own vice and weaknesses?*

How will you answer the question? You should use two approaches:

1. List her unscrupulous acts of deception that put her in power.
2. Explain the reasons for her fall.

Answer the Question

Answer the question that is asked—not some other question. This may seem obvious, but students frequently get off track. Do not write a summary of the material, include irrelevant information, or repeat the same idea over and over again. Focus on the question and write with purpose.

The following is an example of an incorrect response to the question stated above. It is a summary of the material rather than a direct answer:

> Empress Wu became the only woman to rule China in name as well as fact. Her rule lasted for 45 years. She began her rise to power as a concubine of the third T'ang emperor.

Organize Your Answer

Think before you write. This is perhaps the most important step in test-taking, but it is the one that students least want to take the time to do. Plan what you are going to say before you say it.

Brainstorm Ideas. Reread the question, and jot down a word or phrase to note the ideas that you want to include in the answer. Number your ideas in the order in which you want to discuss them. Upon reconsidering, you may find that some of your brainstorming ideas overlap and that others are an example of a larger idea. This is a chance for you to look at your possibilities and come up with a plan. When you use a plan, the writing is a lot easier and more logical.

Establish your purpose in the first sentence, and direct your writing to answer the question. List specific details that support, explain, prove, and develop your point. In a concluding sentence, reemphasize your arguments and restate your purpose. Divide your writing with numbers or subheadings whenever possible, because they simplify the answer for the reader and show the organization. If time runs short, use an outline or a diagram to express your remaining ideas.

The following example shows the plan for answering the question on Empress Wu. The brainstormed ideas have already been organized into a concise, working outline. Remember to think before you write; it is the most important step.

<u>Rose</u>
1. Left convent
2. Plots vs. wife (Sorcery, daughter, poison)
3. Made empress
4. After his death - 2 sons
5. Took Power
6. Monks made her divine ruler

<u>Fell</u>
1. Made ministers mad
2. Rewarding lovers & favorites
   Cosmetics peddler
   Young brothers (governorship)

Use a Formal Writing Style

A college professor, not your best friend, will be reading and grading your answer. Be respectful, direct, and formal. Do not use slang expressions. Do not use phrases such as *as you know* or *well*. They may be appropriate in conversation but not in formal writing.

Avoid empty words and thought. Adjectives such as *good, interesting,* and *nice* say little. Be direct and descriptive in your writing.

State your thesis or main point, supply proof, and use transitional phrases to tie your ideas together. Words such as *first, second,* and *finally* add transition and help to organize your answer. Other terms, such as *however* and *on the other hand,* show a shift in thought. Remember, you are pulling ideas together, so use phrases and words to help the reader see relationships.

The following example illustrates a poor response to the question on Empress Wu. Note the total lack of organization, the weak language, the slang phrase, and the failure to use transition words:

Empress Wu was very sneaky. She did many dishonest things. She told lies about the empress that were so bad that the emperor dumped the empress. Well, then Wu rose like a bird to fill the new shoes.

Be Aware of Appearance

Research has shown that, on the average, essays written in a clear, legible hand receive a grade-level higher score than essays written somewhat illegibly.[3] Be particular about appearance and considerate of the reader. Proofread for correct grammar, punctuation, and spelling.

Predict and Practice

Predict possible essay items by using the table of contents and subheadings of your text to form questions. Practice brainstorming to answer these questions.

---

[3]Charles A. Sloan and Iris McGinnis, "The Effects of Handwriting on Teachers' Grading of High School Essays," Eric #ED220836, 1978.

Copyright ©1999 by Addison-Wesley Educational Publishers Inc.

Review old exams for an insight into both the questions and the kinds of answers that received good marks. Outline answers to possible exam questions. Do as much thinking as possible to prepare yourself to take the test before you sit down to begin writing.

Notice Key Words

Following is a list of key words of instruction that appear in essay questions, with hints for responding to each word:

Compare: List the similarities.
Contrast: Note the differences.
Criticize: State your opinion and stress weaknesses.
Define: State the meaning and use examples so that the term is understood.
Describe: State the characteristics so that the image is vivid.
Diagram: Make a drawing that demonstrates relationships.
Discuss: Define the issue and elaborate on the advantages and disadvantages.
Evaluate: State positive and negative views and make a judgment.
Explain: Show cause and effect and give reasons.
Illustrate: Provide examples.
Interpret: Explain your own understanding of and opinions on a topic.
Justify: Give proof or reasons to support an opinion.
List: Record a series of numbered items.
Outline: Sketch the main points with their significant supporting details.
Prove: Use facts to support an opinion.
Relate: Connect items and show how one influences another.
Review: Give an overview with a summary.
Summarize: Retell the main points.
Trace: Move sequentially from one event to another.

Write to Earn Points

Essay exam grades seem much more subjective and mysterious than multiple-choice test grades. Some students feel that they deserve to pass for filling the page with writing. They wonder what they did wrong if such a paper is returned with a substandard score.

Students need to know that professors use objective measures to grade essay tests. The professor is looking for a certain number of points to be covered for a passing score. If the minimum number of points are not made, the paper fails. Answer an essay question to earn points; do not waste your time including personal experiences or irrelevant facts. Stick to the question, and demonstrate to the professor that you know the material.

The following is the checklist the professor will use to score the essay on Empress Wu:

Rose (60 points)	*Grades*
1. Left convent	All passing exams must have items on both her rise and fall:
2. Plots against wife	
3. Installed as empress	C = Minimum of 5 items
4. Sons on throne	B = Minimum of 6 items
5. Took power	A = Minimum of 7 items included
6. Monks made her divine	

> ***Fell (40 points)***
>
> 1. Ministers angry
> 2. Rewarding lovers
> 3. Examples—peddler and brothers

Read an "A" Paper for Feedback

When your professor returns a multiple-choice exam, you should reread the items and analyze your errors to figure out what you did wrong. An essay exam, however, is not so easy to review. Sometimes essay exams have only a grade on the front and no other comments. The professor may discuss in class what was needed for an A answer, but without seeing it pulled together, a perfect paper is difficult to visualize.

Ask to see an A paper. Maybe it will be yours. If so, share it with others. If not, ask your classmates or professor. The A paper becomes a model from which you can learn. Compare this paper with your own, and draw conclusions about the professor's expectations. Study and learn from the model so that you will not repeat the same mistakes.

EXERCISE 9

Read and assign a grade of A, B, C, D, or F to each of the following essay responses to the Empress Wu question. Explain your reasons for each grade and include any suggestions you would offer to the student who wrote the paper.

PAPER 1

Empress Wu did many bad things in order to get the power. The things she did were against the people in power. She did not want to stay with the Buddhists because she wanted to be with the new emperor. He died and her sons became puppets. She worked against the people who did not like her.

She was finally forced out of power because she had lovers. One of the lovers became a governor. The two brothers that she liked were decapitated. She fell from power and thus was no longer the Empress.

PAPER 2

Empress Wu rose to power through tricks and deception. She was intelligent enough to devise a way to meet the new emperor, get him attracted to her, and thus escape her lifetime sentence in the convent. She rose in the new emperor's favor and plotted dishonestly against his wife. Wu falsely accused the emperor's wife of sorcery, murdering her own daughter, and plotting to poison her husband. Wu was soon made empress and given great power. When the emperor died, she ruled through her two sons. Finally, she took the throne herself. Buddhist monks helped her devise a scheme using the scriptures to validate her power. They said she was a divine incarnation of the Buddha.

Wu fell from power because of her weakness for men as lovers. She rewarded her lovers with power and thus angered her ministers. She made a cosmetics peddler abbot, architect, and then commander-in-chief. Her final appointment of a younger brother of two of her favorites to an important governorship was too much for the ministers. They forced her from power.

Remember that you need to brainstorm before you write. Jot down the ideas that you will use to answer the question, and then number them. Stick to the question, organize your response, and use logic.

Copyright ©1999 by Addison-Wesley Educational Publishers Inc.

POINTS TO PONDER

▲ Gain points by being aware of how tests are constructed and what is expected in the test-taking situation.

▲ Get plenty of sleep the night before a test.

▲ Arrive early for a test and know what to expect.

▲ Concentrate and schedule your time.

▲ Seek feedback so that you will not repeat the same mistakes.

▲ Use the five thinking stragegies of good readers.

▲ Understand the major question types: main idea, details, implied meaning, purpose, and vocabulary.

▲ For essay exams, organize your response and answer the question directly.

PERSONAL FEEDBACK 2

Name_____

1. Do you prefer multiple-choice or essay exams? Why?

   _____

2. What are the weaknesses of your essay responses?

   _____

   _____

3. How did your last English course prepare you for essay exam responses? _____

   _____

4. Describe an activity that could be done in this course to help you on essay responses. _____

   _____

5. Name a student who writes excellent essay responses.

   _____

6. Have you ever outlined a possible essay question before a test? If so, for what class? _____

7. Describe the best paper you have ever written.

   _____

   _____

8. Since grading essay responses is more subjective than grading multiple-choice items, what system do you think professors use to arrive at accurate grades?

   _____

EXPLORE THE NET

- Does your college or state require you to take a standardized test at the end of this course or before graduation? If so, what information is available on the Internet concerning the test? Is a sample test available?
- Find information on one of the many tests that are given to students seeking admission to graduate schools. Describe the registration procedures, cost, and the types of questions that will appear on the test.

For additional readings and exercises, visit the Longman English Skills Web page at:

http://longman.awl.com/englishpages

For a user name and password, please see your instructor.

Copyright ©1999 by Addison-Wesley Educational Publishers Inc.

Efficient Reading

◆ *What is your reading rate?*
◆ *How fast should you read?*
◆ *How can you increase your reading speed?*

Copyright ©1999 by Addison-Wesley Educational Publishers Inc.

What Is Your Reading Rate? ◆◆◆◆◆◆◆◆◆◆◆◆

If you are not zipping through a book at 1,000 words per minute, does it mean that you are a slow reader? No, of course not. You do not need to be reading as fast as you can turn the pages, yet many college students are concerned about their reading rate. While professors focus primarily on improving comprehension, students also want to increase speed. This chapter explains factors that contribute to a fast or slow reading rate and suggests techniques that can help you improve your reading efficiency.

EXERCISE 1

Read the following selection at your normal reading speed. Time your reading so that you can calculate your words-per-minute rate. Use a stopwatch or a watch with a second hand. Record your starting time in minutes and seconds. When you have completed the selection, record your finishing time in minutes and seconds. Answer the questions that follow and use the chart to determine your rate.

Starting time: _____ *minutes* _____ *seconds*

STEROIDS, THE DRUG OF "CHAMPIONS"

In 1988, at the Seoul Olympics, sprinter Ben Johnson of Canada burst out of the starting blocks to win the 100 meter dash, leaving American Carl Lewis in the dust. Three days later the gold medal was awarded to Lewis because traces of stanozolol were found in Johnson's urine. Stanozolol use is banned in international sports because it is an anabolic (tissue-building) steroid. Anabolic steroids burst upon the athletic scene in Olympic competition in the 1950s, when it was learned that Soviet weightlifters were using them to increase their strength. The Americans quickly followed suit and the drugs were soon being used in any sport that required strength (as does virtually every sport). At first steroids were used primarily by elite athletes looking for the final edge that might put them over the top. Soon, however, they found their way into local gyms where body builders of mediocre abilities and grand egos were wolfing down pills in hopes of looking good around the pool.

The major benefit of steroids seems to be to allow muscles to recover more quickly, so that the athlete can train harder. As athletes were reporting remarkable results with steroids, the medical community began testing the effects of the drugs and the drugs were soon banned. Medical researchers reported a variety of remarkable side effects of steroid use including liver cancer, heart disease, and kidney damage. One problem with the drugs is that, along with tissue building, they also "masculinize." The masculinization is particularly acute for women who may grow facial hair as their voices deepen and their breasts decrease in size. They may, indeed, gain muscle mass, but the masculizing effects may be impossible to reverse. In adolescents, steroids hasten maturation and may cause growth to stop and the loss of hair in boys. Strangely, in men, the high levels of steroids in the body may cause the body's own production of male hormones to cease, resulting in enlarged breasts and shrunken testes.

Anabolic steroids also can cause behavioral changes by increasing the aggressiveness of the user. The aggressiveness may be manifest by more vigorous training but also by hostile and sometimes violent social interaction. Interestingly, much of what we know about steroid use comes from observations of abusers since the medical community cannot administer such doses for athletes because of ethical considerations.

(387 words)

—*Biology: The World of Life* by Robert Wallace

Finishing time: _____ *minutes* _____ *seconds*

Reading time in seconds = _____

Words per minute = _____ *(see Time Chart)*

Time Chart

Time in Seconds and Minutes	Words per Minute
40	581
50	464
60 (1 min.)	387
120 (2 min.)	194
130	179
140	165
150	155
160	145
170	137
180 (3 min.)	129
190	122
200	116
210	110
220	106
230	101

Answer the following with *T* (true) or *F* (false).

___F___ 1. Carl Lewis used steroids at the Seoul Olympics.

___T___ 2. Steroid use was once accepted in international sports.

___T___ 3. A high level of steroids in men may cause increased aggression.

___F___ 4. A high level of steroids in women may cause enlarged breasts.

___T___ 5. Liver cancer can be a side effect of steroids.

   (Each scored item counts 20 points)

   Comprehension = _____%

What Is an Average Reading Rate?

Rate calculations vary according to difficulty of the material. Research indicates, however, that on relatively easy material, the average adult reading speed is approximately 250 words per minute at 70 percent comprehension. For college students, the rate is sometimes estimated at closer to 300 words per minute.

   Since this selection was not particularly difficult, the average adult reading speed of 250 words per minute at 70 percent comprehension would apply. If you are reading below this rate, you may have trouble finishing standardized tests and finishing assignments. The suggestions on page 252 can help you become a more efficient reader.

PERSONAL FEEDBACK 1

Name_____

1. When you read the timed reading, how many times did you have to reread?

   _____

Copyright ©1999 by Addison-Wesley Educational Publishers Inc.

2. If your mind wandered during the timed reading, what were you thinking about?

_____

3. Describe why reading speed is or is not a problem for you.

_____

4. What kind of easy reading would you choose for practicing and improving your reading rate?

_____

5. Describe any previous instruction that you have had on improving your reading rate.

_____

6. What do you think is the greatest misconception about reading speed?

_____

How Can You Increase Your Reading Speed? ◆◆◆◆◆◆◆◆◆◆◆◆

Be Aggressive—Attack!

Grab that book, sit up straight, and try to get some work done. Don't be a passive reader who lets the words go by like cars on a country road. Be active. Look for meaning with a strong intellectual curiosity, and try to get something out of what you have read. Drive for the main idea.

Faster reading does not mean poorer comprehension. Moderate gains in speed usually result in improved comprehension because the reader is doing more concentrating and more thinking.

The following exercises are designed to help increase your awareness of speed and give you a sense of haste. Time yourself on each exercise and then compare your time with those of other members of the class. If possible, do these exercises as a group, with one person calling out the time at five-second intervals.

EXERCISE 2 In the lists below, the key word is in boldface in the column at the left. It is then repeated in the group of words to the right. As rapidly as possible, locate the identical word, check it, and then move to the next line. Try to do most of this visually rather than saying each word to yourself. When you have finished each list, record your time and compare your performance with that of fellow classmates.

List 1

1. **lip**	lid	long	left	lip	lap
2. **stand**	start	stand	strong	torn	stop
3. **wander**	willow	wanton	waiting	wander	worry
4. **vain**	vale	vain	vane	vague	value

5. **most**	mort	most	might	host	mast
6. **divide**	divine	devoted	divide	have	doing
7. **someone**	somewhere	someone	sooner	somehow	somebody
8. **week**	weak	meek	week	leak	seek
9. **hazy**	hazy	hazard	hamper	lazy	dizzy
10. **mold**	mole	mound	mold	mind	hold
11. **sight**	height	right	might	sight	light
12. **aide**	aid	aide	add	also	hide
13. **reform**	remake	reclaim	malformed	reform	form
14. **bubble**	raffle	baffle	bubble	rubber	blubber
15. **scarce**	source	sacred	scarce	scorn	serious
16. **fabulous**	famous	fabulous	fashion	false	fasten
17. **reservation**	preservation	occupation	realization	reservation	reserve
18. **reality**	really	reaction	finality	reality	rational
19. **tranquilizer**	transfer	relaxation	tranquilizer	transcribe	transit
20. **phenomena**	pneumonia	phenomena	paralysis	feminine	phrases

Time in seconds = _____

List 2

1. **wing**	wig	wring	wing	with	ring
2. **cram**	crash	carry	ram	ham	cram
3. **like**	mike	like	land	load	hike
4. **sandal**	saddle	sandal	ramble	soften	sweet
5. **prime**	proud	prim	prime	prissy	rime
6. **manage**	mingle	manager	mangle	manner	manage
7. **rash**	rash	rush	race	lush	rich
8. **trace**	trance	trace	trade	train	trail
9. **saline**	saloon	salmon	saline	short	slowly
10. **revenge**	regain	ravenous	rancid	revamp	revenge
11. **tired**	tried	trend	tread	tired	torn
12. **withdrawn**	without	withdraw	within	withdrawn	witness
13. **powerful**	power	potential	powerful	potent	palate
14. **indignant**	indigenous	indigent	distinguish	indignant	indulge
15. **remember**	dismember	remain	reminisce	remission	remember
16. **condescending**	condemning	condense	concise	coherent	condescending
17. **magnanimous**	magnificent	magnanimous	magnetic	malformed	magnify
18. **humorous**	human	hormone	hammock	hammer	humorous
19. **civilization**	civilized	citizenry	civic	civilization	centered
20. **ingenious**	ingenuous	injurious	ingenious	ignoble	engine

Time in seconds = _____

Concentrate

Our eyes cannot actually read. We read with our minds. Thus, getting information from the printed page ultimately comes down to concentration. The faster you read, the harder you must concentrate. It is like driving a car at 80 miles per hour as opposed to 40 miles per hour. You are covering more ground at 80, and it requires total concentration if you are to keep the car on the road. Faster reading is direct, purposeful, and attentive. There is no time to think about anything except what you are reading.

As Clayton Pinette at the University of Maine says, "Concentration requires

Copyright © 1999 by Addison-Wesley Educational Publishers Inc.

lots of energy. Health, rest, and physical and mental well-being are necessary for good concentration. Rest breaks are important and so are personal rewards."[1]

Both external and internal distractions interfere with concentration. External distractions are the physical things around you. Are you in a quiet place? Is the television going? Can you hear people talking on the telephone? Are you being interrupted by someone asking you questions? Most external distractions can be controlled by prior planning. Be careful in selecting your time and place to study. Choose a quiet place and start at a reasonable hour. Set yourself up for success.

Internal distractions, on the other hand, are much more difficult to control. They are the things that are going on in your mind that keep you from concentrating. Again, prior planning will help. Keep a "To Do" list as mentioned in Chapter 1. Making a list and knowing that you will check back over it will help you stop worrying about your duties and responsibilities. Make an effort to spend more time *doing* something than *worrying* about something.

Visualizing can also help concentration. If you are reading about ostriches, visualize ostriches. As much as possible, try to see what you read as a movie. Use the five senses to improve your comprehension.

EXERCISE 3

In the lists below, the key word is in boldface. Among the words to the right, locate and mark the one that is most similar to the key word in meaning. In this exercise, you are not just looking at the shapes of words, but you are looking quickly for meaning. This will help you think fast and effectively. When you have finished each list, record your time, check your answers, and compare your performance with those of others in the class.

List 1

1. **recall**	read	guide	✓remember	fail	forgive
2. **sanitary**	new	fine	equal	✓clean	straight
3. **physician**	health	✓doctor	coward	elder	teacher
4. **motor**	car	horse	wagon	shine	✓engine
5. **first**	✓primary	last	finally	only	hard
6. **look**	stick	serve	✓glance	open	wait
7. **usual**	✓common	neat	best	cruel	kindness
8. **quick**	noisy	near	✓fast	finish	give
9. **annoy**	logic	make	win	✓disturb	set
10. **shout**	✓cry	action	most	fear	force
11. **friend**	family	mother	soldier	farmer	✓comrade
12. **carry**	plan	instruct	✓take	deal	rank
13. **sincere**	style	✓genuine	safe	future	simple
14. **valuable**	✓dear	unstable	truthful	ancient	broken
15. **diminish**	season	promote	forward	✓reduce	marry
16. **anxious**	appear	sight	✓nervous	mean	helpful
17. **liquid**	clear	running	pipes	kitchen	✓fluid
18. **prestige**	program	✓status	mission	natural	report
19. **core**	side	nation	✓heart	event	process
20. **harness**	✓control	appear	build	mark	attend

Time in seconds = _____

[1]Clayton Pinette, personal communications, February 1994.

List 2

1. **ill**	sin	die	skill	✓sick	mind
2. **calm**	envy	breeze	✓peaceful	early	far
3. **nice**	✓pleasant	needed	new	smooth	plastic
4. **emotion**	drain	✓feeling	heat	silent	search
5. **close**	cost	tall	mild	flow	✓near
6. **gun**	knife	✓rifle	handle	metal	hold
7. **expert**	rule	sort	believer	follower	✓specialist
8. **obtain**	✓get	feature	delay	injure	adapt
9. **discuss**	sense	divide	order	✓talk	find
10. **moisture**	✓dampness	sample	screen	dark	dirty
11. **village**	mountain	✓town	river	country	moving
12. **bravery**	origin	voluntary	✓courage	means	social
13. **loyal**	client	✓faithful	definite	legal	scale
14. **convert**	swim	chief	movement	policy	✓change
15. **celebrate**	attain	learn	century	✓rejoice	statement
16. **argument**	fund	✓quarrel	meeting	democracy	voice
17. **preserve**	opportunity	solar	system	✓save	signal
18. **hilarious**	✓funny	horrible	drama	sensible	even
19. **imitate**	difficult	confer	strike	language	✓copy
20. **danger**	general	fair	position	✓risk	army

Time in seconds = _____

Stop Regressions

A **regression** is the act of going back and rereading what you have just finished. Does this ever happen to you? Certainly some textbook material is so complex that it requires a second reading, but most of us are guilty of regressing even when the material is not that complicated. The problem is simply "sleeping on the job." The reader's mind takes a nap or starts thinking about something else while the eyes keep moving across the page. Hence half-way down the page, the reader wonders, "What am I reading?" and plods back to reread and find out. Then, after an alert rereading, the meaning is clear, but valuable time has been lost.

Regression can be a habit. You know that you can always go back and reread. Break yourself of the habit. The next time you catch yourself going back to reread because your mind has been wandering say, "Halt, I'm going to keep on reading." This will put more pressure on you to pay attention the first time.

Sleeping through only one or two paragraphs in an entire chapter probably won't hurt your comprehension that much. Sleeping through much more than that, however, could be quite harmful. Remember, reading the assignment twice takes double the time. Try to reread only when it is necessary because of the complexity of the material.

Avoid Vocalization

Vocalization means moving your lips as you read. It takes additional time and is generally a sign of an immature reader. A trick mentioned by specialists to stop lip movement is to put a slip of paper in your mouth. If the paper moves, your lips are moving, and you are thus alerted to stop the habit.

Subvocalization, on the other hand, refers to the little voice in your head that reads out loud for you. Even though you are not moving your lips or making any sounds, you hear the words in your mind as you read. Some experts say that sub-

Copyright ©1999 by Addison-Wesley Educational Publishers Inc.

vocalization is necessary for difficult material while others say that fast readers are totally visual and do not need to subvocalize. The truth is probably in between the two. You may find that in easy reading you can eliminate some of your subvocalization and only hear the key words, whereas on more difficult textbook material, the subvocalization reinforces the words and gives you better reading comprehension. Since your work will be primarily with textbook reading, perhaps you should not concern yourself with subvocalization at this time. In fact, you might need to read particularly difficult textbook passages out loud in order to fully understand them.

Expand Fixations

Your eyes must stop for you to read. These stops last for a fraction of a second and are called **fixations.** If you are reading a page that has twelve words to a line and you need to stop at each word, you have made twelve fixations, each of which takes a fraction of a second. If, however, you can read two words with each fixation, you will make only half the stops and thus increase your total reading speed.

You might say, "How can I do this?" and the answer has to do with peripheral vision. To illustrate, hold up your finger and try to look only at that finger. As you can see, such limited vision is impossible. Because of peripheral vision, you can see many other things in the room besides your finger. Research has shown that the average reader can see approximately 2.5 words per fixation.

Read the following phrase:

in the barn

Did you make three fixations, one on each word, or did you fixate once? Now read the following word:

entertainment

How many fixations did you make? Probably one, but as a beginning reader in elementary school, you most likely read the word with four fixations, one for each syllable. Your use of one fixation for *entertainment* dramatizes the progress that you have already made as a reader and indicates the ability of the eyes to take in a number of letters at one time. The phrase *in the barn* has nine letters, whereas *entertainment* has thirteen. Does it make any sense to stop three times to read nine letters and once to read thirteen? Again, the reason we do so is habit and what we have taught ourselves to do. If you never expected nor tried to read more than one word per fixation, that is all you are able to do.

The key to expanding your fixations is to read phrases or thought units. Some words seem to go together automatically and some don't. Words need to be grouped according to thought units. Your fixation point, as shown in the following example, will be under and between the words forming the thought unit, so that your peripheral vision can pick up what is on either side of the point.

Read the following paragraph by fixating at each indicated point. Notice how the words have been divided into phrase units.

FASTER READING

A faster   reading speed   is developed   through   practice
and concentration.   Your reading rate   also depends
on how much   you know   about a subject.

EXERCISE 4

In the lists below, the key phrase is boldface. Among the words on the line below, locate and mark the phrase that is most similar to the key phrase in meaning. Record your time, check your answers, and compare your performance with those of others in the class. This exercise will help you increase your eye span and grasp meaning quickly from phrases.

List 1

1. **to have your own**
   wish for more   share with others   ✓to keep for yourself   harmed by fire
2. **finish a task**
   lessen the impact   cleaning the attic   turn on the lights   ✓complete a job
3. **sing a song**
   ✓hum a tune   work for pleasure   leave for vacation   wish on a star
4. **manage a business**
   lost your job   lock the door   seek employment   ✓run a company
5. **sit for a while**
   make ends meet   ✓rest in a chair   learn new ways   fall into bed
6. **clear and concise**
   engage in conversation order a change   ✓easy to understand   complex and difficult
7. **reach a goal**
   ✓achieve an objective call a meeting   change your mind   open a hearing
8. **free your mind**
   leave a spot   ✓clear the head   turn the motor   remember a date
9. **walk down the road**
   meet in the car   support rapid transit   call the taxi   ✓stroll in the street
10. **hold some money back**
    rush to the bank   drop a dime   ✓accumulate a savings   remain at work

Time in seconds = _____

List 2

1. **sense a disaster**
   sleep with ease   ✓feel danger near   yearn for adventure   seek your fortune
2. **hurry to leave**
   walk in the rain   spill the coffee   lower the rent   ✓rush out the door
3. **seek legal advice**
   ✓engage an attorney   earn a living   move your address   give to charity
4. **forget to call**
   scream and yell   open an account   send by mail   ✓neglect to phone
5. **offer your services**
   get in the way   ✓ask to help   quit your job   waste your time
6. **listen to music**
   play in a band   buy a piano   ✓hear a tune   turn off the radio
7. **notice a change**
   ✓see a difference   buy a new shirt   work on a project   meet new people
8. **lose money gambling**
   pay for a product   ✓not win a bet   cut expenses   make an offer
9. **clean up a spill**
   go in the kitchen   add more water   ✓wipe away a stain   tear a rag
10. **leap with delight**
    sing a high note   turn the page   ask for help   ✓jump for joy

Time in seconds = _____

Copyright ©1999 by Addison-Wesley Educational Publishers Inc.

Use a Pen as a Pacer

Using a pen to follow the words in a smooth, flowing line can help you set a rhythmical pace for your reading. In elementary school you were probably taught never to point at words, so this advice may be contrary to what you have learned. However, it can be an effective speed-reading technique.

The technique of using a pen as a pacer is demonstrated in the following paragraph. Use a pen to trace the lines shown, so that it goes from one side of the column to the other and returns in a Z pattern. Note that since you are trying to read several words at a fixation, it is not necessary for your pen to go to the extreme end of either side of the column. After you have finished, answer the comprehension questions with *T* (true) or *F* (false) and compare your speed with that of others.

EXAMPLE   Summarizing while Reading

When you begin to read with concentration,
you should stop after key passages
and restate the main ideas to yourself.
You should try to find relationships

between principles presented in the text

and your own experiences or information

previously acquired. You should try

making up questions that are answered

in the material you are reading,

questions that might appear on an exam.

All of these activities serve to encode

the material in depth and therefore

to improve your retention. These activities

are different forms of elaborative rehearsal,

which is known to strengthen memory.

(93 words)

—*Introductory Psychology* by Morris Holland

Time in seconds = _____

___T___ 1. Restating the main ideas as you are reading improves memory.

___F___ 2. Stopping to summarize after key passages harms concentration.

EXPLANATION The answers are (1) *true* and (2) *false*. Although it may seem awkward at first, practice using a pen to read in a *Z* pattern on light material such as the newspaper or magazines to get accustomed to the technique. You will find that it not only forces you to move your eyes faster, but also improves your concentration and keeps you alert and awake.

Try using your pen as a pacer for the first five or ten minutes of your reading to become familiar with the feeling of a faster, rhythmical pace. When your hand becomes tired, stop the technique, but try to keep reading at the same pace. If, later in the reading, you feel yourself slowing down, resume the technique until you have regained the pace. This is a simple technique that does not involve expensive machines or complicated instruction. The best thing about it is that *it works!* Pacing with the Z pattern *will* increase your reading speed

Read the following passage using your pen as a pacer in the Z pattern. Answer the comprehension question with *T* (true) or *F* (false), and then record your reading time and compare your performance with that of other students.

PASSAGE 1

NATURAL GAS SAFETY

Natural gas   is odorless   so,   in the early days
of using   natural gas   to heat buildings   and cook,
someone would occasionally   light a match   without realizing that
a gas leak   had filled   the air   with gas.   Poof!
Inventors quickly   began designing devices   that would detect
the presence   of natural gas   in the air   and sound
an alarm.   However,   the best solution   was not
a detection device.   Instead,   a gas   that could be
easily smelled   was added   to the odorless   natural gas
so that   a leak   could be detected   easily   by a human's
built-in   gas detector,   the nose!

(69 words)

—*A Creative Problem Solver's Toolbox* by Richard Fobes

Time in seconds = _____

_____T_____ 1. Another gas was mixed with natural gas to create a smell.

_____T_____ 2. Originally natural gas was odorless.

PASSAGE 2

ALLERGIC REACTIONS

Certain seasons   of the year,   when pollen   is produced,
bring anxiety   and apprehension   to many people.
Others must,   at all times,   avoid certain wines,
cheeses, or oysters.   Yet others   cannot be around
cat dander   or dust.   The reason is   these people
are allergic   to something   associated with
these conditions.   (You won't   be pleased
to learn   that household dust   often contains
tiny mites   that are kicked up   into the air

Copyright ©1999 by Addison-Wesley Educational Publishers Inc.

by vacuuming or sweeping, and then drawn
into the delicate respiratory tract
by breathing the dust.) The body
has ways of cleansing itself of intruders
or incompatible substances, such as by violent rushes
of air or profuse production of cleansing fluids.
And so we sneeze and cough and our eyes and noses run
when we encounter some irritant.

(127 words)

—*Biology: The World of Life* by Robert Wallace

Time in seconds = _____

___T___ 1. Sweeping can cause an allergic reaction.

___T___ 2. Tiny mites live in household dust.

PASSAGE 3

TYPING KEYBOARD

The earliest typewriters usually jammed when a key
was pressed too soon after the previous key
was released. Most people weren't willing
to tolerate this flaw, so early typewriters
were used mostly by blind people and others
who couldn't write easily by hand. Christopher Sholes
created a clever supporting enhancement that overcame
this jamming tendency. He arranged the letters
on the keys awkwardly! He put the frequently
typed letters E, T, O, N, R, and I on keys
that required finger movement to reach them,
and assigned frequently-typed pairs of letters,
such as E and D, to the same finger. His innovation worked!
It successfully slowed down a person's typing speed,
thereby reducing the tendency for his typewriters to jam.
Unfortunately, because Sholes' typewriters became so popular,
this awkward keyboard arrangement is the one
we still use today!

(139 words)

—*The Creative Problem Solver's Toolbox* by Richard Fobes

Time in seconds = _____

___F___ 1. Our present typing keyboard was adopted to enhance speed.

___T___ 2. Early typewriters were used by blind people.

PASSAGE 4

LANGUAGE DEVELOPMENT

Frederick II, a king who lived almost 800 years ago in Europe, wanted to carry out an experiment. He was interested in learning what human language was the "most natural." He knew that as a child grew up, the child inevitably learned the language spoken by the people around it. Frederick thought this was hiding what would have been the "natural" language of the child. He reasoned that if he could get rid of the effects of this spoken language, the child would still speak, but would speak the "basic, natural" human language. Speaking a language, in his theory, was built in. You can see that the king wasn't all that well informed on the collaboration of environment and heredity. But, then, no one was in those days.

The king instructed a group of foster mothers not to speak at all to the babies they were caring for. It was okay to meet the baby's physical needs, but the foster mothers were not allowed to play with them, babble at them, sing to them, or speak to them. Frederick II figured that the children would "naturally" speak Hebrew, Greek, Latin, or perhaps Arabic. One of those was thought to be the "original" human language.

All the children spoke no language at all. They all died. "For they could not live without the petting and joyful faces and loving words of their foster mothers."

(232 words)

—*Psychology: What It Is/How to Use It* by David Watson.

Time in seconds = _____

___F___ 1. In his experiment Frederick II found that children will speak the original human language if left alone.

___F___ 2. The children died from lack of food.

PASSAGE 5

THAT WONDERFUL YOU

You may have noticed that there are certain areas of the human body that are not discussed very much. One of these neglected areas is the armpit, but paradoxically, a neglected armpit will generate discussion. This is because the armpit has a number of large sweat glands that produce the scent that is so distinctly you. Its scent-laden secretion is a mixture of watery sweat and a thick, dark yellow oil. The secretion itself actually has a musky, not unpleasant fragrance. However, its finer qualities are rarely appreciated because, once it is trapped in underarm hair, it is acted upon by bacteria that quickly decompose it into something with an aura reminiscent of goat. Most people tend to give up projecting their own odor preferring to be odor-free, or perfumed, rather than risk the result of bacterial action on their scent.

Underarm secretions are largely steroids, the chemical group that includes the sex hormones estrogen and testosterone. Many people are intensely sensitive to such smells.

Other sweat glands of the body also secrete an oily mixture that mark us individually and this is why dogs are used to catch us when we escape from prison. (Dogs can perceive odors at up to hundreds of millions lower concentrations than humans.) The dense aggregations of sweat glands on the soles of the feet may release half a fluid ounce of sweat per day. If even one-thousandth of this penetrated the seams of the shoes, millions of molecules would be left behind with each footstep, making tracking us quite simple for

Copyright ©1999 by Addison-Wesley Educational Publishers Inc.

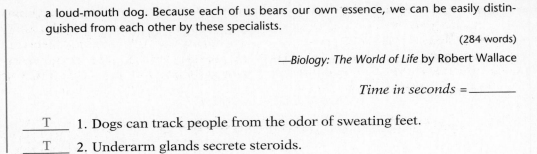

a loud-mouth dog. Because each of us bears our own essence, we can be easily distinguished from each other by these specialists.

(284 words)

—*Biology: The World of Life* by Robert Wallace

Time in seconds = _____

____T____ 1. Dogs can track people from the odor of sweating feet.

____T____ 2. Underarm glands secrete steroids.

Preview Before Reading

Do not start reading without looking over the material and thinking about what you need to accomplish. Think about the title and glance over the material for key words and phrases. Read the boldface and italic type. Decide what you think the selection is going to be about and what you want to know when you finish it. A few minutes spent on such an initial survey will help you read more purposefully and thus more quickly.

Activate your schema. What is your prior knowledge on the subject? Pull out your computer chip and prepare to add new information or change existing ideas.

Set a Time Goal for an Assignment

For each of your textbooks, estimate the approximate number of words per page. Write this estimate in the front of your book so that you can refer to it during the course. Knowing your reading rate, you can approximate how many minutes it will take you to read a page. Remember, this speed will vary with different textbooks according to the difficulty of the material. Toward the middle of the book, as you become more familiar with the subject, you will read faster than you did in the beginning.

Each time you sit down to do an assignment, count the number of pages that you need to complete. Calculate the amount of time it will probably take you, and then look at the clock and write down your projected finishing time. Make your goal realistic and pace yourself so that you can make it. Having an expectation will help you speed up your reading and improve your concentration. Do not become an all-night victim of Parkinson's Law, which states that the job expands to fit the time available. Don't allow yourself all night or all weekend to read twenty-five pages. Set a goal and then try to meet it. Rather than leisurely sauntering through an assignment, develop a sense of urgency.

Be Flexible

Inefficient readers are overconscientious, too often giving equal time to all words and all types of reading. As mentioned, you should be able to read a newspaper article in much less time than it would take you to read a science or economics passage, especially if you have already heard the highlights on the radio. One is more difficult and less familiar than the other. Don't read everything at the same rate. Be willing to switch gears and select the appropriate speed for the job.

Sometimes you may need to look over material for a detail or a specific point. In this case, don't read all the words. Skim until your eyes locate the information you need and then move on to the next task. This is a case of adjusting your speed to your purpose. For example, if you are told to read a history chapter for an exam, you should read it carefully and spend some time studying it. On the other hand, if you have been told to write a half-page summary of five articles in the library, you can probably just skim the material for the main ideas and a few supporting details. Again, adjust your speed to your purpose.

Practice

You cannot improve your running speed unless you get out and run. The same is true with reading. To learn to read faster, you need to practice faster reading techniques every day. As explained in the following paragraph, *wishing* and *willing* are not the same:

> The *wish* to learn is diffuse and general. The *will* to learn is concentrated and specific. The wish to learn means that we repeat a thing again and again hoping for something to happen. The will to learn means that we dig down and analyze, that we try to find out exactly what is wrong and exactly how to put it right.
>
> —*Streamline Your Mind* by James Mursell

POINTS TO PONDER

▲ The average adult reading speed is approximately 250 words per minute at 70 percent comprehension.
▲ Be an aggressive reader.
▲ Learn to control internal and external distractions so that you can concentrate.
▲ **Regressing** is a crutch; stop doing it.
▲ Rapid readers experience very little subvocalization.
▲ Expand your **fixations** into phrases or thought units.
▲ Use a pen as a pacer.
▲ Survey material before you read it.
▲ Pace yourself; set time goals for the completion of an assignment.
▲ Be flexible and adjust your speed to your purpose.
▲ Practice faster reading.

TIMED READING 1

Use your pen as a pacer and time your reading of the following selection.

Starting time: _____ *minutes* _____ *seconds*

DARKNESS AT NOON

Blind from birth, I have never had the opportunity to see myself and have been completely dependent on the image I create in the eye of the observer. To date it has not been narcissistic.

There are those who assume that since I can't see, I obviously also cannot hear. Very
5   often people will converse with me at the top of their lungs, enunciating each word very carefully. Conversely, people will also often whisper, assuming that since my eyes don't work, my ears don't either.

Copyright ©1999 by Addison-Wesley Educational Publishers Inc.

For example, when I go to the airport and ask the ticket agent for assistance to the plane, he or she will invariably pick up the phone, call a ground hostess and whisper: "Hi,
10 Jane, we've got a 76 here." I have concluded that the word "blind" is not used for one of two reasons: Either they fear that if the dread word is spoken, the ticket agent's retina will immediately detach, or they are reluctant to inform me of my condition of which I may not have been previously aware.

On the other hand, others know that of course I can hear, but believe that I can't
15 talk. Often, therefore, when my wife and I go out to dinner, a waiter or waitress will ask Kit if "*he* would like a drink" to which I respond that "indeed *he* would."

This point was graphically driven home to me while we were in England. I had been given a year's leave of absence from my Washington law firm to study for a diploma in law degree at Oxford University. During the year I became ill and was hospitalized.
20 Immediately after admission, I was wheeled down to the X-ray room. Just at the door sat an elderly woman—elderly I would judge from the sound of her voice. "What is his name?" the woman asked the orderly who had been wheeling me.

"What's your name?" the orderly repeated to me.

"Harold Krents," I replied.
25 "Harold Krents," he repeated.

"When was he born?"

"When were you born?"

"November 5, 1944," I responded.

"November 5, 1944," the orderly intoned.
30 This procedure continued for approximately five minutes at which point even my saint-like disposition deserted me. "Look," I finally blurted out, "this is absolutely ridiculous. Okay, granted I can't see, but it's got to have become pretty clear to both of you that I don't need an interpreter."

"He says he doesn't need an interpreter," the orderly reported to the woman.
35 The toughest misconception of all is the view that because I can't see, I can't work. I was turned down by over forty law firms because of my blindness, even though my qualifications included a cum laude degree from Harvard College and a good ranking in my Harvard Law School class.

The attempt to find employment, the continuous frustration of being told that it was
40 impossible for a blind person to practice law, the rejection letters, not based on my lack of ability but rather on my disability, will always remain one of the most disillusioning experiences of my life.

Fortunately, this view of limitation and exclusion is beginning to change. On April 16, the Department of Labor issued regulations that mandate equal-employment oppor-
45 tunities for the handicapped. By and large, the business community's response to offering employment to the disabled has been enthusiastic.

I therefore look forward to the day, with the expectation that it is certain to come, when employers will view their handicapped workers as a little child did me years ago when my family still lived in Scarsdale.
50 I was playing basketball with my father in our backyard according to procedures we had developed. My father would stand beneath the hoop, shout, and I would shoot over his head at the basket attached to our garage. Our nextdoor neighbor, aged five, wandered over into our yard with a playmate. "He's blind," our neighbor whispered to her friend in a voice that could be heard distinctly by Dad and me. Dad shot and missed; I did
55 the same. Dad hit the rim; I missed entirely; Dad shot and missed the garage entirely. "Which one is blind?" whispered back the little friend.

I would hope that in the near future when a plant manager is touring the factory with the foreman and comes upon a handicapped and nonhandicapped person working together, his comment after watching them work will be, "Which one is
60 disabled?"

(729 words)

—"Darkness at Noon" by Harold Krents, *The New York Times*, 26 May 1976

Finishing time: _____ *minutes* _____ *seconds*

Total time: _____ *minutes* _____ *seconds*

Rate = _____ *words per minute (see time chart)*

Time Chart

Time in Seconds and Minutes	Words per Minute	Time in Seconds and Minutes	Words per Minute
60 (1 min.)	729	240 (4 min.)	182
120 (2 min.)	365	250	175
130	336	260	168
140	314	270	162
150	292	280	156
160	273	290	151
170	257	300 (5 min.)	146
180 (3 min.)	243	310	141
190	230	320	137
200	219	330	133
210	208	340	129
220	199	360 (6 min.)	122
230	190		

Answer the following with *T* (true) or *F* (false).

___F___ 1. The author indicated that the number 76 means deaf.

___T___ 2. The author studied law at Harvard and Oxford.

Copyright ©1999 by Addison-Wesley Educational Publishers Inc.

_____F_____ 3. When the neighbor was watching, the author made the basket and his father missed.

_____F_____ 4. The author indicates that he has to use a wheelchair at work.

_____F_____ 5. The author indicates that he works at the Department of Labor.

Comprehension = (% correct) _____

TIMED READING 2

Use your pen as a pacer and time your reading of the following selection.

Starting time: _____ minutes _____ seconds

REMEMBERING LOBO

We called her *Lobo*. The words means "wolf" in Spanish, an odd name for generous and loving aunt. Like all names it became synonymous with her, and to this day returns me to my childself. Although the name seemed perfectly natural to us and to our friends, it did cause frowns from strangers throughout the years. I particularly remember one hot after-
5   noon when on a crowded streetcar between the border cities of El Paso and Juárez, I momentarily lost sight of her. "Lobo! Lobo!" I cried in panic. Annoyed faces peered at me, disappointed at such disrespect to a white-haired woman.

Actually the fault was hers. She lived with us for years, and when she arrived home from work in the evening, she'd knock on our front door and ask, "*¿Dónde estan mis*
10   *lobitos?*" "Where are my little wolves?"

Gradually she became our lobo, a spinster aunt who gathered the four of us around her, tying us to her for life by giving us all she had. Sometimes to tease her we would call her by her real name. "*¿Dónde esta Ignacia?*" we would ask. Lobo would laugh and say, "She is a ghost."
15   To all of us in nuclear families today, the notion of an extended family under one roof seems archaic, complicated. We treasure our private space. I will always marvel at the generosity of my parents, who opened their door to both my grandmother and Lobo. No doubt I am drawn to the elderly because I grew up with two entirely different white-haired women who worried about me, tucked me in at night, made me tomato soup or
20   hot *hierbabuena* (mint tea) when I was ill.

Lobo grew up in Mexico, the daughter of a circuit judge, my grandfather. She was a wonderful storyteller and over and over told us about the night her father, a widower, brought his grown daughters on a flatbed truck across the Rio Grande at the time of the Mexican Revolution. All their possessions were left in Mexico. Lobo had not been
25   wealthy, but she had probably never expected to have to find a job and learn English.

When she lived with us, she worked in the linens section of a local department store. Her area was called "piece goods and bedding." Lobo never sewed, but she would talk about materials she sold, using words I never completely understood, such as *pique* and *broadcloth*. Sometimes I still whisper such words just to remind myself of her. I'll always
30   savor the way she would order "sweet milk" at restaurants. The precision of a speaker new to the language.

Lobo saved her money to take us out to dinner and a movie, to take us to Los Ange-les in the summer, to buy us shiny black shoes for Christmas. Though she never married and never bore children, Lobo taught me much about one of our greatest challenges as
35   human beings: loving well. I don't think she ever discussed the subject with me, but through the years she lived her love, and I was privileged to watch.

40   She died at ninety-four. She was no sweet, docile Mexican woman dying with perfect resignation. Some of her last words before drifting into semiconsciousness were loud
words of annoyance at the incompetence of nurses and doctors.

   "No sirven." "They're worthless," she'd say to me in Spanish. "They don't know
what they're doing. My throat is hurting and they're taking X-rays. Tell them to take care
45 of my throat first."

   I was busy striving for my cherished middle-class politeness. "Shh, shh," I'd say.
"They're doing the best they can."

   "Well, it's not good enough," she'd say, sitting up in anger.

   Lobo was a woman of fierce feelings, of strong opinions. She was a woman who lit-
50 erally whistled while she worked. The best way to cheer her when she'd visit my young
children was to ask for help. Ask her to make a bed, fold laundry, set the table or dry
dishes, and the whistling would begin as she moved about her task. Like all of us, she
loved being needed. Understandable, then, that she muttered in annoyance when her
body began to fail her. She was a woman who found self-definition and joy in visibly
showing her family her love for us by bringing us hot *té de canela* (cinnamon tea) in the
middle of the night to ease a cough, by bringing us comics and candy whenever she
returned home. A life of giving.

(748 words)

—Nepantla: Essays from the Land in the Middle by Pat Mora

Finishing time: _____ *minutes* _____ *seconds*

Total time: _____ *minutes* _____ *seconds*

Rate = _____ *words per minute (see time chart)*

Time Chart

Time in Seconds and Minutes	Words per Minute	Time in Seconds and Minutes	Words per Minute
60 (1 min.)	748	180 (3 min.)	249
70	641	190	236
80	561	200	224
90	499	210	214
100	449	220	204
110	408	230	195
120 (2 min.)	374	240 (4 min.)	187
130	345	250	180
140	221	260	173
150	299	270	166
160	281	280	160
170	264	300 (5 min.)	150

Answer the following with *T* (true) or *F* (false).

____T____ 1. The children called her Lobo because she called them her little
wolves.

____T____ 2. Lobo's real name was probably Ignacia.

Copyright ©1999 by Addison-Wesley Educational Publishers Inc.

_____F_____ 3. Lobo lived in the house of the author's grandmother.

_____F_____ 4. The author's primary purpose in writing this essay was to compare the goodness of her aunt to the weakness of the main character in "The Boy Who Cried Wolf."

_____T_____ 5. Lobo's family emigrated to the United States during the Mexican Revolution.

_____F_____ 6. Lobo's husband was dead, and she had no children.

_____T_____ 7. The author says she learned about loving and giving from her aunt's example rather than her words.

_____F_____ 8. Lobo worked in a fabric and bedding store because she did not like to do housework.

_____T_____ 9. According to the author Lobo enjoyed feeling useful and needed.

_____F_____10. Lobo died a bitter old woman with her fighting spirit diminished.

Comprehension = (% correct) _____

TIMED READING 3

Use your pen as a pacer and time your reading of the following selection.

Starting time: _____ *minutes* _____ *seconds*

CHILDBIRTH IN EARLY AMERICA

Childbirth in colonial America was a difficult and sometimes dangerous experience for women. During the seventeenth and eighteenth centuries, between 1 and 1.5 percent of
5   all births ended in the mother's death—as a result of exhaustion, dehydration, infection, hemorrhage, or convulsions. Since the typical mother gave birth to between five and eight children, her lifetime chances of dying in childbirth ran as high as one in eight. This meant that if a woman had eight female friends, it was likely that one would die in childbirth. In their letters, women often referred to childbirth as "the Dreaded apparition."

10   In addition to her anxieties about pregnancy, an expectant mother was filled with apprehensions about the survival of her newborn child. The death of a child in infancy was far more common than it is today. In the healthiest seventeenth century communities, 1 infant in 10 died before the age of 5. Puritan minister Cotton Mather saw 8 of his 15 children die before reaching the age of 2.

15   Given the high risk of birth complications and infant death, it is not surprising to learn that pregnancy was surrounded by superstitions. It was widely believed that if a mother-to-be looked upon a "horrible spectre" or was startled by a loud noise her child would be disfigured. If a hare jumped in front of her, her child was in danger of suffering a harelip. There was also fear that if the mother looked at the moon, her child might become a lunatic or sleepwalker. A mother's ungratified longings, it was thought, could
20   cause a miscarriage or leave a mark imprinted on her child's body. At the same time, however, women were expected to continue to perform work until the onset of labor, since hard work supposedly made for an easier labor.

In colonial America, the typical woman gave birth to her children at home, while female kin and neighbors clustered at her bedside to offer support and encouragement.
25   Most women were assisted in childbirth not by a doctor but by a midwife. Most midwives were older women who relied on practical experience. Skilled midwives were highly valued. Communities tried to attract experienced midwives by offering a salary or a rent-free house.

30   During labor, midwives administered no painkillers, except for alcohol. Pain in child-birth was considered God's punishment for Eve's sin of eating the forbidden fruit in the Garden of Eden. Women were merely advised to "arm themselves with patience" and prayer and to try, during labor, to restrain "those dreadful groans and cries which do so much discourage their friends and relations that are near them."

35   After delivery, new mothers were often treated to a banquet. Women from well-to-do families spent three to four weeks in bed, while women from poorer families were generally back at work in one or two days.

(500 words)

—*America and Its Peoples* by James Martin et al.

Finishing time: _____ *minutes* _____ *seconds*

Total time: _____ *minutes* _____ *seconds*

Rate = _____ *words per minute (see time chart)*

Time Chart

Time in Seconds and Minutes	Words per Minute	Time in Seconds and Minutes	Words per Minute
40	750	170	176
50	600	180 (3 min.)	167
60 (1 min.)	500	190	158
70	428	200	150
80	375	210	143
90	333	220	136
100	300	230	130
110	272	240 (4 min.)	125
120 (2 min.)	250	250	120
130	231	260	115
140	214	270	111
150	200	280	107
160	188	300 (5 min.)	100

Answer the following with *T* (true) or *F* (false).

___F___ 1. Approximately 1 in 10 women died in childbirth.

___T___ 2. The pain of childbirth was given a religious interpretation.

___T___ 3. According to the passage, women in colonial America dreaded child-birth.

___F___ 4. Women in colonial America generally rested in bed for several weeks prior to childbirth.

___F___ 5. Midwives were not respected by the community because they were not doctors.

Comprehension = (% correct) _____

Copyright ©1999 by Addison-Wesley Educational Publishers Inc.

EXPLORE THE NET

- Describe any step-by-step lessons that are offered for faster reading.
- What programs for improving reading rate are advertised for purchase?

For additional readings and exercises, visit the Longman English Skills Web page at:

http://longman.awl.com/englishpages

For a user name and password, please see your instructor.

Copyright ©1999 by Addison-Wesley Educational Publishers Inc.

CHAPTER

9 *Analytical Reasoning*

◆ *What is good thinking?*
◆ *What are the characteristics of unsuccessful students?*
◆ *What are the characteristics of successful students?*
◆ *What is involved in good problem solving?*
◆ *How do graphic illustrations condense complex information?*

Identify Analytical Thinking ◆◆◆◆◆◆◆◆◆◆◆

According to researchers, good thinkers have developed a logical and sequential pattern of working through complex material, whereas poor thinkers lack this "habit of analysis." Good thinkers work persistently, believing that they will find the answer. They draw on their old knowledge to solve new problems and thus relate, interpret, and integrate what they already know with what they want to learn. Poor thinkers, on the other hand, merely collect facts and are unaware of relationships. They cannot put old and new information together to draw conclusions. They seem to have no logical method for problem solving.

Each time you master a textbook, you have learned how to think about a subject. This process offers you both immediate and future benefits. For example, after you struggle through and finally understand an introductory biology text, the same habits of thinking and capturing meaning will transfer to the next biology course, which then will be easier to understand because of your experience. Another future benefit is the ability to apply your learned thinking skills to a new and different task. For instance, the very act of thinking through the complexities of biology will make it easier for you to tackle a chemistry, physics, or anthropology book. Thinking, like everything else, requires practice, and the more you do, the better you become. You gradually develop the ability to educate yourself.

Two researchers, Bloom and Broder, studied both academically successful and unsuccessful college students at the University of Chicago.[1] They described the thinking processes of each.

Before reading further, think of a student you know personally who is not successful in school. Check to see if the following characteristics describe that student.

An Unsuccessful Student

1. Has no method of attacking new material.
2. Misunderstands or skips directions.
3. Fails to keep the purpose in mind.
4. Is unable to apply present knowledge to new situations.
5. Is passive in thinking and answers questions on the basis of few clues.
6. Uses "impression" or "feeling" to arrive at answers.
7. Is careless in considering details and jumps around from one to another.
8. After making a superficial attempt to reason, gives up and guesses.

Do you know a very successful student? How many of the following characteristics describe that student?

A Successful Student

1. Is careful and systematic in attacking the problem.
2. Can read directions and immediately choose a point at which to begin reasoning.
3. Keeps sight of goals while thinking through the problem.
4. Pulls out key terms and tries to simplify the material.
5. Breaks larger problems into smaller subproblems.
6. Is active and aggressive in seeking meaning.
7. Applies relevant old knowledge to the problem.
8. Is persistent and careful in seeking solutions.

---

[1] B. S. Bloom and L. Broder, *Problem-Solving Process of College Students* (Chicago: University of Chicago Press, 1950).

What kind of student are you? Go back to both lists and circle the characteristics that apply to you.

In studying these characteristics you will see that learning to comprehend what you read is learning to reason and to associate meaning. To understand the ideas in college textbooks, you have to work harder than you do when reading newspapers or magazines. Absorbing the meaning from college texts frequently requires a laborious, step-by-step analysis of details and their relationship to the whole. For example, understanding and explain the functioning of a part of the body or the evolution of a volcano can be extremely complex.

Successful students attack their studying aggressively and systematically, and persist to a logical conclusion. As you can see, Bloom and Broder's list of characteristics might just as easily apply to successful problem solving in everyday life as to success in the academic world. These characteristics thus contribute not only to college success but to the long-lasting personal success that is the ultimate reason for going to college. Start developing them!

The two lists by Bloom and Broder also describe test-taking characteristics. Too often students look for gimmicks in test-taking, but a well-constructed test should not be based on tricks. A high score should reflect the student's ability to think through the problems and come up with logical solutions. Again, the characteristics that describe the successful student also describe the successful test taker. After all, test-taking is thinking.

PERSONAL FEEDBACK 1

Name_____

1. If you won the lottery, what would you do with the money?

   _____

2. Why were you glad to leave high school?

   _____

3. What do you miss most about high school?

   _____

4. What does *delayed gratification* mean and how does it apply to college?

   _____

5. What causes you the most stress?

   _____

6. How can a professor make you feel that you are an important part of the class?

   _____

7. Describe a problem at home, work, or school that you enjoyed systematically attacking and solving.

   _____

   _____

8. What do you feel is your greatest problem-solving strength?

   _____

Copyright ©1999 by Addison-Wesley Educational Publishers Inc.

Engage in Problem Solving

Another researcher, Whimbey, studied good and poor readers. He noted two prominent features of poor college readers.

> First, there is one-shot thinking rather than extended, sequential construction of understanding; and second, there is a willingness to allow gaps of knowledge to exist, in effect, an attitude of indifference toward achieving an accurate and complete comprehension of situations and relations.[2]

Whimbey and other researchers believe that all students can learn the characteristic behaviors of good readers by increasing their analytical reasoning skills through problem solving. Through analytical reasoning they break problems into small parts and use logic to arrive at a solution. Breaking a complex word problem into sequential steps for solution requires thinking skills similar to those used in breaking a paragraph down to get a main idea, draw a conclusion, or trace the details of a process.

EXAMPLE Read the following word problem and think about how you would figure out the answer.

> Mary is shorter than Carol but taller than Kathy. Sue is taller than Mary but shorter than Carol. Which girl is tallest?

Although the problem may seem rather confusing at first reading, when it is broken down in sequential steps, the answer is simple. The best way to solve this problem is to draw a diagram so that you can visualize the relative height of each girl. Reread the problem and place each girl in a position on a vertical line:

Mary is shorter than Carol
┌─Carol
└─Mary

but taller than Kathy.
┌─Carol
├─Mary
└─Kathy

Sue is taller than Mary, but shorter than Carol.
┌─Carol
├─Sue
├─Mary
└─Kathy

EXPLANATION The diagram indicates that the tallest girl is Carol.

Whimbey found that analytical reasoning skills can be taught through practice. He devised a variety of word problems similar to those that follow to help students learn. The thinking strategies used to solve these problems apply in every academic task, not just in reading textbooks. Break each problem below into parts and sequentially work toward a solution. You may want to do the first exercise with someone else so that you can discuss the steps leading to a solution, and then try the rest on your own.

EXERCISE 1

Make notes or diagrams to help you solve the following problems.

Jack 1. George and Scott are the same age. Beth is younger than George, and Jack is older than Scott. Tom is older than Scott but younger than Jack. Who is the oldest? (Do your figuring next to the diagram above.)

---

[2]Arthur Whimbey, *Intelligence Can Be Taught* (New York: E. P. Dutton, 1975), 55.

____c____ 2. Which set of letters is different from the other three?

                a. LMOP   b. EFHI   c. RSTV   d. JKMN

___HBI___ 3. According to the pattern, which letters should come next in the series?

          B C D B E F B G __ __ __

___9:10___ 4. An airplane left New York at 4:25 and arrived in Miami 4 hours and 45 minutes later. What time did it arrive in Miami?

___7, 6, 8___ 5. According to the pattern, which numbers should come next in the series?

          2 1 3 2 4 3 5 4 6 5 __ __ __

___VW5___ 6. According to the pattern, what numbers and letters should come next in the series?

          G H 2 K L 3 P Q 4 __ __ __

___one___ 7. In how many days of the week are there more than three letters and less than five letters preceding the part of the word that is the same in all seven?

__11,12,33__ 8. According to the pattern, what numbers should come next in the series?

          1 2 3 6 4 5 6 15 7 8 9 24 10 __ __ __

9. Tim, Larry, and Dave got different scores on a history test. Tim scored higher than Larry but lower than Dave. Their last names, not in order, are Lewis, Davis, and Conners. Davis got the lowest score and Lewis got the highest. What are the last names of Tim and Larry?

Tim Conners and Larry Davis

___six___ 10. How many letters are in either the rectangle or the square but not in both?

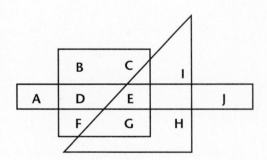

Copyright ©1999 by Addison-Wesley Educational Publishers Inc.

EXERCISE 2

Collaborate with a "study buddy" to answer the following questions. Share your "steps in thinking" with each other.

___b___ 1. Which set of letters is different from the other three?

          a. GHIF   b. MNOK   c. RSTQ   d. CDEB

___south___ 2. Face the south and turn to your right. Make another right turn and then an about-face. In which direction are you now facing?

___UWX___ 3. According to the pattern, which letters should come next in the series?

          KL NO QR T __ __ __

_3:55_ 4. A train arrived at its destination at 7:45, which was 3 hours and 50 minutes after its departure. What time was its departure?

_13,14,16_ 5. According to the pattern, which numbers should come next in the series?

$$1 \quad 2 \quad 4 \quad 5 \quad 7 \quad 8 \quad 10 \quad 11 \quad \_ \quad \_ \quad \_$$

6. Write the word *manage*. If deleting the first three letters or the last three letters leaves an actual word, circle the second *a* in the original word. If not, circle the first *a*.

man@ge

_26,31,36_ 7. According to the pattern, what numbers should come next in the series?

$$1 \quad 6 \quad 11 \quad 16 \quad 21 \quad \_ \quad \_ \quad \_$$

_K_ 8. Which letter in the alphabet is as far away from *M* as *R* is from *P*?

9. Ellen, Carolyn, and Betsy each finished the road race at a different time. Their last names, not in order, are King, Wilson, and Harris. Wilson finished before Harris but after King. Betsy came in before Carolyn and Ellen was last. What are the last names of Betsy and Ellen?

Betsy King and Ellen Harris

10. Fran, Sally, and Marsha collected old books from different countries. Together they had a total of eighteen books. Six of the books are from Spain, with one more than that being the total from the Orient and one less being the total from Holland. Sally has two books from Spain, and Fran has an equal number from the Orient. Marsha has twice as many books from the Orient as Fran has. Both Marsha and Fran have only one book each from Holland, and Fran has only one from Spain. How many books does Sally have? How many does Marsha have?

Sally has six and Marsha has eight.

	Holland	Spain	Orient	Total
Fran				
Sally				
Marsha				
Total				

Do you prefer working alone or did you benefit more from working with a "study buddy"? Answers will vary.

Analytical Reasoning in Textbooks

Apply analytical reasoning to every page of every textbook you read. Reading is problem solving, and reading is thinking. Each time you answer a question about what you have read, you are displaying the characteristics of a successful student. Get in the habit of carefully and systematically working through complex ideas. Simplify the material, and break it into smaller, more manageable ideas. Draw on what you already know, and actively and aggressively seek to understand.

To help you visualize complex ideas, textbooks frequently include maps, charts, diagrams, and graphs. These illustrations condense a lot of information into one picture. The reader is supposed to refer to such graphic illustrations while reading; the material should then be easier to understand.

Included in this chapter are several exercises on graphic illustrations and problems that require logical and sequential thinking. Before doing the exercises, read the following hints.

◆◆◆ READER'S TIP

THINKING ABOUT MAPS, CHARTS, GRAPHS, AND DIAGRAMS

1. Read the title to determine the subject.
2. Read any information in italics or boldface.
3. Read the footnotes to determine the source of the information.
4. Read the labels to determine what each mark, arrow, figure, or design means.
5. Figure out the legend, the key on a map that shows what the markings represent.
6. Notice if numbers are written in some unit of measurement, such as percents, dollars, thousands, millions, or billions.
7. Notice the trends and the extremes. What is the average, and what are the highs and lows?
8. Refer back and forth to the text to follow a process or label parts.
9. Draw conclusions based on the information.
10. Do not read more into the illustration than is supported by fact. In other words, don't draw conclusions that cannot be proved.

EXERCISE 3   Collaborate with a "study buddy" to answer the following questions.

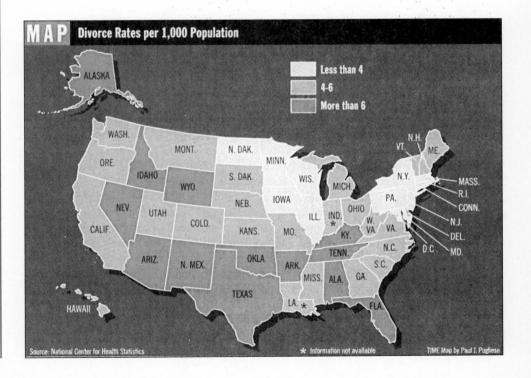

MAP   **Divorce Rates per 1,000 Population**

Less than 4
4–6
More than 6

Source: National Center for Health Statistics   ★ Information not available   TIME Map by Paul J. Pugliese

Copyright ©1999 by Addison-Wesley Educational Publishers Inc.

The purpose of the map is to show <u>the divorce rate in populations of 1,000</u>
<u>for each state in the United States.</u>

Use the map to answer the following with *T* (true), *F* (false), or *CT* (can't tell).

_____T_____ 1. More states have a divorce rate of four to six per thousand than over six per thousand.

_____CT_____ 2. Nevada and Florida have an equal number of divorces per 1,000 population.

_____F_____ 3. The map indicates that Louisiana and Indiana did not have any divorces during the period reported.

_____T_____ 4. More states in the Southeast had a divorce rate higher than six per thousand than states in the Northeast.

_____T_____ 5. Alaska had a higher divorce rate than Hawaii.

6. Although the map does not show reasons, why would you guess that the divorce rate is higher in Nevada and Texas than it is in Illinois and Pennsylvania?

<u>Answers will vary</u>

 **EXERCISE 4**

Collaborate with a "study buddy" to review the chart and answer the questions that follow. Notice that numbers are in both thousands and percents.

Minority Populations in America in 1994 and Projected for 2000 and 2050

	Number (Thousands)	Percentage of Population
1994		
African American	31,192	12.0
Latino	26,077	10.0
Asian American	8,438	3.2
American Indian	1,907	0.7
2000		
African American	33,741	12.2
Latino	31,166	11.3
Asian American	11,407	4.1
American Indian	2,055	0.7
2050		
African American	56,346	14.4
Latino	88,071	22.5
Asian American	38,064	9.7
American Indian	3,701	0.9

Source: U.S. Bureau of the Census (1995a).

—*Sociology* by Richard Appelbaum and William Chambliss

The purpose of this chart is to <u>show the number and percentage of four</u>
<u>minority populations in America in 1994 and project those for 2000 and 2050.</u>

Use the chart to answer the following with *T* (true), *F* (false), or *CT* (can't tell).

    F   1. By the year 2000 there will be an estimated 2,549 more African Americans in the population than in 1994.

    T   2. The greatest estimated minority group increase between the periods covered before and after 2000 is Latino.

    F   3. The ranking of minority groups by percentage of the population is estimated to remain the same in 1994, 2000, and 2050.

    CT   4. Immigration is the primary force in the increase in the Latino population.

    F   5. From 1994 to 2050 the estimated increase in the American Indian population is 2 percent.

    6. Although the chart does not show reasons, why would you guess that the Latino population is predicted to increase by a greater percent by 2050 than the African American population?

    <u>Answers will vary.</u>

EXERCISE 5

Collaborate with a "study buddy," first to explain the information on the graph and then to answer the questions.

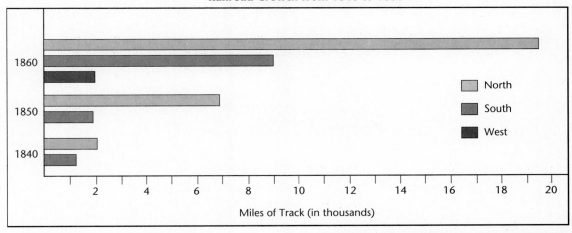

Railroad Growth from 1840 to 1860

—*America and Its People* by James Martin et al.

The purpose of this graph is to show <u>the growth of railroads in sections of the</u> <u>United States from 1840 to 1860.</u>

Use the graph to answer the following with *T* (true), *F* (false), or *CT* (can't tell).

    F   1. In 1850 the South had only 200 miles of track.

    T   2. In 1840, 1850, and 1860, the North surpassed the South and West in total miles of track.

    T   3. The West had no railroad track in 1840.

Copyright ©1999 by Addison-Wesley Educational Publishers Inc.

_____F_____ 4. The North had three times as much railroad track as the South in 1860.

_____CT_____ 5. An overemphasis on agriculture led the South to neglect transportation improvements.

6. Although the bar graph does not show reasons, why would you guess the South had fewer miles of track than the North during the years from 1840 to 1860?

Answers will vary.

EXERCISE 6

Collaborate to study the graph and to answer the questions.

GROWTH IN GOVERNMENT EMPLOYEES

The number of government employees has grown rapidly since 1950. The real growth, however, has been in the state and local sector, with its millions of teachers, police officers, and other service deliverers. Many state and local employees and programs, though, are supported by federal grants-in-aid. (Note that the figures for federal employment do not include military personnel.)

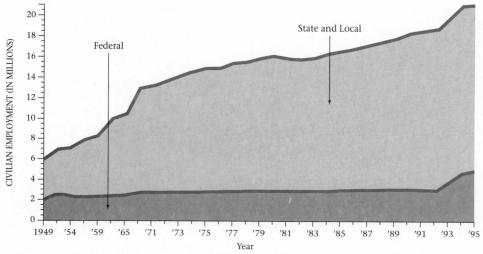

SOURCE: *Budget of the United States Government, Fiscal Year 1997: Historical Tables* (Washington, DC: U.S. Government Printing Office, 1996), Table 17-5.

—*Government in America* by George Edwards et al.

The purpose of this graph is to show the growth in the number of state and local as well as federal employees from 1949 to 1995.

Use the graph to answer the following with *T* (true), *F* (false), or *CT* (can't tell).

_____T_____ 1. In 1979 the number of civilian federal employees was approximately 2 million.

_____CT_____ 2. Presidents and Congress have used political pressure to restrict the number of federal employees while governors have not done the same for state and local employees.

_____T_____ 3. The biggest jump since 1949 in federal civilian employees was in the 90s.

___T___ 4. From 1949 to 1995 the number of state and local employees increased by over 14 million.

___F___ 5. In 1965 the number of state and local employees increased by more than eight times the number of federal employees.

6. Although the line graph does not show reasons, why would you guess that the number of state and local employees has increased more than the number of federal employees from 1949 to 1995?

Answers will vary.

EXERCISE 7 Collaborate with a "study buddy" to understand the following math problem and then to apply that understanding to solve two similar problems. Use logic and sequential thinking to study the step-by-step solution to the word problem example. Notice how the amounts are symbolized in an equation.

A bank teller has 25 more five-dollar bills than ten-dollar bills. The total value of all the money that the teller has is $200. How many of each type of bill does he have?

Let x be the number of ten-dollar bills, so that $x + 25$ is the number of fives. The value of all the tens is given by the number of tens (x) times the value per bill ($10), or

$$\text{value of tens} = 10x$$

In the same way,

$$\text{values of fives} = 5(x + 25)$$

The total value of all the money is $200.

The value of fives	plus	the value of tens	is	$200.
↓	↓	↓	↓	↓
$5(x + 25)$	$+$	$10x$	$=$	200

Solve this equation:

$$5x + 125 + 10x = 200$$
$$15x + 125 = 200$$
$$15x = 75 \quad \text{Add} - 125$$
$$x = 5 \quad \text{Multiply by } 1/15$$

Since x represents the number of tens, the teller has 5 tens and 30 fives (5 + 25).

—*Beginning Algebra* by Margaret Lial and Charles Miller

Use the pattern and logic shown in the example to solve the following problems.

1. A bank teller has some five-dollar bills and some twenty-dollar bills. The teller has five more of the twenties. The total value of the money is $725. How many of each kind of bill does the teller have? The teller has 5 more twenties than fives. The teller has: $20(x + 5) + 5x = \$725$.

2. A woman has $1.70 in dimes and nickels; she has two more dimes than nickels. How many of these coins does she have? 2 more dimes than nickels = $1.70. She has 10 nickels, and 12 dimes (2 + 10).

Copyright ©1999 by Addison-Wesley Educational Publishers Inc.

EXERCISE 8 Read the passage and use the drawing to help visualize your thoughts.

THE KINDEST CUT

After thanking the donor for a bouquet of flowers and sniffing them appreciatively, the next step is to find a vase and put them in water. The florist usually sends a message to cut off an inch or two of stem first; purists even instruct that this should be done while the stem is immersed in water.

Three stems were cut from the same plant at the same time. Stem 1 was placed in water immediately. Stem 2 was left for half an hour, and then a two-inch length was cut off the bottom end. It was then placed in water. Stem 3 was also left for half an hour and then placed in water without further treatment.

Stem 3 is distinctly wilted, whereas the other two look normal.

The figure shows why Stems 1 and 2 have fared so much better: in both, the column of water in the xylem is continuous with the water in the container. As the leaves transpire, the water lost from the plant is replaced by pulling more water into the xylem from the container. While Stems 2 and 3 were left out of water, transpiration from the leaves pulled the water column in the xylem up into the stem, leaving room for air to enter the base of the xylem. Cutting Stem 2 the second time removed this air-filled xylem, permitting the water still in the xylem to link up with the water in the container. However, Stem 3 was left with an air bubble at the base of its xylem, which blocks the entry of water from the container. As the leaves transpire, they lose water faster than the dwindling xylem contents can replace it. Water is pulled out of other cells in the leaves until they no longer fill their walls. Without this internal support the walls buckle and the plant wilts.

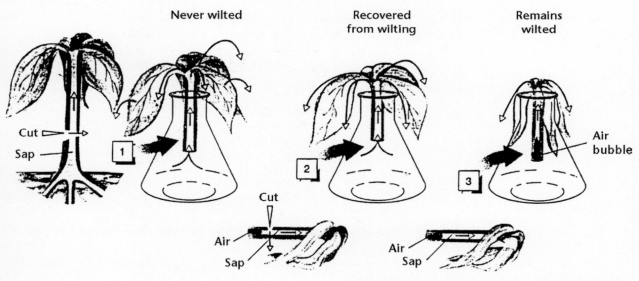

—*A Journey into Life* by Karen Arms and Pamela Camp

Use the passage and the diagram to answer the following questions with *T* (true) or *F* (false).

___T___ 1. Stem 2 would not be receiving water unless it had been cut a second time.

___T___ 2. The flow of water in Stem 1 is not blocked by an air bubble.

_____T_____ 3. The xylem is in the stem of the plant.

_____T_____ 4. The xylem of Stem 2 was blocked before the second cut.

_____T_____ 5 If cut immediately above the air bubble and placed in water, Stem 3 might recover freshness.

EXERCISE 9   Answer the following questions and then analyze your responses in order to learn about yourself.

PSYCHOLOGICAL TIME

Attitudes toward time vary from one culture to another. In one study, for example, the accuracy of clocks was measured in six cultures—Japan, Indonesia, Italy, England, Taiwan, and the United States. Japan had the most accurate and Indonesia had the least accurate clocks. A measure of the speed at which people in these six cultures walked found that the Japanese walked the fastest, the Indonesians the slowest.

WHAT TIME DO YOU HAVE?

For each statement, indicate whether the statement is true (*T*) or untrue (*F*) of your general attitude and behavior.

_____ 1. Meeting tomorrow's deadlines and doing other necessary work comes before tonight's partying.

_____ 2. I meet my obligations to friends and authorities on time.

_____ 3. I complete projects on time by making steady progress.

_____ 4. I am able to resist temptations when I know there is work to be done.

_____ 5. I keep working at a difficult, uninteresting task if it will help me get ahead.

_____ 6. If things don't get done on time, I don't worry about it.

_____ 7. I think that it's useless to plan too far ahead because things hardly ever come out the way you planned anyway.

_____ 8. I try to live one day at a time.

_____ 9. I live to make better what *is* rather than to be concerned about what *will* be.

_____10. It seems to me that it doesn't make sense to worry about the future, since fate determines that whatever will be, will be.

_____11. I believe that getting together with friends to party is one of life's important pleasures.

_____12. I do things impulsively, making decisions on the spur of the moment.

_____13. I take risks to put excitement in my life.

_____14. I get drunk at parties.

_____15. It's fun to gamble.

_____16. Thinking about the future is pleasant to me.

_____17. When I want to achieve something, I set subgoals and consider specific means for reaching those goals.

_____18. It seems to me that my career path is pretty well laid out.

Copyright ©1999 by Addison-Wesley Educational Publishers Inc.

____19. It upsets me to be late for appointments.

____20. I meet my obligations to friends and authorities on time.

____21. I get irritated at people who keep me waiting when we've agreed to meet at a given time.

____22. It makes sense to invest a substantial part of my income in insurance premiums.

____23. I believe that "A stitch in time saves nine."

____24. I believe that "A bird in the hand is worth two in the bush."

____25. I believe it is important to save for a rainy day.

____26. I believe a person's day should be planned each morning.

____27. I make lists of things I must do.

Interpretation

This time test measures seven different factors. If you selected true (*T*) for all or most of the questions within any given factor, you are probably high on that factor. If you selected untrue (*F*) for all or most of the questions within any given factor, you are probably low on that factor.

Count the number of true (*T*) responses for each area.

1–5 ____, 6–10 ____, 11–15 ____, 16–18 ____, 19–21 ____, 22–25 ____, 26–27 ____

The first factor, measured by questions 1–5, is a future, work motivation, perseverance orientation. These people have a strong work ethic and are committed to completing a task despite difficulties and temptations. The second factor (questions 6–10) is a present, fatalistic, worry-free orientation. High scorers on this factor live one day at a time, not necessarily to enjoy the day but to avoid planning for the next day or anxiety about the future.

The third factor (questions 11–15) is a present, pleasure-seeking, partying orientation. These people enjoy the present, take risks and engage in a variety of impulsive actions. The fourth factor (questions 16–18) is a future, goal-seeking, and planning orientation. These people derive special pleasure from planning and achieving a variety of goals.

The fifth factor (questions 19–21) is a time-sensitivity orientation. People who score high are especially sensitive to time and its role in social obligations. The sixth factor (questions 22–25) is a future, practical action orientation. These people do what they have to do—take practical actions—to achieve the future they want.

The seventh factor (questions 26–27) is a future, somewhat obsessive daily planning orientation. High scorers on this factor make daily "to do" lists and devote great attention to specific details.

Source: From "Time in Perspective" by Alexander Gonzalez and Philip G. Zimbardo. Reprinted with permission from *Psychology Today* magazine. Copyright © 1985 (Sussex Publishers, Inc.)

—*Essentials of Human Communication* by Joseph DeVito

Using your rankings on the scale, write a brief description of your attitude and behavior regarding time.

I am _____

_____

_____

POINTS TO PONDER

▲ Reading is thinking.
▲ Good thinkers have developed a logical and sequential pattern of working through complex material
▲ Good thinkers work persistently, believing they will find the answer.
▲ Good thinkers draw on old knowledge to solve new problems.
▲ Good thinkers are active and aggressive in seeking meaning.
▲ Good thinkers break larger problems into smaller problems.
▲ Good thinkers pull out key terms and simplify problems.

SELECTION 1   *Psychology*

THINKING BEFORE READING

Preview for content and organizational clues. Activate your schema and anticipate what you will learn.

Do you know the first name of ten fellow classmates?

Who is the shyest person you know?

Are you embarrassed to talk to new people?

THINKING DURING READING

As you read, predict, picture, relate, monitor, and correct.

ANALYTICAL REASONING

In this passage, you will be using your analytical reasoning skills as you read. Throughout this selection, the original reading selections are interspersed with boxed workbook exercises.

COPING WITH SHYNESS

When I was very young my parents often had relatives and friends visit our house. I never wanted to say hello to them and I tried hiding in my room, the closet, or the base-

Copyright ©1999 by Addison-Wesley Educational Publishers Inc.

ment. When I had to sit down at meals with these people I would be polite, but I would have very little to say.

5   As I grew up I avoided parties and gatherings unless I knew most of the people. I was afraid to talk to girls and never did have a date until I was a senior in high school. I remember how embarrassed I used to become when I went out on a date. If there was any talk of sex I started blushing and could not look the other person in the eye.

In college I spent many nights alone in my dorm room. It was depressing, but it was 10 easier than going out and facing the world. I used that time to study my music. I became an excellent flautist and started performing for larger and larger audiences. I wonder if the people listening to me would believe that I am shy?

Shyness is universal. It affects the young and the old, men and women, celebrities and ordinary people, and even college students. Shyness affects the way we act and com-15 municate with other people. It involves a lack of social skills combined with a high level of anxiety. The lack of social skills usually includes a negative self-image (low self-esteem) and problems in interpersonal relations (listening, self-disclosure, expression of feelings, trust, and social attractiveness). Nonassertiveness, or not standing up for your own rights, is also a contributor to the syndrome we call shyness.

Shyness Scale

Before continuing, it may be interesting to determine your own level of shyness. Answer each of the following questions either true or false.

Stop and respond to these items

_____ 1. I feel relaxed even in unfamiliar social situations.

_____ 2. I try to avoid situations which force me to be very sociable.

_____ 3. It is easy for me to relax when I am with strangers.

_____ 4. I have no particular desire to avoid people.

_____ 5. I often find social occasions upsetting.

_____ 6. I usually feel calm and comfortable at social occasions.

_____ 7. I am usually at ease when talking with someone of the opposite sex.

_____ 8. I try to avoid talking to people unless I know them well.

_____ 9. If the chance comes to meet new people, I often take it.

_____10. I often feel nervous or tense in casual get-togethers in which both sexes are present.

_____11. I am usually nervous with people unless I know them well.

_____12. I usually feel relaxed when I am with a group of people.

_____13. I often want to get away from people.

_____14. I usually feel uncomfortable when I am in a group of people I don't know.

_____15. I usually feel relaxed when I meet someone for the first time.

_____16. Being introduced to people makes me tense and nervous.

_____17. Even though a room is full of strangers, I may enter it anyway.

_____18. I would avoid walking up and joining a large group of people.

_____19. When my superiors want to talk with me, I talk willingly.

_____20. I often feel on edge when I am with a group of people.

_____21. I tend to withdraw from people.

_____22. I don't mind talking to people at parties or social gatherings.

_____23. I am seldom at ease in a large group of people.

_____24. I often think of excuses in order to avoid social engagements.

_____25. I sometimes take the responsibility for introducing people to each other.

_____26. I try to avoid formal social occasions.

_____27. I usually go to whatever social engagements I have.

_____28. I find it easy to relax with other people.

The following directions for scoring appear in the psychology text. Use your analytical thinking skills to determine how you did on the test.

> The above scale is called the social avoidance and distress (SAD) scale and was developed by David Watson and Ronald Friend. In order to obtain your score, determine how many of your answers agree with the following answers: 1 F, 2 T, 3 F, 4 F, 5 T, 6 F, 7 F, 8 T, 9 F, 10 T, 11 T, 12 F, 13 T, 14 T, 15 F, 16 T, 17 F, 18 T, 19 F, 20 T, 21 T, 22 F, 23 T, 24 T, 25 F, 26 T, 27 F, 28 F. The mean or *average,* score for males is approximately eleven and for females, approximately eight. People with scores below average tend to be confident and relaxed in social situations. People with high scores tend to avoid social interactions, prefer to work alone, talk less, and are more worried, and less confident about social relationships.

My score is _____ which means _____ .

Copyright ©1999 by Addison-Wesley Educational Publishers Inc.

Did you figure out how to compute your score? Probably the easiest way to check your answers is to have someone call them out for you. Add the number of correct answers for your score. A high score means you are shy. Scoring a zero on this test means you should audition for a job as a talk show host. You may be the next Oprah Winfrey or Geraldo Rivera!

SITUATIONAL STRESS

20 Most people are shy in specific circumstances. This is called situational shyness. Many people, like the flautist at the beginning of the chapter, don't have enough confidence in their own social skills to comfortably interact with other people. They have trouble starting conversations, speaking up for their rights, saying "no," or disagreeing with other people. It may be certain people, or certain places, that lead to this situational shyness.

25 Susan had been in college for three years. She dated frequently and had many friends and a variety of interests. She never considered herself a shy person. She enjoyed going to movies, concerts, parties, or just sitting around talking with her friends. As a student, Susan had maintained a B average, but many people who knew her felt she could do better. Susan's problem in school was that she
30 was afraid to ask questions in large lecture classes. If she missed an important point or didn't understand the professor, she would just sit back and hope that someone else would ask the question she was thinking about. A friend who had seen Susan ask many intelligent questions in smaller classes asked her why she didn't raise her hand in the larger classes. Susan would explain: "I wasn't sure
35 my question was important," or "I didn't want to look foolish."

Susan was shy only in large lecture classes. This is an example of situational shyness. By contrast, some people are shy in almost all social situations. It is painful for them to meet strangers, to ask a question in class, and to participate in conversations. Because they avoid social interactions, they have few friends and are often lonely.

The Need to Relax

40 One major contributor to shyness is anxiety; reducing shyness begins with reducing anxiety. You may be unable to cope with shyness if you are constantly anxious when you are around other people. This fear may have developed in a number of ways. You may have had a bad social experience in the past that makes you feel anxious now. For example, if you had to make a speech in school, forgot what you were going to say, and were
45 laughed at by your schoolmates, you may now associate speechmaking with this negative consequence. You may also have developed your anxiety by watching and listening to another person who had a bad experience in a similar social situation.

. . . Anxiety that has been learned can be unlearned. One way to do this is through relaxation exercises that are incompatible with anxiety. Joseph Wolpe described this
50 incompatibility as *the principle of reciprocal inhibition: If a response that inhibits anxiety can be made to occur in the presence of an anxiety-evoking stimulus, it will weaken the connection between the stimulus and the anxiety.*

The principle is based on a classic study of children's fears by Mary Clover Jones, in which a child was given attractive foods while a feared object was progressively brought
55 closer and closer to the child. The object soon became associated with the food and the child's anxiety was reduced.

Currently, two common types of behaviors have been used by therapists to inhibit anxiety: relaxation and assertiveness. Each act of assertion or relaxation in a situation will

60 weaken the relationship between the situation and anxiety. The technique of desensitiza-
tion is based on the principle of reciprocal inhibition.

Social Attractiveness

Increasing your social attractiveness will help you cope with shyness. Few of us look like
movie stars, but there are always ways to maximize appearance. By wearing clothes that
look good on you and dressing for success, you may be able to improve your social
attractiveness.

65 But social attractiveness is more than just physical appearance. Going to different
activities is part of social attractiveness. At first, you may just want to go somewhere that
is familiar and comfortable, but eventually you should attempt to go to other places that
interest you. The first time you might want to try going with a friend.

Once you meet people, be prepared to have something to talk about. If you are wor-
70 ried that you will have nothing to say, you will feel anxious and withdraw. If you prepare
yourself, you will feel less anxious and have more rewarding social encounters.

Improving Your Self-Image

Reducing shyness can also come from improving your self-image. Your self-image (or self-
esteem) is your evaluation of your self-worth. People with a good self-image appear confident and satisfied. People with a poor self-image appear overly sensitive and are often
75 shy.

Your self-image is largely determined by the way you compare yourself to other people. To whom do you compare yourself? It is important to choose appropriate models for
comparison. A female choosing a beautiful actress as a model might well feel physically
inferior. When people have poor self-images, it is usually the result of their own evalua-
80 tion of themselves. You can improve your self-image by changing some of the negative
thoughts you have about yourself.

First, it is essential to start thinking positively about yourself. List your strengths and
set goals that realistically reflect these strengths. Try to find something you really excel in,
and emphasize it. Start with some small tasks and build up to more important major
85 objectives. The more successes you have, and the more often you think about your successes and your strengths, the more social confidence you will have. The more you focus
on negative thoughts, the less social confidence you will have.

Try to eliminate negative self-statements like "I'm a failure." Don't say bad things
about yourself or allow other people to attack you as a person. If people or activities
90 lower your self-image, either challenge or eliminate the source of these bad feelings.

Asserting Yourself

Alex really enjoyed going to movies and plays and would often wait in line for
hours to get student-price tickets. Yesterday, he had been waiting in line for
concert tickets when he saw a person cutting in line in front of him. He didn't
say anything, figuring others would not allow line-cutting and would kick the
95 person out of the line. Besides, it would only mean waiting a few minutes longer
and he really didn't feel like bothering anybody.

Alex was not assertive. Reducing shyness involves becoming more assertive. Assertive
behavior has been defined as "behavior which enables a person to act in his own best
interests, to stand up for himself without undue anxiety, to express honest feelings com-
100 fortably, or to exercise his own rights without denying the rights of others." The line-cutting incident is a classic example of nonassertive behavior. Nonassertive people allow
others to take advantage of them; they do not stick up for their own rights. This generally
leads to frustration, unhappiness, or anxiety.

Alex could have been assertive by calmly approaching the person who had cut in line
105 and simply stating: "I saw you cut in line. The line forms at the rear. People have been
waiting here for hours. Please go to the end of the line." The response is direct, nonag-
gressive, and allows Alex to stick up for his own interests.

Copyright ©1999 by Addison-Wesley Educational Publishers Inc.

Students who are able to be assertive at school have many advantages because they are able to ask for help, express their feelings, and stand up for their rights. How assertive
110 are you at school? You can get an idea by checking the statements below that accurately describe how assertively you handle situations at school.

Assertiveness Scale

Stop and check each item that describes your behavior.

_____ If I think a grade I was given was unfair or wrong, I discuss my feelings with the instructor and ask that it be changed.

_____ I refuse unreasonable requests from my friends and fellow students.

_____ If I miss a class one day, I ask other students for a copy of their notes.

_____ If a friend asks me to go to a movie when I have to study, I am able to say no.

_____ If I am confused by what the teacher says, I ask for clarification.

_____ If someone sitting next to me in class talks and bothers me, I ask him or her to be quiet.

_____ If I can't find a room I am looking for on campus, I ask a stranger for help.

How many items did you check on the above list? The following will explain your score: Checking 6 to 7 items indicates an above average level of assertiveness, 3 to 5 items an average level, and 0 to 2 items a level of assertiveness below average.

_____ 1. According to this test of assertiveness, I am

    a. above average
    b. average
    c. below average

_____ 2. This means _____.

Certain nonverbal communication skills are essential to becoming assertive. You must have good eye contact with the person you are talking to; staring at someone or never looking at them leads to communication problems. Your facial expression must be
115 consistent with the message you are trying to send; you can't express dissatisfaction while smiling. Nervous hand gestures and constant movement also distract from your intended message. Don't stand too close or too far away from the recipient; inappropriate body positioning and posturing can indicate a tentativeness in communicating your thoughts. In fact, you must use your body posture to emphasize important points.
120 How you verbalize your message may be as important as what you say. The message should be presented with a loudness that is appropriate to the circumstances and at a rate of speech that is not too fast or too slow. Try to avoid distracting verbal habits like "um" or "you know." Emotional tones should also be consistent with the emotion being expressed.

PRACTICE IN ANALYTICAL REASONING

125 The exercises at the end of this selection differ from the usual format because they require you to get up from your desk and take action. You will be conducting experiments with

yourself and others. What could be more interesting than applying your analytical thinking skills to your own personality! Pretend you are a scientific researcher and systematically engage in the recommended behaviors. Record your findings.

130   **Experiment 1: Experimenting with Your Image.** You are more likely to have positive social experiences if you sound confident, strong, and successful than if you sound uncertain, weak, and timid. The image that you present to others strongly affects their response.

Image is a perception. You have an image of yourself, and others form an image of
135   you. You can change the way others see you by engaging in the following behaviors. Do each exercise with a different person. Record the effects of your changed behavior on the other person.

1. Intentionally raise or lower your voice during part of your conversation.

   Effects of a raised voice: _____

   Effects of a lowered voice: _____

2. Experiment with the amount of eye contact you have during a conversation. Try staring at the person as well as making no eye contact.

   Effects of staring: _____

   Effects of no eye contact: _____

3. Vary your rate of speech from very fast to very slow.

   Effects of fast speech: _____

   Effects of slow speech: _____

4. Imagine that you are an actor playing the role of a self-assured, emotionally expressive, and successful person who doesn't really care about the impression he or she makes on others. Start a conversation with someone and pretend you are that actor.

   Effects of your self-assured role: _____

5. In which of the above situations did you feel the most comfortable? _____

6. In which of the above situations did you feel the least comfortable? _____

7. How did the above situations affect your self-image? _____

   _____

Experiment 2: Initiating Conversations. A common problem for an unassertive person is initiating conversations. You may want to start a conversation by mentioning a com-
140   mon experience that you share with another person. Paying a compliment or requesting information are other ways to initiate a conversation.

In order to practice initiating conversations, try each of the following exercises—in order—first with someone of the same sex and then with someone of the opposite sex. In each case, avoid negative thoughts, act with confidence, and do not worry about what
145   the other person may think. When you have finished, evaluate your efforts.

1. Ask someone for the correct time, and then make a comment about a class or meeting you have to attend.

2. Ask to borrow another student's pen. When you return it, ask a question about class, campus, or school.

3. Stop a stranger on the street and ask for directions to a nearby store, movie theater, or park. Then follow with another question about the quality of the store, what's playing at the movie theater, and the like.

Copyright ©1999 by Addison-Wesley Educational Publishers Inc.

4. While waiting in a line for a movie or concert, or while walking out of a class, start a conversation with a stranger. Find an opportunity to discuss why you like or don't like something.

5. Identify two people whom you would like to know better. Find an opportunity to initiate conversation with each of them, and include in your conversation a request for a favor.

6. Which of the above exercises was the most rewarding? Why? _____

_____

7. Which of the above exercises was the least rewarding? Why? _____

_____

—*Using Psychology* by Morris Holland

Connect

Social psychologists study factors that draw people together. Have you ever wondered why your friends are your friends? Read the following findings by researchers and think about your own personal relationships. List five of your close friends. For each, explain how proximity, exposure, and similarity played a part in your friendship.

ATTRACTION AND PERSONAL RELATIONSHIPS

PROXIMITY

Regular interaction or familiarity seems to increase liking; often, the people we interact with the most are simply those who are literally closest to us. A classic study by Festinger, Schachter, and Back found that residents of an apartment complex tended to interact with—and like—those who happened to live on the same floor more than those who lived on other floors or in other buildings. (These researchers did not analyze this phenomenon in terms of the development of in-group versus out-group perceptions and biases, but such an analysis might prove interesting.) Likewise, when classroom seating is alphabetical, students are more likely to be friends with people who share the same last initial.

There are two major explanations for the relation between proximity and liking. First is simple availability. Assuming that most people are nice enough once you get to know them, it follows that proximity will determine who you get to know and, therefore, like. A second explanation is based on the **mere exposure effect**—simple familiarity increases liking for a person or object that is not, necessarily, intrinsically likeable. The mere exposure effect has been demonstrated in the laboratory with stimuli as neutral as nonsense syllables, which people find more pleasing after they have read them several times. It seems reasonable to conclude that repeated exposure to people in proximity to us leads us to like them more. (Presumably, there are some limits to this phenomenon, as when repeated exposure to someone who initially irritates us just makes things worse!)

SIMILARITY

Liking goes with likeness; whether you like someone seems to depend on whether the person is like you. As we have already seen, people of similar levels of physical attractiveness seem to wind up together; similarity along other dimensions also affects attraction. Byrne has demonstrated that we tend to prefer people who share our attitudes and opinions, perhaps because these people provide evidence that our attitudes and opinions are "correct."

—*Psychology* by Henry Roediger et al.

EXPLORE THE NET

- Find an article on overcoming shyness that you feel adds relevant information to what has already been offered in this selection.
- What are some of the self-help books and materials that are available on coping with shyness?

For additional readings and exercises, visit the Longman English Skills Web page at:

http://longman.awl.com/englishpages

For a user name and password, please see your instructor.

SELECTION 2   *Biology*

THINKING BEFORE READING

Preview for content and organizational clues. Activate your schema and anticipate what you will learn.

How is the organizational pattern for this selection different?

When you feel the symptoms, what do you do to prevent catching a cold?

What do you do to "cure" a cold?

VOCABULARY PREVIEW

Are you familiar with these words?

scientific reasoning	inductive logic	deductive logic	sampling	replicates
testimony	predictability	intuitions	hypothesis	null

What do you do if you replicate a scientific study?

How do inductive and deductive logic differ?

What kind of logic did Sherlock Holmes use?

Your instructor may give a true-false vocabulary review before or after reading.

THINKING DURING READING

As you read, predict, picture, relate, monitor, and correct.

SCIENTIFIC LOGIC

Scientific reasoning flows along two philosophical channels: inductive reasoning and deductive reasoning. **Inductive logic** occurs when a great number of individual observa-

Copyright ©1999 by Addison-Wesley Educational Publishers Inc.

THE FAR SIDE

By GARY LARSON

Testing whether or not animals "kiss."

—*The Far Side* © 1985 Farworks, Inc. Used by permission of
Universal Press Syndicate. All rights reserved.

tions suggests that a general principle may be true. For instance, suppose you interviewed 25 women on campus concerning their feelings about legalized abortion and
5 every one said she opposed it. From this sample you might be tempted to make the general statement that *all* women are opposed to legalized abortion. Obviously, you are taking a risk when you make such general statements. The smaller the sample of people interviewed or subjects tested, the greater the risk. Science goes to great lengths to reduce the possibility of these inductive errors, or **sampling errors**, by insisting that all
10 scientific studies include as many *replicates* (additional subjects) as time or money allows. For that reason, personal *testimony* is the worst and most unreliable kind of scientific evidence of all. A single person's opinion or experiences (Like: "Well, I've been taking megadoses of vitamin C for two years now and I haven't had a cold yet!") are usually viewed with great suspicion.

15 **Deductive logic** is even riskier. It attempts to use general statements to predict specific situations. For instance, suppose you are operating from the general premise:

"Malamute huskies are good sled dogs." (General statement)
"Kima is my new malamute puppy." (Fact)
"Therefore, Kima will be a good sled dog when she grows up." (Prediction)

20 You are using a general statement to predict something about your own dog. Your prediction might come true. But it might not. The predictability is only as good as the general statement. As it turns out, Kima came from a highly inbred line of malamutes, and by age two she was horribly crippled with hip dysplasia (her thighbones did not fit into her hip joints).

25 Scientists use inductive logic during experiments aimed at revealing general patterns. They use deductive experiments when they are testing the predicting power of their theories or hypotheses.

Yet it is not quite fair to believe, as many people do, that scientists are strictly logical beings. Induction and deduction enter their work primarily after the research has been
30 done, when they are writing up the results for publication in journals and textbooks. The actual process of scientific research has much more in common with the creative arts than most people suspect. The scientist leaps out of bed in the dead of night to cry "Aha!" and rush to the laboratory with a new hypothesis or an experiment or an insight that might make sense of a jumble of data. Dreams and hunches and intuitions all play
35 parts in the process. The history of science is a history of inspiration as much as it is a history of logic.

LEARNING FOCUS: THE STRUCTURE OF THE SCIENTIFIC METHOD

In order to understand the structure of the scientific method, read the following example based on an actual experiment. Some details have been fictionalized so that it more clearly reveals the structure of the scientific method.

A CURE FOR THE COMMON COLD?

Initial Observation: A young patient being treated for leukemia at the University of Texas was given a lozenge of zinc gluconate to correct the zinc deficiency that commonly accompanies that disease. Instead of swallowing the lozenge, she kept it in her mouth
40 and sucked on it. To everyone's surprise, the symptoms of a cold she was developing vanished within an hour.

Hypothesis: The researchers' hypothesis (tentative explanation) was that prolonged contact between the zinc compound and the tissues lining the throat and mouth may somehow shorten the duration of the cold. However, for research purposes, the hypothe-
45 sis must be reworded to describe the conditions under which no (null) difference appears. That is, because it is impossible to do all the experiments required to prove a positive hypothesis but it takes only one experiment to disprove a negative one, it must become a *null hypothesis.* Since the researchers really expected the zinc lozenges to make a difference, they set up the following testable hypothesis:
50 *Null Hypothesis:* A group of patients given zinc lozenges (the experimental group) will have active cold symptoms for the same length of time as another group given lozenges containing no zinc (the control group).

The Experiment: The researchers divided a population of 64 people who were coming down with colds into two groups: 32 people were given the zinc lozenges (experimental
55 treatment) and 32 were given lozenges that contained no zinc (control treatment). As in most modern research on humans, the study was *double-blind,* meaning that neither the experimental subjects (the patients) nor the researchers knew what kind of lozenges any particular patient received. This practice keeps the expectations of the subjects and researchers from influencing the results. (In a *single-blind* or just plain "blind" experi-
60 ment, only the subjects are kept ignorant.)

Individual Observations: The researchers noted the duration of cold symptoms for each subject. Each measurement of the length of time a subject stayed sick is a single observation.

Look for the Pattern (Generalization): Much of the creative work in science is involved
65 with attempting to find the pattern (if any) in the data generated by an experiment. In this experiment, the recovery patterns for the two groups are then compared to each other to see whether any group differences can be seen. In this example, there may be significant differences between the two treatments. In actual practice, a special branch of applied mathematics, called *statistics,* is used to help design experiments and to deter-
70 mine just how "significant" these differences really are. The total number of sick days for each group and the average length of time members from the respective groups were sick were calculated to see whether a pattern emerged from the data for the two groups. Their results were strikingly different:

Copyright ©1999 by Addison-Wesley Educational Publishers Inc.

Test Results

Group	Number in Group	Total Days with Colds	Average Duration of Cold
Experimental Group Zinc lozenges	32	128	4.28 days
Control Group No zinc	32	352	11.06 days

75 *Conclusion:* The results are compared to the null hypothesis to see whether they discredit it or not. In this example, it does seem that taking the zinc lozenge shortens the duration of cold symptoms. The null hypothesis is not supported.

Now go to the Learning Focus Response to break the information from this experiment down into the components of the scientific method and relate the experimental design to the patterns of deductive and inductive reasoning.

(1,055 words)

—*Focus on Human Biology* by Carl Rischer and Thomas Easton

THINKING AFTER READING

ANALYTICAL REASONING: LEARNING FOCUS RESPONSE

Use analytical reasoning to summarize what you have learned by answering the following questions.

1. What is a null hypothesis? A null hypothesis is a negative statement of the tentative explanation that the scientist wants to test.

2. What was the null hypothesis that was tested by the experiment? The null hypothesis tested by the experiment was that the patients given the zinc lozenges would have the cold symptoms for the same amount of time as the patients without the zinc.

3. What was the actual hypothesis from which the researchers were working? The actual hypothesis from which the researchers were working was that the patients taking the zinc would have cold symptoms for less time than those without zinc.

4. Why and how is a null hypothesis used? A null hypothesis is used in a scientific experiment to test a possible explanation. It is stated in the negative to reduce the number of trials necessary for proof.

5. What is inductive reasoning? Inductive reasoning is logic that uses a large number of individual observations from which to form a general principle that may be true.

6. Describe deductive reasoning. Deductive reasoning is logic that uses a general principle or statement to predict a specific situation.

7. Would you say the zinc lozenge experiment was designed along inductive or deductive lines? Why? <u>The experiment of zinc lozenges was designed along</u> <u>deductive lines because the scientists already suspected that the zinc would</u> <u>shorten the duration of the cold symptoms. However, the doctors probably</u> <u>used inductive reasoning to figure out that the zinc was affecting cold</u> <u>symptoms.</u>

8. If, as a physician, you prescribed zinc lozenges for a patient after reading that study, would you be proceeding along inductive or deductive lines? Explain. <u>You would be using deductive lines because you already believe</u> <u>that zinc shortens the length of a cold, although it may not work on your</u> <u>particular patient.</u>

9. Describe a generalization about efficient study habits that you might make using deductive reasoning. <u>Answers will vary, but an example would be to</u> <u>review your lecture notes immediately after each class to determine if it</u> <u>improves memory as has been suggested in this text.</u>

10. Describe a generalization about the need for sleep that you might make using inductive reasoning. <u>Answers will vary, but an example would be to</u> <u>sleep 5 hours each night for 5 nights and then sleep 7 hours for 5 nights.</u> <u>After each 5-night segment, test for mental alertness in order to form a</u> <u>hypothesis.</u>

VOCABULARY ENRICHMENT

Context Clues: Select the boldface word from the following list that best completes each sentence.

scientific reasoning   inductive logic   deductive logic   sampling   replicate
testimony   predictability   intuition   hypothesis null

1. If a buyer does not deliver the money by noon, the contract will be _____<u>null</u>_____ and void.

2. Systematically accumulating evidence from which to later make a generalization is called _____<u>inductive</u>_____ logic.

3. My _____<u>intuition</u>_____ tells me that my math professor will check homework only once a week.

4. Rather than survey every single student at the university, you can use a statistical table to indicate a smaller number of students that would make an adequate size for _____<u>sampling</u>_____.

5. The witness saw the crime committed and gave _____<u>testimony</u>_____ in court concerning the defendant's role.

6. _____<u>Scientific reasoning</u>_____ involves using logic to seek answers in a systematic and controlled experiment.

Copyright ©1999 by Addison-Wesley Educational Publishers Inc.

7. Colleges use standardized test scores, high school grade point average, and rank in class as measures of ___predictability___ of college success.

8. Scientists sometimes ___replicate___ a previous study using the same method and similar subjects to see if the findings will be the same.

9. When you start with an acceptable generalization and then systematically find evidence for support, the process is called ___deductive___ logic.

10. The students in the group reviewed the evidence and then suggested a reasonable ___hypothesis___ to explain the phenomenon.

ASSESS YOUR LEARNING

Review confusing questions, seek clarification, and make notes in your text to help you remember new information and vocabulary.

EXPLORE THE NET

- What have been the traditional uses for zinc gluconate?
- Find additional research studies that demonstrate the effectiveness of zinc gluconate for treating the common cold.

For additional readings and exercises, visit the Longman English Skills Web page at:

http://longman.awl.com/englishpages

For a user name and password, please see your instructor.

SELECTION 3 *Business*

THINKING BEFORE READING

Preview for content and organizational clues. Activate your schema and anticipate what you will learn.

Why are you motivated to make good grades in college?

If you were a millionaire, would you get a college degree?

This selection will probably tell me _____.

VOCABULARY PREVIEW

Are you familiar with these words?

stifled	inspire	proponent	premise	pinnacle
crux	de-emphasis	hygienic	grievances	verbalizing

How do the prefixes *pre* and *pro* differ?

Are people who get to the pinnacle usually inspired?

What committees in your college are set up to hear student grievances?

Your instructor may give a true-false vocabulary review before or after reading.

THINKING DURING READING

As you read, predict, picture, relate, monitor, and correct.

MOTIVATING YOURSELF[1]

"It is asking too much to suggest that people motivate themselves in the work environment. Motivation should come from the supervisor, special rewards, or the job itself."

Many people would disagree with the above quotation. They would claim that self-motivation is an absolute necessity in many work environments. They would also claim
5   that the more you can learn about motivation, the more you understand yourself and, as a result, the more you will be in a position to inspire your own efforts.

―――――――
[1]Chapman, Elwood N. From Your Attitude Is Showing, 8E by Elwood N. Chapman, © 1987: Adapted by permission of Prentice-Hall, Inc. Upper Saddle River, NJ.

Copyright ©1999 by Addison-Wesley Educational Publishers Inc.

Let's assume that you find yourself in a job where things are not going well. You feel stifled and "boxed in." You may, for example, be much more capable than the job demands. Perhaps too, the pay and benefits are only average, your immediate supervisor

10 is difficult to deal with, and some other factors are not ideal. Even so, you consider the organization a good one and you recognize that by earning promotions your long-term future can be excellent.

How can you inspire yourself to do a better-than-average job despite the temporary handicaps? How can you motivate yourself to live close to your potential despite a nega-

15 tive environment? How can you keep your attitude from showing? How can you keep from injuring important human relationships?

There are many theories or schools of thought on why people are motivated to achieve high productivity on the job. Most of these are studied by managers so that they will be in a better position to motivate the employees who work for them. In this chapter we are

20 going to reverse the procedure. We are going to show you how to motivate yourself. *If your supervisor can be trained to motivate you, why can't you learn to motivate yourself?*

THEORY 1: SELF-IMAGE PSYCHOLOGY

This is frequently called the PsychoCybernetics School. The proponent of this theory is Dr. Maxwell Maltz, a plastic surgeon. The basic idea is that, in order to be properly motivated to achieve certain goals, an individual must recognize the *need* for a good self-

25 image. Dr. Maltz discovered in his work as a plastic surgeon that some patients became much more self-confident and far more motivated after having their faces greatly improved. Why? Maltz came to the conclusion that the image the individual had of himself (or herself) *inside* was more motivating than the changes he had made *outside.* In short, the way an individual *thinks* he or she looks can be more important than the way

30 he or she actually looks to others.

How Can You Use This Theory to Motivate Yourself? Learn to picture yourself in a more complimentary way. First, research has shown that most people who have poor self-images actually *do* look better to others than they do to themselves. If this is true of you, you might try concentrating on your strong features instead of the weak ones, thus

35 developing a more positive outlook and a better self-image.

Second, you might consider improving yourself on the outside as well as on the inside. You may not want to go as far as plastic surgery, but you could change your hairstyle, dress differently, lose or gain weight, exercise, and many other things. According to the theory, however, unless you recognize and accept the improvement, nothing may

40 happen. PsychoCybernetics is, of course, a do-it-yourself project. You do all the work—and you get all the credit, too!

THEORY 2: MASLOW'S HIERARCHY OF NEEDS

This is a very old theory developed by Abraham Maslow in his book *Motivation and Personality.* The premise here is that you have certain needs that must be fulfilled if you are to be properly motivated. These needs are built one on top of the other as in a pyramid.

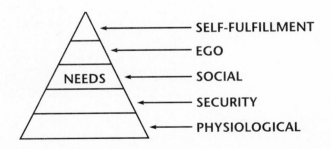

45   The bottom need is physiological—food, good health. The next is safety and security. The third from the bottom is social needs: one needs to be accepted and enjoy the
company of others. Next are ego needs—recognition from others. Finally, at the pinnacle, is one's need for self-fulfillment or self-realization.

        The crux of this theory is that the bottom needs must be fulfilled before the others
50 come into play. In other words, you must satisfy your need for food and security *before*
social needs become motivating. You must satisfy social and ego needs before self-fulfillment is possible.

How Can You Use This Idea to Motivate Yourself to Reach Goals? If you believe
Maslow is right, it would be self-defeating to reverse the pyramid or "skip over" unsatis-
55 fied needs to reach others. Chances are good, however, that your first two needs are
being adequately satisfied so you could make a greater effort to meet new people and
make new friends. This could, in turn, help to satisfy your ego needs. With both your
social and ego needs better satisfied you might be inspired to attempt greater creative
efforts which could eventually lead you to greater self-realization.

Theory 3: Psychological Advantage

60 This school was founded by Saul W. Gellerman. It contends that people constantly seek
to serve their own self-interests, which change as they grow older. People can make their
jobs work for them to give them a psychological advantage over other people at the
same level. The way to create a psychological advantage in a starting job that is beneath
your capacity is to learn all there is about that job. That way, you can use the job as a
65 springboard to something better, a position that will give you more freedom and responsibility.

How Could You Use This to Inspire Yourself? The best way, perhaps, is to be a little
selfish about your job. Work for the organization and yourself at the same time. Instead of
letting your job control you, perhaps pulling you and your attitude down, use it as a
70 launching pad. Use it to build human relations that will be important later on. Study the
structure of your organization so you will understand the lines of progression better than
the other employees. Study the leadership style of your supervisor and others so that you
will have a better one when your turn comes.

Theory 4: Motivation-Hygienic School

This theory was developed by Professor Frederick Herzberg. Basically it claims that unde-
75 sirable environmental factors (physical working conditions) can be dissatisfiers. Factors of
achievement, recognition, and freedom, on the other hand, are satisfiers. All working
environments have both negative and positive factors.

How Can You Take Advantage of This Theory? People who maintain positive attitudes
under difficult circumstances do so through attitude control. They concentrate *only* on
80 the positive factors in their environment. You can, for instance, refuse to recognize the
demotivating factors in your job and concentrate only on those things that will satisfy
your needs better.

        This could mean a de-emphasis on physical factors and more emphasis on psycho-
logical factors such as social, ego, and self-fulfillment needs. One individual puts it this
85 way: "I work in a very old building with poor facilities. Even so I have learned that I can
be happy there because of the work I do and the great people I work with. One quickly
gets used to fancy buildings and facilities and begins to take them for granted anyway."

Copyright ©1999 by Addison-Wesley Educational Publishers Inc.

THEORY 5: THE MAINTENANCE-MOTIVATION THEORY

90   This school is much like Herzberg's hygienic approach and was developed by M. Scott Myers of Texas Instruments, Inc. His research found that employees usually fall into one of two groups: motivation-seekers and maintenance-seekers. In short, some people look for those factors that are motivating to them and are constantly pushing themselves toward fulfillment. Others are concerned with just staying where they are. Maintenance-seekers spend much time talking about working conditions, wages, recreational pro-

95   grams, grievances, and similar matters and do little or nothing to motivate themselves. Motivation-seekers, on the other hand, look beyond such matters.

How Might You Use This to Improve Your Own Motivation? The obvious answer is, of course, to keep yourself out of the maintenance-seeker classification. To do this you should try not to overassociate with those in the maintenance classification. Without your

100   knowing it, they could pull you into their camp. Try also to talk about positive things instead of being a complainer. Verbalizing negative factors often intensifies the dissatisfaction one feels. Turn your attention to things you can achieve on the job—not to the negative factors.

(1,338 words)

—*Your Attitude Is Showing* by Elwood Chapman

THINKING AFTER READING

RECALL: Self-test your understanding. Your instructor may choose to give you a true-false review.

REACT: If you could have plastic surgery, what would you have done and what do you think it would do for you? <u>Answers will vary.</u>

REFLECT: For each of Maslow's five levels of needs, name and describe a person that you know who fits the level. <u>Answer will vary.</u>

 THINK CRITICALLY: Why would a plastic surgeon be the author of a book on self-image and motivation. Write your answer on a separate sheet of paper.

ANALYTICAL REASONING

Use your analytical reasoning skills on the following business problem.

After having worked for the same corporation for over three years, Norman decided that he had made a major mistake. He had been accepted into a formal management training program directly out of college. He had received his first supervisory role before his first year was up, but after that nothing else happened. He had been on a plateau for over two years. In recent months he had been feeling extremely frustrated, stifled, and somewhat hostile. He admitted that his attitude was showing. He admitted that his personal productivity had stagnated.

Norman knew the primary reason for his lack of upward progress. His company had been going through a consolidation process and had put a freeze on hiring new employees. Very few middle- and upper-management positions were opening. Nevertheless, Norman finally came to the uncomfortable conclusion that he had to do something about his situation. He had to force some kind of action, even if it was difficult.

He then sat down and listed the advantages and disadvantages of his role with the company:

Advantages	**Disadvantages**
Good geographical location	Corporation not expanding
Good benefits	Salary only fair
Job security	Limited learning opportunities
Good personnel policies	Overconservative management
Good physical working conditions	Poor supervisor
Little community time	Already made some human relations mistakes
Good home neighborhood	Limited opportunities for upward communication with management
Enjoyable type of work	Boring fellow supervisors

After carefully going over the pros and cons of his job—and considering his three-year investment—Norman decided that he had the following options:

1. Go to the personnel department and discuss his frustration about being on a plateau.
2. Submit a written request for a transfer involving a promotion.
3. Start a serious search for a new job in a new company.
4. Resign with two weeks' notice and start looking for a new job.
5. Talk to his supervisor and ask for more responsibility.
6. Motivate himself so that management will recognize a change in attitude and consider him for the next promotion.
7. Relax, continue present efforts, and wait it out.
8. Motivate himself for three months. Then if nothing happens, resign.
9. After telling his boss his intentions, go to the president of the company with the problem.
10. Go to the president of the company to discuss his personal progress.

Assume you are Norman. First, on a separate sheet of paper, list which of the above options you would consider. Second, put them in the order in which you would undertake them. Third, add any steps you would take that are not on the list. Fourth, justify your decisions.

Copyright ©1999 by Addison-Wesley Educational Publishers Inc.

Name _____

Date _____

COMPREHENSION QUESTIONS

Answer the following with *a, b, c,* or *d,* or fill in the blank. In order to help you analyze your strengths and weaknesses, the question types are indicated.

Main Idea ___b___ 1. The best statement of the main idea is:

    a. Motivation comes from within and cannot be taught.
    b. People can use different theories of motivation to motivate themselves.
    c. People who are not motivated lose their jobs.
    d. Motivation in an organization is the responsibility of management.

Purpose ___c___ 2. The purpose of this selection is to

    a. improve management.
    b. criticize supervisors.
    c. encourage self-motivation.
    d. analyze mistakes.

Detail ___a___ 3. According to Maltz's theory, many people make mistakes by

    a. thinking they look worse than others think they do.
    b. trying to look as good as others.
    c. thinking they look better than they do.
    d. trying to hide their weaknesses from others.

Inference ___c___ 4. In Maslow's "Hierarchy of Needs," winning sales trophies satisfies the

    a. security need.
    b. social need.
    c. ego need.
    d. self-fulfillment need.

Conclusion ___b___ 5. Gellerman's theory of psychological advantage is based primarily on

    a. competition.
    b. self-interest.
    c. group cooperation.
    d. the needs of management.

Conclusion ___c___ 6. According to the motivation-hygienic theory, a person should

    a. work only in a positive environment.
    b. motivate supervisors to clean up the environment.
    c. ignore the negative factors in the environment and focus on the positive factors.
    d. seek a job with only positive factors.

Inference 7. According to the maintenance-motivation theory, someone who wants to stay in a position for a few more years until retirement is a maintenance-seeker. _____

Answer the following with *T* (true) or *F* (false).

Inference ___F___ 8. The author seems to agree with the quotation at the beginning of the selection.

Inference   _T_   9. In Maslow's hierarchy, the need to feel that you are using all of your talents to the best of your ability is the self-fulfillment need.

Conclusion   _F_ 10. Maltz's theory is exactly the opposite of Herzberg's theory.

VOCABULARY

Answer the following with *a, b, c,* or *d* for the word or phrase that best defines the boldface word as used in the selection. The number in parentheses indicates the line of the passage in which the word is located.

_b_ 1. "feel **stifled**" (7–8)

   a. useless
   b. smothered
   c. angry
   d. sick

_a_ 2. "**inspire** yourself" (13)

   a. motivate
   b. force
   c. command
   d. instruct

_c_ 3. "**proponent** of this theory" (22)

   a. scholar
   b. attacker
   c. supporter
   d. manager

_d_ 4. "The **premise** here" (43)

   a. signal
   b. mistake
   c. meaning
   d. supposition

_c_ 5. "at the **pinnacle**" (47–48)

   a. bottom
   b. crucial time
   c. peak
   d. most noticeable point

_a_ 6. "The **crux** of this theory" (49)

   a. crucial point
   b. beginning
   c. solution
   d. reward

_b_ 7. "**de-emphasis** on physical factors" (83)

   a. renewed response
   b. less stress
   c. complete drop
   d. minor stress

_c_ 8. "**hygienic** approach" (89)

   a. scientific
   b. analytical
   c. healthful
   d. resourceful

_d_ 9. "**grievances**, and similar matters" (95)

   a. successes
   b. contests
   c. enrichments
   d. complaints

_b_ 10. "**Verbalizing** negative factors" (101)

   a. hiding
   b. talking about
   c. overlooking
   d. remembering

VOCABULARY ENRICHMENT

A. Study these easily confused words and circle the correct one for each sentence.

   ware: goods sold
   wear: put on clothes
   where: a place

   1. The bookstore surprised us with some new ((wares) wears).

   decent: morally good
   descent: move downward
   dissent: disagreement

Copyright ©1999 by Addison-Wesley Educational Publishers Inc.

2. The (**decent**, **descent**, **dissent**) between the two countries grew into a major confrontation.

allusion: reference in literature
illusion: false idea

3. He is operating under the (**allusion**, **illusion**) that I am going to help him with homework.

B. Refer to Appendix 2 in the back of this text and use the doubling rule to complete the following words.

4. regret + ing = regretting

5. swim + ing = swimming

6. excel + ent = excellent

7. ship + ment = shipment

C. Suffixes   Use the boldface suffix to supply an appropriate word for each group of sentences.

ment: act of, state of, result of action

8. Another _____amendment_____ to the constitution was proposed by the legislature.

9. A growing child needs to eat the right foods so that his or her body gets the proper _____nourishment_____.

10. My _____appointment_____ with the manager was postponed until tomorrow at two o'clock.

ence: action, state, quality

11. The therapist showed great _____persistence_____ in working with the man for hours to achieve a tiny degree of success.

12. The behavior of seemingly untrainable dogs can improve when the dogs are sent to _____obedience_____ school.

13. Who had the greatest _____influence_____ over your life as you were growing up?

able, ible: can do, able

14. To get elected, a political candidate must mix with the public and make himself highly _____visible_____.

15. I need a _____reliable_____ car that I can count on to start each morning.

ASSESS YOUR LEARNING

Review confusing questions, seek clarification, and make notes in your text to help you remember new information and vocabulary.

- What type of information is available on PsychoCybernetics?
- How is Maslow's hierarchy of needs applied in business management?

For additional readings and exercises, visit the Longman English Skills Web page at:

http://longman.awl.com/englishpages

For a user name and password, please see your instructor.

Copyright © 1999 by Addison-Wesley Educational Publishers Inc.

Copyright ©1999 by Addison-Wesley Educational Publishers Inc.

CHAPTER

10 *Inference*

◆ *What is implied meaning?*
◆ *Why would meaning be implied rather than stated directly?*
◆ *What is slanted language or connotation of words?*
◆ *What kinds of clues imply meaning?*
◆ *How do good readers draw conclusions?*

What Is an Inference? ◆◆◆◆◆◆◆◆◆◆

An inference is a meaning that is suggested rather than directly stated. Inferences are implied through clues that lead the reader to make assumptions and draw conclusions. For example, instead of making a direct statement, "these people are rich and influential," an author could imply that idea by describing an impressive residence, expensive heirlooms, and prominent friends. Understanding an inference is what we mean by "reading between the lines" because the suggestion, rather than the actual words, carries the meaning.

Inference from Cartoons

Cartoons and jokes require you to "read" between the lines and make a connection. They are funny because of the unstated, rather than the stated. When listeners "catch on" to a joke, it simply means that they have made the connection and recognize the unstated inference. For example, what inference makes the following joke funny?

Sam: Do you know how to save a politician from drowning?
Joe: No.
Sam: Good.

Taxpayers like to dislike politicians, and this joke falls into that category. As a rule, when you have to explain the inference in a joke, the fun is lost. You want your audience to "make the connection" and laugh uproariously.

EXAMPLE Look at the following cartoon. What do you know about a jury? What is being implied about this one?

"Eleven hamburgers, one frank. Eleven coffees, one tea. Eleven apple pies, one chocolate cake. . . . "

—*Elements of Public Speaking* by Joseph DeVito

EXPLANATION A jury is composed of twelve people who are trying to reach consensus on a verdict of guilty or not guilty. The implication in this cartoon is that eleven of the jurors are in agreement on everything, including what to eat, while one juror is totally opposed. Ordering food implies that the discussion may drag on for a long and difficult time. Frequently, a point that takes some figuring out and taps our imagination has a greater impact on us than one that is obviously stated.

EXERCISE 1

The following cartoon contains many suggestive details that imply meaning. Use the details to figure out the meaning of the cartoon and answer the questions.

'Okay, bring in the new guy . . .'

—Edwards, George. Auth © 1976 *The Philadelphia Inquire*. Reprinted by permission of UNIVERSAL PRESS SYNDICATE. All rights reserved.

1. Who is the "new guy"? <u>The new President of the United States.</u>

2. What is implied by the man in the middle of the cartoon? <u>The man directs the media in order to whip the President into shape.</u>

3. Why is the man labeled *Press* holding a pen? <u>He represents the newspapers.</u>

4. What kind of bird is in the cage, and what does that suggest? <u>The bird is a bald eagle that represents our freedom but has been caged by the media.</u>

5. What is meant by the sign saying *Oval Chamber*? <u>The sign suggests both the oval office of the President and a chamber of horrors.</u>

6. What is suggested by the television camera? <u>The camera represents the television press.</u>

Copyright ©1999 by Addison-Wesley Educational Publishers Inc.

7. What is the main point of the cartoon? <u>The main point is to criticize the</u> <u>press for the aggressive and abusive manner in which the press treats the</u> <u>President. The bias is against the press and sympathetic to the President.</u>

Recognizing Suggested Meaning

In reading, as in everyday life, information may or may not be stated outright. For example, someone's death would seem to be a fact beyond question. An author could simply state, "He is dead," but often it is more complicated than that. In literature and in poetry such a fact might be divulged in a more dramatic manner, and the reader is left to put the clues together and figure out what happened. Read the following excerpt from a story about a shipwrecked crew's struggle to shore. What clues tell you that the oiler is dead?

> In the shallows, face downward, lay the oiler. His forehead touched sand that was periodically, between each wave, clear of the sea.
>
> —"The Open Boat" by Stephen Crane

The oiler's head is face down in the shallow water. When the waves rush in to shore, his face is in the water, and when they wash out, his face or forehead touches the sand. He is bobbing at the water's edge like a dead fish and cannot possibly be alive with his face constantly underwater or buried in the sand. The man must be dead, but the author doesn't directly state that.

Two paragraphs later in the story the author writes:

> The welcome of the land to the men from the sea was warm and generous; but a still and dripping shape was carried slowly up the beach, and the land's welcome for it could only be the different and sinister hospitality of the grave.
>
> —"The Open Boat" by Stephen Crane

The "still and dripping shape" and the "sinister hospitality of the grave" support your interpretation of the clues, even though the author still has not directly stated, "The oiler is dead." Implying the idea is perhaps more forceful than making a direct statement.

PERSONAL FEEDBACK 1

Name_____

1. Who supplied your references for college admission or for your last job?

   _____

2. What professor would you ask to write you a letter of reference for an award or scholarship? Why would you choose that particular professor?

   _____

3. Describe how textbooks differ from literature books.

   _____

4. Katharine Hepburn told Barbara Walters that she would describe herself as an oak tree. As what plant would you choose to describe yourself?

   _____

5. Describe the personal dynamics of your reading class. _____

_____

6. What have you added to the class? _____

_____

7. What have you done to investigate courses for next term? What do you plan to take and why? _____

_____

Connecting with Prior Knowledge

Authors, like cartoonists, use inferences that require linking old knowledge to what is being read at the time. Clues that imply meaning may draw on an assumed knowledge of history, current issues, or social concerns. Just as in making the connection to understand the punch line of a joke, the reader must make a connection in order to understand the inference.

EXAMPLE

THE TREE

It was 390 feet tall. Nothing on earth could match it. It had stood as a slender sapling in the cool coastal air, perhaps moving slightly in a light breeze, on the very day Caesar finally decided to move against Britain. But all that happened a long way from the area that would be called California. Great leaders were born as the tree grew. And they died as the tree became stronger and taller. Wars came and went, as well as plagues and famine. There were great celebrations and deep mourning here and there over the earth. The tree lived through it all.

—*Biology: The World of Life* by Robert Wallace

1. Although not directly stated, what kind of tree is this?

2. How old is the tree?

3. Is the tree still there?

EXPLANATION   From the age, height, and location, the reader could infer that the tree is a giant redwood. The tree dates back to Caesar—about 2000 years ago. The word *was* in the first sentence implies that the tree is no longer there. The following exercises illustrate how authors expect readers to connect with prior knowledge.

Answer the questions that follow each passage.

PASSAGE 1

THE SAVAGE STRUGGLE

The crowd cheered in anticipation of the fight for life. Soon the two gladiators entered the arena, each carrying a short sword.

Where and approximately when is this? <u>Ancient Rome in the Colosseum during the time of Christ, approximately 100 B.C. to 250 A.D.</u>

Copyright ©1999 by Addison-Wesley Educational Publishers Inc.

PASSAGE 2

MANDATORY TESTING

Mandatory testing can further wreak havoc in the lives of those who test positive. Individuals who have tested positive from voluntary testing have been known to say: "Hardly an hour goes by when I don't think about it," "I feel like a leper," or "I am frightened of being rejected." Some have even killed themselves or tried to do so. Many carry their burden secretly for fear of losing friends, lovers, jobs, homes, and health insurance.

—*Sociology* by Alex Thio

Although not directly stated, this article refers to mandatory testing for what?
AIDS

PASSAGE 3

TELLING THE STORY

The account of that morning some weeks later belongs to history. Three planes take off during the night of 6 August from Tinian in the Mariana Islands. Paul Tibbets is the group's commander. Eatherly opens the formation. There are no bombs in his plane; as for the others, no one suspects what a terrible device is hidden inside the *Enola Gay*. A bigger contrivance, they think, nothing more. Eatherly's job is to pinpoint the target with maximum accuracy. He must establish whether weather conditions allow for the center to be Hiroshima, Kokura or Nagasaki, or whether they should continue towards secondary targets. He tells the story of that morning's events in a voice devoid of emotion which suggests that the recitation is the thousandth one.

—"The Man from Hiroshima" by Maurizio Chierici, in *One World, Many Cultures* by Stuart Hirschberg

1. Although not directly stated, what is the "bigger contrivance?"
   The atomic bomb

2. Who are Tibbets and Eatherly? The pilots who dropped the atomic bomb.

Recognizing Slanted Language

Writers choose words to manipulate the reader and thus to control the reader's attitude toward a subject. Such words are referred to as having a particular **connotation** or **slant.** The dictionary definition of a word is its *denotation,* but the feeling or emotion surrounding a word is its *connotation.* For example, a real estate agent showing a run down house to a prospective buyer would refer to the house as "neglected" rather than "deteriorated." Both words mean run down. *Neglected* sounds as if a few things have been forgotten, whereas *deteriorated* sounds as if the place is rotting away and falling apart.

Some words in our society seem to have an automatic positive or negative slant. Words such as *socialist, cult member,* and *welfare state* have a negative emotional effect, while words such as *the American worker, democracy,* and *everyday people* have a positive effect. The overall result of using slanted language is to shift the reader's attitude toward the point of view, positive or negative, advocated by the author.

EXERCISE 3

Label the following phrases as either *P* (slanted positively) or *N* (slanted negatively).

___P___ 1. a well-dressed man

___N___ 2. a ruthless despot

___P___ 3. freedom of the press

___P___ 4. a larger-than-life leader

___N___ 5. corporate raiders

___P___ 6. give sympathy and understanding in return

___N___ 7. ignorant of common courtesy

___P___ 8. efficient office management

___N___ 9. corporate greed

___N___10. further extension of authoritarian rule

___P___11. keen insight and infectious wit

___P___12. a pillar of the community

___N___13. massacres of the Holocaust

___N___14. stooped to serving a cruel master

___N___15. the temperament of a bulldog

___P___16. reminded her of home and hearth

___N___17. an unpredictable candidate with a short memory

___P___18. the home folks of rural America

___P___19. the warm flow of family comfort

___N___20. spoken with malice toward all

EXERCISE 4

Indicate whether the boldface words in the following passages are positive (*P*) or negative (*N*), and explain your answer.

___P___ 1. "Surprisingly well read—especially in history and biography—Truman possessed **sound** judgment, the ability to reach decisions quickly, and a fierce and uncompromising sense of right and wrong."
means wise

—*America: Past and Present* by Robert Divine et al.

___P___ 2. "Even as you sit quietly reading this book, your body is changing at a **dazzling** rate. Certain cells are being created, others are dying, and yet others are being altered." noting wonderment

—*Biosphere* by Robert Wallace et al.

___N___ 3. "An innately shy man, Nixon hoped to enjoy the power of the presidency in **splendid** solitude." noting his kinglike nature

—*America: Past and Present* by Robert Divine et al.

___P___ 4. "It is not every company chairman who bakes cookies for management trainees or rewards top salespeople with furs, jewels, vacations, and pink Cadillacs. But Mary Kay Ash, 64, founder of Mary Kay Cosmetics Inc., does all these things—and such tangible inspiration has paid off **phenomenally**." noting an amazing amount of money

—*Marketing* by Patrick Murphy and Ben Enis

Copyright ©1999 by Addison-Wesley Educational Publishers Inc.

___N___ 5. "The Democrats rallied behind Carter, although the convention delegates displayed a **notable** lack of enthusiasm in renominating him."

so lacking in enthusiasm that it was noticed

—*America: Past and Present* by Robert Divine et al.

Drawing Conclusions

Readers use both stated and unstated ideas to logically draw conclusions. They use the facts, the hints, and prior knowledge to piece together meaning. The facts and clues lead to assumptions, which then lead to conclusions. Read the following passage and explain how the conclusion is suggested.

EXAMPLE

MY HOUSE

My master still went to school every day and, coming home, he'd still bottle himself up in his study. When he had visitors he'd continue to complain about his job.

I still had nothing to eat so I did not become very fat but I was healthy enough. I didn't become sick like Kuro and, always, I took things as they came. I still didn't try to catch rats, and I still hated Osan, the maid. I still didn't have a name but you can't always have what you want. I resigned myself to continue living here at the home of this school-teacher.

—From a story by Natsume Soseki, in *One World, Many Cultures* by Stuart Hirschberg

Conclusion: The narrator of the story is a cat.

What clues suggest this conclusion? _____

EXPLANATION The term "my master" may lead to an initial suspicion of a pet, but the "try to catch rats," clearly suggests a cat. The option of continuing to live in the home supports the idea of a cat. The story, as you might guess, is titled "I Am a Cat."

In the following exercises, identify the clues that lead to the stated conclusions.

PASSAGE 1

CULTS: THE PEOPLE'S TEMPLE

A **cult** is usually united by total rejection of society and extreme devotion to the cult's leader. The People's Temple is a dramatic example. In the 1970s their leader, Jim Jones, preached racial harmony, helped the poor, established drug-rehabilitation programs, staged protest demonstrations against social injustices, and helped elect sympathetic politicians. He moved his cult from San Francisco to Jonestown, Guyana, because, he said, evil people in the United States would try to destroy the Temple. He told his flock that to build a just society required a living God—namely, himself. To prove his dismay, he "healed parishioners by appearing to draw forth cancers" (which actually were bloody chicken gizzards). He claimed that he had extraordinary sexual gifts, required Temple members to turn over all their possessions to him, and insisted that they call him "Dad" or "Father." Then the People's Temple shocked the world. In November 1978 more than 900 members committed mass suicide at the order of their leader.

—*Sociology* by Alex Thio

Conclusion: Jim Jones brainwashed cult members into total submission.

What clues suggest this conclusion? He said evil people would try to destroy the temple, named himself god, healed cancers, took the wealth of the followers, and made them kill themselves.

PASSAGE 2

THE CULTURE OF SOCIAL TIME

My class was scheduled from 10 until noon. Many students came late, some very late. Several arrived after 10:30. A few showed up closer to 11. Two came after that. All of the latecomers wore the relaxed smiles that I came, later, to enjoy. Each one said hello, and although a few apologized briefly, none seemed terribly concerned about lateness. They assumed that I understood.

Back home in California, I never need to look at a clock to know when the class hour is ending. The shuffling of books is accompanied by strained expressions that say plaintively, "I'm starving. . . . I've got to go to the bathroom. . . . I'm going to suffocate if you keep us one more second." (The pain usually becomes unbearable at two minutes to the hour in undergraduate classes and five minutes before the close of graduate classes.)

When noon arrived in my first Brazilian class, only a few students left immediately. Others slowly drifted out during the next 15 minutes, and some continued asking me questions long after that. When several remaining students kicked off their shoes at 12:30, I went into my own "starving/bathroom/suffocation" routine.

—"Social Time: The Heartbeat of Culture" by Robert Levin with Ellen Wolff, in *One World, Many Cultures* by Stuart Hirschberg

Conclusion: The Brazilians do not consider themselves late but rather differ from Americans in their cultural concept of time.

What clues suggest this conclusion? Latecomers were relaxed and happy.

PASSAGE 3

WOMEN OF THE WAR

On November 20, 1837, Sarah Benjamin, then eighty-one years old, applied for a pension as the widow of a Revolutionary War soldier. She declared that she had married Aaron Osborn, a blacksmith, in Albany in 1780. After he enlisted, he insisted that she accompany him to the army. The narrative she dictated in 1837 is the only known autobiographical account left by one of the thousands of women who traveled with the revolutionary army as "camp followers."

For the first eighteen months of their service, Sarah and Aaron Osborn were stationed at West Point, on the Hudson River, where she did washing and sewing for the soldiers. Three other women were also attached to the company—an unmarried black woman and the wives of a sergeant and a lieutenant. This orderly existence changed abruptly in the fall of 1781, when their unit joined others marching hurriedly to Yorktown under the command of General George Washington.

There, she reported, she "busied herself washing, mending, and cooking for the soldiers, in which she was assisted by the other females." At intervals she carried beef, bread, and coffee to the front lines. Once she met Washington himself, who asked whether she was afraid of the cannonballs. Osborn staunchly replied, "It would not do for the men to fight and starve too."

—*A People and a Nation* by Mary Beth Norton et al.

Conclusion: The contributions of women in the American Revolution far exceed the documentation.

What clues suggest this conclusion? Women did washing, cooking, and sewing but only one narrative records this.

Copyright ©1999 by Addison-Wesley Educational Publishers Inc.

PASSAGE 4

NICHOLAS II (1894–1917)

Last of the Romanov tsars, Nicholas II was in almost every respect an unfortunate man. Besides having been influenced by a reactionary father and a strong-willed mother, he was dull, weak, stubborn, insensitive, and totally devoid of the qualities required for successfully administering a great empire. The day following his coronation, in conformity with tradition, he scheduled a banquet celebration for the people of the capital. A huge throng, possibly half a million souls, turned out for the great event. At one point the crowd surged forward and more than a thousand people were trampled to death. But Nicholas and the tsarina attended a ball at the French embassy that night and apparently spent a most enjoyable evening.

—A History of the Western World by Solomon Modell

Conclusion: Nicholas and the tsarina had a total lack of concern for the welfare of the people.

What clues suggest this conclusion? They attended a ball and enjoyed themselves even though more than a thousand people had been trampled to death that day at a celebration of his coronation.

PASSAGE 5

KANGAROO AND ZEBRA

A kangaroo hopping awkwardly along with some bulky object concealed in her pouch met a Zebra, and desirous of keeping his attention upon himself, said:

"Your costume looks as if you might have come out of the penitentiary."

"Appearances are deceitful," replied the Zebra, smiling in the consciousness of a more insupportable wit, "or I should have to think that you had come out of the Legislature."

—Fantastic Fables by Ambrose Bierce

What conclusion does the author imply about legislators?
Legislators have their pockets full of other people's money.

Underline the words that led to your conclusion.

EXERCISE 6

Use a combination of inference skills to read the following passages and answer the questions.

PASSAGE 1

TEXAS TOUGH

Lyndon Baines Johnson was a complex man—shrewd, arrogant, intelligent, sensitive, vulgar, vain, and occasionally cruel. He loved power, and he knew where it was, how to get it, and how to use it. "I'm a powerful sonofabitch," he told two Texas congressmen in 1958 when he was the most powerful legislator on Capitol Hill. Everything about Johnson seemed to emphasize or enhance his power. He was physically large, and seemed even bigger than he was, and he used his size to persuade people. The "Johnson Method" involved "pressing the flesh"—a back-slapping, hugging sort of camaraderie. He also used symbols of power adroitly, especially the telephone which had replaced the sword and pen as the symbol of power. "No gunman," remarked one historian, "ever held a Colt .44 so easily" as Johnson handled a telephone.

A legislative genius, Johnson had little experience in foreign affairs. Reared in the poverty of the Texas hill country, educated at a small teachers' college, and concerned politically with domestic issues, before becoming president LBJ had expressed little interest in foreign affairs. "Foreigners are not like the folks I am used to," he often said, and whether it was a joke or not he meant it. He was particularly uncomfortable around foreign dignitaries and ambassadors, often receiving them in groups and scarcely paying attention to them. "Why do I have to see them?" he once asked. "They're [Secretary of State] Dean Rusk's clients, not mine."

—America and Its People by James Martin et al.

Answer with *T* (true) or *F* (false).

___T___ 1. LBJ had an enormous ego.

___T___ 2. LBJ used the telephone to influence votes.

___F___ 3. LBJ quickly learned to perform in international situations.

___T___ 4. LBJ's background is reflected in both his genius and his flaws.

___F___ 5. LBJ was the right person to be president during the Vietnam War.

___T___ 6. The phrase, *replaced the sword*, suggests a negative connotation.

PASSAGE 2

THE REIGN OF LOUIS XVI (1774–1793)

A plain, fat, rather stupid young man, who loved to hunt and tinker with locks, Louis XVI succeeded his grandfather (whose one legitimate son, Louis XVI's father, died in 1765) at the age of twenty. His modesty and inherent kindness did not serve him well. He was far too simple, possessed an almost total lack of self-confidence, and could be made to change his mind with relative ease. His wife, Marie Antoinette, an Austrian princess, was pretty, not well educated, shallow, and selfish. Totally unconcerned with the people's welfare, she devoted herself to jewels and costly clothes, gambling and flirtation, masques and balls. Not completely satisfied with court life, she insisted on interfering in governmental affairs and sabotaged, to the extent that she could, whatever chance existed for the reformation of French life. Her liberal emperor-brother, Joseph II of Austria, reprimanded her, but his words went unheeded.

—A History of the Western World by Solomon Modell

Answer with *T* (true) or *F* (false).

___F___ 1. Louis XVI and his wife were probably loved and respected by his people.

___F___ 2. Despite his wife's influence, Louis XVI had many of the qualities of great leadership.

___F___ 3. Louis XVI was firm in his decisions.

___T___ 4. Marie Antoinette's extravagance was probably resented by the people.

___T___ 5. Joseph II understood the possible repercussions of Marie Antoinette's actions.

___T___ 6. The reformation of French life would probably have been a benefit to the people.

___F___ 7. The phrase *tinker with locks* suggests hard work.

Copyright ©1999 by Addison-Wesley Educational Publishers Inc.

PASSAGE 3

"LIZZIE BORDEN TOOK AN AX"

Andrew [Borden] was rich, but he didn't live like a wealthy man. Instead of living alongside the other prosperous Fall River citizens in the elite neighborhood known as The Hill, Andrew resided in an area near the business district called the flats. He liked to save time as well as money, and from the flats he could conveniently walk to work. For his daughters Lizzie and Emma, whose eyes and dreams focused on The Hill, life in the flats was an intolerable embarrassment. Their house was a grim, boxlike structure that lacked comfort and privacy. Since Andrew believed that running water on each floor was a wasteful luxury, the only washing facilities were a cold-water faucet in the kitchen and a laundry room water tap in the cellar. Also in the cellar was the toilet in the house. To make matters worse, the house was not connected to the Fall River gas main. Andrew preferred to use kerosene to light his house. Although it did not provide as good light or burn as cleanly as gas, it was less expensive. To save even more money, he and his family frequently sat in the dark.

The Borden home was far from happy. Lizzie and Emma, ages thirty-two and forty-two in 1892, strongly disliked their stepmother Abby and resented Andrew's penny-pinching ways. Lizzie especially felt alienated from the world around her. Although Fall River was the largest cotton-manufacturing town in America, it offered few opportunities for the unmarried daughter of a prosperous man. Society expected a woman of Lizzie's social position to marry, and while she waited for a proper suitor, her only respectable social outlets were church and community service. So Lizzie taught a Sunday School class and was active in the Woman's Christian Temperance Union, the Ladies' Fruit and Flower Mission, and other organizations. She kept herself busy, but she wasn't happy.

In August, 1892, strange things started to happen in the Borden home. They began after Lizzie and Emma learned that Andrew had secretly changed his will. Abby became violently ill. Abby told a neighborhood doctor that she had been poisoned, but Andrew refused to listen to her wild ideas. Shortly thereafter, Lizzie went shopping for prussic acid, a deadly poison she said she needed to clean her sealskin cape. When a Fall River druggist refused her request, she left the store in an agitated state. Later in the day, she told a friend that she feared an unknown enemy of her father's was after him. "I'm afraid somebody will do something," she said.

On August 4, 1892, the maid Bridget awoke early and ill, but she still managed to prepare a large breakfast of johnnycakes, fresh-baked bread, ginger and oatmeal cookies with raisins, and some three-day-old mutton and hot mutton soup. After eating a hearty meal, Andrew left for work. Bridget also left to do some work outside. This left Abby and Lizzie in the house alone. Then somebody did something very specific and very grisly. As Abby was bent over making the bed in the guest room, someone moved into the room unobserved and killed her with an ax.

Andrew came home for lunch earlier than usual. He asked Lizzie where Abby was, and she said she didn't know. Unconcerned, Andrew, who was not feeling well, lay down on the parlor sofa for a nap. He never awoke. Like Abby, he was slaughtered by someone with an ax. Lizzie "discovered" his body, still lying on the sofa. She called Bridget, who had taken the back stairs to her attic room: "Come down quick; father's dead; somebody came in and killed him."

Experts have examined and reexamined the crime, and most have reached the same conclusion: Lizzie killed her father and stepmother. In fact, Lizzie was tried for the gruesome murders. However, despite a preponderance of evidence, an all male jury found her not guilty. Their verdict was unanimous and was arrived at without debate or disagreement. A woman of Lizzie's social position, they affirmed, simply could not have committed such a terrible crime.

Even before the trial started, newspaper and magazine writers had judged Lizzie innocent for much the same reasons. As one expert on the case noted, "Americans were certain that well-brought-up daughters could not commit murder with a hatchet on sunny summer mornings."

Jurors and editorialists alike judged Lizzie according to their preconceived notions of Victorian womanhood. They believed that such a woman was gentle, docile, and physically frail, short on analytical ability but long on nurturing instincts.

Too uncoordinated and weak to accurately swing an ax and too gentle and unintelligent to coldly plan a double murder, women of Lizzie's background simply had to be innocent because of their basic innocence.

—*America and Its People* by James Martin et al.

Answer with *T* (true) or *F* (false).

___T___ 1. Andrew Borden's family suffered from his efforts to save money.

___T___ 2. Abby was probably correct in telling the doctor that her illness was due to poison.

___F___ 3. Andrew was killed when he discovered his wife dead.

___T___ 4. The jury did not carefully consider the evidence against Lizzie.

___T___ 5. The Victorian stereotyping of women worked in Lizzie's favor.

___F___ 6. The author believes that Lizzie was not guilty.

___T___ 7. The quotation marks around the word *discovered* change the connotation of the word.

PERSONAL FEEDBACK 2

Name_____

1. What characteristics do you have that are important for leadership?
_____

2. During this term, what have your leadership roles been?
_____
_____

3. As the term has progressed, how has your thinking about college changed? _____
_____

4. How are your friends and loved ones affecting your academic success?
_____
_____

5. What is most irritating about your roommates or people with whom you live? _____
_____

6. What will you remember the most from this class?
_____
_____

Copyright ©1999 by Addison-Wesley Educational Publishers Inc.

POINTS TO PONDER

▲ Implied meaning is not directly stated but can be deduced from clues.
▲ Jokes and cartoons are funny because of implied meaning.
▲ Inferences require linking old knowledge to what is being read at the time.
▲ Slanted language manipulates the reader's attitude toward a subject.
▲ Conclusions allow you to generalize meaning based on clues and incorporate what you already know with what you have just discovered.

 **SELECTION 1** *Narrative Essay*

THINKING BEFORE READING

Preview the selection for content and organizational clues. Activate your schema and anticipate the story.

Who do you know who has been in combat?

Where is combat occurring in the world today?

VOCABULARY PREVIEW

Are you familiar with these words?

solitude	scrawled	ecstatic	tinged	demeaned
solace	invincible	degraded	momentum	duped

What does the prefix *de* in *demeaned* and *degraded* mean?

What happens when a political campaign gains momentum?

Your instructor may give a true-false vocabulary review before or after reading.

THINKING DURING READING

As you read, predict, picture, relate, monitor, and correct.

MY BROTHER

For a long time I'd planned to go out to the highway overpass and spraypaint a greeting to my brother: "Hi, Roger!" Now he'd be arriving the very next morning; back after three long years at war. He'd sent letters now and then, but I hadn't seen him since I was four-teen. It was dawn. The sky was clear, the sun bright. The air was cool and clean.

Copyright ©1999 by Addison-Wesley Educational Publishers Inc.

5   I leaned over the rail and was struck by the neat four-laned highway below. It was deserted except for a tiny car far in the distance. The dead grasses on either side were colored golden brown by the new sun. This beautiful solitude was itching to blossom into an exciting spring. And I would get to be with my brother again.

       I carefully scrawled my message, upside down, across the bridge. Suddenly I lost my
10   grip and slid forward. The hard concrete below flew up toward my face, taking my breath away. I grabbed the metal rail and barely stopped my body from hurtling over the edge. I finished the sign and hurried back to my car. The radio blasted as I raced down the expressway toward home. My brother would be back tomorrow.

       I was up before the sun again the next morning. Dad and Mom were awake soon
15   thereafter and we left for the airport by seven. Each mile of the trip seemed like a million until the airport was in view. Then I became ecstatic. The time had finally come to be with my brother again.

Driving up the long airport road I remembered playing baseball with him. He was young and strong. His hair flew wildly about his head as he rounded the bases and slid

20   into home plate. He was my hero. He was everything I wanted to be. It's hard to believe that then he was only as old as I am now. When he graduated from high school it was off to the army with plenty of his friends. By now he would have been finishing up college ready to begin an adult life. But that would have to wait until after the service, he had said.

25   I couldn't understand him going to war. He had said he had to do it—it was the law, it was his duty, it was the way things were done. But the reality of war was something else altogether. His letters were so sad, tinged with dread and insanity. The darkest side of human nature slapped him across the face again and again. It demeaned him. He was the vehicle for a great evil but he could find no escape. His only solace was in believing that

30   his family was safe, far from the nightmarish world he had to inhabit. I watched the death and destruction on TV and wondered if I'd be as brave as my brother when it was my time to go. He was my hero.

We pulled up to the parking lot and my Dad paid the attendant fifty cents. We searched through the rows and rows of cars until we found an empty slot. The anticipa-

35   tion had now gripped me completely. I wanted to run and meet him, throw my arms around him, hug him so tightly and never let him go.

There was something very important torn from my life—and my Mom's and Dad's, too—when he left. And what's to be said about his own life? He was so young when he had to make the decision: whether to go or not. He was idealistic and trusting. He was

40   strong and invincible. As we walked into the terminal his flight was landing. We found the proper gate and waited. I knew I would not go to war. And was sure he wouldn't go if he had it all to do over again. I knew by his letters. He never said it—he was too brave—but I knew it anyway. He was degraded, taught to inflict pain, hate and kill. He was forced to undertake a torturous journey and face bloody battlefields, burning towns and

45   frightened children. He learned to act on command and suppress his instinctual conscience and humanity. He learned that the value of human life was nil, that politics was a black magic and that evil gathered momentum until it swallowed up everything in its path. He knew that he could have slowed that momentum had he been smarter, less headstrong, and more brave at age seventeen.

50   But to me he was still a hero. He had been required to make decisions that men twice his age and wisdom could make only with the greatest care. I think he was duped. I think he was chosen because he was young and wanted to be a man; young and unattached; young and inexperienced in life; young and available for war. I think he was stolen, used and discarded. I would like to tell him this, but I know he already knows.

55   My Mom and Dad are crying now as Roger is the last one off the plane. The day is bright and clear, the beginning of spring and the beginning of a new understanding. The shiny black casket is rolled slowly down the long runway. Soon my brother's body will pass under the concrete bridge with the spraypainted plea, "Stop War." Perhaps soon, we will.

(898 words)

—By Rick Theis

THINKING AFTER READING

RECALL: Self-test your understanding. Your instructor may choose to give a true-false review.

REACT: At what point did you suspect the outcome? _____

REFLECT: What makes the story so powerful? _____

THINK CRITICALLY: How does the author's message apply not just to Vietnam but to all wars? Write your answer on a separate sheet of paper.

INFERENCE

1. How does the story make you feel? What does the author do to make you feel this way? _____

2. How would you feel about going to a war zone to fight? _____
   _____

3. How does the author's sign "Stop War" reflect the message of the story?
   The sign is a bitter irony with a message that is too late for his brother, but he wants others to feel the grief and understand the waste.

4. How does the suspense add to your interest in the story? As the arrival progresses, the anticipation rises and you wonder how the brother will appear.

5. What makes the story so powerful for you? _____
   _____

Answer the following with *T* (true) or *F* (false).

___T___ 6. The reader is led to believe in the first paragraph that the message on the bridge is a greeting to the brother.

___T___ 7. The author implies that it takes more courage to protest than to be drafted.

___T___ 8. The author manipulates the language in the story to surprise the reader at the end.

___T___ 9. The author never directly states that the brother is dead.

___T___ 10. The author implies that his brother took orders that were against his instincts.

Copyright © 1999 by Addison-Wesley Educational Publishers Inc.

Name _____

Date _____

COMPREHENSION QUESTIONS

Answer the following with *a, b, c,* or *d,* or fill in the blank. In order to help you analyze your strengths and weaknesses, the question types are indicated.

Main Idea   __b__   1. The best statement of the main idea of this selection is:

        a. Love your brother.
        b. Stop war.
        c. Obey the law.
        d. Die for your country.

Detail   __d__   2. Roger fought in

        a. World War I.
        b. World War II.
        c. the Korean War.
        d. the Vietnam War.

Inference   __b__   3. The upcoming season of the year is

        a. winter.
        b. spring.
        c. summer.
        d. fall.

Purpose   4. The primary purpose of this selection is to <u>arouse antiwar</u> <u>sentiments.</u>

Inference   __b__   5. The author implies that he would have

        a. volunteered for the military himself.
        b. protested having to serve in the military.
        c. encouraged his brother to serve with honor.
        d. served alongside his brother if given the chance.

Inference   __a__   6. The author implies that during the course of the war his brother became

        a. disgusted and disillusioned.
        b. increasingly committed to the military.
        c. proud of his country's efforts.
        d. more idealistic and trusting.

Conclusion   __b__   7. This selection would most likely appear in a publication printed by

        a. the government.
        b. antiwar protesters.
        c. parent-teacher organizations.
        d. the Pentagon.

Answer the following with *T* (true), *F* (false), or *CT* (can't tell).

Inference   __F__   8. Roger was killed during his first year in the war.

Inference   __CT__   9. The parents had encouraged Roger to protest the draft.

Inference   __T__   10. Roger was about three years older than his brother.

VOCABULARY

Answer the following with *a, b, c,* or *d* for the word or phrase that best defines the boldface word as used in the selection. The number in parentheses indicates the line of the passage in which the word is located.

__c__ 1. "This beautiful **solitude**" (7)

    a. wilderness
    b. environment
    c. seclusion
    d. earth

__d__ 2. "**scrawled** my message" (9)

    a. dropped
    b. opened
    c. waved
    d. wrote

__c__ 3. "became **ecstatic**" (16)

    a. alarmed
    b. fearful
    c. overjoyed
    d. angry

__a__ 4. "**tinged** with dread" (27)

    a. colored
    b. written
    c. overcome
    d. crying

__c__ 5. "**demeaned** him" (28)

    a. crippled
    b. frightened
    c. belittled
    d. wounded

__b__ 6. "His only **solace**" (29)

    a. dependence
    b. comfort
    c. conviction
    d. need

__b__ 7. "was strong and **invincible**" (39–40)

    a. moral
    b. unconquerable
    c. loving
    d. frank

__b__ 8. "He was **degraded**" (43)

    a. scandalized
    b. dragged down
    c. stopped
    d. discharged

__c__ 9. "evil gathered **momentum**" (47)

    a. time
    b. members
    c. force
    d. glory

__d__ 10. "he was **duped**" (51)

    a. disappointed
    b. aware
    c. sick
    d. tricked

VOCABULARY ENRICHMENT

IDIOM

An idiom is a phrase used mainly in conversation that has meaning other than the literal meaning of the words themselves. For example, the phrase "My eyes were bigger than my stomach" is an idiom. The exact, literal meaning of the words is anatomically impossible. In our culture, however, the phrase is a creative way of saying, "I took more food on my plate than I can possibly eat." Other languages probably do not have this same expression. Students who learn English as a second language find our idioms confusing when they look for an exact translation.

Idioms are slang phrases, clichés, and regional expressions. Their popularity changes with the times. Grandparents may use idioms that would make a college student shudder. Professional writers try to avoid idioms because they are considered informal.

Write the meaning of the boldface idioms in the following sentences.

1. She is **making a mountain out of a molehill** in continuing to stress the importance of that one test. _making a big deal out of nothing_

Copyright ©1999 by Addison-Wesley Educational Publishers Inc.

2. I knew Lucy could not keep a secret, and now she has **spilled the beans.**
<u>told the secret</u>

3. Lewis successfully quit smoking this time, but he said he had to stop **cold turkey.** <u>without ever taking another puff</u>

4. The fraternity overspent last month, and the treasurer reported that the budget was a hundred dollars **in the red.** <u>in debt</u>

5. I will tell you about the surprise party, but you must **button your lip** when Harold comes into the room. <u>not mention anything about it</u>

6. They all went to the mountains this weekend and left me **holding the bag.**
<u>in charge</u>

7. The computer problem was a **piece of cake,** so we had time to play baseball.
<u>very easy</u>

8. If I can't get the money from Dad, I still have an **ace in the hole.**
<u>a sure option</u>

9. We are going to the beach over Labor Day to **catch some rays.**
<u>get a suntan</u>

10. Jerome is **in the doghouse** with his girlfriend because of last weekend.
<u>viewed with displeasure</u>

ASSESS YOUR LEARNING

Review confusing questions, seek clarification, and make notes in your text to help you remember the new information and vocabulary.

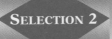
SELECTION 2 ◆ *Literature*

THINKING BEFORE READING

Preview the selection for content and organizational clues. Activate your schema and anticipate the story.

What is an alchemist?

Were alchemists viewed positively or negatively? Why?

VOCABULARY PREVIEW

Are you familiar with these words?

alchemist   baser metals   autopsy   insomnia   hot grog

Can chemists turn baser metals into gold?

What ingredients are in hot grog?

THINKING DURING READING

As you read, predict, picture, relate, monitor, and correct.

THE ALCHEMIST'S SECRET

Sitting quietly in his little herb shop on a crooked street in the shadow of Notre Dame, Doctor Maximus did not look like a very remarkable man. But he was. Five hundred years before, he might have busied himself changing the baser metals into gold. But in Paris of the nineties, it is said, he worked at a more subtle alchemy. He changed dreams into real-
5   ities—provided, of course, you could pay.

The man who came into the gaslit shop this early October evening in 1891 was pre-pared to pay. He stood just inside the door, blotting his forehead with a silk handkerchief although actually the weather was rather cool. He was holding a heart-shaped package tightly under one arm. "You are Monsieur le Doctor Maximus?"
10   The Doctor bowed respectfully.

"I have a problem," said the visitor nervously. "I am told you might help me with it."

"Indeed?" said the Doctor mildly. "Who told you that?"

The newcomer glanced around uneasily at the dim shelves, the leathery tortoise dan-gling from a string, the small stuffed crocodile with its dust-filmed eyes. "Last night we
15   had a dinner guest. A foreign diplomat. First secretary of the—"

"Ah, yes, Pechkoff. It is true I did him a small service."

"He was not very specific, you understand. But after a few glasses of cognac he talked rather freely. I got the impression . . ."

"Yes?"
20   "That if it weren't for your—er—assistance he would still be married, most unhap-pily, to his first wife."

Doctor Maximus took off his glasses and polished the spotless lenses. "She died, I believe, poor woman. Quite suddenly."

"Yes," said the visitor, "she did. So suddenly that there was an autopsy. But they dis-
25   covered nothing wrong."

"Of course not," said Doctor Maximus, smiling gently.

Copyright ©1999 by Addison-Wesley Educational Publishers Inc.

"My wife," said the visitor with a certain agitation, "is a very beautiful woman. Naturally, she has many admirers. She has always ignored them until recently, but now there is one—I don't know which one—a younger man, no doubt. She admits it! She demands
30 that I make some settlement. I will not—"

Doctor Maximus raised his hand. "The details," he murmured, "do not concern me."

The visitor's face was tight and dangerous. "I am not a man to be made a fool of!"

"No," said the Doctor, "I can see that."

35 "Madame," said the visitor abruptly, "is very fond of candy." He unwrapped the heart-shaped package and placed it on the counter. It was a box of chocolates. "I thought perhaps you might—ah—improve the candies at your convenience and then post them to her. She would be very pleased. I have even prepared a card to enclose." He took out a small rectangle of cardboard. On it was printed in neat capitals: FROM AN
40 ADMIRER.

Doctor Maximus took the card and sighed. "My fees are not inconsiderable."

"I did not expect them to be," the visitor said stiffly. He did not flinch when the price was named. He paid it, in gold coins. He blotted his forehead once more with the silk handkerchief. "Will you be able to send the candy tonight?"

45 "Perhaps," said the Doctor noncommittally. "We shall see. And where should it be sent?"

"Ah, yes," said the visitor. "Of course." And he gave Madame's name and address.

Doctor Maximus wrote the information on a slip of paper. Then he scribbled three digits on another slip and handed it over. "You sir, are customer 322. If there are any dif-
50 ficulties, kindly refer to that number. Not," he added, "that there will be any."

With one hand on the doorknob, the visitor hesitated. "It won't be—" he wet his lips—"it won't be painful, will it?"

"Not at all," said Dr. Maximus. He peered over his spectacles in a benign and sympathetic fashion. "You seem rather upset. Do you want me to give you something to
55 make you sleep?"

"No, thank you," said his visitor nervously. "I have my own prescription for insomnia: a hot grog before going to bed."

"Ah, yes," said Dr. Maximus. "An excellent habit."

"Good night," said the visitor, opening the door into the narrow, ill-lit street.

60 "Good-bye," murmured Dr. Maximus.

Taking the box of chocolates in one hand and the slip of paper in the other, he went into the little room at the rear of the shop. From the shelf above his test tubes and retorts he took a big black book, opened it, and looked at the record of the previous transaction. There it was, entered only that afternoon in his spidery handwriting: *Customer 321. Com-*
65 *plaint: the usual. Remedy: six drops of the elixir, to be administered in husband's hot grog at bedtime . . .*

Dr. Maximus sighed. Then, being a man who honored his commitments, he opened the box of chocolates and went to work. There was no great rush. He would post the parcel in the morning.

70 In the herb shop, as in life, you got just about what you paid for. But his motto was, First come, first served.

(867 words)

—"The Alchemist's Secret" by Arthur Gordon

THINKING AFTER READING

INFERENCE QUESTIONS

1. Where did the couple learn of Dr. Maximus? They both learned from Pechkoff, a foreign diplomat who was their dinner guest.

2. How was Dr. Maximus connected to Pechkoff's wife? It is implied that Dr. Maximus supplied the means of killing her.

3. Why was the husband who drank grog unhappy with his wife? <u>She was</u> <u>seeing a younger man and wanted a settlement.</u>

4. How did Dr. Maximus realize that the husband was his next victim? <u>He did</u> <u>not need anything to help him sleep because he drank hot grog at night for</u> <u>insomnia.</u>

5. What can be concluded about Customer 321? <u>It is the wife.</u>

6. Why is the motto, "First come, first served," ironic in this story? <u>It is usually</u> <u>ethical behavior, but here it applies to a very unethical person and situation.</u>

7. Why is the phrase "being a man who honored his commitments" sarcastic? <u>He was a dishonorable murderer, but he killed both as he had promised.</u>

8. What is the theme of this story? <u>Even persons of extreme dishonor develop</u> <u>and live by their own ethical codes.</u>

VOCABULARY ENRICHMENT

FIGURATIVE LANGUAGE

Writers and speakers use figurative language to spark the imagination and make the message more sensual and visual. The words create images in the mind and activate associations stored in memory. Figurative language is challenging because figuring out the meaning demands logical and creative thinking.

A. Simile
   A simile uses the words *like* or *as* to compare two unlike things. The purpose of a simile is to strengthen the message by adding a visual image. Similes usually dramatize the characteristics of nouns. As a reader, you must figure out the unique characteristic the simile is describing. In the sentence, "the new teacher stood like a statue in front of the class," what does the simile add to the meaning? "Like a statue" describes the teacher as "stiff and unmoving." The simile adds humor and visual interest to the sentence.
   Write the meaning of the boldface similes in the following sentences.

   1. Matthew ran **like the wind.** <u>very swiftly</u>

   2. The children rose **like bubbles of carbonated water.** <u>popping up to the</u> <u>top</u>

   3. The late teenager crept to her room **like an autumn leaf that falls without a sound.** <u>silently</u>

   4. The overcooked bread was as hard **as the table.** <u>very hard, as wood</u>

   5. Earleen wept through the movie **like an injured child.** <u>as if wounded</u>

B. Metaphor
   Whereas a simile uses the words *like* or *as* to compare two unlike things, a metaphor does not use those words but instead states the comparison directly. For example, "The soccer player was a tiger," is a metaphor that dramatizes the player's aggressive spirit. If the statement had been, "The girl plays soccer like a tiger," the figure of speech would be a simile, but the meaning would remain the same.
   Write the meaning of the boldface metaphors in the following sentences.

Copyright ©1999 by Addison-Wesley Educational Publishers Inc.

6. Grandpa had a head of **snow** and a warm smile. <u>white hair</u>

7. My roommate was a **pig** when it came to housecleaning. <u>untidy person</u>

8. Sam was the **dove** at the meeting. <u>peacemaker</u>

9. Her troubles were a **stone** around her neck. <u>a weight that held her down</u>

10. The storm was the **thief** of the enchanting summer night. <u>ruined or took away the lovely night</u>

SELECTION 3 *Essay*

THINKING BEFORE READING

Preview for content and organizational clues. Activate your schema, and anticipate the author's opinion.

What is your definition of the word *macho*?

After reading this, I will probably want to _____.

VOCABULARY PREVIEW

Are you familiar with these words?

cringe	promiscuous	exude	sullenness	ennobles
ambiguities	recalcitrant	upbraided	menial	refute

Is a recalcitrant child a pleasure to a parent?

If you agree with an argument, do you refute its message?

Do you cringe at the sight of blood?

Your instructor may give a true-false vocabulary review before or after reading.

THINKING DURING READING

As you read, predict, picture, relate, monitor, and correct.

AMERICANIZATION IS TOUGH ON "MACHO"

What is *macho*? That depends which side of the border you come from.

Although it's not unusual for words and expressions to lose their subtlety in translation, the negative connotations of *macho* in this country are troublesome to Hispanics.

Take the newspaper descriptions of alleged mass murderer Ramon Salcido. That an
5 insensitive, insanely jealous, hard-drinking, violent Latin male is referred to as *macho* makes Hispanics cringe.

"*Es muy macho,*" the women in my family nod approvingly, describing a man they respect. But in the United States, when women say, "He's so macho," it's with disdain.

The Hispanic *macho* is manly, responsible, hardworking, a man in charge, a patri-
10   arch. A man who expresses strength through silence. What the Yiddish language would
call a *mensch*.

The American *macho* is a chauvinist, a brute, uncouth, selfish, loud, abrasive, capable
of inflicting pain, and sexually promiscuous.

Quintessential *macho* models in this country are Sylvester Stallone, Arnold
15   Schwarzenegger and Charles Bronson. In their movies, they exude toughness, independence, masculinity. But a closer look reveals their machismo is really violence masquerad-
ing as courage, sullenness disguised as silence and irresponsibility camouflaged as independence.

If the Hispanic ideal of *macho* were translated to American screen roles, they might
20   be Jimmy Stewart, Sean Connery and Laurence Olivier.

In Spanish, *macho* ennobles Latin males. In English it devalues them. This pattern
seems consistent with the conflicts ethnic minority males experience in this country. Typically the cultural traits other societies value don't translate as desirable characteristics in
America.

25   I watched my own father struggle with these cultural ambiguities. He worked on a
farm for twenty years. He laid down miles of irrigation pipe, carefully plowed long, neat
rows in fields, hacked away at recalcitrant weeds and drove tractors through whirlpools of
dust. He stoically worked twenty-hour days during harvest season, accepting the long
hours as part of agricultural work. When the boss complained or upbraided him for minor
30   mistakes, he kept quiet, even when it was obvious the boss had erred.

He handled the most menial tasks with pride. At home he was a good provider,
helped out my mother's family in Mexico without complaint, and was indulgent with me.
Arguments between my mother and him generally had to do with money, or with his
stubborn reluctance to share his troubles. He tried to work them out in his own silence.
35   He didn't want to trouble my mother—a course that backfired, because the imagined is
always worse than the reality.

Americans regarded my father as decidedly un-*macho*. His character was interpreted
as nonassertive, his loyalty non-ambition, and his quietness, ignorance. I once overheard
the boss's son blame him for plowing crooked rows in a field. My father merely smiled at
40   the lie, knowing the boy had done it, but didn't refute it, confident his good work was
well known. But the boss instead ridiculed him for being "stupid" and letting a kid get

Copyright ©1999 by Addison-Wesley Educational Publishers Inc.

away with a lie. Seeing my embarrassment, my father dismissed the incident, saying ''They're the dumb ones. Imagine, me fighting with a kid.''

I tried not to look at him with American eyes because sometimes the reflection hurt.

45   Listening to my aunts' clucks of approval, my vision focused on the qualities America overlooked. ''He's such a hard worker. So serious, so responsible.'' My aunts would secretly compliment my mother. The unspoken comparison was that he was not like some of their husbands, who drank and womanized. My uncles represented the darker side of *macho.*

50   In a patriarchal society, few challenge their roles. If men drink, it's because it's the manly thing to do. If they gamble, it's because it's how men relax. And if they fool around, well, it's because a man simply can't hold back so much man! My aunts didn't exactly meekly sit back, but they put up with these transgressions because Mexican society dictated this was their lot in life.

55   In the United States, I believe it was the feminist movement of the early '70s that changed macho's meaning. Perhaps my generation of Latin women was in part responsible. I recall Chicanas complaining about the chauvinistic nature of Latin men and the notion they wanted their women barefoot, pregnant and in the kitchen. The generalization that Latin men embodied chauvinistic traits led to this interesting twist of semantics.

60 Suddenly a word that represented something positive in one culture became a negative prototype in another.

      The problem with the use of *macho* today is that it's become an accepted stereotype of the Latin male. And like all stereotypes, it distorts truth.

      The impact of language in our society is undeniable. And the misuse of *macho* hints

65 at a deeper cultural misunderstanding that extends beyond mere word definitions.

(781 words)

—Rose Del Castillo Guilbault, in the *San Francisco Chronicle,* 1989 (from *Literature and Ourselves* by Gloria Henderson et al.)

THINKING AFTER READING

RECALL: Self-test your understanding. Your instructor may choose to give a true-false review.

REACT: What does the author believe are the origins of the word *macho*?

_____

REFLECT: What recent movies promote the negative image of a macho man? Which ones promote a positive macho image?
<u>Answers will vary.</u>

 THINK CRITICALLY: How are males stereotyped in different nationalities? List stereotypical male characteristics for Asians, Arabs, British, French, and Italians.

INFERENCE

1. What is the denotation of *macho*? <u>A manly, responsible, hardworking</u> <u>patriarch who expresses strength through silence.</u>

2. What is the connotation of *macho* in America? <u>Insensitive, insanely jealous,</u> <u>hard-drinking, violent Latin male</u>

3. What does the author mean by saying, "a course that backfired, because the imagined is always worse than the reality"? <u>His wife suspected things worse</u> <u>than the actual problem and thus worried more.</u>

4. How did the daughter feel when her father said, "They're the dumb ones. Imagine, me fighting with a kid." <u>She felt he was weak, and she was</u> <u>embarrassed.</u>

5. What does the author imply about the uncles? <u>They were drinking,</u> <u>womanizing, and disrespectful to their families.</u>

Copyright ©1999 by Addison-Wesley Educational Publishers Inc.

Name _____

Date _____

COMPREHENSION QUESTIONS

Answer the following with *T* (true) or *F* (false).

___F___ 1. The author is concerned because the word *macho* has a negative connotation in Latin countries.

___T___ 2. To the author, *macho* and *mensch* have approximately the same meaning.

___T___ 3. The author believes that Sean Connery would do an honorable job of portraying *macho* on the screen.

___F___ 4. The author was proud of her father because he did not correct the kid about who plowed the crooked rows.

___F___ 5. The author views Jimmy Stewart, Sean Connery and Laurence Olivier in a negative manner.

___T___ 6. The author feels that her father should have been more open in discussing problems with her mother.

___F___ 7. The aunts believed that the author's father was not ambitious.

___F___ 8. The author feels that Sylvester Stallone, Arnold Schwarzenegger, and Charles Bronson are admirable examples of the male ideal.

___F___ 9. The author suggests that her uncles were not hard workers.

___T___ 10. The author feels that the feminist movement changed the connotation of the word *macho*.

VOCABULARY

Answer the following with *a, b, c,* or *d* for the word or phrase that best defines the boldface word as used in the selection. The number in parentheses indicates the line of the passage in which the word is located.

___d___ 1. "makes Hispanics **cringe**" (6)

    a. whisper
    b. think
    c. laugh
    d. wince

___b___ 2. "sexually **promiscuous**" (13)

    a. diseased
    b. immoral
    c. weak
    d. normal

___c___ 3. "**exude** toughness" (15)

    a. absorb
    b. portray
    c. emit
    d. ignore

___a___ 4. "**sullenness** disguised" (17)

    a. somberness
    b. intelligence
    c. honor
    d. violence

___b___ 5. "**ennobles** Latin males" (21)

    a. humiliates
    b. elevates
    c. angers
    d. overlooks

___b___ 6. "cultural **ambiguities**" (25)

    a. clarity
    b. confusions
    c. fears
    d. opportunities

_a_ 7. "**recalcitrant** weeds" (27)

  a. stubborn
  b. hearty
  c. ugly
  d. flourishing

_b_ 8. "**Upbraided** him for minor mistakes" (29–30)

  a. groomed
  b. scolded
  c. laughed at
  d. forgave

_d_ 9. "most **menial** tasks" (31)

  a. meaningful
  b. important
  c. difficult
  d. lowly

_c_ 10. "didn't **refute** it" (40)

  a. exaggerate
  b. prove
  c. deny
  d. continue

VOCABULARY ENRICHMENT

LITERARY DEVICES

A. Personification

In personification, an inanimate object is given human characteristics. Personification can embellish an image and create a mood. In the sentence, "The wind sang through the trees," the word *sang* gives the wind a human characteristic that adds a soft, gentle mood to the message.

Write the meaning, mood, or feeling the boldface personification adds to the message in the following sentences.

1. Her skin **crawled** when the music played. _moved with feeling_

2. The glowing fireplace was the **heart** of the mountain lodge.
   center of life

3. The sun **kissed** the flowers in the meadow. _shone on_

4. The house **stretched** to make room for their new baby brother.
   seemed to expand

5. The stars **flirted** with the drifting sand. _twinkled over_

B. Irony

Irony is saying one thing but meaning another. It may be used to show humor or to be sarcastic and ridicule others. The trick in irony is to be able to recognize that the speaker does not really mean what he or she says. The context in which the statement is made gives clues to the speaker's true attitude. Gullible people have trouble picking up irony and are subsequently sometimes fooled and embarrassed. For example, after a basketball game, someone may say to a player who scored only once in seventeen tries, "You're a great shot." Here irony is used to ridicule the poor shooting.

Complete the story in each of the following sentences by choosing the response that best shows irony.

_b_ 6. Each time the professor called on Larry to answer a question, he gave the wrong response. After class Frances said to Larry,

  a. "We need to study hard."
  b. "Here's the guy with the brains."
  c. "I hope you weren't embarrassed."

Copyright ©1999 by Addison-Wesley Educational Publishers Inc.

_____a_____ 7. Sue missed only one item on a chemistry exam that almost every-one else failed. When congratulated, Sue retorted,

    a. "Maybe next time I'll study."
    b. "I'm glad I studied."
    c. "My major is chemistry."

_____b_____ 8. As newlyweds, Betsy and Fred moved to a tiny New York apart-ment. When their parents came to visit, a sign on the door said,

    a. "Welcome to our new place."
    b. "Welcome to the Caribbean Hilton."
    c. "Welcome to our friends and family."

_____c_____ 9. Because George's apartment was so dirty, his friends called him

    a. the Slob.
    b. George the Unclean.
    c. Mother's Helper.

_____a_____ 10. Chris was known to be cheap, so friends started calling him

    a. Mr. Rockefeller.
    b. Mr. Scrooge.
    c. Mr. Chips.

ASSESS YOUR LEARNING

Review confusing questions, seek clarification, and make notes in your textbook to help you remember the new information and vocabulary.

Copyright ©1999 by Addison-Wesley Educational Publishers Inc.

Critical Reading

◆ *What is an author's purpose or intent?*
◆ *What is point of view?*
◆ *What is bias?*
◆ *What is tone?*
◆ *How do you distinguish between fact and opinion?*
◆ *What are fallacies?*

—Library Bernard Boruch Zakleim, Courtesy San Francisco Art Commision

What Do Critical Readers Do? ◆◆◆◆◆◆◆◆◆◆◆

Critical readers evaluate what they read. They use direct statements, inferences, prior knowledge, and language clues to assess the value and validity of what they are reading. Critical readers do not accept the idea that "If it's in print, it must be true." They do not immediately accept the thinking of others. Rather, they think for themselves, analyze different aspects of written material in their search for truth, and then decide how accurate and relevant the printed words are.

Recognize the Author's Purpose or Intent

Authors write with a particular **purpose** or **intent** in mind. For example, you might be instructed to write a scientific paper on environmental pollution with the ultimate purpose of inspiring classmates to recycle. In writing the paper, you must both educate and persuade, but your overriding goal is persuasion. Therefore, you will choose and use only the facts that support your argument. Your critical reading audience will then carefully evaluate your scientific support, recognizing that your purpose was to persuade and not really to educate, and thus decide whether to recycle all or some combination of paper, glass, aluminum, and plastic. The author's reason for writing can alert the reader to be accepting or suspicious. The three common purposes for writing are:

◆ **To inform.** Authors use facts to inform, to explain, to educate, and to enlighten. The purpose of textbooks is usually to inform or explain, but sometimes an author might venture into persuasion, particularly on topics such as smoking or recycling.

◆ **To persuade.** Authors use a combination of facts and opinions to persuade, to argue, to condemn, and to ridicule. Editorials in newspapers are written to argue a point and persuade the reader.

◆ **To entertain.** Authors use fiction and nonfiction to entertain, to narrate, to describe, and to shock. Novels, short stories, and essays are written to entertain. Sometimes an author may adopt a guise of humor in order to entertain and achieve a special result.

EXAMPLE　For each of the following topic sentences, decide whether the main purpose is to inform (*I*), to persuade (*P*), or to entertain (*E*).

　　_P_　1. Telling secrets in the form of public confessions on television talk shows is detrimental to building healthy, satisfying relationships. Such talk shows reveal the worst in human behavior and should be taken off the air.

　　_I_　2. Self-disclosure in communication means revealing information about yourself, usually in exchange for information about the other person.

　　_E_　3. Daytime viewers don't seem too surprised to find that Sam has been married to two other women while he has been dating Lucinda who is carrying his third child and is having an affair with Sam's best friend.

EXPLANATION　The purpose of the first sentence is to persuade or condemn such programs for the harm they can cause the participants. The purpose of the second sentence is simply to inform or educate by giving a definition. The last sentence exaggerates in order to entertain.

EXERCISE 1 Identify the main purpose of the following as being to inform (*I*), to persuade (*P*), or to entertain (*E*).

___E___ 1. Lucy and Rachel were both eleven years old when they met in the textile mill for work. When they were not changing the bobbins on the spinning machines, they could laugh with each other and dream of trips back home.

___I___ 2. Samuel Slater opened a new textile mill in Rhode Island in 1790 and employed seven boys and two girls between the ages of seven and twelve. The children were whipped with a leather strap and sprayed with water to keep them awake and alert. Consolidating such a workforce under one roof, the children could produce three times as much as whole families working at home.

___P___ 3. The textile mills of the late eighteenth century in America were not unlike the sweat shops of Central America today. Children were employed for pennies under the supervision of an adult who was concerned about profit. Today, however, enlightened Americans are buying the product of the labor of foreign children. Perhaps Americans should think before buying.

___I___ 4. Gap, Incorporated has been successful in developing a three-tiered organization, but not in providing the variety that consumers need. Styles and the variety of products are limited by a singular corporate mindset.

___I___ 5. In response to a drop in profits, Gap, Incorporated opened Old Navy stores targeted at discount shoppers. This created a three-tiered organization. The company's Banana Republic is designed to appeal to high-end shoppers, The Gap to a middle market searching for quality casual clothing, and Old Navy for the bargain hunters.

___E___ 6. How can my daughter be surprised to see her outfit on two other girls at the party? The girls all shop at the same stores, The Gap and Banana Republic. They want socially acceptable labels with individual differences.

EXERCISE 2 Read the passage below and notice how the author uses humor for a serious purpose. Then answer the questions that follow with *T* (true) or *F* (false), or fill in the blank.

IMPROVE EDUCATION, MAKE GRADE SCHOOL LAST

There is a tremendous concern in this country about our educational system. At least 1,567 commissions are studying it; 18,732 professors are now writing books critical of it, and every politician running for office is demanding a change in it.

I myself have opted for the Makepiece Plan, put forward by Harvey Makepiece of the Society for the Abolishment of the Three-Chocolate-Milk Lunch.

Makepiece told me, "It's obvious that 5- and 6-year-olds are not ready for grade school. Their minds and bodies are too fragile to take on the different tasks that their teachers assign to them. They should have more leisure and fun before they get down to work.

"What do you suggest?" I asked him.

"We send them to college first and let them work off their high spirits."

"I'm not sure I follow."

Copyright ©1999 by Addison-Wesley Educational Publishers Inc.

"Let first graders have their first taste of school in college. Give them a chance to join sororities and fraternities, go to football games, frolic on the campus and have panty raids in the dorms. College is not the time for serious school work, and it is the perfect place for children from the ages of 5 to 9 to have a good time and get used to attending classes, where they can sleep, flirt or cheat on their studies.

"Very few demands are made on college students. They can cut classes, spend their days in the student union and their evenings listening to rock music."

"And then what?" I said.

"After four years of college a child is ready to tackle high school. High school, as you know, is just a little tougher than college, and a child would have to get down to work. Not too much work, but enough to get him or her interested in books. The student would still have an opportunity to attend football games, date once in a while if he or she wanted to, go to an occasional dance and drive around in a car after 3 o'clock.

"But high school would still give the youth a feeling that life is not a bowl of cherries and that he or she is going to have to take education seriously.

"Also, the student would have to work hard because he or she knows that there are only a certain number of places open in grade school, and to be able to go on to the school of his or her choice would mean making the grades to qualify."

"Then," I said, "What you're advocating is that grade school be the last one a student must attend."

"That's correct. After the pleasures of college and the joys of high school, a student should be mature enough to face life in the tough world of grade school. There are no fraternities or sororities to distract them. Social life is at a bare minimum, teachers in grade school don't take any back talk from their students, and corporal punishment is permitted. Lower public schools have no football teams or extracurricular activities. If the truth be known, it's an eight-year grind, and no one accepts any excuses from a kid who can't make it from grades one to eight."

"But grade school is so long," I protested. "Do you think teen-agers could go the distance without dropping out?"

"No one drops out of grade school. All of them are prepared to come to grips with it, particularly when a grade school diploma will be the highest one that any student can receive. A grade school education under my system is what every parent in this country will want for his kid."

"But what about graduate school?" I asked.

"Those who want to go on to graduate school could enroll in kindergarten."

"You're advocating a complete reversal of the American educational system," I said. "Do you think this country is ready for it?"

"After what we've seen of our students for the past ten years, this country is ready for anything."

—Art Buchwald in the *Atlanta Journal*

1. The author's purpose is to <u>draw attention to how little work students do in high school and college.</u>

___F___ 2. The quoted numbers of commissions studying education and professors writing books on the subject are probably accurate.

___T___ 3. The author feels that students are forced to work the hardest in grade school.

___T___ 4. The author feels that college students take social activities more seriously than studying.

___T___ 5. The author feels that teachers are more demanding in grade school than in high school.

___F___ 6. The author blames educational weaknesses on lack of funding.

Through humor the author has made a serious point about education. By exaggerating the proposed solution, he shows weaknesses in student attitudes and expectations in the upper grades as well as their strengths in the lower grades.

Recognize the Author's Point of View or Bias

If you were reading an article analyzing Bill Clinton's achievements as President, you would ask, "Is this written by a Republican or a Democrat?" The answer would help you understand the point of view or bias from which the author is writing and thus help you evaluate the accuracy and relevance of the message.

Point of view refers to the opinions and beliefs of the author or of the reader, and a critical reader must recognize how those beliefs influence the message. Students sometimes find the term "point of view" confusing because, when discussing literature, "point of view" refers to the first, second, or third grammatical person that the author is using as the narrative voice. In this chapter, however, point of view refers to an opinion or position on a subject. For example, does the author write from the point of view of a believer or a nonbeliever in aliens?

Bias is a word that is closely related to *point of view*. However, the term *bias* tends to be associated with prejudice, and thus it has a negative connotation. A bias, like a point of view, is an opinion or a judgment. Either may be based on solid facts or on incorrect information, but a bias suggests that an author leans too heavily to one side in unequally presenting evidence and arguments. All authors write from a certain point of view, but not all authors have the same degree of bias.

Since both writers and readers are people with opinions, their biases interact on the printed page. Thus, critical readers need to recognize an author's bias or point of view as well as their own. For example, a reader might fail to understand an author's position on legalization of prostitution because the reader is totally opposed to the idea. In such a case, the reader's bias or point of view on the subject can interfere with comprehension.

EXAMPLE   Respond to the following statement by describing the author's point of view or bias, as well as your own.

> African animals are endangered and should not be used for fur coats. Minks, however, are a different story and should be considered separately. Minks are farmed animals that are produced only for their fur.

Explain the author's point of view/bias. _____

Explain your own position on the topic. _____

EXPLANATION The author implies that minks are not endangered and should be used for fur coats. Your position may be the same, or you may feel that being on the endangered list is not the only issue. You may feel that animals should not be used for clothing.

EXERCISE 3   The following statements adamantly express only one side of an issue. Read each statement, and mark whether you agree (*A*) or disagree (*D*). Then describe the point of view/bias of the author and your own position.

_____ 1. Teenage drinking causes accidents and deaths. The legal drinking age in all states should be raised to twenty-one. The fact that a citizen can be drafted into the military at eighteen years of age has no connection with the age at which he can legally consume alcohol.

Copyright ©1999 by Addison-Wesley Educational Publishers Inc.

Explain the author's point of view/bias. <u>For raising the drinking age</u>
<u>to 21</u>

Explain your own point of view/bias. _____

_____ 2. The billions of dollars that are allocated to the space program would
be better spent relieving the suffering of the poor and sick here on
earth. We have not solved our problems on this planet, so why should
we be eager to expand to other worlds?

Explain the author's point of view/bias. <u>Against spending money on</u>
<u>the space program</u>

Explain your own point of view/bias. _____

_____ 3. An overwhelming amount of this nation's land is owned by the government in the form of national parks and forests. This is especially
true in the West. Much of this land is not needed for public recreation and could be sold to private enterprise, with the proceeds going
to pay off part of the national debt.

Explain the author's point of view/bias. <u>Wants to reduce government</u>
<u>ownership of land</u>

Explain your own point of view/bias. _____

 **EXERCISE 4**

Read the following description of Napoleon Bonaparte from a freshman history
textbook. Keep in mind that Napoleon is generally considered one of the great
heroes of France and one of the greatest conquerors of the world. Does this passage say exactly what you would expect? Analyze the author's point of view, and
answer the questions that follow with *T* (true) or *F* (false).

PASSAGE 1

Napoleon was a short, swarthy, handsome man with remarkable, magnetic eyes. Slender
as a youth, he exhibited a tendency toward obesity as he grew older. He was high-strung,
and his manners were coarse. Militarily, he has been both denigrated and extolled. On
the one hand, his success has been attributed to luck and the great skill of his professional
lieutenants; on the other, he has been compared with the greatest conquerors of the
past. Politically, he combined the shrewdness of a Machiavellian despot with the majesty
of a "sun king." It is generally conceded that he was one of the giants of history. He had
an exalted belief in his own destiny, but as an utter cynic and misanthrope felt only contempt for the human race. He once exclaimed, "What do a million men matter to such as
I?" The world was Napoleon's oyster. He considered himself emancipated from moral
scruples. Yet this man, who despised humanity, was worshiped by the millions he held in
such contempt. To his soldiers he was the invincible hero, a supreme ruler over men, literally a demi-god. He came from nowhere, but was endowed with an extraordinary mind
and the charisma required for masterful leadership. He used democracy to destroy
democracy. He employed the slogans of revolution to fasten his hold on nations. His
great empire collapsed, but his name will never be forgotten.

—A History of the Western World by Solomon Modell

___F___ 1. The author wants to present Napoleon as a demi-god.

___F___ 2. The author shows Napoleon as the greatest military leader in history.

___T___ 3. The author feels that Napoleon effectively used propaganda for his own benefit.

___T___ 4. The author wants to show the differences between the public and the private views of Napoleon.

___F___ 5. The author feels that Napoleon adhered to a strict moral code.

___F___ 6. The author feels that Napoleon matured into a handsome, well-mannered gentleman.

___F___ 7. The author believes that Napoleon's success was due primarily to good luck.

___T___ 8. The author feels that Napoleon had little regard for the average person.

___F___ 9. The author feels that Napoleon is undeserving of a prominent place in history.

___T___10. The author feels that Napoleon used ruthless tactics to get what he wanted.

The author gives a cynical description of Napoleon. For example, he relates a quote attributed to Napoleon that shows him in an unfavorable light. The critical reader needs to be aware that other accounts show Napoleon as a great leader who was concerned for his soldiers and wanted the best for France.

Read the passage below for a somewhat different view of Napoleon. Then answer the questions that follow.

PASSAGE 2

Few men in Western history have compelled the attention of the world as Napoleon Bonaparte did during the fifteen years of his absolutist rule in France. Schooled in France and at the military academy in Paris, he possessed a mind congenial to the ideas of the Enlightenment—creative, imaginative, and ready to perceive things anew. His primary interests were history, law, and mathematics. His particular strengths as a leader lay in his ability to conceive of financial, legal, or military plans and then to master their every detail; his capacity for inspiring others, even those initially opposed to him; and his belief in himself as the destined savior of the French. That last conviction eventually became the obsession that led to Napoleon's undoing. But supreme self-confidence was just what the French government lacked since the first days of the revolution. Napoleon believed both in himself and in France. That latter belief was the tonic France now needed, and Napoleon proceeded to administer it in liberally revivifying doses.

—Western Civilizations by Edward McNall Berns et al.

1. How does the author turn Napoleon's shortcoming into an advantage?
   Although it later became an obsession, Napoleon's belief that he was the destined savior of France gave the country the self-confidence it needed after the revolution.

2. How does the view of this author compare with the stance of the previous author? Reference the passage to support your answer. The second author sees Napoleon in a more favorable light than the first.

Copyright ©1999 by Addison-Wesley Educational Publishers Inc.

PASSAGE 3

THE ARABS' IMAGE

All that the average American ever hears about Arab countries concerns their polygamy, the status of their women, and the Islamic movements behind the Iranian revolution. Americans see Arabs as desert bedouins in flowing robes. Such stereotypes do not make distinctions between rich and poor Arab countries, or between Arabs who have lived since the dawn of history on the banks of rivers where they planted crops, and those who are desert nomads. American portrayals of Arabs take no account of the universities and research centers all over the Arab world, or of the programs of economic growth and social development there.

The American media choose to ignore all of this, preferring the racist caricatures that spring from Western chauvinism that holds the civilizations of the East in contempt. Arabs appear as blood-thirsty terrorists and dissolute tribal sheiks who squander their vast wealth among the women of their harems. The scriptwriters apparently get their information, more imaginary than real, straight from the *Arabian Nights* and the tales of Ali Baba.

—"The Arabs' Image" by Mustafa Nabil, in *Connections* edited by Judith Stanford

1. What is the author's point of view on America's image of Arabs? <u>The image is wrong and based on fiction rather than fact.</u>

2. How are Arabs misrepresented and by whom? <u>The American media misrepresent them as terrorists or extravagant sheiks.</u>

3. Why do you agree or disagree with the author? _____

Recognize the Author's Tone

The author's **tone** describes the writer's attitude toward the subject. An easy trick to distinguish tone is to think of tone of voice. When someone is speaking, voice sounds usually indicate whether the person is angry, romantic, or joyful. In reading, however, you cannot hear the voice, but you can pick up clues from the choice of words and details.

Critical readers need to "tune in" to the author's tone, and thus let attitude become a part of evaluating the message. For example, an optimistic tone on water pollution might cause suspicion that information has been overlooked, whereas an extremely pessimistic article on the same subject might overwhelm the reader, causing him or her to discount valuable information.

EXAMPLE   Identify the tone of the following passage.

Caesar Chavez had himself felt the pain of the poor immigrant farmworkers. As a child, he sometimes slept with his family in the car, or they camped under bridges. He attended more than 30 schools as a child. He knew the hardships and excuses all too well, and he wanted a change in the system.

_____c_____ 1. The author's tone is

    a. nostalgic.
    b. ironic.
    c. angry.

EXPLANATION   The details show that Chavez suffered through his own difficult times, and he doesn't want to hear the "excuses." The tone is angry.

READER'S TIP

THINKING ABOUT TONE

The following is a list of words that are frequently used to describe the author's tone, with explanations in parentheses:

- ❖ cheerful, joyous, happy (feeling good about the topic)
- ❖ angry, bitter, hateful (feeling bad and upset about the topic)
- ❖ objective, factual, straightforward (using fact without emotions)
- ❖ subjective, opinionated (expressing opinions and feelings)
- ❖ humorous, jovial (being funny)
- ❖ serious, sincere (being honest and concerned)
- ❖ optimistic (looking on the bright side)
- ❖ pessimistic (looking on the negative side)
- ❖ ironic (the opposite of what is expected; a twist at the end)
- ❖ sarcastic (saying one thing and meaning another)
- ❖ hypocritical (saying one thing and doing another)
- ❖ cynical (expecting the worst from people)
- ❖ formal (using an official style)
- ❖ informal (using a slang style)
- ❖ sentimental, nostalgic (remembering the good old days)
- ❖ mocking, scornful (ridiculing the topic)
- ❖ arrogant (acting conceited or above others)

EXERCISE 5

Mark the letter that identifies the tone for each of the following sentences.

_____ c _____ 1. Baseball was invented as an urban game in order for owners to make money, players to become arrogant, and spectators to drink over-priced beer.

    a. objective
    b. nostalgic
    c. humorous

_____ c _____ 2. The Puritans came to the new land for religious freedom, yet they allowed little freedom to their followers. Anne Hutchinson was banished from the colony for preaching that salvation can come through good works.

    a. optimistic
    b. sentimental
    c. ironic

_____ c _____ 3. When I study now, I'm in a lab with 50 noisy computers. What happened to the quiet chair in a corner with a table for your books, papers, and pencils?

    a. objective
    b. bitter
    c. nostalgic

Copyright ©1999 by Addison-Wesley Educational Publishers Inc.

_____b_____ 4. According to a recent study in a book called *Living Well*, sexually active partners who do not use contraceptives stand an 85 percent chance of conceiving within a year.

     a. subjective
     b. objective
     c. sarcastic

_____b_____ 5. If given the funding, scientists could trace most aggressive behavior, crime, and violence to either too much testosterone or low blood sugar.

     a. sentimental
     b. subjective
     c. objective

EXERCISE 6

Read the passages below and answer the questions that follow.

PASSAGE 1

TECHNO-BORES

Techno-bores are like chemically altered bores in that their condition (infatuation with technology—often computers) blinds them to the possibility that *your* reality simply isn't theirs. Details about the latest software or synthesizer are lost on you.

    The curious thing about computer-obsessed bores is that their behavior appears to have been directly influenced by the machines they love—you can see little floppy disks spinning in their eyes when they speak; their sentences come out in a robotic cadence. Don't even consider launching a personal question in the direction of a techno-bore— you may cause a short circuit.

          —"The Ten Most Memorable Bores" by Margot Mufflin

1. What is the tone of the passage? <u>humorous</u>
2. What clues reveal the author's tone? <u>chemically altered, blind to reality,</u>
<u>disks spinning in eyes, etc.</u>

PASSAGE 2

COLLEGE CLONES

Has anyone else noticed that the very same students people college classrooms year after year? Has anyone else found the same bodies, faces, personalities returning semester after semester? Forgive me for violating my students' individual "personhoods," but reality makes it so tempting to see them as types. Doubtless you will recognize at least some of them. They have twins, or perhaps clones, on your campus, too.

    There is the eternal Good Time Charlies (or Charlene), who makes every party on and off campus, who by November of his freshman year has worked his face into a case of terminal acne, who misses every set of examinations because of "mono," who finally burns himself out physically and mentally by the age of 19 and drops out to go home and recuperate, and who returns at 20 after a long talk with Dad to major in accounting.

    —"How Do We Find the Students in a World of Academic Gymnasts and Worker Ants?"
                   by James T. Baker

___c___ 1. The author's tone is

  a. bitter.
  b. nostalgic.
  c. humorous.
  d. sympathetic.

___b___ 2. The tone of the phrase "Forgive me for violating my students' individual 'personhoods'" is

  a. respectful.
  b. sarcastic.
  c. optimistic.
  d. objective.

PASSAGE 3

TAKING THE TEST

For the next two weeks I ate bacon cheeseburgers almost daily, a series of last meals. Every time the phone rang, at home or at the office, I felt an electric anxiety. My doctor had promised he would not call, but I kept hoping he'd break our agreement and phone to say I was negative. That way I could sleep at night. He didn't call. I grew more obsessed daily. Even though for hours at a time I'd forget to anticipate my test results, my fear would ambush me like a bowel-loosening punch in the gut. I told myself that I wouldn't die the very day the doctor told me the bad news. My HIV-positive friends, and those who had been diagnosed with AIDS, were still alive—mostly. They'd coped. I'd cope too. Cold comfort.

—"Taking the Test" by David Groff

___b___ 1. The author's tone is

  a. bitter.
  b. fearful.
  c. sarcastic.
  d. intellectual.

___c___ 2. The author's primary purpose is

  a. to argue.
  b. to criticize.
  c. to describe.
  d. to entertain.

PASSAGE 4

POPULATION GROWTH AND RESOURCES

In 1988, a billion and a half people inhabited the earth. Now the population exceeds five billion and is growing fast—in essence, the world must accommodate a new population roughly equivalent to that of the United States and Canada *every three years.* Understanding ecosystems and how civilization is living on capital provides the appropriate context for analyzing the population problem. It immediately exposes the myth that the impact of the population stems primarily from poor people in poor countries who do not know enough to limit their reproduction. Numbers per se are not the measure of overpopulation; instead it is the *impact* of people on ecosystems and nonrenewable resources. While developing countries severely tax their environments, clearly the populations of rich

Copyright ©1999 by Addison-Wesley Educational Publishers Inc.

countries leave a vastly disproportionate mark on the planet. The birth of a baby in the United States imposes more than a hundred times the stress on the world's resources and environment as a birth in, say, Bangladesh. Babies from Bangladesh do not grow up to own automobiles and air conditioners or to eat grain-fed beef. Their life-styles do not require huge quantities of minerals and energy, nor do their activities seriously undermine the life-support capability of the entire planet.

—"Population, Plenty, and Poverty" by Paul Ehrlich and Anne Ehrlich

_____d_____ 1. The authors' tone is

      a. sarcastic.
      b. humorous.
      c. hopeful.
      d. serious.

_____T_____ 2. The authors' point about how the few consume the most is ironic.

_____F_____ 3. The authors' purpose is to condemn poor countries for not putting limits on reproduction.

Distinguish Fact from Opinion

The reader who cannot distinguish between fact and opinion will always remain gullible. By contrast, the critical reader realizes that most writing contains a combination of facts and opinions, and is able to tell one from the other. A **fact** is a statement that can be proven true or false, whereas an **opinion** is a statement of feeling that cannot be proven right or wrong.

EXAMPLE

Mark the following statements as *F* (fact) or *O* (opinion).

_____F_____ 1. George Washington was the first president of the United States.

_____O_____ 2. George Washington was the best president of the United States.

_____F_____ 3. The author states that George Washington was the best president of the United States.

_____O_____ 4. It is a fact that George Washington was the best president of the United States.

The first and third are statements of fact that can be proven, but the second and fourth are opinions, even though the fourth tries to present itself as a fact. In psychology, for example, it is a fact that Freud believed the personality is divided into three parts; however, it is only an opinion that there are three parts of the human personality. Others may feel that the personality should be divided into two parts or ten parts,

Dr. Beatrice Mendez-Egle, a professor at the University of Texas-Pan American, further clarifies the distinction between fact and opinion with the following definitions and table:

A **fact** is an observation that can be supported with incontrovertible evidence. An **opinion**, on the other hand, is a commentary, position, or observation based on fact but which represents a personal judgment or interpretation of these facts.

Fact	Opinion
3/4 of the students in this class are making A's.	This class is really smart.
The temperature in the class is 78°.	This classroom is always hot and stuffy!
Clinton won the presidency with a lower percentage of popular votes than Michael Dukakis got in 1988.	Bill Clinton doesn't deserve to be president because fewer than half of the voters who voted in the 1992 presidential election voted for him.

The first two opinions are clearly judgments that would probably be obvious to most readers. The third opinion, however, is mixed with fact and thus the judgment portion of "doesn't deserve to be president" needs the sharp eye of a critical reader to recognize it as an opinion. In order to achieve a certain purpose, a writer can support a particular bias or point of view and attempt to confuse the reader by blending facts and opinions so that both sound like facts.

 **EXERCISE 7**

Mark the following statements from textbooks as *F* (fact) or *O* (opinion).

___O___ 1. "Much of our lives, in fact, is spent filling out questionnaires, taking tests, and being interviewed."

—*Psychology and You* by David Dempsey and Philip Zimbardo

___F___ 2. "Veins, by definition, are blood vessels that carry blood back toward the heart from capillary beds."

—*Biological Principles* by Gideon Nelson

___O___ 3. "If Adams was inept politically, he was deft diplomatically, and in foreign affairs he was expected to shine."

—*The American Pageant* by Thomas Bailey and David Kennedy

___F___ 4. "To register as a taste, molecules of a substance must dissolve in the mucus of a taste bud and trigger off nerve impulses in the hair cells."

—*Biological Principles* by Gideon Nelson

___F___ 5. "Adler, too, believed that early childhood experiences shaped the human personality, but he emphasized the social nature of the child's urges and believed that they could, for the most part, be brought under rational control."

—*Psychology and You* by David Dempsey and Philip Zimbardo

___F___ 6. "Several Southern states adopted formal protests; in South Carolina flags were lowered to half-mast."

—*The American Pageant* by Thomas Bailey and David Kennedy

___O___ 7. "An applicant who is publicly shy and withdrawn, for example, would probably not be hired as a sales representative or an airline flight attendant."

—*Psychology and You* by David Dempsey and Philip Zimbardo

___F___ 8. "The hedonistic theory was first set forth by the Greek philosopher Epictetus, who believed that all human action could be explained by the desire to seek pleasure or avoid pain."

—*Psychology and You* by David Dempsey and Philip Zimbardo

Copyright ©1999 by Addison-Wesley Educational Publishers Inc.

_____O_____ 9. "A great deal of knowledge about the structure of the brain has accumulated through the years, and more is probably known about the human brain than about any other vertebrate's brain."

—*Biological Principles* by Gideon Nelson

_____O_____ 10. "Despite this trend toward the diffusion of power, it would be naive to believe that wealth and power are no longer linked."

—*Sociology: Human Society* by Melvin DeFleur et al.

Recognize Valid and Invalid Support for Arguments

When evaluating persuasive writing, critical readers realize that support for an argument or a position can be in the form of both facts and opinions. For example, valid reasons for a career change or a vacation destination can be a combination of both facts and feelings. The trick for a critical reader is to recognize which reasons validly support the point and which merely confuse the issue with an illusion of support.

A **fallacy** is an error in reasoning that can give an illusion of support. On the surface, a fallacy can appear to add support, but closer inspection shows it to be unrelated and illogical. For example, valid reasons for buying running shoes might be comfort and price, whereas invalid reasons might be that "everybody has them" and a sports figure said to buy them.

Fallacies are particularly prevalent in **propaganda,** a form of writing designed to convince the reader by whatever means possible. Propaganda can be used to support a political cause, advertise a product, or engender enthusiasm for a college event.

Experts have identified and labeled over 200 fallacies or tricks of persuasion. The following list contains some of the most common ones.

Testimonials: Celebrities who are not experts state support.
Example: Tiger Woods appears in television advertisements endorsing a particular credit card.

Bandwagon: You will be left out if you do not join the crowd.
Example: All the voters in the district support Henson for Senator.

Transfer: A famous person is associated with an argument.
Example: George Washington indicated in a quote that he would have agreed with us on this issue.

Straw Person: A simplistic exaggeration is set up to represent the argument.
Example: The professor replied, "If I delay the exam, you'll expect me to change the due dates of all papers and assignments."

Misleading Analogy: Two things are compared as similar that actually are distinctly different.
Example: Studying is like taking a shower; most of the material goes down the drain.

Circular Reasoning: The conclusion is supported by restating it.
Example: Papers must be turned in on time because papers cannot be turned in late.

EXERCISE 8

Identify the letter for the fallacy in each of the following statements: (a) testimonial, (b) bandwagon, (c) transfer, (d) straw person, (e) misleading analogy, (f) circular reasoning.

_____c_____ 1. The monument of Mexico should be restored because Michelangelo created monuments.

___e___ 2. The first semester of college is like the premiere of a Batman movie because both require the use of imagination.

___f___ 3. Customs booklets warn that Cuban cigars are not legally allowed in the United States because the government will not let you bring them into the country.

___a___ 4. The soft drink must be good because Sinbad's ads say that he enjoys it.

___b___ 5. Purchase tickets immediately because everyone in school has signed up for the event and soon it will be sold out.

___d___ 6. A student who is late for class would probably be late for a job interview and thus be a failure.

EXERCISE 9

To practice your critical thinking skills, read the textbook passages below, and then answer the questions that follow.

PASSAGE 1

ELIZABETH OF RUSSIA (1741–1762)

Elizabeth was Peter the Great's daughter. She is said to have been ignorant, charming, extravagant, capricious, and nymphomaniacal. She ascended the throne as a result of a palace revolution and ruled for some twenty-two years. Because of her dependence on the service nobility, the class from which members of the palace guard were chosen, their power increased considerably during her reign. To the same degree, German influence at court was drastically reduced. One reason, among others, was Elizabeth's hatred for Frederick the Great of Prussia, who is reputed to have made rather uncomplimentary remarks about her moral character. Legend has it that he was not far wrong; the empress apparently made a practice of selecting handsome young men from her palace guard as her lovers. She also felt a great need for ostentatious display. It is said that while her peasants went hungry Elizabeth accumulated fifteen thousand gowns. She knew little, however, about geography; she thought one could travel from Russia to Britain entirely by land.

—*A History of the Western World* by Solomon Modell

Answer the following with *T* (true) or *F* (false), or with *a*, *b*, *c*, or *d*.

___T___ 1. The author wishes to show Elizabeth as a selfish ruler, interested in herself rather than the people.

___T___ 2. The author suggests that the status of the service nobility increased, in part due to Elizabeth's sexual desires.

___F___ 3. The author's tone is primarily objective.

___F___ 4. The author respects Elizabeth's accomplishments.

___F___ 5. The author uses the example about geography to verify Elizabeth's extravagance.

___c___ 6. All of the following words are negatively slanted *except*

    a. ostentatious.
    b. capricious.
    c. charming.
    d. nymphomaniacal.

Copyright ©1999 by Addison-Wesley Educational Publishers Inc.

Mark the following statements as *F* (fact) or *O* (opinion).

___F___　7. "She ascended the throne as a result of a palace revolution. . . ."

___O___　8. "To the same degree, German influence at court was drastically reduced."

___O___　9. "She also felt a great need for ostentatious display."

PASSAGE 2

KILLING BOBCATS

The reasons for killing such an endangered species are varied. Ranchers often cite the bobcat as a chicken killer (while choosing to overlook its role in controlling rodents). Among many cultures, including our own, such killing is often taken to be a symbol of maleness or manhood. If the cats were run down on foot and then throttled with bare hands, perhaps a case could be made for this argument, but they have very little chance of escaping trained hounds and high-powered rifles. Sometimes the reason given for such killing is economic. Perhaps the hides can be sold. If the demand exists, it will be met, whether the poachers are African tribesmen killing the last of the rhinos or Louisiana citizens spotlighting alligators at night. The sale of such skins is not restricted throughout most of the world and one can find all sorts of spotted-cat skin on the proud backs of status-conscious Europeans any cool Saturday afternoon. They are also showing a resurgence in the United States. A Siberian lynx coat was recently advertised in Los Angeles for over $70,000. The high price was stated to be due to the fact that the animal was so rare.

—Biology: The World of Life by Robert Wallace

Answer the following with *T* (true) or *F* (false).

___T___　1. The author's purpose is to ridicule people who kill rare animals.

___F___　2. The author implies that the bobcat serves no useful purpose for society.

___T___　3. The author implies that killing animals with high-powered rifles is connected with a false sense of manhood.

___F___　4. The author's tone is sympathetic.

___T___　5. The author suggests that the buyer of the $70,000 lynx coat is as guilty as the hunter.

___F___　6. In using the phrase "Louisiana citizens spotlighting alligators at night," the author intends for the slant to be positive.

Mark the following statements as *F* (fact) or *O* (opinion).

___F___　7. "Ranchers often cite the bobcat as a chicken killer. . . ."

___F___　8. "The sale of such skins is not restricted throughout most of the world. . . ."

___F___　9. "The high price was stated to be due to the fact that the animal was so rare."

PASSAGE 3

A DEAD LAKE

Lake Erie was once one of the world's most beautiful lakes. Its waters were pure and abounded with life. It provided food, and lent its beauty to man for literally thousands of years. What man, camped beside it in earlier times, spending leisurely days swimming and fishing and reveling in its quiet sunrises, could have guessed its fate? The growing human population, however, was demanding new goods. The production of those goods required great amounts of water. So factories were set up along the banks of the immense lake—factories that would use the water as a coolant, and the lake itself as a dump. Thus millions of tons of poisons of all sorts were poured directly into the water. After all, this was the cheapest means of disposal. Cheap production increased profits. But the question is, did the industrialists have the *right* to pour their garbage into a lake they didn't own? As their profits increased, the lake was changed to the extent that it became dangerous to swim in it or drink from it. The industrialists, of course, when threatened with belated lawsuits in recent years, argued that their dumping of poisons into the lake resulted in cheaper goods for people, and *that,* after all, is what the people *really* wanted. You can immediately see that the question can be extended to apply to industries that vomit their poisonous fumes into the air. Whose air is it, after all?

Because of new demands being placed on the earth's fresh water, it is very likely that you will come to change your feelings toward the uses of fresh water before long. Whereas you may have, somewhere around the second grade, learned that water is something people drink and plants need, you may soon come to think of it in terms of its mining and allocation.

—*Biology: The World of Life* by Robert Wallace

Answer the following with *T* (true) or *F* (false).

___T___ 1. The author's purpose is to warn the reader of a very real threat.

___F___ 2. The author's tone is humorous.

___T___ 3. The author implies that Lake Erie was sacrificed for greed.

___T___ 4. The author suggests that the industrialists shifted the blame unfairly in their response to the Lake Erie lawsuits.

___F___ 5. The author feels that a larger portion of the air and water supply should be allocated for industrial needs than for human needs.

___T___ 6. In using the phrase "vomit their poisonous fumes into the air," the author intends for the slant to be negative.

Mark the following statements as *F* (fact) or *O* (opinion).

___O___ 7. "Lake Erie was once one of the world's most beautiful lakes."

___F___ 8. ". . . factories were set up along the banks of the immense lake. . . ."

___F___ 9. "Cheap production increased profits."

PASSAGE 4

SIMPLICITY

Clutter is the disease of American writing. We are a society strangling in unnecessary words, circular constructions, pompous frills and meaningless jargon.

Who really knows what the average businessman is trying to say in the average business letter? What member of an insurance or medical plan can decipher the brochure that tells him what his costs and benefits are? What father or mother can put together a child's toy—on Christmas Eve or any other eve—from the instructions on the box? Our national tendency is to inflate and thereby sound important. The airline pilot who wakes us to announce that he is presently anticipating experiencing considerable weather wouldn't dream of saying that there's a storm ahead and it may get bumpy. The sentence is too simple—there must be something wrong with it.

Copyright ©1999 by Addison-Wesley Educational Publishers Inc.

But the secret of good writing is to strip every sentence to its cleanest components. Every word that serves no function, every long word that could be a short word, every adverb which carries the same meaning that is already in the verb, every passive construction that leaves the reader unsure of who is doing what—these are the thousand and one adulterants that weaken the strength of a sentence. And they usually occur, ironically, in proportion to education and rank.

During the late 1960's the president of Princeton University wrote a letter to mollify the alumni after a spell of campus unrest. "You are probably aware," he began, "that we have been experiencing very considerable potentially explosive expressions of dissatisfaction on issues only partially related." He meant that the students had been hassling them about different things. As an alumnus I was far more upset by the president's syntax than by the students' potentially explosive expressions of dissatisfaction. I would have preferred the presidential approach taken by Franklin D. Roosevelt when he tried to convert into English his own government's memos, such as this blackout order of 1942:

> Such preparations shall be made as will completely obscure all Federal buildings and non-Federal buildings occupied by the Federal government during an air raid for any period of time from visibility by reasons of internal or external illumination.

"Tell them," Roosevelt said, "that in buildings where they have to keep the work going to put something across the windows."

—*On Writing Well*, 6/e by William Zinsser

Answer the following with *T* (true) or *F* (false), or with *a*, *b*, *c*, or *d*.

___T___ 1. The author's main purpose is to criticize wordy writing.

___T___ 2. The author quotes Roosevelt to show how simply the blackout order could have been stated.

___F___ 3. The author quotes the president of Princeton to show that educated people usually communicate clearly.

___F___ 4. The author feels that the airline pilot avoids using the word *storm* because it may frighten the passengers.

___T___ 5. The overall tone of the passage is serious.

___d___ 6. All of the following words are negatively slanted *except*

    a. clutter.
    b. jargon.
    c. decipher.
    d. brochure.

Mark the following statements as *F* (fact) or *O* (opinion).

___O___ 7. "Clutter is the disease of American writing."

___O___ 8. "We are a society strangling in unnecessary words. . . ."

___O___ 9. " . . . the secret of good writing is to strip every sentence to its cleanest components."

PASSAGE 5

THEODORE ROOSEVELT AND THE ROUGH RIDERS

Brimming with enthusiasm, perhaps a bit innocent in their naiveté, the Rough Riders viewed Cuba as a land of stars, a place to win great honors or die in the pursuit. Like many of his men, TR believed "that the nearing future held . . . many chances of death, of honor and renown.'' And he was ready. Dressed in a Brooks Brothers uniform made especially for him and with several extra pairs of spectacles sewn in the lining of his Rough Rider hat, Roosevelt prepared to meet his destiny.''

In a land of beauty, death often came swiftly. As the Rough Riders and other soldiers moved inland toward Santiago, snipers fired upon them. The high-speed Mauser bullets seemed to come out of nowhere, making a *z-z-z-z-eu* as they moved through the air or a loud *chug* as they hit flesh. Since the Spanish snipers used smokeless gunpowder, no puffs of smoke betrayed their positions.

During the first day in Cuba, the Rough Riders experienced the "blood, sweat and tears'' of warfare. Dr. Church looked "like a kid who had gotten his hands and arms into a bucket of thick red paint.'' Some men died, and others lay where they had been shot dying. The reality of war strikes different men differently. It horrifies some, terrifies others, and enrages still others. Sheer exhilaration was the best way to describe Roosevelt's response to death and danger. Even sniper fire could not keep TR from jumping up and down with excitement.

On July 1, 1898, the Rough Riders faced their sternest task. Moving from the coast toward Santiago along the Camino Real, the main arm of the United States forces encountered an entrenched enemy. Spread out along the San Juan Heights, Spanish forces commanded a splendid position. As American troops emerged from a stretch of jungle, they found themselves in a dangerous position. Once again the sky seemed to be raining Mauser bullets and shrapnel. Clearly the Heights had to be taken. Each hour of delay meant more American casualties.

The Rough Riders were deployed to the right to prepare to assault Kettle Hill. Once in position, they faced an agonizing wait for orders to charge. Most soldiers hunched behind cover. Bucky O'Neill, however, casually strolled up and down in front of his troops, chain-smoked cigarettes, and shouted encouragement. A sergeant implored him to take cover. "Sergeant,'' Bucky remarked, "the Spanish bullet isn't made that will kill me.'' Hardly had he finished the statement when a Mauser bullet ripped into his mouth and burst out of the back of his head. Even before he fell, Roosevelt wrote, Bucky's "wild and gallant soul has gone out into the darkness.''

—America and Its People by James Martin et al.

Answer the following with *T* (true) or *F* (false) or with *a, b, c,* or *d.*

    F   1. The author's main purpose is to persuade.

    T   2. The author feels that the Rough Riders had a glorified view of war.

    T   3. The author shows sarcasm in mentioning the "Brooks Brothers uniform.''

    T   4. In view of his subsequent death, Bucky O'Neill's remark about a Spanish bullet was ironic.

    F   5. The overall tone of the passage is humorous.

    c   6. All of the following phrases are negatively slanted *except*

        a. sheer exhilaration.
        b. jumping up and down.
        c. sternest task.
        d. casually strolled.

Mark the following statements as *F* (fact) or *O* (opinion).

    F   7. " . . . the Spanish snipers used smokeless gunpowder. . . .''

    O   8. "Dr. Church looked 'like a kid who had gotten his hands and arms into a bucket of thick red paint.'''

    F   9. "Some men died, and others lay where they had been shot dying.''

Copyright ©1999 by Addison-Wesley Educational Publishers Inc.

PASSAGE 6

MEANWHILE, HUMANS EAT PET FOOD

The first time I witnessed people eating pet foods was among neighbors and acquaintances during my youth in the South. At that time it was not uncommon or startling to me to see dog-food patties sizzling in a pan on the top of a stove or kerosene space heater in a dilapidated house with no running water, no refrigerator, no heat, no toilet and the unrelenting stench of decaying insects. I simply thought of it as the unfortunate but unavoidable consequence of being poor in the South.

The second time occurred in Cleveland. Like many other Southerners, I came to seek my fortune in one of those pot-at-the-end-of-the-rainbow factories along Euclid Avenue. Turned away from one prospective job after another ("We didn't hire hillbillies," employers said), I saw my nest egg of $30 dwindle to nothing. As my funds diminished and my hunger grew, I turned to pilfering food and small amounts of cash. With the money, I surreptitiously purchased, fried and ate canned dog and cat food as my principal ration for several weeks.

I was, of course, humiliated to be eating something that, in my experience, only "trash" consumed. A merciless pride in self-sufficiency kept me from seeking out public welfare or asking my friends or family for help. In fact, I carefully guarded the secret from everyone, because I feared being judged a failure. Except for the humiliation I experienced, eating canned pet food did not at the time seem to be particularly unpleasant. The dog food tasted pretty much like mealy hamburger, while the cat food was similar to canned fish that I was able to improve with mayonnaise, mustard or catsup. My later experience as a public assistance caseworker in Richmond, a street-based community worker in South Philadelphia, and my subsequent travels and studies as a medical sociologist throughout the South, turned up instances of people eating pet food because they saw it as cheaper than other protein products. Throughout the years, similar cases found in the Ozarks, on Indian reservations and in various cities across the nation have also been brought to my attention.

My experience and research suggest that human consumption of pet food is widespread in the United States. My estimate, one I believe to be conservative, is that pet foods constitute a significant part of the diet of at least 225,000 American households, affecting some one million persons. Who knows how many more millions supplement their diet with pet food products? One thing that we can assume is that current economic conditions are increasing the practice and that it most seriously affects the unemployed, poor people, and our older citizens.

There are those who argue that we do not have enough hard data on the human consumption of pet foods. Must we wait for incontrovertible data before we seriously seek to solve the problems of hunger and malnutrition in America? I submit that we have data enough.

—"Meanwhile, Humans Eat Pet Food" by Edward Peeples, Jr.

Answer the following with *T* (true) or *F* (false).

_____F_____ 1. The author's purpose is to change laws governing the sale of pet food.

_____F_____ 2. The author's overall tone is humorous.

_____T_____ 3. The author has probably been referred to as a hillbilly.

_____T_____ 4. The author writes from the point of view of one who has been poor, as well as from that of a professional caseworker.

_____T_____ 5. The term "trash" is used to refer to people.

POINTS TO PONDER

▲ Critical readers evaluate the accuracy and relevance of the printed word before accepting it.

▲ Authors write with a particular *purpose* or *intent* in mind.

▲ *Point of view* refers to the writer's opinions and beliefs.

▲ Both writers and readers bring *bias* to the printed page.

▲ *Tone* refers to the author's attitude toward the subject.

▲ A *fact* is a statement that can be proven true or false.

▲ An *opinion* is a statement of feeling that cannot be proven right or wrong.

▲ A *fallacy* is an error in reasoning that is designed to give the illusion of support.

▲ *Propaganda* is a form of writing that uses fallacies to convince readers.

SELECTION 1   *Narrative Essay*

THINKING BEFORE READING

Preview for content and organizational clues. Activate your schema and anticipate what you will learn.

What celebrities have died of drug-related causes?

Were drugs sold in your high school?

What are the social consequences of drugs in a community?

I want to learn _____.

VOCABULARY PREVIEW

Are you familiar with these words?

ambivalence	stupefied	convulse	miraculously	audibly
gnashing	irreverent	freak	speculated	casualty

What does the prefix in *ambivalence* mean?

What is property and casualty insurance?

What does the root word in *speculated* mean?

Your instructor may give a true-false vocabulary review before or after reading.

THINKING DURING READING

As you read, use the five thinking strategies of a good reader: predict, picture, relate, monitor, and correct.

Copyright ©1999 by Addison-Wesley Educational Publishers Inc.

AS THEY SAY, DRUGS KILL

The fastest way to end a party is to have someone die in the middle of it.

At a party last fall I watched a 22-year-old die of cardiac arrest after he had used drugs. It was a painful, undignified way to die. And I would like to think that anyone who shared the experience would feel his or her ambivalence about substance abuse dissolv-
5   ing.

This victim won't be singled out like Len Bias as a bitter example for "troubled youth." He was just another ordinary guy celebrating with friends at a private house party, the kind where they roll in the keg first thing in the morning and get stupefied while watching the football games on cable all afternoon. The living room was littered
10   with beer cans from last night's party—along with dirty socks and the stuffing from the secondhand couch.

And there were drugs, as at so many other college parties. The drug of choice this evening was psilocybin, hallucinogenic mushrooms. If you're cool, you call them "'shrooms."
15   This wasn't a crowd huddled in the corner of a darkened room with a single red bulb, shooting needles into their arms. People played darts, made jokes, passed around a joint and listened to the Grateful Dead on the stereo.

VIOLENT FALL

Suddenly, a thin, tall, brown-haired young man began to gasp. His eyes rolled back in his head, and he hit the floor face first with a crash. Someone laughed, not appreciating the
20   violence of his fall, thinking the afternoon's festivities had finally caught up with another guest. The laugh lasted only a second, as the brown-haired guest began to convulse and

choke. The sound of the stereo and laughter evaporated. Bystanders shouted frantic suggestions:

"It's an epileptic fit, put something in his mouth!"

25   "Roll him over on his stomach!"

"Call an ambulance; God, somebody breathe into his mouth."

A girl kneeling next to him began to sob his name, and he seemed to moan.

"Wait, he's semicoherent." Four people grabbed for the telephone, to find no dial tone, and ran to use a neighbor's. One slammed the dead phone against the wall in frus-

30 tration—and miraculously produced a dial tone.

But the body was now motionless on the kitchen floor. "He has a pulse, he has a pulse."

"But he's not breathing!"

"Well, get away—give him some f—ing air!" The three or four guests gathered

35 around his body unbuttoned his shirt.

"Wait—is he OK? Should I call the damn ambulance?"

A chorus of frightened voices shouted, "Yes, yes!"

"Come on, come on, breathe again. Breathe!"

Over muffled sobs came a sudden grating, desperate breath that passed through

40 bloody lips and echoed through the kitchen and living room. "He's had this reaction before—when he did acid at a concert last spring. But he recovered in 15 seconds . . . ," one friend confided.

The rest of the guests looked uncomfortably at the floor or paced purposelessly around the room. One or two whispered, "Oh my God," over and over, like a prayer. A

45 friend stood next to me, eyes fixed on the kitchen floor. He mumbled, just audibly, "I've seen this before. My dad died of a heart attack. He had the same look. . . ."

I touched his shoulder and leaned against a wall, repeating reassurances to myself. People don't die at parties. People don't die at parties.

Eventually, no more horrible, gnashing sounds tore their way from the victim's

50 lungs. I pushed my hands deep in my jeans pockets wondering how much it costs to pump a stomach and how someone could be so careless if he had this reaction with another drug. What would he tell his parents about the hospital bill?

Two uniformed paramedics finally arrived, lifted him onto a stretcher and quickly rolled him out. His face was grayish blue, his mouth hung open, rimmed with blood, and

55 his eyes were rolled back with a yellowish color on the rims.

The paramedics could be seen moving rhythmically forward and back through the small windows of the ambulance, whose light threw a red wash over the stunned watchers on the porch. The paramedics' hands were massaging his chest when someone said, "Did you tell them he took psilocybin? Did you tell them?"

60   "No, I . . . "

"My God, so tell them—do you want him to die?" Two people ran to tell the paramedics the student had eaten mushrooms five minutes before the attack.

It seemed irreverent to talk as the ambulance pulled away. My friend, who still saw his father's image, muttered, "That guy's dead." I put my arms around him half to com-

65 fort him, half to stop him from saying things I couldn't believe.

The next day, when I called someone who lived in the house, I found that my friend was right.

My hands began to shake and my eyes filled with tears for someone I didn't know. Weeks later the pain has dulled, but I still can't unravel the knot of emotion that has

70 moved from my stomach to my head. When I told one friend what happened, she shook her head and spoke of the stupidity of filling your body with chemical substances. People who would do drugs after seeing that didn't value their lives too highly, she said.

NO LESSONS

But others refused to read any universal lessons from the incident. Many of those I spoke to about the event considered him the victim of a freak accident, randomly struck down

Copyright ©1999 by Addison-Wesley Educational Publishers Inc.

75 by drugs as a pedestrian might be hit by a speeding taxi. They speculated that the student must have had special physical problems; what happened to him could not happen to them.

Couldn't it? Now when I hear people discussing drugs I'm haunted by the image of him lying on the floor, his body straining to rid itself of substances he chose to take.

80 Painful, undignified, unnecessary—like a wartime casualty. But in war, at least, lessons are supposed to be learned, so that old mistakes are not repeated. If this death cannot make people think and change, that will be an even greater tragedy.

(1,004 words)

—By Laura Rowley, from *Models for Writers* edited by Alfred Rosa and Paul Eschholz

THINKING AFTER READING

RECALL: Self-test your understanding. Your instructor may choose to give a true-false review.

REACT: How would this incident have affected you?

_____

REFLECT: What type of drug awareness programs would be most effective for

high school students? _____

_____

 THINK CRITICALLY: Are you convinced by what the author says about drugs? Why or why not? Write your answer on a separate sheet of paper.

CRITICAL READING
Answer the following with *T* (true) or *F* (false), or with *a, b, c,* or *d.*

____F____ 1. The story is told from the victim's point of view.

____T____ 2. The author's purpose is to persuade.

____T____ 3. The author's tone is disgust.

____c____ 4. All of the following words are negatively slanted *except*

     a. secondhand couch.
     b. gnashing sounds.
     c. ordinary guy.
     d. speeding taxi.

Mark the following statements as *F* (fact) or *O* (opinion).

____O____ 5. "The fastest way to end a party is to have someone die. . . ."

____F____ 6. "The living room was littered with beer cans. . . ."

____O____ 7. "People who would do drugs after seeing that don't value their lives. . . ."

Name _____

Date_____

COMPREHENSION QUESTIONS

Answer the following with *a, b, c,* or *d,* or fill in the blank. In order to help you analyze your strengths and weaknesses, the question types are indicated.

Main Idea ___d___ 1. The best statement of the main idea of this selection is:

    a. Drugs are addictive.
    b. Drug users should seek professional help.
    c. Drugs are destroying our society.
    d. Drugs are dangerous.

Inference ___b___ 2. The author mentions Len Bias, who was a talented basketball player, to indicate that

    a. drug abuse is a problem for the rich and famous.
    b. the victim she describes will not be considered important.
    c. both the famous and the unknown are affected by drugs.
    d. drug victims teach us a lesson.

Inference ___c___ 3. The author's description suggests that the people at the party were

    a. unstable drug addicts.
    b. high school students experimenting with drugs.
    c. average young people.
    d. close friends that she had known for years.

Inference 4. The author dramatizes the partygoers' hesitance to tell the paramedics about the psilocybin to show how they let their own concerns override the needs of the victim.

Inference ___b___ 5. The author mentions the hospital bills to emphasize

    a. the fear of parents.
    b. what runs through the mind in a crisis.
    c. the high cost of medical attention for drug abusers.
    d. the group's need to share financial responsibility.

Detail ___b___ 6. When the author told her friends about the overdose, most were

    a. convinced not to take drugs.
    b. unaffected.
    c. consumed by grief.
    d. eager to fight against drugs.

7. The phrase "he chose to take" is particularly meaningful because he took the drug of his own free will, even after his body had warned him, and thus ended his own life. He did it to himself.

Answer the following with *T* (true) or *F* (false).

Inference ___T___ 8. The friend whose father had died of a heart attack was correct in his assessment of the situation.

Inference ___T___ 9. The author feels that the victim had been forewarned of the danger of drugs to his system.

Copyright ©1999 by Addison-Wesley Educational Publishers Inc.

Inference _____F____10. The author is optimistic about the lessons to be learned from the victim's death.

VOCABULARY

Answer the following with *a, b, c,* or *d* for the word or phrase that best defines the boldface word as used in the selection. The number in parentheses indicates the line of the passage in which the word is located.

__b__ 1. "her **ambivalence**" (4)

    a. hatred
    b. uncertainty
    c. attraction
    d. belief

__a__ 2. "get **stupefied**" (8)

    a. groggy
    b. argumentative
    c. aggressive
    d. defensive

__d__ 3. "began to **convulse**" (21)

    a. swallow
    b. breathe heavily
    c. cough
    d. contract muscles

__c__ 4. "**miraculously** produced" (30)

    a. immediately
    b. finally
    c. marvelously
    d. hesitantly

__a__ 5. "just **audibly**" (45)

    a. barely heard
    b. religiously
    c. nervously
    d. quietly

__b__ 6. "**gnashing** sounds" (49)

    a. depressing
    b. grinding
    c. surprising
    d. deadly

__c__ 7. "**irreverent** to talk" (63)

    a. unnecessary
    b. not applicable
    c. disrespectful
    d. insane

__a__ 8. "**freak** accident" (74)

    a. abnormal
    b. sudden
    c. horrible
    d. major

__b__ 9. "They **speculated**" (75)

    a. wished
    b. guessed
    c. thought
    d. were told

__d__10. "wartime **casualty**" (80)

    a. assignment
    b. hero
    c. battle
    d. death

VOCABULARY ENRICHMENT

A. Study the similar-sounding words and choose one for each sentence.

accent: speech pattern
ascent: climb upward

  1. My roommate speaks with a slight (**accent**, ascent).

elicit: draw out
illicit: improper

  2. The police suspected (**elicit**, **illicit**) activities in the apartment.

eminent: well known
imminent: about to happen

3. The guest speaker was an (**eminent**, **imminent**) geologist from Russia.

B. Use context clues, word parts, and, if necessary, the dictionary, to write the meaning for each of the boldface words from a sociology textbook.

4. Immigrant children were **assimilated** into American society through the school system. <u>incorporated or made part of</u>

5. In order to live together in harmony, society demands **conformity** from its members. <u>similarity of action</u>

6. The study investigated the **correlation** between intelligence and wealth. <u>close relationship</u>

7. For his leadership in the community, he was held in high **esteem.** <u>regard; respect</u>

8. Rather than being members of her own **peer** group, most of her friends were ten years older. <u>persons of equal age or rank</u>

9. Society has become increasingly more **urban** as people leave the farms to look for jobs. <u>citified</u>

10. Through money, some people hope to achieve a higher social **status.** <u>position; standing</u>

C. Identify the boldface phrase as simile, metaphor, or personification and explain the meaning.

11. George Washington was the **father of the country** but he had no children of his own. <u>metaphor; first President</u>

12. Glaciers are melting **like warm ice cream** because pollution is trapping heat to the earth. <u>simile; becoming runny</u>

13. Some birds migrate over two continents, perhaps **singing their songs** in both English and Spanish. <u>personification; only people sing songs and speak English and Spanish</u>

14. In order to avoid 200 mile an hour winds that strike **like tornadoes,** one can climb Mount Everest only during two months of the year. <u>simile; fiercely, with great force</u>

15. Poetry **speaks to** both the heart and the brain. <u>personification; appeals to</u>

ASSESS YOUR LEARNING

Review confusing questions, seek clarification, and make notes in your text to help you remember new information and vocabulary.

Copyright ©1999 by Addison-Wesley Educational Publishers Inc.

Connect

Experiments have shown that, even in the face of an obviously correct decision, group members will conform to go along with an incorrect group decision. Read the following and reflect on your experiences with group conformity. Describe a group in which you are a member and explain the group's values. List five examples, either positive or negative, of ways in which you feel you conform with the group.

CONFORMITY

Social pressure is not confined to explicit attempts to convince you of something (persuasion) or to get you to do something by asking or telling you to do it (compliance or obedience). **Conformity** is yielding to group pressure when there is no direct order to do so. Every group has social norms, or implicit rules, that its members obey. Although we may prefer to see ourselves making our own choices, most of our behavior is dictated by group norms. Although adolescents typically take pride in rebelling against their parents' values and behavior patterns, the more thoughtful rebels recognize that the rebel group itself imposes constraints of speech, dress, and action.

Experiments have demonstrated how others' opinions can affect individuals' behavior. A powerful demonstration was devised by Asch (1956). Subjects saw a standard line, and had to decide which of the other lines was the same length as the standard. Typically, the subject made his or her decision after a number of other subjects announced theirs; and following a few trials in which the first few subjects (actually experimental confederates) made the obviously correct decision, there followed some trials in which the confederates unanimously chose the wrong alternative. A large percentage of the actual subjects (75 percent) went along with the group on at least one trial, despite the evidence of their own senses, whereas subjects who performed alone hardly ever erred.

—*Psychology* by Henry Roediger et al.

EXPLORE THE NET

- What type of information is available on drug abuse hotlines?
- Which drug rehabilitation treatment centers are located in your area or state, and what is the cost of treatment?

For additional readings and exercises, visit the Longman English Skills Web page at:

http://longman.awl.com/englishpages

For a user name and password, please see your instructor.

SELECTION 2 ◆ *Psychology*

THINKING BEFORE READING

Preview for content and organizational clues. Activate your schema and anticipate what you will learn.

What personality characteristics does your astrological sign indicate?

Would you ever go to a fortune teller?

What famous people seek the advice of astrologers?

This selection will probably tell me _____.

VOCABULARY PREVIEW

Are you familiar with these words?

universally	collaborated	conception	constellation	precise
slant	vague	irrelevant	consistently	woefully

What constellations can you name and locate?

Why does an architect need to be precise, relevant, and consistent?

If your project is woefully underbudgeted, what is your financial situation?

Your instructor may give a true-false vocabulary review before or after reading.

THINKING DURING READING

As you read, use the five thinking strategies of a good reader: predict, picture, relate, monitor, and correct.

ASTROLOGY—THE EARLIEST THEORY OF PERSONALITY

These are the questions we will deal with:

Is there any truth in astrology?
Why do people believe in astrology?

Astrology, the world's oldest theory of personality, is almost universally rejected by
5   scientists. For example, two hundred leading American and European scientists recently collaborated on a book, *Objections to Astrology* (Prometheus Books), in which they pointed out that a gravitational force from the doctor and nurses in the delivery room is greater than the distant stars, that the moment of conception made more sense as a point of influence than the time of birth, and that astrology is based on magical think-
10   ing—such as Mars is red, like blood, so people born under the "sign" of Mars are aggressive. But some people still believe in astrology—or half-believe.

Astrology claims that there are basically twelve different human types, and that finding out the astrological sign of a person allows one to describe and explain that person. "Claire is an Aquarius. She acts that way because she is an Aquarius." It even attempts to
15   predict what a person will do.

Astrology began in the Near East more than five thousand years ago. Ancient peoples charted the course of the planets, the stars, and our sun and moon. They noticed that some very important events in their lives—for example, annual floods and changing seasons—were marked by changes in the patterns of the heavenly bodies. Some early
20   astronomers thought: "The heavens seem to control the weather and the crops—surely they also control human lives!"

In astrology "the heavens" are divided into twelve "houses," each controlled by a particular constellation. The fate and acts of each human being are controlled by how the stars were arranged at the moment of that person's birth. Thus astrology is a theory that
25   has twelve major groups, or types.

Since fate is determined at the moment of birth, a good astrologer should be able to predict the exact course of any person's life. Astrologers try to make up a precise map of

Copyright ©1999 by Addison-Wesley Educational Publishers Inc.

"the heavens" as they were on the exact day and hour of the person's birth. This is called a *horoscope,* which means "map of the hour."

Do Astrologers Really Use Astrology?

30   When an astrologer makes up a horoscope for a person, does the astrologer stick strictly to business? Does the astrologer pay attention only to the matching of birth hour with the positions of "the stars," or do other things make a difference? In other words, do astrologers really practice astrology, or do other factors influence the predictions they make?

35   Two researchers selected eighteen astrologers who advertised that they do horoscopes by mail. The psychologists wrote letters to the astrologers that were supposedly coming from a couple who were thinking about getting married and were asking for advice about whether to marry or not. All of the letters gave the same information about the birth hour of each person. Half of the letters added a sentence noting that the couple
40   had been having a lot of arguments. The other half of the letters added a line stating that the couple really enjoyed being together and got along very well. So half the letters were negative and half were positive in their tone. Whether the astrologer got a positive or negative letter was determined by flipping a coin.

       Did the slant—positive or negative—of the letter from the couple influence the kind
45   of advice they got from the astrologer? Yes. Out of nine answers to the positive letter, six encouraged the couple to get married. One discouraged them, one was vague, and one was irrelevant. Out of nine answers to a negative letter, only one was encouraging. Six were vague, and two predicted disaster. Clearly, the tone of the letter sent by the couple influenced the marriage prediction made by the astrologers. So it looks as though the
50   astrologers' advice was based on their reaction to the tone of the letters sent by the couple, rather than on the theory of astrology. In fact, out of all eighteen, only one astrologer consistently stuck to the prediction of astrology and ignored the tone of the letters.

Criticisms of Astrology

Scientific critics of astrology point out that it is based on belief in magic instead of the
55   cause-and-effect kind of thinking used in science. They note that no one has shown a cause-and-effect relation between the heavens and human actions. Actually, scientists have noted that astrologers are often woefully ignorant of modern astronomy. They make whopping errors in figuring out the correct positions of "the stars." Also, astrology ignores both the biological nature of humans and the effect of the social environment on
60   them.

       With all of these problems, why do many people still believe in astrology? Imagine this situation: A couple who have been having a lot of arguments ask the advice of their astrologer about whether they should get married or not. The astrologer notices that they don't seem to be getting along very well, so the advice given is not to get married.
65   But the people do it anyway. Two years later they get divorced. Now the woman says: "Listen, I know from personal experience that astrology is true. If I had only followed the advice of my horoscope, I wouldn't have married him and wouldn't be divorced today." If astrologers usually base their advice on common sense instead of astrology, then some of the advice is going to be okay. Astrologers are probably as good as most people at
70   making commonsense predictions about people.

       A second reason that astrological predictions are sometimes believed is that they are so vague they can fit a whole range of different situations. Here is an actual quote from an astrological forecast in a daily newspaper: "General tendencies: get into all the various aspects of any plan that can improve your financial situation, whether requiring your own
75   individual efforts, or those of others operating on your behalf." First, notice that this is commonsense advice. Second, notice that there is practically no situation involving money to which these words cannot apply. They apply if your boss is thinking of raising

—*Celestial Map—Northern Hemisphere,* Albrecht Durer, The Metropolitan Museum of Art, Harris Brisbane Dick Fund, 1951. (51.537.1)

your salary, if a friend is doing your income tax for you, or if your aunt is thinking of
putting you in her will. Also, all of us need money. Therefore the general advice of this
80   "prediction" affects everyone. So anyone who *wanted* to believe in the astrologer's suggestion could easily find examples of how the advice "just fit me exactly."

      Why would someone want to believe? Astrology is mysterious and therefore interest-
ing. It is also simple. It does not require the kind of complex understanding of human
behavior that you have been learning as you read this book. Most people find other peo-
85   ple and themselves pretty hard to explain. You have to master books like this to understand the modern viewpoint. And astrology has become a fad. Twenty years ago anyone
who believed in it would have been considered badly educated. Today, it's trendy to ask:
"What's your sign?"

(1,176 words)

—*Psychology: What It Is/How to Use It* by David Watson

THINKING AFTER READING

RECALL: Self-test your understanding. Your instructor may choose to give a
true-false review.

REACT: Do you believe in astrology? Why or why not?

REFLECT: Both Nancy Reagan and Hillary Clinton are reported to have con-
sulted psychics for advice. Why do you think such bright and prominent women
would believe in psychics?

THINK CRITICALLY: Look in a newspaper or magazine and read your horoscope
for the day or month. Summarize the message and evaluate its relevance to you.
How do you feel the author of the horoscope arrived at the message? Write your
answer on a separate sheet of paper.

Copyright ©1999 by Addison-Wesley Educational Publishers Inc.

CRITICAL READING
Answer the following with *T* (true) or *F* (false), or with *a, b, c,* or *d.*

____F____ 1. The author seems to believe in astrological predictions.

____T____ 2. The author's purpose is to discuss the validity of astrology.

____F____ 3. The author's tone is humorous.

____c____ 4. All of the following words are negatively slanted *except*

     a. vague.
     b. woefully ignorant.
     c. cause-and-effect thinking.
     d. badly educated.

Mark the following statements of *F* (fact) and *O* (opinion).

____F____ 5. "Astrology claims that there are basically twelve different human types. . . . "

____O____ 6. "Twenty years ago anyone who believed in it would have been considered badly educated."

____F____ 7. "Today, it's trendy to ask: 'What's your sign?' "

Name _____

Date _____

COMPREHENSION QUESTIONS

Answer the following with *a, b, c,* or *d,* or fill in the blank. In order to help you analyze your strengths and weaknesses, the question types are indicated.

Main Idea   ___b___ 1. The best statement of the main idea of this selection is:

    a. Astrology was the beginning of a study of personality theory.
    b. Astrology is a theory of personality that some people believe but scientists reject.
    c. Astrology divides personality into twelve main groups or types.
    d. Early astronomers believed that the heavens controlled the weather, the crops, and human lives.

Detail   ___d___ 2. In describing personality, astrology claims to rely on all of the following *except*

    a. the exact day and hour of birth.
    b. the gravitational force of distant stars.
    c. the control of a particular constellation.
    d. the moment of conception.

Inference   ___d___ 3. The author uses the research study requesting advice on getting married to demonstrate that astrologers

    a. stick to the stars when making predictions.
    b. calculate horoscopes by the exact moment of birth.
    c. are unbiased in their predictions.
    d. do not predict exclusively from a study of the stars.

Inference   4. If astrological predictions were totally scientific, the researchers would have received eighteen replies concerning marriage that were

    ___the same_____.

Detail   ___a___ 5. Scientists criticize astrologers for

    a. miscalculating star positions.
    b. using cause-and-effect relations.
    c. considering the biological nature of humans.
    d. studying the effect of social environment on humans.

Inference   ___d___ 6. The author suggests that people believe in astrology for all of the following reasons *except*

    a. the advice is sometimes true.
    b. the advice is vague enough to fit many circumstances.
    c. people want to believe it because it is simple.
    d. people need a reliable scientific basis for decision making.

Inference   ___c___ 7. The author believes that astrology

    a. needs further study to determine its value.
    b. can become a valid science with a few changes.
    c. is a hoax.
    d. has not remained true to its early Near Eastern development.

Copyright © 1999 by Addison-Wesley Educational Publishers Inc.

Answer the following with *T* (true), *F* (false), or *CT* (can't tell).

Inference ___T___ 8. The author feels that astrological advice is influenced more by common sense than by the position of the stars.

Detail ___CT___ 9. More people believe in astrology today than at any other time in history.

Detail ___T___ 10. Astrology claims to base personality type on the "house" in which you were born.

SUMMARY

Write a summary of this selection on a separate sheet of paper.

VOCABULARY

Answer the following with *a, b, c,* or *d* for the word or phrase that best defines the boldface word as used in the selection. The number in parentheses indicates the line of the passage in which the word is located.

___d___ 1. "almost **universally** rejected" (4)

    a. carelessly
    b. logically
    c. never
    d. generally

___c___ 2. "**collaborated** on a book" (6)

    a. competed
    b. wrote separately
    c. worked jointly
    d. reported

___a___ 3. "the moment of **conception**" (8)

    a. becoming pregnant
    b. being born
    c. acquiring knowledge
    d. experiencing thought

___d___ 4. "controlled by a particular **constellation**" (22–23)

    a. religious tenet
    b. gravitational pull
    c. sign
    d. pattern of stars

___a___ 5. "make up a **precise** map" (27)

    a. exact
    b. large
    c. neat
    d. conclusive

___c___ 6. "Did the **slant**" (44)

    a. error
    b. purpose
    c. bias
    d. subject

___b___ 7. "one was **vague**" (46)

    a. interesting
    b. unclear
    c. supporting
    d. positive

___a___ 8. "one was **irrelevant**" (46–47)

    a. inapplicable
    b. negative
    c. confusing
    d. understandable

___d___ 9. "**consistently** stuck to" (52)

    a. seldom
    b. infrequently
    c. mildly
    d. steadily

___a___ 10. "often **woefully** ignorant" (57)

    a. deplorably
    b. knowingly
    c. purposefully
    d. slightly

VOCABULARY ENRICHMENT

A. Use context clues and word parts to write the meaning of the boldface words in the following paragraph from a psychology book.

An organism can **replenish** its water **deficit** in two ways—by drinking and by recovering water from the kidneys before it is **excreted** as urine. A water deficit motivates the organism to drink and also sets off a homeostatic mechanism by stimulating the release of the antidiuretic hormone (ADH) from the pituitary gland. ADH regulates the kidneys so that water is reabsorbed into the bloodstream and only very concentrated urine is formed. (After a night's sleep, you may notice that your urine is a darker color and has a stronger odor than it does at other times of the day; your body has recovered water from your kidneys to **compensate** for the fact that you have not consumed fluids while you were sleeping.) This **homeostatic** mechanism can maintain the body's water balance only to a certain point, however. When the water deficit is too great, thirst becomes intense and the organism is **impelled** to find water.

—*Introduction to Psychology* by Rita Atkinson et al.

1. replenish: <u>refill</u>
2. deficit: <u>shortage</u>
3. excreted: <u>eliminated</u>
4. compensate: <u>make up for or overcome</u>
5. homeostatic: <u>equal balance or state of equilibrium</u>
6. impelled: <u>forced</u>

B. Create your own analogies for each type of relationship. Think of a second word that establishes the indicated relationship, and then finish the analogy with a similar comparison.

7. Degree: *Damp* is to _____<u>wet</u>_____ as _____<u>cool</u>_____ is to _____<u>cold</u>_____.

8. Part to whole: *Toes* are to _____<u>feet</u>_____ as _____<u>finger</u>_____ is to _____<u>hand</u>_____.

9. Cause and effect: *Careless* is to _____<u>accident</u>_____ as _____<u>anger</u>_____ is to _____<u>fight</u>_____.

10. Classification: *Airplane* is to _____<u>transportation</u>_____ as _____<u>sweater</u>_____ is to _____<u>clothing</u>_____.

C. Choose one of the following transitional words or phrases to complete each sentence.

however   for instance   thus   in addition   in a like manner

11. Freud was the first to conceptualize a theory of personality, _____<u>thus</u>_____ he is considered the father of psychoanalysis.

12. Freud's theories were considered by many to be too sexual and caused some of his followers to leave; _____<u>for instance</u>_____, a group of his followers who broke away were known as neo-Freudians.

13. Karen Horney was a neo-Freudian who, _____<u>in addition</u>_____, became the first American female psychologist.

14. Carl Jung began with Freud studying personality; _____<u>however</u>_____, later in life he focused on learning theory.

15. Although the neo-Freudians discarded some of the negativity of Freud, they retained Freud's belief that the subconscious affects the personality

Copyright ©1999 by Addison-Wesley Educational Publishers Inc.

and, <u>in a like manner</u>, popularized their own theories through research and publication.

ASSESS YOUR LEARNING

Review confusing questions, seek clarification, and make notes in your text to help you remember new information and vocabulary.

Connect

Have you ever had an experience in which you felt the intervention of super-natural forces? Read the following passage written by someone who believes in angels. Describe any experience that you have had or that a friend has mentioned that suggested a supernatural force.

ANGELS ALL AROUND US

I found it fascinating that, although angel incidents varied, the *reaction* of those involved was almost always the same, and twofold: first, a hesitancy about sharing, then, once that was overcome, an awe that, even years later, was still powerfully aroused by the memory of the incident.

F. S. Smythe, who attempted to climb Mount Everest in 1933, wrote of the same "friendly presence" in his account of the expedition. "A strange feeling possessed me that I was accompanied by another. In its company I could not feel lonely, nor could I come to any harm. It was always there to sustain me on my solitary climb up the snow-covered slabs. (When) I halted and extracted some mint cake from my pocket, it was so near and so strong that instinctively I divided the mint into two halves and turned round with one half in my hand to offer it to my companion."

Another respondent told me of a time when she was seventeen and, for several nights in a row, felt a presence at the foot of her bed. "I didn't actually see anything," she explained. "It was more the kind of feeling you get when you're aware of someone looking at you when you're in traffic, or reading, or sitting with your back to a doorway."

She sensed that there were two angels standing side by side, facing her. Their mission seemed to be one of simple reassurance, and the young girl felt warm, sheltered, and at peace.

—*Angels All Around Us* by Joan Webster Anderson

EXPLORE THE NET

- Find instruction on astrology for beginners to locate information on how to get started reading the stars.
- Read your daily or monthly horoscope in three different sources. Summarize the information and point out the differences.

For additional readings and exercises, visit the Longman English Skills Web page at:

http://longman.awl.com/englishpages

For a user name and password, please see your instructor.

SELECTION 3	*Business*

THINKING BEFORE READING

Preview for content and organizational clues. Activate your schema and anticipate what you will learn.

Who do you know who has a female boss?

Are female bosses more likely to be nitpickers than male bosses?

This selection will probably tell me _____.

VOCABULARY PREVIEW

Are you familiar with these words?

disdain	conventional	competent	apparent	shuns
clout	echelons	expertise	flounder	relentless

What does the noun form of *flounder* mean?

What does taking out a conventional loan on a house mean?

What is your area of expertise?

Your instructor may give a true-false vocabulary review before or after reading.

THINKING DURING READING

As you read, use the five thinking strategies of a good reader: predict, picture, relate, monitor, and correct.

THE JOB MAKES THE PERSON

"I'd never work for a woman," a woman draftsman told me. "They are too mean and petty."

Research on female workers has for years looked for sex differences on the job. Women, the surveys show, have lower aspirations than men, less commitment to work, and more concern with friendships than with the work itself. And many people assume
5   that women make poor leaders because their personalities do not allow them to be assertive. Women who do make it to management positions are presumed to fit the mold of the dictatorial, bitchy boss.

To explain why more women don't seek or find career success, many people concentrate on supposed personality differences between the sexes: women's "motive to
10   avoid success" or incapacity to handle power. Or they look at childhood training and educational training: how women learn to limit their ambitions and hide their accomplishments. Because women learn that high achievement means a loss of traditional femininity, they choose to preserve the latter and sacrifice the former.

When I began to study women in work organizations three years ago, I also was
15   looking for sex-related individual differences that would explain women's absence from high-status, powerful jobs. If women were ever going to make it in a man's world, the conventional wisdom said, we would have to get them when they're young and make sure they don't pick up any motives to avoid success or other bad habits. When I looked more closely at how real people in organizations behave, however, the picture changed. I
20   could find nothing about women in my own research and that of others that was not equally true of men in some situations. For example, some women do have low job aspi-

Copyright ©1999 by Addison-Wesley Educational Publishers Inc.

rations, but so do men who are in positions of blocked opportunity. Some women managers are too interfering and coercive, but so are men who have limited power and responsibility in their organizations. Some women in professional careers behave in
25 stereotyped ways and tend to regard others of their sex with disdain, but so do men who are tokens—the only member of their group at work.

So I dropped my search for sex differences, and I concentrated instead on three aspects of a business organization that do the most to explain the conventional wisdom about women: opportunity, power, and tokenism.

OPPORTUNITY

30 Are women less ambitious and committed to work than men? According to one large corporation I investigated, they are. This company has surveyed 111 hourly employees in white-collar jobs about their attitudes toward promotion. Sure enough, the men showed greater motivation to advance in rank than the women, and the men had higher self-esteem, considering themselves more competent in the skills that would win them pro-
35 motions. The women seemed much less interested in advancement, sometimes saying that they cared more about their families.

Yet in this company, like many, there were dramatic differences in the actual opportunities for promotion that men and women had. Men made up only a small proportion of white-collar workers; most were clustered in professional roles with steps toward man-
40 agement positions. Over two thirds of the women were secretaries or clerks in dead-end jobs. They could hope to advance two or three steps up to executive secretary, and there

they would stop. Only rarely had a secretary moved up into professional or managerial ranks. No wonder the women found promotion a far-fetched idea.

45   If the company had looked at women in high-ranking jobs, the apparent sex differ-ence in work attitudes would have vanished utterly. In my interviews, I found that ambi-tion, self-esteem, and career commitment were all flourishing among women in sales jobs, which are well-paid and on the way to top management. Indeed, one successful young woman in the sales force told me she hoped someday to run the company.

Lack of opportunity to succeed, not a personality style that shuns success, is often
50   what separates the unambitious from the climbers—and the women from the men. The great majority of women hold jobs that have short, discouraging career ladders—secre-tarial, clerical, factory work. When the jobs include opportunities for advancement, women want to advance. But jobs without such opportunities depress a person's ambi-tion and self-esteem, for men as well as women.

GOSSIP AT THE DEAD END

55   Opportunity also determines what kinds of relationships a person forms on the job. Work-ers who have few prospects of moving up and out compensate by making close friends. The very limitations of the job ensure that those friends will be around for a while, and one better make sure that at least the social side of an unchallenging job is pleasurable. Being well-liked becomes another meaning of success to people in dead-end work, and if
60   you've got the best stories to offer the office, you can add a bit of excitement to mun-dane work. So it often looks as if women are "talk-oriented," not "task-oriented," in their jobs. Some employers point to the gossipy office coffee klatch as a direct result of women's natural concern with people, rather than with achievement. Instead, I think it is more accurate to say that female socializing reflects the jobs they have.

65   Highly mobile jobs demand that a person be most concerned with the work. Such jobs make close friendships with co-workers less likely. The corporate world requires its participants to be willing to relocate, to surpass rivals without hesitation, to use other people to advance in status. The aggressive, striving junior executive is as much a creation of his place in the organization hierarchy as is the talkative, unambi-
70   tious secretary.

POWER

One of the reasons given to explain why so few women have organizational authority is that people don't like female bosses. In a 1965 *Harvard Business Review* survey of almost 2,000 executives, few respondents of either sex said that they or others would feel com-fortable about working for a woman, although the women were more ready to do so
75   than the men. Over half of the men felt that women were "temperamentally unfit" for management, echoing the stereotype of the ineffective lady boss who substitutes picki-ness about rules for leadership.

In fact, there is no solid evidence of lasting differences in the leadership styles of men and women. Nor is there evidence that people who work for women have lower morale.
80   Research points in the other direction: those who have worked for a woman boss are much more likely to be favorably disposed toward female leaders.

One clear factor distinguishes good leaders from bad, effective from ineffective, liked from disliked. It is not sex, but power. It is not a matter of personality, but of clout.

Just because people have been given formal authority by virtue of position and title,
85   they do not necessarily have equal access to power in the organization. It is not enough to be the most skillful handler of people in the world. One also needs system-granted power to back up one's demands and decisions and to ensure the confidence and loyalty of subordinates.

System power comes from having influence in the upper echelons of the organi-
90   zation, through membership in informal inner circles and by having high status. As a number of social-psychological studies have shown, people who bring such signs of status and influence into a group tend to be better liked—not resented—and to get

Copyright ©1999 by Addison-Wesley Educational Publishers Inc.

their way more often. Organization members, as my interviews revealed, prove to be very knowledgeable about who is in and who is out, and when I asked them to
95 describe desirable bosses, they decidedly preferred those with power to those with style or expertise.

TOKENISM

I studied what happens to women when they do manage to get closer to the top, and I uncovered a range of familiar situations. Male managers who could not accept a woman as a colleague without constantly reminding her that she was "different." Women who
100 could not make themselves heard in committee meetings and who felt left out. Bright women who hid their accomplishments. A female sales executive who felt that most women should not be hired for jobs like hers. A woman scientist who let another woman in her unit flounder without help. A woman faculty member who brought cookies to department meetings and mothered her colleagues.
105   All the characters were there, dressed in their sex roles. Yet I saw that even so the play was not about sex. It was about numbers. These women were all tokens, alone or nearly alone in a world of male peers and bosses. When people take on a token status— whether they are female scientists or male nurses or black executives in a white company—they share certain experiences that influence their behavior.
110   Tokens, by definition, stand out from the crowd. In one company I studied, the first 12 women to go to work among 400 men set the rumor mill in motion. They caused more talk and attracted more attention, usually for their physical attributes, than new male employees. The men tended to evaluate the women against their image of the ideal female rather than the ideal colleague, and the women, under relentless scrutiny, felt
115 they could not afford to make mistakes.

THE JOB MAKES THE WOMAN

What I am suggesting is that the job makes the man—and the woman. People bring much of themselves and their histories to their work, but I think we have overlooked the tremendous impact of an organization's structure on what happens to them once they are there.
120   If my approach is right, it suggests that change will not come from changing personalities or attitudes, and not from studying sex or race differences. Change will come only from interrupting the self-perpetuating cycles of blocked opportunity, powerlessness, and tokenism.
  Take the case of Linda S., a woman who had been a secretary in a large corporation
125 for 16 years. Five years ago, she would have said that she never wanted to be anything but a secretary. She also would have told you that since she had recently had children she was thinking of quitting. She said secretarial work was not a good enough reason to leave the children.
  Then came an affirmative-action program, and Linda was offered a promotion. She
130 wavered. It would mean leaving her good female friends for a lonely life among male managers. Her friends thought she was abandoning them. She worried whether she could handle the job. But her boss talked her into it and promised to help, reassuring her that he would be her sponsor.
  So Linda was promoted, and now she handles a challenging management job most
135 successfully. Seeing her friends is the least of her many reasons to come to work every day, and her ambitions have soared. She wants to go right to the top.
  "I have 15 years left to work," she says. "And I want to move up six grades to corporate vice president—at least."

(1,810 words)

—Rosabeth Moss Kanter from *Understanding Diversity* by Carol Harvey and
M. June Allard

THINKING AFTER READING

RECALL: Self-test your understanding. Your instructor may choose to give a true-false review.

REACT: What has been your experience with knowing, observing, or working for a female boss? _____

REFLECT: List the assumptions about women workers that are stated in the beginning and beside each, list evidence presented that substantiates or refutes those assumptions. _____

_____

_____

 THINK CRITICALLY: As a new manager of a business organization, what strategies would you use to motivate employees in dead-end jobs?

CRITICAL READING

1. Why does the author begin the selection with "I'd never work for a woman," a woman draftsman told me. "They are too mean and petty"?
   To catch the reader's attention _____

2. What is the purpose of the first five paragraphs? To explain misconceptions in previous research on sex differences and to introduce the author's focus.

3. What is the purpose of the anecdote about Linda S. at the end of the selection? Does the story offer valid proof of the argument? The author uses it as an example to prove her point about opportunity, but it is not valid proof.

4. What is the author's bias on female bosses? What is your bias? No different than male leadership.

5. How would you evaluate the statement, supported by the 1965 *Harvard Business Review* survey, that people do not like female bosses? Most had probably never known a female boss and were responding to a stereotype.

Copyright ©1999 by Addison-Wesley Educational Publishers Inc.

Name _____

Date _____

COMPREHENSION QUESTIONS

Answer the following with *a, b, c,* or *d.* In order to help you analyze your strengths and weaknesses, the question types are indicated.

Main Idea ___c___ 1. The best statement of the main idea of this selection is:

    a. More women than men work in jobs that lack advancement opportunities.
    b. Surveys have shown that people do not want to work for female bosses.
    c. Work attitudes are molded more by the job itself than by sex or racial differences.
    d. Men have not given women credit for their ability to succeed in high-ranking jobs.

Inference ___b___ 2. The tone of the passage is

    a. angry.
    b. objective.
    c. sarcastic.
    d. humorous.

Inference ___c___ 3. The author feels that the major problem with the company's method of surveying 111 hourly white-collar workers was

    a. more women than men were surveyed.
    b. the women cared more about their families than the men.
    c. the opportunities for advancement were not equal for the men and women surveyed.
    d. the men had higher self-esteem and would thus be more likely to win promotions.

Inference ___d___ 4. The author feels that the major reason women workers are often considered more talk-oriented than task-oriented is because

    a. women bring a strong sense of community to the workplace.
    b. women make close friends easily and have a natural concern for others.
    c. female socializing is acceptable on the job.
    d. women use friendship to compensate for lack of advancement opportunities in dead-end jobs.

Detail ___a___ 5. The author defines the system-granted power that a leader needs to be successful within an organization as

    a. being an informal member of the top group of decision makers.
    b. being a skillful handler of people.
    c. having the courage to back up one's demands and make decisions.
    d. having the style, personality, and desire to lead.

Inference ___c___ 6. The author implies all of the following about women *except*

    a. they must work harder to advance.
    b. they are regarded by colleagues as different.
    c. they are hired because the majority of the employees want change.
    d. their experiences as tokens influence their behaviors.

Inference   __d__   7. The conclusion, "Women are in dead-end jobs, therefore most women are not ambitious in seeking professional advancement," is an example of an error in reasoning called

        a. straw person.
        b. transfer.
        c. misleading analogy.
        d. circular reasoning.

Mark the following as a statement of fact (*F*) or opinion (*O*).

__O__   8. Highly mobile jobs demand that a person be most concerned with the work.

__F__   9. Research points in the other direction: those who have worked for a woman boss are much more likely to be favorably disposed toward female leaders.

__O__ 10. Opportunity also determines what kinds of relationships a person forms on the job.

VOCABULARY

Answer the following with *a, b, c,* or *d* for the word or phrase that best defines the boldface word as used in the selection. The number in parentheses indicates the line of the passage in which the word is located.

__b__   1. "regard . . . with **disdain**" (25)

        a. anger
        b. scorn
        c. competition
        d. uncertainty

__a__   2. "explain the **conventional** wisdom" (28)

        a. traditional
        b. scientific
        c. unspoken
        d. incorrect

__a__   3. "more **competent** in the skills" (34)

        a. qualified
        b. highly paid
        c. interested
        d. flexible

__a__   4. "**apparent** sex difference" (44–45)

        a. obvious
        b. unwanted
        c. unnoticed
        d. natural

__c__   5. "**shuns** success" (49)

        a. courts
        b. overlooks
        c. avoids
        d. loses

__a__   6. "Not . . . personality, but of **clout**" (83)

        a. influence
        b. charm
        c. education
        d. intelligence

__c__   7. "upper **echelons** of the organization" (89–90)

        a. limits
        b. values
        c. ranks
        d. point of view

__b__   8. "style or **expertise**" (96)

        a. experience
        b. know-how
        c. leadership
        d. personality

Copyright ©1999 by Addison-Wesley Educational Publishers Inc.

____c____ 9. "**flounder** without help" (103) ____b____10. "under **relentless** scrutiny" (114)

    a. quit   a. unnecessary
    b. get fired   b. persistent
    c. struggle   c. needless
    d. beg   d. untimely

VOCABULARY ENRICHMENT

Select the word from the following list that best completes each sentence.

disdain	conventional	competent	apparent	shuns
clout	echelons	expertise	flounder	relentless

1. The couple chose a ____conventional____ wedding format with a white dress and formal attire.

2. Few employees in a large corporation have the ____clout____ to be able to comfortably call the president and ask for advice.

3. The protesters showed their ____disdain____ for the flag by cutting and burning it.

4. The paparazzi were ____relentless____ in their pursuit of Princess Diana for pictures to sell to the tabloids.

5. Workers who are ____competent____ can get the job done without supervision and do not need to look for excuses.

6. Often a professional athlete has a high level of ____expertise____ in more than one sport.

7. Success is more likely to come to a person who welcomes work rather than ____shuns____ it.

8. The clues indicated an ____apparent____ accident rather than suggesting a devious murder.

9. Mentors are frequently assigned to new students so they will not ____flounder____ without someone to call for help.

10. In a sport such as golf, only a few players in the top ____echelons____ make the cut to play in the major tournaments.

ASSESS YOUR LEARNING

Review confusing questions, seek clarification, and make notes in your text to help you remember new information and vocabulary.

EXPLORE THE NET

- What other books has Rosabeth Moss written on organizational change?
- What type of information is available on the *Harvard Business Review?*

For additional readings and exercises, visit the Longman English Skills Web page at:

http://longman.awl.com/englishpages

For a user name and password, please see your instructor.

Copyright ©1999 by Addison-Wesley Educational Publishers Inc.

Independent Textbook Assignments

◆ *Can you apply what you have learned?*
◆ *Can you organize for textbook study?*
◆ *How well can you prepare for an exam?*

Copyright ©1999 by Addison-Wesley Educational Publishers Inc.

Apply What You Have Learned ◆◆◆◆◆◆◆◆◆◆

Do you know now how to study an actual textbook chapter on your own, prepare for a test on the chapter, and then do well on the exam? This chapter provides two longer textbook selections for you to "show off" what you have learned. Your job as an efficient independent learner is to read, study, and learn. For each selection, your instructor has provided both multiple-choice and essay questions for your exams.

Take control and organize your study according to the strategies outlined in this text. Preview, set goals, and activate your schema before you begin to read. Use the five thinking strategies of good readers while you are reading, annotating, and taking notes. After reading, recall what you have read and predict possible exam questions. Study and use time management techniques to make sure that you are 100 percent prepared on each examination date.

Independent Assignment 1: Psychology ◆◆◆◆◆◆◆◆◆◆

Before reading the chapter, read the following article on smoking to activate your schema. Annotate the article and take notes on some of the compelling facts.

THE JOY OF SMOKING

It is interesting to watch an old film in which the lead characters smoke. Generally, lead characters today don't smoke. Smoking is increasingly characteristic of poorer and less-educated people, or those who started before the hazards were known. (Interestingly, it seems to me that there are regional differences. You don't see many people smoking in Florida, Colorado, and California, while you may see it more often in Missouri, Illinois, and Pennsylvania.)

Smoking is hard to explain even on the basis of smell and cost, but on the basis of health it is incomprehensible. The American Cancer Society tells us that a person aged 25 who smokes two packs of cigarettes a day will live about $8\frac{1}{2}$ years less than a non-smoker. Furthermore, the end of the smoker's life may be marked by extreme pain due to lung cancer, as well as cancer of the mouth, bladder, pancreas, and esophagus. Even in the absence of cancer, the smoker may be severely debilitated by emphysema when thickened bronchioles and alveolar walls cause trapped air to permanently inflate the lungs. The inefficiency of the damaged lungs may affect both the heart (increasing the risk of coronary heart disease and heart attacks) and brain (bringing on behavioral changes, including sluggishness and irritability). Pregnant women who smoke increase the risk of stillbirths, and those who deliver tend to have smaller, sicker children.

Fortunately, if you quit in time, the damage is largely reversible. Within a year you are markedly at less risk for coronary heart disease and 10 to 15 years later, you are at no greater risk for premature death and coronary heart disease than a nonsmoker. The coughing may stop after a few weeks and, unless the damage is too great, lung function is likely to improve over time. The bottom line is simple: if you smoke, quit.

—*Biology: The World of Life* by Robert Wallace

What is ironic about the title? _____

Do you agree that there are regional differences in smoking behaviors? _____

_____

Why do you think it is so difficult for people to quite smoking? _____

_____

If you were helping a smoker quit, what techniques would you use? _____

_____

What additional research data could you add on the hazards of smoking? _____

_____

Compare your notes with those of a classmate. Did you both write down the

same facts? _____

THINKING BEFORE READING

Preview the chapter by reading the subheadings, boldface print, and inserted questions. What focus do you predict this chapter will take on smoking?

How much time do you predict you will need to read, annotate, and take notes on this chapter?

Do you plan to take notes using an informal outline format or a system of note-taking?

THINKING DURING READING

As you read, predict, picture, relate, monitor, and correct. In addition, since you will need to study this material for an exam, annotate and take notes on what you want to remember in each section.

For the first few sections, compare your notes with the notetaking examples. Although the format may differ, is the content about the same? When you have finished the chapter, compare your notes with those of fellow classmates.

SMOKING: HAZARDOUS TO YOUR HEALTH

According to the U.S. Department of Health and Human Services, cigarette smoking is the single most preventable cause of death and disease in the United States. It will adversely affect the health of one out of every three people who smoke cigarettes. Most people know that smoking is bad for their health and that the more they smoke, the more at risk they are. It is therefore not surprising that most professionals in the medical field are concerned with the prevention of smoking and with encouraging those already smoking to stop.

Compare notes.

U.S. Health Dept.
Smoking most preventable cause of death
& disease in U.S.

SMOKING PREVENTION

The first puff on a cigarette is rarely pleasant. Why, then, do people ever start smoking? The answer is complex, since the initiation of smoking involves psychological, social, and biological factors. Although for some people smoking is an expression of rebellion against their parents or society, most people begin to smoke in response to social pressures from peers or in imitation of role models such as family members, movie stars, and athletes. Once a person begins to smoke, there is additional biological pressure to continue smok-

Copyright ©1999 by Addison-Wesley Educational Publishers Inc.

The single most preventable cause of death and disease in the United States is cigarette smoking. Posters like this one with Brooke Shields attempt to get young people to quit smoking by pointing out that smoking is also bad for your looks and smell.

ing because of the addictive effects of nicotine. Therefore, one way to reduce the number of smokers is to prevent people from taking their first puff.

Those concerned with the prevention of smoking face a tough uphill battle in having to contend with the effects of peer pressure and the advertising budgets of the large tobacco companies. Smoking provides adolescents with immediate short-term reinforcements from their peers, while the long-term health disadvantages do not seem at all relevant to them. Therefore, the most successful techniques geared toward prevention of smoking in young people have focused on the short-term detrimental effects of tobacco use, such as coughing, bad breath, difficulty in breathing, dependence on an addictive substance, and the effects on personal appearance and hygiene. Most young people do not realize that smoking makes them smell as well as taste like cigarette smoke until the facts are converted to down-to-earth terms like, "Who wants to kiss a dirty ashtray?" Another successful technique involves using peer role models to teach specific social skills that enable young people to resist the social pressure to start smoking.

Compare notes.

Why smoke?
  Psy, soc, & bio. factors
  Soc = peer pressure & imitation of role models
  Bio = addicted to nicotine
Prevention
  Stop youth by negative ads

CESSATION OF SMOKING

Question: What's the best way to stop smoking?

It is difficult for many people to quit smoking, since the same social pressures that help initiate the habit also help to maintain it. These social pressures, combined with the ritual of smoking and the fact that nicotine is an addictive substance, make smoking an especially hard habit to break. The maintenance of smoking behaviors can be viewed as the result of both positive and negative reinforcement. Most smokers tend to associate smoking with pleasant things, such as good food, friends, and sex, as well as the "high" that nicotine gives them, so smoking is positively reinforced by these factors. When smokers are deprived of their cigarettes for a few hours, they start to go through an extremely unpleasant physical withdrawal. When they are finally able to smoke, the nicotine reduces these symptoms, and smoking is thereby negatively reinforced. Any program designed to help smokers break their habit must therefore combat both the positive and the negative reinforcement obtained from smoking.

Several approaches are currently being used to help people quit smoking. In addition to ad campaigns designed to alert the general public to the dangers of cigarette smoking, both cognitive and behavioral techniques have been developed.

One cognitive approach used to break the smoking habit is **covert sensitization,** a form of cognitive classical conditioning. With this technique, smokers are asked to mentally associate something extremely unpleasant with smoking. For example:

> Imagine that your favorite brand of cigarettes is sitting on a table in front of you. Now imagine that a housefly lands on the cigarettes and lays her eggs inside the cigarettes. The eggs hatch and little maggots begin to crawl around inside each cigarette. You now pick up the cigarette and put it in your mouth. You light up and draw in your first breath with the maggots still inside. The heat of the cigarette forces the maggots to crawl into your mouth and down your throat and start to eat at your body from the inside out.

If you were a smoker who used this imagery to try to make yourself sick every time you felt like having a cigarette, there is a good chance that you would be able to combat some of the positive associations that cigarette smoking might have for you.

Compare notes.

How to stop?
  Smoking assoc. with positives & negatives
Covert sensitization
  Cognitive classical conditioning
  Change mental assoc. to the unpleasant
  Result: imaging makes you sick & thus fights
    positive assoc.
Ex. maggots in throat

Another approach to trying to eliminate the positive reinforcement of smoking behavior is **stimulus control**. With this technique, the individual is made aware of stimuli leading to the unwanted behavior and these stimuli are then controlled or reduced. The smoker is asked to make a list of the situations in which he or she normally smokes. By doing so, the individual is made aware of the specific situations, or stimuli, that trigger smoking behavior. Once the smoker is aware of these specific situations, he or she can be extra aware of the tendency to smoke at these times and more able to combat the urge to smoke. Or the smoker can substitute another behavior (preferably something that is not equally "addicting") or can try to avoid the situations altogether. For example, if a smoker tends to light up right after meals and snacks, he or she could reduce the number

Copyright ©1999 by Addison-Wesley Educational Publishers Inc.

of meals per day or could have a pencil handy after meals and doodle on a napkin instead of smoking.

Although covert sensitization and stimulus control have been used successfully in reducing the number of cigarettes smoked each day, they have not been very successful in helping people quit completely. More successful strategies have included reinforcement for not smoking, aversion therapies, and slow withdrawal using nicotine gum.

If an appropriate reinforcer can be found, reinforcement for *not* smoking can be very effective. Basically, this technique involves choosing one or several alternative behaviors to smoking and trying to reinforce those behaviors. Ideally, these behaviors should be incompatible with smoking. Many forms of physical exercise fit this criteria—you certainly can't smoke when you're swimming. The most common reinforcer used is money. The subject makes a large monetary deposit and is then paid for doing things other than smoking. This type of approach has been successful for some people.

Question: Is this how they help people stop smoking in smoking clinics such as the Schick centers?

Most commercial smoking clinics use **aversion therapy** . . . to help people stop smoking. In this approach, smoking behavior is paired with some kind of aversive stimulus, such as electric shock or an abundance of cigarette smoke. In typical electrical shock aversion therapy, electrodes are attached to smokers' hands or wrists. The smokers are then asked to begin smoking cigarettes. Each time they take a puff, they receive an unpleasant shock. The electrical shock becomes paired with the cigarette, and the smoker is classically conditioned to feel uncomfortable around cigarettes. Some researchers using this method have reported up to 70 percent abstinence after one year. However, most controlled research on smoking and electrical shock has found no difference between the shock group and a control group. This ineffectiveness has been attributed to the fact that once smokers are no longer hooked up to the shock device, they know that they won't get a shock if they smoke. In conditioning terms, they have failed to generalize the associations learned in the laboratory to the real world.

A type of aversion therapy that gets around this generalization problem uses cigarette smoke as the aversive stimulus. The most widely used technique is called "rapid smoking," in which the smoker takes a puff every 6 seconds (10 puffs per minute) while concentrating on the negative sensations produced by the rapid smoking. If the smoker gets sick, so much the better. Rapid smoking, accompanied by long-term support or therapy, has been a highly successful cessation technique. The one major drawback is that it can produce a moderate amount of stress on the heart and lungs; therefore, it should be used only under the supervision of a medical doctor.

Another cessation strategy is to deal with the physical addiction to nicotine experienced by cigarette smokers. If they can become less dependent on this addictive substance, they will have a better chance at quitting smoking altogether. Use of nicotine gum is one way to slowly withdraw smokers from the dependency of nicotine.

Freedom from dependence on nicotine is, of course, not enough to prevent former smokers from wanting to smoke; both nicotine gum and sheer willpower must be used in conjunction with other techniques to help smokers eliminate their psychological need for cigarettes. For instance, two common problems faced by those trying to kick the habit are fear of weight gain and lack of replacements for the rituals associated with smoking. They often find themselves wondering, "What can I put in my mouth?" and "What can I do with my hands?" Therefore, an effective smoking cessation program must consist not only of techniques for physically kicking the habit but also of suggestions for controlling weight and for countering the social pressures and replacing the rituals associated with smoking.

—*Psychology in Action* by Karen Huffman et al.

THINKING AFTER READING

Recall what you have read with a "study buddy" and prepare to take an examination on the material.

1. What are the major points in this chapter? _____

_____

2. What essay questions might be asked about this chapter? _____

_____

3. What multiple-choice or true-false questions might be asked? _____

_____

4. What will be your time schedule for studying the material in this chapter?

_____

5. When is the exam and how much will it count toward your final grade?

_____

THINKING AFTER THE EXAM

PERSONAL FEEDBACK 1

Name_____

1. How would you evaluate your grade on the exam?

_____

2. Did you make the grade that you studied to get? Why or why not?

_____

3. What on the exam came as a surprise to you?

_____

4. What was on the exam that was not included in your notes?

_____

5. How will you study differently next time?

_____

6. How will you manage your time differently next time?

_____

7. Did you study with a "study buddy"? Why or why not?

_____

Copyright ©1999 by Addison-Wesley Educational Publishers Inc.

Independent Assignment 2:
History ◆◆◆◆◆◆◆◆◆◆◆◆

THINKING BEFORE READING

Preview the chapter by reading the subheadings. Write down your time plan for reading, annotating, notetaking, and studying this chapter.

THINKING DURING READING

As you read, predict, picture, relate, monitor, and correct. In addition, since you will need to study this material for an exam, annotate and take notes on what you want to remember in each section. Use the study questions in the bulleted lists to test your comprehension.

THE SURGE WESTWARD

Early in April 1846, 87 pioneers led by George Donner, a well-to-do 62-year-old farmer, set out from Illinois for California. As this group of pioneers headed westward, they never imagined the hardship that awaited them. The pioneers' 27 wagons were loaded not only with necessities, but with fancy foods, liquor, and such luxuries as built-in beds and stoves.

In Wyoming, the party decided to take a shortcut, having read in a guidebook that pioneers could save 400 miles by cutting south of the Great Salt Lake. At first the trail was "all that could be desired," but soon huge boulders and dangerous mountain passes slowed the expedition to a crawl. During one stretch, the party traveled only 36 miles in 21 days. In late October, the Donner party reached the eastern Sierra Nevada and prepared to cross the Truckee Pass, the last remaining barrier before they arrived in California's Sacramento Valley. They climbed the high Sierra ridges in an attempt to cross the pass, but early snows blocked their path.

Trapped, the party built crude tents covered with clothing, blankets, and animal hides, which were soon buried under 14 feet of snow. The pioneers intended to slaughter their livestock for food, but many of the animals perished in 40-foot snowdrifts. To survive, the Donner party was forced to eat mice, their rugs, and even their shoes. In the end, surviving members of the party escaped starvation only by eating the flesh of those who died.

Finally, in mid-December, 17 men and women made a last-ditch effort to cross the pass to find help. They took only a six-day supply of rations, consisting of finger-sized pieces of dried beef—two pieces per person per day. During a severe storm two of the group died. The surviving members of the party "stripped the flesh from their bones, roasted and ate it, averting their eyes from each other, and weeping." More than a month passed before seven frostbitten survivors reached an American settlement. By then, the rest had died and two Native-American guides had been shot and eaten.

Relief teams immediately sought to rescue the pioneers still trapped near Truckee Pass. The situation that the rescuers found was unspeakably gruesome. Surviving members of the Donner party were delirious from hunger and overexposure. One survivor was found in a small cabin next to the cannibalized body of a young boy. Of the original 87 members of the party, only 47 survived.

It took white Americans a century and a half to expand as far west as the Appalachian Mountains, a few hundred miles from the Atlantic coast. It took another 50 years to push the frontier to the Mississippi river. By 1830, fewer than 100,000 pioneers had crossed the Mississippi.

During the 1840s, however, tens of thousands of Americans ventured beyond the Mississippi River. Inspired by the new vision of the West as a paradise of plenty, filled with

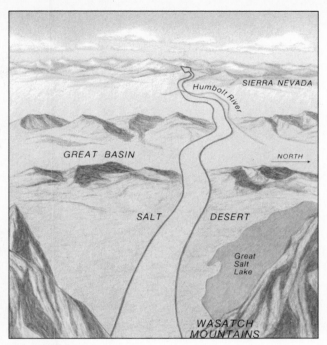

Donner Party
Western emigrants like the Donner party were ill-prepared for the dangers of travel to the far West.

fertile valleys and rich land, thousands of family chalked GTT ("Gone to Texas") on their gates or painted "California or Bust" on their wagons and joined the trek westward. By 1850 pioneers had pushed the edge of American settlement all the way to Texas, the Rocky Mountains, and the Pacific Ocean.

◆ What happened to the Donner party?
◆ How did the survivors reach California?
◆ Trace the route of the Donner party on a current map.

PATHFINDERS

In 1803, the year that the United States purchased the Louisiana territory from France, President Thomas Jefferson appointed his personal secretary, Meriwether Lewis, and William Clark, a former U.S. military officer, to explore the area's northern portion. Between 1804 and 1806, Lewis and Clark and about 45 other men traveled up the Missouri River, across the Rocky Mountains, and along the Columbia River as far as the Pacific before returning to St. Louis.

In 1806, as Lewis and Clark returned from their 8000-mile expedition, a young army lieutenant named Zebulon Pike left St. Louis to explore Louisiana territory's southern portion. Traveling along the Arkansas River, Pike saw the towering peak that bears his name. He and his party then traveled into Spanish territory along the Rio Grande and Red River. Pike's description of the wealth of Spanish towns in the Southwest attracted American traders to the region.

Pike's report of his expedition, published in 1810, helped to create one of the most influential myths about the Great Plains; that is, that the plains were nothing more than a "Great American Desert," a treeless and waterless land of dust storms and starvation. "Here," wrote Pike, is "barren soil, parched and dried up for eight months of the year . . . [without] a speck of vegetation."

◆ What did Lewis and Clark do?
◆ What areas did Zebulon Pike explore?

Copyright ©1999 by Addison-Wesley Educational Publishers Inc.

Margaret Reed
Margaret Reed was one of only 47 survivors of the
original party of 87 pioneers to reach California.

MOUNTAIN MEN

Fur traders and trappers quickly followed in the footsteps of Lewis and Clark, who
brought back reports of rivers and streams teeming with beaver and otter in the northern
Rockies. Starting in 1807, keelboats ferried fur trappers up the Missouri River. By the
mid–1830s these "mountain men" had marked out the overland trails that would lead
pioneers to Oregon and California.

    The Rocky Mountain Fur Company played a central role in opening the western fur
trade. Instead of buying skins from the Native Americans, the company ran ads in St.
Louis newspapers asking for white trappers willing to go to the wilderness. In 1822, it
sent a hundred trappers along the upper Missouri River. Three years later the company
introduced the "rendezvous" system, under which trappers met once a year at an
agreed-upon meeting place to barter pelts for supplies. "The rendezvous," wrote one
participant, "is one continued scene of drunkenness, gambling, and brawling and fighting, as long as the money and the credit of the trappers last."

◆ How did the Rocky Mountain Fur Company open the western fur trade?

TRAILBLAZING

The Santa Fe and Oregon trails were the two principal routes to the far West. William
Becknell, an American trader, opened the Santa Fe Trail in 1821. His 800-mile journey
from Missouri to Santa Fe took two months. When he could find no water, Becknell drank
blood from a mule's ear and the contents of a buffalo's stomach. Ultimately, the trail tied
the New Mexican Southwest economically to the United States and hastened American
penetration of the region.

    The Santa Fe Trail served primarily commercial functions. From the early 1820s until
the 1840s, an average of 80 wagons and 150 traders used the trail each year. Mexican
settlers in Santa Fe purchased cloth, hardware, glass, and books. On their return east,
American traders carried Mexican blankets, beaver pelts, wool, mules, and silver. By the
1830s, traders had extended the trail into California with branches reaching Los Angeles
and San Diego.

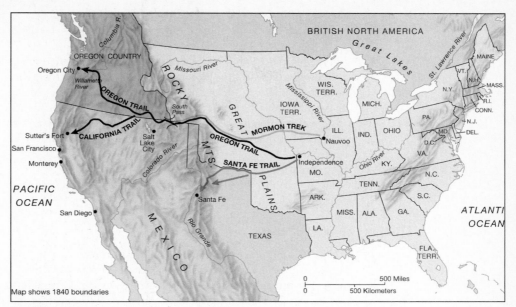

Western Trails

◆ What is the historical importance of the Santa Fe Trail?

SETTLING THE FAR WEST

During the 1840s thousands of pioneers headed westward toward California and Oregon. In 1841, the first party of 69 pioneers left Missouri for California, led by an Ohio schoolteacher named John Bidwell. The members of the party knew little about western travel: "We only knew that California lay to the west." The hardships the party endured were nearly unbearable. They were forced to abandon their wagons and eat their pack animals, "half roasted, dripping with blood." But American pioneering of the far West had begun. The next year another 200 pioneers went west. Over the next 25 years, 350,000 more made the trek along the overland trails.

◆ Outline the order, according to approximate years, in which significant western settlement occurred.

LIFE ON THE TRAIL

Each spring, pioneers gathered at Council Bluffs, Iowa, and Independence and St. Joseph, Missouri, to begin a 2000-mile journey westward. For many families, the great spur for emigration was economic. The financial depression of the late 1830s, accompanied by floods and epidemics in the Mississippi Valley, forced many to pull up stakes and head west. Said one woman: "We had nothing to lose, and we might gain a fortune." Most settlers traveled in family units. Even single men attached themselves to family groups.

At first, pioneers tried to maintain the rigid sexual division of labor that characterized early nineteenth-century America. Men drove the wagons and livestock, stood guard duty, and hunted buffalo and antelope for extra meat. Women got up before dawn, collected wood and "buffalo chips" (animal dung used for fuel), hauled water, kindled campfires, kneaded dough, and milked cows. The demands of the journey forced a blurring of gender-role distinctions for women who, in addition to domestic chores, performed many duties previously reserved for men. They drove wagons, yoked cattle, and loaded wagons. Some men did such things as cooking, previously regarded as women's work.

Accidents, disease, and sudden disaster were ever-present dangers. Diseases such as

Copyright © 1999 by Addison-Wesley Educational Publishers Inc.

typhoid, dysentery, and mountain fever killed many pioneers. Emigrant parties also suffered devastation from buffalo stampedes, prairie fires, and floods. At least 20,000 emigrants died along the Oregon Trail.

Still, despite the hardships of the experience, few emigrants ever regretted their decision to move west. As one pioneer put it: "Those who crossed the plains . . . never forgot the ungratified thirst, the intense heat and bitter cold, the craving hunger and utter physical exhaustion of the trail. . . . But there was another side. True they had suffered, but the satisfaction of deeds accomplished and difficulties overcome more than compensated and made the overland passage a thing never to be forgotten."

◆ Why did settlers go west?
◆ What were the hardships and divisions of labor for pioneers on the trail west?

MANIFEST DESTINY

In 1845 an editor named John L. O'Sullivan referred in a magazine to America's "manifest destiny to overspread the continent allotted by Providence for the free development of our yearly multiplying millions." One of the most influential slogans ever coined, the term *manifest destiny* expressed the romantic emotion that led Americans to risk their lives to settle the far West.

The idea that America had a special destiny to stretch across the continent motivated many people to migrate west. Manifest destiny inspired a 29-year-old named Stephen F. Austin to talk of grandly colonizing the Mexican province of Texas with "North American population, enterprise and intelligence." It led expansionists—united behind the slogan "54°40' or fight!"—to demand that the United States should own the entire Pacific Northwest all the way to Alaska. Aggressive nationalists invoked the idea to justify the displacement of Native Americans from their land, war with Mexico, and American expansion into Cuba and Central America. More positively, the idea of manifest destiny also inspired missionaries, farmers, and pioneers, who dreamed only of transforming plains and fertile valleys into farms and small towns.

◆ What is manifest destiny?
◆ What is the historical significance of manifest destiny?

—America and Its People by James Martin et al.

THINKING AFTER READING

Recall what you have read with a "study buddy" and prepare to take an examination on the material.

1. What are the major points in this chapter?

2. What essay questions might be asked about this chapter?

3. What multiple-choice or true-false questions might be asked?

4. What will be your time schedule for studying the material in this chapter?

5. When is the exam and how much will it count toward your final grade?

THINKING AFTER THE EXAM

PERSONAL FEEDBACK 2

Name_____

1. How would you evaluate your grade on the exam? _____

2. Did you make the grade that you studied to get? Why or why not?_____
   _____

3. What on the exam came as a surprise to you?_____
   _____

4. What was on the exam that was not included in your notes? _____
   _____

5. How will you study differently next time? _____
   _____

6. How will you manage your time differently next time? _____
   _____

7. Did you study with a "study buddy"? Why or why not? _____
   _____

8. How did your studying and performance on this exam differ from the previous exam on "The Joy of Smoking"?_____
   _____

Copyright ©1999 by Addison-Wesley Educational Publishers Inc.

Copyright ©1999 by Addison-Wesley Educational Publishers Inc.

1 *Pronunciation Review*

There are twenty-six letters in the English alphabet. These letters, however, make many more than twenty-six sounds. When you are trying to sound out a new word, knowing a few principles of phonics will help.

Phonics is the use of letter–sound relationships in pronouncing unknown words. With a knowledge of phonics, you can sound out parts of a word and then blend the parts to make a whole. The whole usually approximates the sound of the word. If the word is already in the reader's speaking vocabulary, the approximation will be sufficient to trigger the reader to recall the exact pronunciation. If an exact pronunciation is needed, the reader can check the dictionary for the phonetic spelling.

Principles of Phonics ◆◆◆◆◆◆◆◆◆◆◆

Do All Letters Make Sounds?

Say *time.* How many sounds do you hear? How many letters are there? There are four letters, but only three sounds because the final *e* is not heard. Sometimes the number of sounds and the number of letters are the same, and sometimes they are not.

Say each word below slowly, and listen for the sounds. In the blank next to the word, write the number of sounds you hear.

ball __3__   heel __2__   hen __3__   ride __3__

ate __2__   sand __4__   con __3__   play __3__

can __3__   top __3__   boy __3__   snow __3__

The Short Vowel Sounds

The letters *a, e, i, o,* and *u* are vowels.[1] You will always remember the short vowel sounds if you memorize the beginning sound of the following key-word pictures.

a =   apple

---

[1]The letter *y* can serve as a consonant or vowel. When *y* comes at the beginning of a word as in *yellow,* it is a consonant. The letter *y* in the middle of a word usually stands for a short *i* vowel sound as in *gym.* As the last sound in a short word such as *my,* the letter *y* usually stands for a long *i* vowel sound. In a longer word such as *baby,* the final *y* usually stands for a long *e* vowel sound.

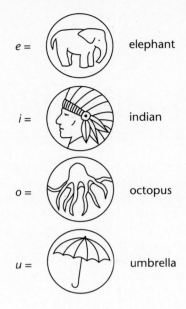

e = elephant

i = indian

o = octopus

u = umbrella

Say each of the following words, and put a check next to each word that has a short vowel sound.

flag ⎯✓⎯   cup ⎯✓⎯   hair ⎯⎯⎯   pig ⎯✓⎯

feed ⎯⎯⎯   meat ⎯⎯⎯   top ⎯✓⎯   nine ⎯⎯⎯

can ⎯✓⎯   egg ⎯✓⎯   flip ⎯✓⎯   us ⎯✓⎯

The Long Vowel Sounds

Notice the difference in the *o* sound in *got* and *go*. The *o* in *got* is short, as in *octopus,* whereas the *o* in *go* is a long vowel sound.

When a vowel says its name, as the *o* in *go,* it is called the *long sound* of the vowel. These long sounds are formed in several ways.

Compare the sound of *a* in *man* and in *main*. The first *a* is short and the second *a* is long. Study the following word pairs. How does the additional letter change the sound of the vowel?

ran   rain
got   goat
met   meat
bat   bait
fed   feed

When a word has two vowels together, usually the first vowel is long and the second is silent.

Now compare the sound of the *a* in *at* and in *ate*. The first *a* is short and the second *a* is long. Study the word pairs below. How does the final *e* affect the preceding vowel?

us   use
pin   pine
rip   ripe
mad   made
not   note

When a word has a vowel followed by a consonant, the final e is short and the preceding vowel is long.

Mark the following vowels as short (ăt) or long (ātę). Cross out the silent vowels.

māil	pīę	bōat	bŭt
pĕt	kītę	dīmę	cōal
făst	mĭlk	lēaf	dĭd

The Consonant Sounds

The letters other than *a, e, i, o,* and *u* are consonants. A vowel can be pronounced by itself, but a consonant needs a vowel to make a complete sound. Study the first sound of the following words to learn the sound of the consonants.

ball	sun	tap	pipe	vase
fish	rat	moon	kite	wagon
lamp	hat	dog	jug	zipper

Tricky Consonant Sounds

1. *C (cat* versus *cigar)*: When *c* is followed by *e, i,* or *y,* it usually has the soft sound of the *s* in *sun,* as in *cell, city, bicycle, ace,* and *cent.* When *c* is followed by *a, or,* or *u,* it usually has the hard sound of the *k* in *kite,* as in *cast, cocoa, curb, Dracula,* and *come.*
2. *G (gate* versus *giraffe)*: When *g* is followed by *e, i,* or *y,* it usually has the soft sound of *j* in *jump,* as in *germ, ginger, cage,* and *giant.* When *g* is followed by other letters, it has the hard sound of the *g* in *gate,* as in *drug, gag, tugboat,* and *piglet.*
3. *Q (queen)*: The *u* always follows the *q* to make the *kw* sound, as in *quart, quick,* and *quiz.*
4. *X (box)*: When *x* is at the end of a word, it usually has a *ks* sound, as in *ax, ox,* and *fox.*
5. *Y (yard* versus *gym)*: When *y* begins a word, it is a consonant, as in *yellow* and *yell.* At the end of a word, however, *y* is a vowel, as in *very, sadly,* and *many.*

Consonant Blends

Two or three consonant letters that appear together and keep their own sounds are called *consonant blends.* When you say the word, you can hear each consonant in the blend. Blends can be found in the beginning, middle, or end of a word. Study the following blends and listen to the sounds.

black	brown	prize	snip	spring
clean	crab	train	spider	square
fly	dry	scum	still	string
glee	fry	skip	sweet	hunt
plum	green	smoke	scrub	thank
			sand	held

Consonant Digraphs

When two consonants are next to each other but make only one speech sound, they are called *consonant digraphs.* Some digraphs take the sound of a single letter, whereas others form a new sound.

Copyright ©1999 by Addison-Wesley Educational Publishers Inc.

shell	laugh	church
that	phone	
what		

Silent Consonants

In several unusual cases, a consonant can be silent. Study the following examples, and note the letter combinations in which only one consonant is heard.

putt	gnat	autumn
lamb	sight	psalm
debt	ghost	isle
duck	knit	castle
scene	calf	wrap

Double Vowel Sounds

When two vowels appear next to each other in a word, they can have only the sound of the first vowel, have a new single sound, or have more than one single sound.

Sound of the First Vowel Only	*New Single Sound*	*More Than One Sound*
aid	haul	out
tray	boy	dough
sea	coin	cousin
dead		soup
week		room
soap		foot

Compound Words

When small words are put together to make a longer word, the result is called a *compound word*. Study the examples.

after + noon = afternoon
to + day = today
birth + day = birthday

Show the parts of the following compound words by drawing a line between the short words.

every|thing	under|pass	watch|man	land|slide
cross|road	butter|fly	some|time	moon|light
cow|boy	pea|nut	pocket|book	oat|meal

Counting the Syllables in a Word

A syllable is a part of a word. Each syllable has a vowel sound. To tell how many syllables a word has, count the vowels that make sounds. Remember that final *e*s are usually silent. If two vowels come together, they usually count as only one sound. In addition, remember that *y* at the end of a word is usually a vowel. Study the following examples, and note the number of syllables in each word.

c<u>o</u>nt<u>e</u>st   __2__   b<u>a</u>ggag¢   __2__   c<u>o</u>mpla<u>i</u>n   __2__   d<u>i</u>ctionary   __4__

k<u>i</u>ndergart<u>e</u>n   __4__   <u>a</u>mbulanc¢   __3__   f<u>ou</u>ndation   __3__   v<u>i</u>ctory   __3__

Count the number of syllables in the following words.

<u>i</u>njury	__3__	diplom<u>a</u>tic	__4__	democr<u>a</u>cy	__4__
org<u>a</u>nization	__5__	refreshments	__3__	kangaroo	__3__
disapp<u>o</u>intment	__4__	est<u>a</u>blishment	__4__	discovery	__4__
correspond<u>e</u>nt	__4__	scissors	__2__	comb<u>i</u>nation	__4__

Dividing Words Between Syllables

To divide a word into syllables, first mark the vowel and consonant sounds in the word. Be sure to allow for consonant blends. Then follow one of the two basic patterns:

> Pattern 1. Vowel consonant/consonant vowel (vc/cv)
>
> di|nner   chi|ldren
> vc|cv   vc|cv
>
> si|ster   ga|rden
> vc|cv   vc|cv
>
> ba|sket   en|ter|tain|ment
> vc|cv   vc|cv|cv|cvc|cv
>
> Pattern 2. Vowel/consonant vowel (v/cv)
>
> be|for¢   mu|sic
> v|cv   v|cv
>
> la|dy   rea|son
> v|cv   v|cv
>
> ho|tel   ba|by
> v|cv   v|cv

Divide the following words into syllables using the vc/cv and v/cv patterns.

o|ver	win|dow	pre|pare
v|cv	vc|cv	v|cv
De|cem|ber	re|cess	po|ta|to
v|cvc|cv	v|cv	v|cv|cv
yes|ter|day	doc|tor	gra|vy
v|cv|cvc|cv	vc|cv	v|cv

Long versus Short Vowels

No rule will enable you to pronounce all words correctly, but there are two rules that will help you.

1. If a syllable ends with a consonant sound, the vowel sound in the syllable is usually short. It is called a *closed syllable*.

> dĭ|nněr   fŏr|gĕt
> v|cv   v|cv
>
> wĭn|dŏw   hă|ppĕn
> v|cv   v|cv

Copyright ©1999 by Addison-Wesley Educational Publishers Inc.

2. If a syllable ends with a vowel sound, that vowel sound is usually long. It is called an *open syllable*.

hō|tĕl   ō|pĕn
v|cv   v|cv

hā|lō   mō|lăr
v|cv   v|cv

Divide the following words into syllables using the vc/cv and v/cv patterns. Mark the long and short vowel sounds using the rule for open and closed syllables.

yel|low   vol|ca|no   va|cant
vc|cv   vc|cv|cv   v|cv

Mo|hawk   No|vem|ber   la|bel
vc|cv   vc|vc|cv   v|cv

hel|lo   pas|sen|ger   sim|mer
vc|cv   vc|cvc|cv   vc|cv

an|no|tate   plen|ti|ful   traf|fic
vc|cv|cv   vc|cv|cv   vc|cv

Using Phonics to Decode and Pronounce Words

Use what you have learned about phonics to pronounce the following words. Many may be new to you. Use the vc/cv and v/cv patterns to divide them into syllables. Be aware of blends and silent letters. Then rewrite the word using the letters that you hear. Mark each vowel sound as long or short.

prenatal	prē|nā|tăl v|cv|cv	hallucinogen	hăl|lū|cĭ|nō|gĕn
aversion	ā|vĕr|sion	fiscal	fĭs|căl
engram	ĕn|grăm	rubella	rū|bĕl|lă
castigate	căs|tĭ|gāte	peptide	pĕp|tīde
scurrilous	scŭr|rĭ|lous	mitosis	mī|tōs|sĭs
olfactory	ŏl|făc|tŏ|rȳ	inadvertent	ĭn|ăd|vĕr|tĕnt
independent	ĭn|dē|pĕn|dĕnt	aspirant	ăs|pī|rănt

Using the Dictionary's Phonetic Spelling

The phonetic spelling of a word in the dictionary may seem like a foreign language at first. The symbols represent sounds that are all explained in a key. After you learn a few basic principles, the symbols will help you rather than confuse you.

Pronunciation Key

Every dictionary contains a pronunciation key. In a standard dictionary, a short form of the key is usually found at the bottom of each page spread, and the complete list of symbols is in the front of the book. Many of the sounds, especially the short and long vowels, will be familiar to you. For the letters with unfamiliar marks, you will need to sound out the sample word to understand the sound and duplicate it in your new word. The following is the short pronunciation key. Say each sample word and listen for the sound of the highlighted letters.

a hat	**i** it	**oi** oil	**ch** child	a in about
ā age	**ī** ice	**ou** out	**ng** long	e in taken
ä far	**o** hot	**u** cup	**sh** she	ə = { i in pencil
e let	**ö** open	**u̇** put	**th** thin	o in lemon
ē equal	**ô** order	**ü** rule	**ᵮH** then	u in circus
ėr term			**zh** measure	

Accents

An accent mark placed after a syllable indicates that you should stress that syllable when you pronounce the word. For example, the word *minute* can have one of two meanings, depending on how it is pronounced. With the accent on the first syllable, *min' it,* the word means sixty seconds. With the accent on the second, *mi nut',* it means very tiny. This heavy accent mark is called the *primary accent*. Some words contain a secondary accent mark, which means that another syllable receives some stress but not as much as the one with the primary accent. The word *playoff (pla' of')* is an example.

The Schwa

The schwa is an upside-down *e*. It stands for a weak vowel sound that is like a short *u* in *up*. The schwa can stand for all five vowel letters. It is an unstressed sound and usually is an unaccented syllable. Say the following words and listen for the schwa sound.

tomato	tə mā´tū
plaza	plaz´ə
pencil	pĕn´səl

Use the pronunciation key above to help you pronounce each of the following familiar words presented in phonetic spelling. Then write the correct spelling of each word.

kē	*key*	frē	free
flī	fly	lōd	load
kēp	keep	stēp	steep
kōl	coal	thrō	throw
bēm	beam	stā´pəl	staple

Copyright ©1999 by Addison-Wesley Educational Publishers Inc.

2 *Spelling Confusing Words*

A United States president once said, "Damn a man who can't spell a word but one way." Nevertheless, college professors tend to expect one official spelling for a word. Unfortunately, there are no "golden rules" of spelling that yield perfect results. There are a few spelling rules, but none is without exception. The following four rules may help you get through some rough spots.

RULE 1. Use *i* before *e* except after *c:*

believe	ceiling	receipt
grief	conceited	priest
cashier	yield	piece

Exceptions: Height, either, leisure, efficient

RULE 2. Drop the final *e* when adding a suffix that begins with a vowel:

hope + ing = hoping

believe + ing = believing

nice + est = nicest

Keep the final *e* when adding a suffix that begins with a consonant:

use + ful = useful

retire + ment = retirement

lone + ly = lonely

RULE 3. When a word ends in a consonant plus *y*, change the *y* to *i* to add a suffix:

lazy + ness = laziness

penny + less = penniless

marry + es = marries

RULE 4. Double the final consonant when all of the following apply:

a. The word is one syllable or is accented on the last syllable.
b. The word ends in a consonant preceded by a vowel.
c. The suffix begins with a word.

hop + ing = hopping

skip + ing = skipping

repel + ent = repellent

Copyright ©1999 by Addison-Wesley Educational Publishers Inc.

3 *Word Parts: Prefixes, Roots, and Suffixes*

Word Part	Meaning	Example
Prefixes		
a-, an-	without, not	atypical, anarchy
ab-	away, from	absent, abnormal
ad-	toward	advance, administer
ambi-, amphi-	both, around	ambiguous, amphibious
anna	year	annual
anti-, contra-, ob	against	antisocial, contradict
bene-, eu-	well, good	benefactor, eulogy
bi-, du-, di-	two or twice	bicycle, duet, dichotomy
cata-, cath-	down, downward	catacombs
cent, hecto	hundred	centipede
con-, com-, syn	with, together	congregate, synthesis
de-	down, from	depose, detract
dec, deca	ten	decade
demi-, hemi-, semi-	half	hemisphere, semicircle
dia-	through	diameter, diagram
dis-, un-	not, opposite of	dislike, unnatural
dys	ill, hard	dystrophy
ex-	out, from	exhale, expel
extra-	beyond, outside	extralegal
hyper-	above, excessive	hyperactive
hypo-	under	hypodermic
il-, im-, in-	not	illogical, impossible
in-	in, into	inside, insert, invade
infra-	lower	infrared
inter-	between	intercede, interrupt
intra-	within	intramural
juxta	next to	juxtaposition
mal, mis	wrong, ill	malformed, mislead
mill	thousand	milligram
nove, non	nine	novena, nonagon
oct, octo	eight	octopus
omni-, pan-	all	omnipotent, pantheist
per-	through	perennial, pervade
peri-, circum-	around	perimeter, circumvent
poly-, multi-	man	polygamy, multiply
post-	after	postscript
pre-, ante-	before	prepared, antebellum
pro-	before, for	promoter
proto-	first	prototype
quad, quatra, tetra	four	quadrilateral, tetrad
quint, penta	five	quintuplet
re-	back, again	review, reply
retro-	backward	retrogress, retrospect

Copyright ©1999 by Addison-Wesley Educational Publishers Inc.

Word Part	Meaning	Example
sequ-	follow	sequence
sex, hexa	six	sextet
sub-	under	submarine, subway
super-	above, over	supervise
temp, tempo, chrono	time	tempo, chronological
trans-	across	translate, transcontinental
tri	three	triangle
uni-, mono-	one	unicorn, monocle
vice-	in place of	viceroy

Roots

alter, hap	to change	alteration, mishap
ama, philo	to love	amiable, philosophy
amina	breath, spirit	animate
aqua	water	aquarium, aqualung
aster, astro	star	disaster, astronomy
aud	to hear	audible, auditory
auto, ego	self	autonomy, egotist
bio	life	biology
cap	head	caption, capitulate
cap, capt	to take	capture
card, cor, cord	heart	cardiac, core, cordial
cosmo	order, universe	cosmonaut
cresc	to grow, increase	crescendo
cryp	secret, hidden	cryptogram
dent	teeth	dental
derma	skin	dermatologist
duc, duct	to lead	reduce, conduct
equ, iso	equal	equivocal, isometric
err, errat	to wander	erratic
ethno	race, tribe	ethnic
fac, fact	to do, make	manufacture
fract	to break	fracture
frater	brother	fraternity
gene	race, kind, sex	genetics, gender
grad, gres	to go, take steps	graduation, digress
gyn	woman	gynecologist
hab, habi	to have, hold	inhabit, habitual
helio, photo	sun, light	heliotrope, photograph
homo	man	homo sapiens
lic, list, liqu	to leave behind	derelict, relinquish
lith	stone	monolith
loc	place	location, local
log	speech, science	logic, dialogue
loquor	to speak	loquacious, colloquial
lum	light	illuminate
macro	large	macrocosm
manu	hand	manual, manuscript
mater	mother	maternity
med	middle	mediate
meter	to measure	barometer
micro	small	microscope
miss, mit	to send, let go	admit, permission
morph	form	morphology
mort	to die	immortalize

Word Part	Meaning	Example
mut, mutat	to change	mutation
nat	to be born	natal, native
neg, negat	to say no, deny	negative, renege
nym, nomen	name	synonym, nomenclature
ocul	eye	oculist, monocle
ortho-	right, straight	orthodox, orthodontist
osteo	bone	osteopath
pater	father	paternal
path	disease, feeling	pathology, antipathy
phag	to eat	esophagus, phagocyte
phobia	fear	claustrophobia
phon, phono	sound	symphony, phonics
plic	to fold	duplicate, implicate
pneuma	wind, air	pneumatic
pod, ped	foot	tripod, pedestrian
pon, pos	to place	depose, position
port	to carry	porter, portable
pseudo	false	pseudonym
psych	mind	psychology
pyr	fire	pyromaniac
quir	to ask	inquire, acquire
rog	to question	interrogate
scrib, graph	to write	prescribe, autograph
sect, seg	to cut	dissect, segment
sol	alone	solitude
soma	body	somatology, psychosomatic
somnia	sleep	insomnia
soph	wise	sophomore, philosophy
soror	sister	sorority
spect	to look at	inspect, spectacle
spir	to breathe	inspiration, conspire
tact, tang	to touch	tactile, tangible
tele	distant	telephone
ten, tent	to hold	tenant, intent
tend, tens	to stretch	extend, extension
the, theo	god	atheism, theology
therma	heat	thermometer
tort	twist	torture, extort
ven, vent	to go, arrive	convention, advent
verbum	word	verbosity, verbal

Suffixes

-able, -ible	capable of	durable, visible
-acy, -ance, -ency, -ity	quality or state of	privacy, competence, acidity
-age	act of, state of	breakage
-al	pertaining to	rental
-ana	saying, writing	Americana
-ant	quality of, one who	reliant, servant
-ard, art	person who	wizard, braggart
-arium, orium	place for	auditorium
-ate	cause to be	activate
-ation	action, state of	creation, condition
-chrome	color	verichrome
-cide	killing	homicide

Copyright ©1999 by Addison-Wesley Educational Publishers Inc.

Word Part	Meaning	Example
-er, -or	person who, thing which	generator
-esque	like in manner	picturesque
-fic	making, causing	scientific
-form	in the shape of	cuneiform
-ful, -ose, -ous	full of	careful, verbose
-fy, -ify, -ize	to make, cause to be	fortify, magnify, modify
-hood, -osis	condition or state of	childhood, hypnosis
-ics	art, science	mathematics
-ism	quality or doctrine of	conservatism
-itis	inflammation of	appendicitis
-ive	quality of, that which	creative
-latry	worship of	idolatry
-less	without	homeless
-oid	in the form of	tabloid
-tude	quality or degree of	solitude
-wards	in a direction	backwards
-wise	way, position	clockwise

Acknowledgments

Copyright ©1999 by Addison-Wesley Educational Publishers Inc.

Text and Illustration Credits

Copyright © 1994 by Houghton Mifflin Company. Reproduced by permission from *The American Heritage Dictionary, Third Paperback Edition.*

Appelbaum, Richard and William Chambliss. From *Sociology* by Richard Appelbaum and William Chambliss. Reprinted by permission of Addison-Wesley Educational Publishers Inc.

Arms, Karen and Pamela S. Camp. From *Biology: A Journey Into Life,* Second Edition by Karen Arms and Pamela S. Camp, copyright © 1991 by Saunders College Publishing, reprinted by permission of the publisher.

Auth © 1976 *The Philadelphia Inquirer.* Reprinted with permission of UNIVERSAL PRESS SYNDICATE. All rights reserved.

Brown, Les. From *Live Your Dreams* by Les Brown. Copyright © 1992 by Les Brown Unlimited, Inc. Reprinted by permission of William Morrow & Company, Inc.

Brum, Gil, Larry McKane, and Gerry Karp. From *Biology: Exploring Life* by Gil Brum, Larry McKane, and Gerry Karp. Copyright © 1989, 1994 by John Wiley & Sons, Inc. Reprinted by permission of John Wiley & Sons, Inc.

Chapman, Elwood N. From *Your Attitude Is Showing, 8E* by Elwood N. Chapman, © 1987. Adapted by permission of Prentice-Hall, Inc., Upper Saddle River, NJ.

Conger & Galambos. From *Adolescence & Youth* by Conger & Galambos. Reprinted by permission of Addison-Wesley Educational Publishers Inc.

DeVito, Joseph. From *Essentials of Human Communication* by Joseph DeVito. Reprinted by permission of Addison-Wesley Educational Publishers Inc.

Dworetsky, John. From *Psychology* by John P. Dworetsky. Copyright © 1997, 1994, 1991, 1988, 1985, 1982 West Publishing Company; © 1997 Brooks/Cole Publishing Company, Pacific Grove, CA, a division of International Thomson Publishing Inc. By permission of the publisher.

Feldman et al. From *Understanding Psychology, 4E* by Feldman et al. Copyright © 1996 The McGraw-Hill Companies. Reprinted by permission of The McGraw-Hill Companies.

Fobes, Richard. From *The Creative Problem Solver's Toolbox* by Richard Fobes. Copyright © 1993 Richard Fobes. Reprinted by permission of Solutions Through Innovation.

Gerow, Josh. From *Essentials of Psychology* by Josh Gerow. Reprinted by permission of Addison-Wesley Educational Publishers Inc.

Gilbert and McCarter. From *Living With Art, 2/E, 4E* by Gilbert and McCarter. Copyright © 1995 The McGraw-Hill Companies. Reprinted by permission of The McGraw-Hill Companies.

Gordon, Arthur. "The Alchemist's Secret" by Arthur Gordon. Copyright © 1952 Arthur Gordon. Reprinted by permission.

Guilbault, Rose Del Castillo. "Rose: Americanization Is Tough on 'Macho'" by Rose Del Castillo Guilbault, originally appeared in *The San Francisco Chronicle.* Reprinted by permission of the author.

Harris, Sydney. "Opposing Principles Help Balance Society" from *Clearing The Ground* by Sydney J. Harris. Copyright © 1982, 1983, 1985, 1986 by The Chicago Sun-Times, Field Newspaper Syndicate, News-America Syndicate, and Sydney J. Harris. Reprinted by permission of Houghton Mifflin Company. All rights reserved.

Holland, Morris, *Psychology: An Introduction to Human Behavior,* Second Edition. Copyright © 1978 by D. C. Heath and Company. Used with permission of Houghton Mifflin Company.

Huffman, Karen et al. From *Psychology In Action, 3E* by Karen Huffman, Mark Vernoy, and Barbara Williams. Copyright © 1987 John Wiley & Sons, Inc. Reprinted by permission of John Wiley & Sons, Inc.

Kanter, Rosabeth Moss. "The Job Makes the Person" by Rosabeth Moss Kanter from *Understanding Diversity* by Carol P. Harvey and M. June Allard. Reprinted by permission of Addison-Wesley Educational Publishers Inc.

Kishlansky, Mark. From *The Unfinished Legacy* by Mark Kishlansky et al. Reprinted by permission of Addison-Wesley Educational Publishers Inc.

Koten, John. From "You Aren't Paranoid If You Think Someone Eyes Your Every Move" by John Koten, *The Wall Street Journal,* March 29, 1985. Reprinted by permission of The Wall Street Journal, copyright © 1985 Dow Jones & Company, Inc. All Rights Reserved Worldwide.

Krents, Harold. "Darkness At Noon" by Harold Krents, *New York Times,* May 26, 1976. Copyright © 1976 by The New York Times Company. Reprinted by permission.

Lakein, Alan. From *How To Get Control Of Your Time And Your Life* by Alan Lakein. Copyright © 1973 by Alan Lakein. Reprinted by permission of David McKay Co., Inc., a division of Random House, Inc.

Lee, Joann Faung Jean. From *Asian American Experiences in the United States: Oral Histories of First to Fourth Generation Americans from China, the Philippines, Japan, India, the Pacific Islands, Vietnam and Cambodia.* Copyright © 1991 Joann Faung Jean Lee by permission of McFarland & Company, Inc., Publishers, Jefferson, NC 28640.

Martin, James Kirby. From *America and Its People* by James Kirby Martin et al. Reprinted by permission of Addison-Wesley Educational Publishers Inc.

By permission. From *Merriam-Webster's Collegiate® Dictionary,* Tenth Edition © 1997 by Merriam-Webster, Incorporated.

By permission. From *Merriam-Webster's Third New International® Dictionary, Unabridged* © 1993 by Merriam-Webster, Incorporated.

Mora, Pat. From "Remembering Lobo" by Pat Mora in *Nepantla: Essays from the Land in the Middle.* Reprinted by permission of The University of New Mexico Press.

Morehead, Philip D. and Morehead, Andrew T. From *The New American Roget's College Thesaurus* by Philip D. Morehead and Andrew T. Morehead. Copyright © 1958, 1962 by Albert H. Morehead. Copyright © 1978, 1985, renewed 1986 by Philip D. Morehead and Andrew T. Morehead. Used by permission of Dutton Signet, a division of Penguin Putnam Inc.

Norton, Mary Beth et al., *A People and a Nation: A History of the United States,* Fourth Edition. Copyright © 1994 by Houghton Mifflin Company. Excerpted with permission.

Peeples, Jr., Edward H. From ". . . Meanwhile, Humans Eat Pet Food" by Edward H. Peeples, Jr., *New York Times,* December 16, 1975. Copyright © 1975 by The New York Times Company. Reprinted by permission.

Rischer, Carl and Thomas Easton. *From Focus on Human Biology* by Carl Rischer and Thomas Easton. Reprinted by permission of Addison-Wesley Educational Publishers Inc.

Roediger, Henry L. et al. From *Psychology, 3E* by Henry L. Roediger et al. Reprinted by permission of Addison-Wesley Educational Publishers Inc.

Rowley, Laura. "As They Say, Drugs Kill" by Laura Rowley. Copyright © 1992 by St. Martin's Press, Inc. From *Models for Writers, 4E* by Rosa & Eschholz. Reprinted with permission of St. Martin's Press, Inc.

Salinas, Marta. "The Scholarship Jacket" by Marta Salinas from *Nosotras: Latina Literature Today* (1986) edited by Maria del Carmen Boza, Beverly Silva, and Carmen Valle. Reprinted by permission of Bilingual Press/Editorial Bilingüe, Arizona State University, Tempe, AZ.

Schwartz, David J. From *The Magic of Thinking Big* by David J. Schwartz. Copyright © 1959, 1987. Reprinted with permission of Prentice-Hall, Inc., Upper Saddle River, NJ.

Scupin, Raymond. From *Cultural Anthropology: A Global Perspective, 3E* by Raymond Scupin. Copyright © 1998. Reprinted by permission of Prentice-Hall, Inc., Upper Saddle River, NJ.

Thio, Alex. From *Sociology* by Alex Thio. Reprinted by permission of Addison-Wesley Educational Publishers Inc.

Wallace, Robert. From *Biology: The World of Life* by Robert Wallace. Reprinted by permission of Addison-Wesley Educational Publishers Inc.

Wolf, Robin. From *Marriages and Families in Diverse Society* by Robin Wolf. Reprinted by permission of Addison-Wesley Educational Publishers Inc.

Zinsser, William. From *On Writing Well, 6E* by William K. Zinsser. Copyright © 1976, 1980, 1985, 1988, 1990, 1994, 1998 by William K. Zinsser. Published by HarperCollins. Reprinted by permission.

Photograph Credits

Page

1 John Coletti/Stock Boston, Inc.
2 Wendy Rosin Maleck/PhotoEdit
16 Michael Newman/PhotoEdit
18 Michael Newman/PhotoEdit
23 John Moore/The Image Works
32 Anna Kaufman/Stock Boston, Inc.
38 Ken Robert Buck/Stock Boston, Inc.
45 Courtesy of the Pilgrim Society, Plymouth, Massachusetts
49 Magellan Geographix/Corbis Media
50 Bob Krist/Corbis Media
55 *Library II*, 1960, Jacob Lawrence, Courtesy of the artist and Francine Seders Gallery, Seattle, Washington
83 Jack Vartoogian
99 Michael Kagan/Monkmeyer Press
105 M. Situk/The Image Works
113 *Cortador de Caña*, Rafael Tufiño, From the collection of the Museum of History, Anthropology and Art of the University of Puerto Rico
121 Corbis-Bettmann
122 Library of Congress
127 *Atlanta Journal/The Atlanta Constitution*, Richmond Newspapers, Inc./Staff Photo
129 Mark Antman/The Image Works
155 Jean-Claude LeJeune/Stock Boston, Inc.
161 Corbis-Bettmann
162 Corbis-Bettmann
169 Larry Kolvoord/The Image Works
177 Hugh Rogers/Monkmeyer Press
196 Historical Pictures/Stock Montage, Inc.
204 ©Merlin D. Tuttle/Bat Conservation International
211 Robert Brenner/PhotoEdit
223 Jose L. Paleaz/The Stock Market
249 Jean Claude LeJeune/Stock Boston, Inc.
265 Charles Kennard/Stock Boston, Inc.
271 The Stock Market
286 Comstock
294 *The Far Side* ©1985 Farworks, Inc. Used by permission of Universal Press Syndicate. All rights reserved.
299 Mark Antman/The Image Works
309 Grantpix/Monkmeyer Press
310 Sicron
311 The Washington Post Writer's Group
323 Wayne Miller/Magnum
329 Lionel Delevingne/Stock Boston, Inc.
332 Ronnie Kaufman/The Stock Market
339 *Library*, Bernard Boruch Zakleim, Courtesy San Francisco Art Commission

Copyright ©1999 by Addison-Wesley Educational Publishers Inc.

360 Richard Sobol/Stock Boston, Inc.
369 *Celestial Map–Northern Hemisphere*, Albrecht Durer, The Metropolitan Museum of Art, Harris Brisbane Dick Fund, 1951. (51.537.1)
376 Frank Grant/International Stock Photography, Ltd.
385 David Pollack/The Stock Market
388 American Lung Association
394 Donner Memorial State Park

Index

Accents, 405

Acronyms, 109–110, 158–159

"Actions for Success," from *The Magic of Thinking Big*, by David Schwartz, 17–19

"Alchemist's Secret, The," by Arthur Gordon, 328–332

"Americanization Is Tough on 'Macho,'" by Rose Del Castillo Guilbault, 332–338

"America's First Age of Reform," from *America and Its People*, by James Martin et al., 160–168

Analogies, 77–79, 202, 209, 373

Analytical reasoning, 271–307

Anderson, Joan Webster, "Angels All Around Us," 374

"Angels All Around Us" by Joan Webster Anderson, 374

Annotating, 178–180

Applied level of reading, 35

Arguments, 352–353

"As They Say, Drugs Kill," by Laura Rowley, from *Models for Writers*, edited by Alfred Rosa and Paul Eschholz, 356–359

Association, 57

"Astrology—The Earliest Theory of Personality," from *Psychology: What It Is/How We Use It*, by David Watson, 367–374

Attitude, 3

"Attraction and Personal Relationships," from *Psychology*, by Henry Roediger et al., 292

Average reading rate, 251

Bar graph, 279

"Becoming Healthy," from *Psychology: Introduction to Human Behavior*, by Morris Holland, 153–160

Bennett, Lerone, Jr., "Timbuktu," from *Before the Mayflower*, 195–203

Bias, 343–346

"Blacks in Blue: The Buffalo Soldiers in the West," from *America: Past and Present*, by Robert Divine et al., 119–127

Brown, Les, "Making Choices for Success," from *Live Your Dreams*, 4–5

Brum, Gil, Larry McKane, and Gerry Karp, "Echolocation: Seeing in the Dark," from *Biology: Exploring Life*, 203–210

Cartoons, 310–312

Cause and effect, 149–152

Chapman, Elwood, "Motivating Yourself," from *Your Attitude Is Showing*, 298–307

Charts, 278–279

"Childbirth in Early America," from *America and Its People*, by James Martin et al., 268–269

relating comparisons, 29

Collaboration, 16

Comparison and Contrast, 146–149

relating comparisons, 29

Compound words, 402

Concept cards, 57–58

Conclusions, 316

"Conformity," from *Psychology*, by Henry Roediger et al., 366

Confused words, 64–65, 79–80, 110, 127, 159–160, 202, 217–218, 305–306, 364–365

Consonants, 401–402

Content essay exams, 241–245

Context clues, 58–64, 110, 118, 126, 174–175, 208–209, 218, 297–298, 365, 372–373, 382

"Coping with Shyness," from *Using Psychology*, by Morris Holland, 285–293

Critical reading, 339–383

"Criticisms of the Milgram Experiment," from *Essentials of Psychology*, by Josh Gerow, 175

"Darkness at Noon," by Harold Krents in *The New York Times*, 263–266

Definitions with examples, 142–144

Detail test questions, 232–233

Details, 130

Major details, 130–138

Minor details, 133–138

Supporting details, 129–175

DeVito, Joseph

"How Do You Fight?," from *Essentials of Human Communication*, 219–220

"Effectiveness in Interpersonal Conflict," from *Essentials of Human Communication*, 210–219

Copyright ©1999 by Addison-Wesley Educational Publishers Inc.

Diagrams, 282–283
Dictionary, 58, 69–74
Digraphs, 401–402
Distractors, 100–102
Divine, Robert et al., "Blacks in Blue: The Buffalo Soldiers in the West," from *America: Past and Present*, 119–127
Drawing conclusions, 316
"Dress Codes and Symbolism," from *Cultural Anthropology: A Global Perspective*, by Raymond Scupin, 48–54
Dworetzky, John, "Obedience," from *Psychology*, 168–179

"Echolocation: Seeing in the Dark," from *Biology: Exploring Life*, by Gil Brum, Larry McKane, and Gerry Karp, 203–210
Effects, 149–152
"Effectiveness in Interpersonal Conflict," from *Essentials of Human Communication*, by Joseph DeVito, 210–219
Efficient reading, 250–270
Equipment for success, 14
Eschholz, Paul, 356–359
Essay exams, 241–245
Etymology, 72–74
Examples, 142–144
Excellence, 3

Facts, 350–352
Figurative language, 331–332
Fixations, 256

Gaps in understanding, 30
General and specific words, 84–85
General topic for sentences, 86–88
General and support sentences, 88–91
General and specific phrases, 85–86
Gerow, Josh, "Criticisms of the Milgram Experiment," from *Essentials of Psychology*, 175
Glossary, 58, 74
Gordon, Arthur, "The Alchemist's Secret," 328–332
Guide words, 70
Guilbault, Rose Del Castillo, "Americanization Is Tough on 'Macho,'" 332–338

Hoffman, Karen et al., "Smoking: Hazardous to Your Health," from *Psychology*, 387–391
Holland, Morris
    "Become Healthy," from *Psychology: Introduction to Human Behavior*, 153–160
    "Coping with Shyness," from *Using Psychology*, 285–293
"How Do You Fight?", from *Essentials of Human Communication*, by Joseph DeVito, 219–220

"Hypnosis," from *Psychology:What It Is/How to Use It*, David Watson, 37–43

Idioms, 327–328
Implied meaning test questions, 233–234
Independent textbook assignments, 385–397
Inference, 309–338
Intent, 340–343
Interpretive level, 35
Invalid support for arguments, 352–353
Irony, 337–338

"Job Makes the Person," by Rosabeth Moss Kanter, 375–378
"Jones Morgan, 110, "Thought To Be Last of Buffalo Soldiers," from *The Atlanta Journal-Constitution*, 127
"Joy of Smoking, The," from *Biology: The World of Life*, by Robert Wallace, 386–387

Kanter, Rosabeth Moss, "The Job Makes the Person," 375–378
Krents, Harold, "Darkness at Noon" in *The New York Times*, 263–266

Lakein, Alan, "Making the Most of Priorities," from *How to Get Control of Your Time and Your Life*, 6–7
Lecture notes, 193–194
Levels of importance, 130–133
Levels of reading comprehension, 35
Line graphs, 280–281
Listing, 139–141
Literal level, 35

Main idea, 83–128
    of longer selections, 102
    questioning for, 93
    stated main ideas, 94–97
    unstated main ideas, 97–100
Main idea test questions, 230–231
Major details, 133–138
"Making Choices for Success," from *Live Your Dreams*, by Les Brown, 4–5
"Making the Most of Priorities," from *How to Get Control of Your Time and Your Life*, by Alan Lakein, 6–7
Maps, 277–278
Mapping, 191–193
Martin, James, et al.,
    "America's First Age of Reform," from *America and Its People*, 160–168
    "Childbirth in Early America," from *America and Its People*, 268– 269
    "Surging Westward," from *America and Its People*, 392–396
    "Squanto," from *America and Its People*, 43–48

Math word problems, 281
Metaphors, 331, 365
Minor details, 133–138
Monitoring understanding, 30
Mora, Pat, "Remembering Lobo," from *Nepantla: Essays from the Hand in the Middle*, 266–268
"Motivating Yourself," from *Your Attitude Is Showing*, by Elwood Chapman, 298–307
Multiple meanings of a word, 64–65, 79–80, 110, 127, 159–160, 202, 217–218, 305–306, 364–365
Multiple-choice and true-false tests, 237–241
"My Brother," by Rick Theis, 322–328

Networking with students, 15
Notetaking, 181–183

"Obedience," from *Psychology*, by John Dworetzky, 168–179
Opinion, 350–352
Outlining, 187–191

Parts of speech, 70
Patterns of organization, 138–152
Pen as a pacer, 258
Personification, 337, 365
Perspective, 48–54
Phonics, 399, 404
Phrases, general and specific, 85–86
Picture images, 29
Point of view, 343–346
Prefixes, 67–68, 117–118, 409–412
Previewing, 24–29
Prior knowledge, 27, 313
Problem solving, 274
Pronunciation, 70, 399–405
Purpose, 340–343
Purpose test questions, 234–236

Questionnaires, 283–284
Question types, 229–237

Reading, stages of, 23–55
Reading comprehension, level of, 35
Reading speed, 252–263
Recalling, 32–33
Regressions, 255
Relating comparisons, 29
"Remembering Lobo," by Pat Mora, from *Nepantla: Essays from the Hand in the Middle*, 266–268
Rischer, Carl, and Thomas Easton, "Scientific Logic," from *Focus on Human Biology*, 293–298
Roediger, Henry, et al.
   "Attraction and Personal Relationships," from *Psychology*, 292

"Conformity from Psychology," from *Psychology*, 366
Roots, 66–67, 126, 218–219, 409–412
Rosa, Alfred, 356–359
Rowley, Laura, "As They Say, Drugs Kill," from *Models for Writers*, edited by Alfred Rosa and Paul Eschholz, 360–362

Salinas, Marta, "The Scholarship Jacket," from *Growing Up Chicana/o: An Anthology*, 111–119
Schema, 27
Schwa, 405
Schwartz, David, "Actions for Success," from *The Magic of Thinking Big*, 17–19
"Scientific Logic," from *Focus on Human Biology*, by Carl Rischer and Thomas Easton, 293–298
"Scholarship Jacket," from *Growing Up Chicana/o: An Anthology*, by Marta Salinas, 111–119
Scupin, Raymond, "Dress Codes and Symbolism," from *Cultural Anthropology: A Global Perspective*, 48–54
Sentences
   general topic for, 86–88
Similar sounding words, 64–65, 79–80, 110, 127, 159–160, 202, 217–218, 305–306, 364–365
Simile, 331, 365
Slanted language, 314–316
"Sleeping and Dreaming," from *Psychology: What It Is/How to Use It*, by David Watson, 104–110
"Smoking : Hazardous to Your Health," from *Psychology*, by Karen Hoffman et al., 387–391
Spelling, 70, 306, 406
"Squanto," from *America and Its People*, James Martin et al., 43–48
Stages of reading, 23–55
Standardized reading tests, 227
Stated main ideas, 94–97
Student success, 1–21
Suffixes, 68–69, 306, 409–412
Suggested meaning, 312
Summarizing, 184–187
Supporting details, 129–175
"Surging Westward," from *America and Its People*, by James Martin et al., 392–396
Syllabus, 9–12

Tape recorder, 17
Test questions, 232–234
Test-taking strategies, 223–247
   implied meaning, 233–234
   main idea, 230–231
   multiple-choice, 237–241
   predicting, 17

Copyright ©1999 by Addison-Wesley Educational Publishers Inc.

Test-taking strategies (*continued*)
  purpose, 234–236
  true-false, 237–241
  vocabularly, 236–237
Textbook learning, 177–221
Theis, Rick, "My Brother," 322–328
Thesaurus, 74–76
Thinking strategies, 28–31
"Timbuktu," from *Before the Mayflower*,
  by Lerone Bennett, Jr., 195–203
Time management, 6–9
Time order and sequence, 144–146
Time savers, 9
To-do list, 7–8
Tone, 346–350
Transitional words, 166–168

Unstated main ideas, 97–100

Valid support for arguments,
  352–353
Videos, 17

Vocabulary, 55–81
Vocabulary test questions, 236–237
Vocalization, 255–256
Vowels, 399–405

Wallace, Robert, "The Joy of Smoking,"
  from *Biology: The World of Life*,
  386–387
Watson, David
  "Astrology—The Earliest Theory of
  Personality," from *Psychology: What
  It Is/How to Use It*, 367–374
  "Hypnosis" from *Psychology:What It
  Is/How to Use It*, 37–43
  "Sleeping and Dreaming" from *Psychology: What It Is/How to Use It*,
  104–110
Word history, 70
Word origins, 72–74, 159, 201–202
Word parts, 58, 65–69, 66–67, 117–118,
  126, 218–219, 409–412